The Malady of the Christian Body

The Malady of the Christian Body

A Theological Exposition of Paul's First Letter to the Corinthians, Volume 1

Brian Brock
   and
Bernd Wannenwetsch

Foreword by
Stanley Hauerwas

CASCADE *Books* · Eugene, Oregon

THE MALADY OF THE CHRISTIAN BODY
A Theological Exposition of Paul's First Letter to the Corinthians, Volume 1

Copyright © 2016 Brian Brock and Bernd Wannenwetsch. All rights reserved. Except for brief quotations in critical publications or reviews, no part of this book may be reproduced in any manner without prior written permission from the publisher. Write: Permissions, Wipf and Stock Publishers, 199 W. 8th Ave., Suite 3, Eugene, OR 97401.

Cascade Books
An Imprint of Wipf and Stock Publishers
199 W. 8th Ave., Suite 3
Eugene, OR 97401

www.wipfandstock.com

PAPERBACK ISBN: 978-1-4982-3418-4
HARDCOVER ISBN: 978-1-4982-3420-7
EBOOK ISBN: 978-1-4982-3419-1

Cataloguing-in-Publication data:

Names: Brock, Brian, 1970–. | Wannenwetsch, Bernd, 1959–.

Title: The malady of the Christian body : a theological exposition of Paul's first letter to the Corinthians, volume 1 / Brian Brock and Bernd Wannenwetsch; foreword by Stanley Hauerwas.

Description: Eugene, OR: Cascade Books, 2016 | Includes bibliographical references and index(es).

Identifiers: ISBN 978-1-4982-3418-4 (paperback) | ISBN 978-1-4982-3420-7 (hardcover) | ISBN 978-1-4982-3419-1 (ebook)

Subjects: LCSH: Bible. Corinthians—Commentaries.

Classification: BS2675.53 .B75 2016 (print) | BS2675.53 .B75 (ebook)

Manufactured in the U.S.A.   11/07/16

New Revised Standard Version Bible, copyright 1989, Division of Christian Education of the National Council of the Churches of Christ in the United States of America. Used by permission. All rights reserved.

Contents

Foreword by Stanley Hauerwas | ix

Preface | xiii

Acknowledgments | xxiii

Abbreviations | xxv

1 Corinthians 1 | 1
  Called to Differentiated Unity · 1
  Paul as Apostle, Parent, and Midwife · 3
  Fostering Doxological Perception · 9
  Ecclesial Unity and the Proximity of Grace · 16
  Rivalry vs. *Oikodome* · 18
  Butchering Christ's Body · 21
  The Consolations of Kenotic Preaching and Wisdom · 23
  Praising the Folly of the Cross · 27
  Relating Creaturely and Divine Wisdom · 29
  The Crucifixion of Pragmatic and Rationalist Christianities · 31
  Jesus Christ, the Substance of the Virtues · 37

1 Corinthians 2 | 39
  Human Knowledge That Demonstrates God's Power · 39
  Outgrowing the Holy Spirit · 44
  The Spirit Is among You · 48
  The Unending Tutelage of the Spirit · 51
  Excursus: Paul and Discernment Today; the Genre of Commentary · 53

1 Corinthians 3 | 63
  Factionalism as Immaturity and Starvation · 63
  Factionalism as Façade · 65
  Factionalism as the Abominating Sacrilege · 70
  Factionalism as Self-Deception · 71
  Factionalism as Parochialism · 72

1 Corinthians 4 | 76

Escaping from Human Judgment into Praise · 76
Scripture as the Limit of Factionalism · 80
Having and Holding Christ's Gifts · 81
Be Like Your Father · 85
Excursus: Moral Dimensions of Characterization and Scripture's Plain Sense · 87

1 Corinthians 5 | 91

Taking Pride in Sin · 91
Grief over the Fractured Body · 94
Empirical Knowledge and Moral Discernment · 97
Baptism, Eucharist, and Poisonous Tolerance · 102
The Lack That Poisons the Bread of Life · 105
Excursus: The Dynamic Nature of Pauline Reasoning · 108

1 Corinthians 6 | 111

Courts as Accelerators of Dissension · 111
The Forms of Justice as Reconciliation · 113
Excursus: Familial Language as Political · 118
Released by Baptism from the Quest for Individual Justice · 121
Possessed by Our Possessiveness · 123
The Dual Bodiliness of Christian Existence · 125
Fleeing the Bondage of Generation Porn · 129

1 Corinthians 7 | 136

Bodies between Chastity and *Porneia* · 136
Chastity vs. Control, Repression, or Repudiation · 142
Excursus: Sex and the Apostle · 145
The Place of Chastity · 147
Excursus: Theology and Phenomenology · 156
Christian Discernment in Intensified Time · 158

1 Corinthians 8 | 169

Conscience: Self-Knowledge as Loving Social Knowledge · 169
Knowing Nonexistent Gods? · 173
Appetite for Destruction · 179

1 Corinthians 9 | 190
    Paul the "Light Traveler"? · 190
    The Fruits of Spiritual Labor · 195
    Boasting of the Gospel's Freedom · 203
    Excursus: Supererogation · 205
    The Rewards of Watching the Gospel at Work · 207
    Excursus: Paul's Formation of the Self · 211
    Becoming and Being Made All Things · 214
    Fitness for the Gospel · 221

Bibliography | 227

Name Index | 235

Subject Index | 239

Scripture Index | 249

Foreword

AFTER THE LITURGY ON a recent Sunday I found myself in conversation with a relatively new member of the Church of the Holy Family. She was a convert from Judaism. She is a wonderful, lively person who is not hesitant to put forward her own views about almost anything. I like her very much though some in the church may find her "a bit much." In fact, she told me that she had recently been asked not to be part of a group in the church because she was too vocal. She confessed she found this to be quite hurtful. She observed she had thought that the church was the one place in contemporary life that might be free of conflict.

I wanted to be sympathetic, but my first response was to recommend she read First Corinthians. I told her if she did she would discover that the church has always been in conflict. The question has never been whether Christians were free of conflict, but as Brian Brock and Bernd Wannenwetsch make clear in this marvelous commentary, given what Christians are about, conflict is necessary if we are to discover who we are as well as what we believe. Indeed, if we were free of conflict we would not be able to discover that through the work of the Holy Spirit we have been made members of the one body of Christ.

Brock and Wannenwetsch's reading of the first half of First Corinthians should put to rest any presumption that the first century of the life of the church was a "golden age." The language of a "golden age" suggests that there was a time when Christians got it right, but the church at Corinth clearly puts that supposition to rest. Some of the perverse behavior by Christians in Corinth can be attributed to their being human beings, but some of their objectionable behavior was imaginable because of the new world the Spirit had made imaginable through Paul's ministry.

The Christians of Corinth were after all the firstborn of a new age. It should not be surprising therefore that questions of authority quickly became central. Moreover, fundamental theological questions could not be avoided. How could you get "right" that God was fully present in Jesus Christ without in any way compromising that God is fully present in creation? The Christians in Corinth heard the Gospel in which it is declared that all things have been made new and they ran with it—some ran too fast, assuming that what had happened in Christ called into question even everyday familial practices. Paul had to find a way to say all things are new but not in the way you think.

What is remarkable about this remarkable commentary is that it models Paul's task. Brock and Wannenwetsch with clear vision have set out to give us a theological reading of First Corinthians as a theological exercise in the formation of the church. That may seem not all that significant, but as they make clear, a theological reading is required if we are to believe as we should that this letter Paul wrote to the Corinthians is also written for us.

Therefore the very character of Brock and Wannenwetsch's commentary is a witness to their understanding that by the work of the Holy Spirit First Corinthians is now scripture. They wisely, however, do not make explicit the methodological presuppositions their theological convictions entail until they provide an Excursus at the end of chapter 2. The Excursus makes explicit the significance of their theological reading of First Corinthians in distinction from the "normal" way of commenting on scripture.

By "normal" I refer to the attempt to use the historical reconstruction of texts to tell us, for example, what Paul *really* meant when he wrote about who should exercise authority in the church. Brock and Wannenwetsch make clear that such a strategy is often an attempt to free ourselves from the reality that Paul is now writing directly to us. I am a bit hesitant to call attention to the Excursus because it may tempt some to read the Excursus before reading the commentary on the first two chapters. To skip ahead is not unforgiveable, but I recommend that you wait until you finish the first two chapters, because Brock and Wannenwetsch have written this commentary to make your reading of Corinthians have a compelling immediacy that can be lost if you think they are only trying to score points in a scholarly debate.

What they have done is not easily done, but I believe you will discover their reading of Paul's letter is one we desperately need as Christians today. Brock and Wannenwetsch challenge our reading habits that tempt us to read Paul as a "thinker," that is, as someone who had some ideas about the human condition and how communities should be ordered. Paul writes to heal the wounded body that was the Corinthian church by helping the Christians at Corinth be for the world a witness to the wounded body of Christ. Paul did not know that his letter to the Corinthians would be for us God's word, but that is what it now is. We are indebted to Brock and Wannenwetsch for reminding us that we are the church at Corinth.

One last observation. Paul's letters are full of his gratitude for those who have traveled with him or cared for him on his journeys. I think it is no accident that the quality of this commentary has everything to do with its being written by friends. We need one another, in or out of conflict.

That is why I told my friend from Holy Family that she should not cease making her views known. If she became quiet, then how would we know who we are?

—Stanley Hauerwas

Gilbert T. Rowe Professor Emeritus of
Divinity and Law, Duke Divinity School

Preface

A biblical commentary needs no introduction. Its life arises out of the liveliness it helps its readers discover in the authoritative text it engages. This is why we rightly judge commentaries not by any conclusions they may have generated but by the persuasiveness with which difficult passages have been handled. From the outset, then, we as authors would encourage potential readers of these volumes simply to turn to a favorite passage to see if our treatment seems compelling enough to warrant further reading. In the end our commentary will ultimately be judged by its fidelity to Paul's Letter to the First Corinthians and the illumination it draws from it. This is as it should be.

Our intention in offering this preface is to contribute to the reader's experience by calibrating expectations about what might reasonably be expected from a pair of books presenting themselves as "theological exposition." We begin by breaking with the academic convention of opening with an introduction summarizing the methodological rules and substantive conclusions that will be found in the pages to come. Readers will soon discover that *The Malady of the Christian Body* and *The Therapy of the Christian Body* are commentary neither of the type we have come to expect from the modern guild of critical biblical scholars nor of the type that has recently emerged in reaction to it, which attempts to merge the "two horizons" of theology and modern biblical criticism in all their diversity. What unites representatives of both genres is the agreement that, after the rise of modern criticism, a proper approach to commentary must begin by presenting a defensible method, and it is setting out this method that is the central task of an introduction. In the modern period it is this initial display of hermeneutic methodology that has become the primary signal that one is pursuing "scholarly" commentary rather than more pastoral or devotional styles of exegesis. As risky as it is to resist this widely held consensus, resist we must.

How can a reluctance to rely on method not itself be a hermeneutic position, the reader rightly asks, that commits us to a position in which the subjectivity of the reader is the only standard of interpretation? If we refuse to make a rational method the measure of proper interpretation do we not necessarily enter the domain of postmodernist reader responsivity? What is distinctive about the road traveled in this commentary is its refusal of this either/or, a procrustean bed into which all modern biblical commentary has been forced by well over a century of heated debates about critical method. In this commentary we will neither deploy a hermeneutic to generate a reading of the text nor stridently assert the irrelevance of method. Our basic approach is best characterized as a stance rather than a method. We have held ourselves to an ethos of non-evasion: a posture toward scripture that allows us to admit that we come to the text with all sorts of hermeneutical, theological, and cultural sensibilities, but which we seek to see reconfigured through close engagement with Paul's Letter to the First Corinthians. We sought to let scripture determine what of the knowledge we brought to the text *fit* with it and, equally importantly, how our previously held ideas would need to be transformed if they were to conform to scripture.

For these reasons it was only as we neared the end of the commentary process on First Corinthians that we were prepared to offer an account of which of our methodological presumptions survived our reading of the epistle. This we do in our leave-taking of Paul (see the discussion of 16:21–24 in *The Therapy of the Christian Body*). As we began we were acutely aware of how little we understood of what it meant to write theological commentary in our time (which we discuss in our engagement with 2:13–15) or even how to define the "plain sense" of scripture (taken up as we engage 4:14–21). If pressed for a nutshell description of our approach to First Corinthians, we might characterize it as exegesis submitted from the outset to Paul's own rule of faith as described in the second chapter: "I resolved to know nothing among you except Jesus Christ, and him Crucified" (v. 2).

Such an approach does, like all reading, rely on a set of distinct practices. Often our most significant insights were prompted as we discussed the theological issues raised by the often striking divergences among various English and German translations of the Greek original text. We found these insights were most productively served by a stable routine in which we devoted the first few days in each of our weeklong working sessions to direct exposure to the text. This initial wrestling continued until we could articulate to our own satisfaction a reading that took account of the most obvious textual features and problems in a given chapter. This we came to call the "spine" of the chapter, which we then wrote up as a first provisional draft in rough prose. We would then expose what we had been given to understand of a passage of Paul's letter to the "fire" of comparison, consulting other commenters past and present. This we typically undertook by way of a survey of patristic, medieval, reformation, and modern commentaries, and in that order. In some cases, this would lead us to modify our account, even forcing us on several occasions to begin again. Perhaps more surprisingly, this comparative exercise occasionally left us with a more profound conviction that we had been given insights into passages and moves in the argument others may have overlooked. In these cases the work of comparison allowed us to sharpen these insights or interpretative directions by contrasting them with alternative accounts. This approach evolved over time into a division of labor in which one of us would arrive equipped with previous readings of a stable selection of choice commentaries, while the other remained intentionally "innocent" of those secondary sources in order to preserve a freshness of reading.

Our reliance on the "empty hands" approach to the text also introduced an unmistakably spiritual aspect to our exegetical practice. We found that our writing could only be properly pursued in a series of quasi-monastic retreats, which we undertook in spaces that were physically bounded by the hanging of the full text of Corinthians on the walls of our various working rooms, and temporally delimited by prayer. Though this approach was certainly demanding—not least because such time must be stolen from institutions no longer conducive to such a style of working—we found these sessions spiritually explosive and invariably left more excited and invigorated than we had come. To pursue theological study in such a manner took us beyond anything we had previously experienced in our academic work and can legitimately be called revelatory in its power to expose our vocations, our churches, the created world, and our God in a new light.

This approach was underpinned by a set of doctrinal and theological assumptions, such as the Reformation understanding of scripture with its dual emphasis on the letter and the illuminating presence of the Spirit of Jesus Christ (discussed in the methodological excursus that concludes chapter 4). Several other insights were especially helpful to us in shaping our approach to First Corinthians, the most important coming from our teacher Hans Ulrich: "Every word of scripture demands its own hermeneutic." See what happens when you submit to the words as they run. Do not leap ahead, in the book or the canon. Do not evade the text before you. Let it set the terms for your reading. Following Ulrich's maxim tied our commentating activity strictly to the text of scripture in a determined attempt to allow its own discernible and unique contours to shape how it would be approached.

What unique interpretative problems would *this* particular epistle pose? This crucial question is all too often dissipated by modern habits of reading that assume that most of the exegetical work that needs to be done is accomplished with the discovery of some macro-structure that will henceforth orient our expectations about what we will hear from specific verses or tracts. We are self-consciously aware that, like any other Christian reader, we come to this text already shaped by previous exegetical traditions. It is precisely *as* those who have already been traditioned in significant ways by Christian belief and practice that we deliberately chose to pay attention to what God might do to us as readers through the words of scripture—what God might do if we were to give up the obvious evasive movements and the predictable textual glosses.

Our working assumption was that by attending closely enough to the form of Paul's belief as articulated in this epistle we would be led in *unanticipated* ways into the entirety of scripture. It was in hope of these new connections being revealed that we refused to explain any passage in the letter by referring to other books in the Bible unless Paul's own argument explicitly guided us further afield. While as radical in its implications as Cartesian suspicion, such mobility of thought is not achieved by attempting to doubt everything that we already know. Instead, it intentionally takes up a stance determined to hold what we think we know so loosely that the Word might be allowed genuinely to reshape us and our knowledge along with us. This can happen only when we take up and consider each word as we would a precious stone, examining not only its initially appearing surface, but also its hidden side and the complex web of connections it has with the words that surround it.

Bearing in mind the predicament of postmodern literary criticism, which constantly teeters on the edge of breaking texts down into nearly infinite segmentations, we have been acutely aware of the price that may have to be paid when giving up the unified hermeneutic method of the interpreter, geared as it is to yielding cohesive interpretation. The proliferation of hermeneutics that Ulrich encourages is therefore only possible as a *disciplined* and *theological* reading, understood as an articulation of faith in Jesus Christ. Such faith trusts the unity of the text to lie not in the *hermeneutic we apply* but in *who it is that we trust* as we read, in the way Martin Luther modeled when commenting on Paul's Letter to the Galatians. "Paul treats the argument of this epistle in every word. He has nothing in his mouth but Christ. Therefore in every word there is a fervor of spirit and life."[1]

The foregoing suggests that, if it is at all legitimate to describe us as having a hermeneutic, it would have to be called a hermeneutic of discovery. Our attention to this tract of scripture has sought to discern the reality to which Paul witnesses: God and the distinctive character of his working. While theological exegetes need to apply themselves to learning the familiar practices that serve serious interpretation, such as studying the text in the original language and being aware of current scholarly discussions, these

---

1. Martin Luther, *Lectures on Galatians Chapters 1–4* (1535), in LW 26:32.

practices cannot themselves yield scripture's meaning.² At their best they can bring into view important considerations about the way the words of scripture run that allow us better to discern where critical theological questions lie. The exegesis we are seeking to exemplify also demanded that we learn the discipline of refusing to engage textual or historical puzzles as ends in themselves. Since historical problems are raised at almost every turn when reading an ancient text, addressing these problems can only be responsibly done if we remain aware of how such investigations at the same time also threaten to become an external source of explanation. We have come to appreciate the demands historical and exegetical puzzles place on our reading as patience-building stumbling blocks slowing us down in order to teach us better to understand how the Spirit is working in and through these divinely given texts.³ Exegesis so conceived cannot be understood as a self-instigated program or project. It grows from a confession that we have been invited or even forced to read in a particular way. Our hope, and indeed our experience, has been that by committing ourselves to these habits of non-evasive reading we will discover new constellations of ideas arising from the specific wording of this singular epistle.

One of the effects of this approach was to discover that Paul's engagement with the Corinthian Christians in his first letter to them is constituted by two distinct and interrelated movements. In this first volume, *The Malady*

---

2. In this we continue ancient Christian practice. We all learn to speak from others as children, Augustine notes, and so we should neither expect people to read scripture without being taught to read nor allow this teaching to be equated with or substituted for the working of the Spirit. "Let us not tempt the one in whom we have placed our trust, or we may be deceived by the enemy's cunning and perversity and become unwilling even to go to church or to hear and learn the gospel, or to read the biblical text or listen to it being read and preached, preferring to wait until 'we are caught up into the third heaven, whether in the body or out of the body' (in the words of the apostle) [2 Cor 12:2], and there to hear 'words that cannot be expressed, which a human being may not utter' or see the Lord Jesus Christ in person and hear the gospel from him rather than from men." Augustine, *On Christian Teaching*, Preface, 11 (5).

3. This emphasis on the limited significance of historical insight is an updated appropriation of a realization of ancient Christians. Augustine's observation about the difficulties of interpreting the first book of the Bible indicates the challenge that continues to face a theological reader of the First Letter to the Corinthians within the context of modern scholarly conventions: "I have, to the best of my ability, winkled out and presented a great variety of possible meanings to the words of the book of Genesis which have been darkly expressed in order to put us through our paces. I have avoided affirming anything hastily in a way that would rule out any alternative explanation that may be a better one . . . Let those people now restrain themselves, who are so puffed up with their knowledge of secular literature, that they scornfully dismiss as something crude and unrefined these texts which are all expressed in a way designed to nourish devout hearts." Augustine, *Literal Meaning of Genesis*, 20.40 (187).

of the Christian Body, we trace the first movement, the Apostle's critical engagement with the maladies of a Corinthian church torn by factionalism, boasting, and false tolerance. Our title is not meant to suggest that Paul's first nine chapters are concerned only with rebuking the Corinthian Christians for the obvious problems on display in their community. Diving deeply into the reasons why ecclesial rivalry is toxic for the church does take the Apostle deep into questions of idolatry, sexuality, legal conflict, dressing, and eating among Christians. But it is a measure of his enduring power as a theologian and apostle that his criticism is thoroughly constructive and implacably resists disputes about these practices being reduced to a merely moral plane. By keeping his treatments of these problems firmly tied to doctrine and the Christian confession of faith Paul shows how such moral disputes are never theologically neutral, but are precisely the forum in which the church must learn what the gospel of Jesus Christ entails in its particular time and place.

On close inspection it becomes obvious that the Apostle is reconfiguring the basic frameworks within which the Corinthians understand the church, politics, law, theology, and their own lives, *by way of* engaging the moral conflicts so evidently on display in the Corinthian church. He continually breaks down and reconfigures all the boundaries and distinctions held by the Corinthians that allowed them to keep a range of problems comfortably isolated from one another. Once we begin to see and appreciate the way Paul attacks and reconfigures the illegitimate boundaries that are creating the conflict among the Corinthians we will inevitably see how it implicates some of our own boundaries. We will see how this dealing with the Corinthians invites corresponding shifts in our own understanding of not only moral problems, but God, the church, and the world. This should not surprise those who acknowledge Paul as our apostle as well as the apostle of the Corinthian church.

Not content simply to correct, however constructively, Paul in chapter 8 of his First Letter to the Corinthians begins to set out in luminous colors his understanding of the peace Jesus Christ has brought into a world estranged and at war. This peace is configured bodily, occupies space in the world, and is characterized by a distinctive political ethos.[4] In *The Therapy of the Christian Body* we find Paul setting out this positive vision more ex-

---

4. This formulation signals our intention to move beyond another unnecessary polarization that has come to determine much of the debate about the relation of Paul to Christian ethics: between readings often called "apocalyptic" or emphasizing "justification" and the primacy of Christ's working in the defeat of the powers and principalities, and those foregrounding the location of Christian moral agency in the church understood as the body of Christ (as championed by proponents of the New Perspective on Paul and by post-MacIntyrian virtue ethicists). The debate is outlined in some detail in Miller, *The Practice of the Body of Christ*.

plicitly and moving a bold step beyond his engagements with the problems that have ensnared the local congregation, offering a sweeping (re-)direction of the Corinthians' vision toward what God is working among them (ch. 10). The Apostle is determined to raise the Corinthians' awareness of the ways in which the Spirit is transforming them into a life-giving community whose preaching and mission are unencumbered by self-absorption (ch. 9) and whose worship is mutually attentive (ch. 11). In the course of this therapeutic reorientation of the Corinthian believers Paul reaches deep into his understanding of the peaceful politics of a pneumatically arranged church (ch. 12), the love that is at its heart (ch. 14), and the eschatology that orients it (ch. 15).

We see it as a matter of great promise that neither the malady nor the therapy described by Paul looks much like the dominant coping strategies being proposed today as responses to the malaise of the contemporary church. The Apostle offers us instead a number of theological escape routes from the conceptual impasses that sustain the deadening entrenchments of our own churches. To take one example, for Paul the factions in the church at Corinth are disastrous first and foremost because the ensuing infighting amounts to a "butchering up" of Christ himself (see 1:13), and not because they undermine the moral authority of the institutional church. Accordingly, the therapy for this affliction is not an invasive treatment prescribed or performed by the Apostle but is effected through his exhortation to the congregation to attend to the self-healing capacities of that body as specifically the *body of Christ*. Factionalism is not healed by "greater tolerance" or "better leadership" but by a deeper realization of the organic connectivity in the body of Christ, understood as a nervous system made up of spiritual gifts that continuously flow from the Son through the Spirit into the community and from there back towards the center, Christ.

Though Paul himself rarely draws on medical imagery, it was this structure of his argument that suggested the metaphor of "malady and therapy" as a truthful reflection both of the ways in which the Apostle engages the conflicts and shortcomings he finds among the Corinthians and his patient service as a midwife for their overcoming. While there are moments in his argument when Paul discusses the individual *Christian's* body, such as when he addresses the effects of certain dietary (chs. 8, 10) or sexual practices (ch. 7) on what he wishes to make them understand as the "temple of the holy Spirit," these concerns are always rooted within the wider concern the Apostle has with the *oikodome* (building up) of *the Christian body*—the social organism that the individuals' use of their bodies inevitably affects. Our understanding of "malady" and "therapy," therefore, assumes the Apostle to be working within an ancient understanding of medicine that, as Ivan

Illich has pointed out, differs substantially from the rationality of modern "organ-centered" medicine: Paul's skill as a practitioner is displayed in the way he sensitively "feels into" the organic whole of the body in order to detect blockages of the healthy flow of powers that are preventing the body from living up to its genuine liveliness and destiny.

Following this route helped us see why the dominant modern approaches to First Corinthians so often project odd divisions and produce such isolated segmentations of the text. More problems are created than solved by treating the letter as a string of discussions about discrete topics susceptible of distillation into a "Pauline sexual ethic," a "Christian dietary ethic," and so on; rather, what we are offered in this letter is best described as an "Apostolic ecclesiology." This ecclesiology sheds penetrating light on a whole range of concerns in the Christian life, including those that we tend to label "moral." What is crucial to see, however, is that one of the overwhelming problems of Christian faith is the isolation of such discussions from an overriding concern of the believer for the social body of Christ as a holy, living organism. It is in this way that Paul teaches us theologically to interrogate the interpretative habits and fixed horizons of understanding that characterize not only most modern commentaries on the epistle but the approaches of most Christian readers of the text today.

The main lines of our approach can be encapsulated under three broad headings.

I. Reading the Apostle over against Ourselves

Our exposition of Paul's letter seeks not only to display but also to narrate the development of an approach in which the apostolic status of the text permeates our reading strategies in ever-deepening ways. In pursuit of this aim, we have come to understand the need to adopt a self-critical approach that grants the Apostle the right to probe, criticize, and unmask our reading horizons. We thus present the activity of reading his letter as a form of "suffering apostolic authority." In and through or even before discovering what Paul wishes to say, the very presence of apostolic authority forces us to come to terms with the obstacles we put in the way of Paul as well as the difficulties involved in relinquishing them. An essential aspect of this strategy is the acknowledgment of our overt, hidden, or even preconscious moral kinship with the Corinthians, Paul's historical first addressees. While acknowledging the importance of our indubitable historical distance from them, we have found it equally important to resist the usual response to this distance, the disengaged perspective of purely historical exegesis. Instead, we have pursued proactive modes of discovering "the Corinthians within ourselves"—sometimes with painfully surprising results. It was our surprise at the power and frequency of such discoveries that revealed to us the poverty of the common interpretative strategy of separating what "Paul once said" from what he "says to us today."

II. Reading the Apostle as Fellow Travelers

Another important discovery arose as we gradually discovered how indispensable teaming up with a theologically congenial coauthor was for our approach to First Corinthians. As we discussed the text line by line and word by word it became ever more obvious that such a demanding task could not be completed without mutual encouragement, especially when it came to facing our hidden alliances with the Corinthians and our own capacity to put obstacles in the way of understanding. As we read together we discovered we were representing to each other not merely an additional pair of eyes, but distinct church traditions—mainline traditional European (German Lutheran) and the Holiness movement–influenced Congregationalism of the new world (United States). Setting out on our joint endeavor we knew we shared many theological positions; but only along the way could we realize how important the differences in our ecclesial upbringing were in helping us see the horizons within which we approached Paul as well as the ways these horizons proved obstructive or constructive in our attempts to make sense of specific passages. We thus offer our commentary as a worked example of how exegetical theology might be undertaken in self-consciously ecclesial and corporate fashion.

III. Reading the Apostle Dramatically

A duplex narratival development unites the commentary's two volumes. At one level we offer a progressive, linear, and almost homiletic treatment of the text in which the argument of each chapter is explained as we come to it, often verse by verse, and in which readers are offered theological evaluations of popular translations and interpretative "hot spots." In the course of this treatment the rich vocabulary that characterizes Paul's theological palette is progressively set out, organized around his core terminology. At the same time we also narrate an overarching drama of our progressive discovery of Paul's fatherly and apostolic dealing not only with the Corinthians but also with us. We repeatedly found that the Paul who first struck us as sounding distinctly misogynist, pedagogically harsh, or as oscillating wildly between theological obscurity and abstraction, is in fact choosing each word out of solicitude for the wellbeing of the church. We thus display how readers of the epistle might admit and directly face their potential distaste for some of Paul's words in order to discover in the Apostle a genuine mediator of God's kindly redeeming activity. Having undergone a whole series of interpretative "conversions" of this type we felt our conviction nourished that the divine condescension is operative even at the level of the individual words of scripture. The linguistic details of scripture are not only theologically significant but even revelatory when we let ourselves attend closely to them, and to what they evoke in us, often rewarding us with surprise discoveries.

We hope that drawing attention to the unity of this commentary in a set of narratives will alert readers to expect something of the feel of a mystery novel. Why does Paul seem so insufferably ironic and condescending here or so oddly contradictory and disjointed there? We wrote as we discovered our way through these puzzles, a bit like the early Egyptologists who, as they climbed deeper into the tombs of the pharaohs, had sequentially to untangle interpretative puzzles as they were led into ever more magnificent chambers and vistas of knowledge. To convey this adventure of discovery has been one of the core aims of this commentary, one on which, to conclude, we can only invite readers to embark with us.

Acknowledgments

We would like to thank the Faculty of Theology of the University of Oxford, Harris Manchester College, Oxford, the Kirby Laing Institute for Christian Ethics, Tyndale House, Cambridge, and Blacknall Presbyterian Church, Durham, North Carolina, for their financial assistance, logistic aid and hospitality in support of this project. We received an early boost to the project when in 2007 at our very first meeting in Cambridge to sit down and write we unexpectedly ran into the author of one of our favorite commentaries on 1 Corinthians, Richard Hays, with whom we spent a wonderful evening talking about Paul and music. We are also grateful for the feedback received from (primarily British) colleagues in Systematic Theology and New Testament Studies during a colloquium in Oxford in January 2010 on an early draft of the project as well as invitations from Andrew Clarke in 2009 and Grant Macaskill in 2016 to present portions of the work in the New Testament Research Seminar in Aberdeen. It was a special delight to offer a "double act" presentation of a chapter of this work to a joint faculty and staff event hosted by the student theological society at Duke Divinity School in 2009 and organized by its president, Matthew Nickoloff. The feedback offered by graduate students on later drafts in the Theological Ethics Research Seminar in Aberdeen 2010–2012 was especially valuable, with special thanks to Tyler Atkinson for his extensive comments on several points of Greek grammar, and David Robinson, whose editorial work and detailed criticisms of the whole manuscript we much appreciated. Stephen Barton was extremely generous with expert advice only a New Testament scholar could give and offered detailed comments on the whole draft, though any surviving errors are entirely our own. An intensive session with our colleagues Tom Greggs, Don Wood, Philip Ziegler, Paul Nimmo, and Michael Mawson catalyzed a much-needed repositioning of the Preface. Daniel Patterson's extensive editorial work on the final draft was indispensable in clarifying some obscure passages and in enabling the manuscript to be brought to press in a timely fashion. Finally, we are especially grateful to our editors at Cascade Books, Charlie Collier and Rodney Clapp, whose unstinting enthusiasm for this book shone through at all the critical moments.

Portions of this volume have appeared in the following publications:

Brian Brock, "Discipline, Sport and the Religion of Winners: Paul on Running to Win the Prize," *Studies in Christian Ethics* 25 (2012) 4-19.

Bernd Wannenwetsch, "Owning Our Bodies? The Politics of Self-Possession and the Body of Christ (Hobbes, Locke, and Paul)," *Studies in Christian Ethics* 26 (2013) 50-65.

Bernd Wannenwetsch and Brian Brock, "Hearing Paul for Us Today in I Corinthians," *Lutheran Forum* 46 (2012) 9-13.

Bernd Wannenwetsch and Brian Brock, "Ein moralisches Angebot für die 'Generation Porno,'" *Salzkorn* 242 (2010) 92-97.

Abbreviations

The symbol ">" denotes a cross reference, as in (>2:9–10).

The following abbreviations are used for frequently cited works.

ACT	Anthony C. Thiselton, *First Corinthians: A Shorter Exegetical and Pastoral Commentary*
ACT2	Anthony C. Thiselton, *The First Epistle to the Corinthians*
CD	Karl Barth, *Church Dogmatics*, Bromiley and Torrance, eds., 14 vols.
CKB	C. K. Barrett, *A Commentary on the First Epistle to the Corinthians*
CSEL	Corpus Scriptorum Ecclesiasticorum Latinorum, 99 vols.
DBWE	Dietrich Bonhoeffer, *Dietrich Bonhoeffer's Works in English*, Green, ed., 17 vols.
DEG	David E. Garland, *1 Corinthians*
GB	Gerald Bray, ed., *1–2 Corinthians*
JC	John Calvin, *The First Epistle of Paul the Apostle to the Corinthians*
JK	Judith L. Kovacs, trans. and ed., *1 Corinthians: Interpreted by Early Christian Commentators*
JMO	Jerome Murphy-O'Connor, *Keys to First Corinthians: Revisiting the Major Issues*
LW	Martin Luther, *Luther's Works*, American Edition, Pelikan and Lehmann, eds., 55 vols.
PG	J. P. Migne, ed., *Patrologiae cursus completus: Series graeca*, 161 vols.
PL	J. P. Migne, ed., *Patrologiae cursus completus: Series latina*, 221 vols.
Pusey	E. B. Pusey, ed., *A Library of Fathers of the Holy Catholic Church: Anterior to the Division of the East and West*, 48 vols.

RBH	Richard B. Hays, *First Corinthians*
RFC	Raymond F. Collins, *First Corinthians*
SC	Sources chrétiennes, 548 vols.
ST	Thomas Aquinas, *The Summa Theologica*, Fathers of the English Dominican Province
Staab	K. Staab, ed., *Pauluskommentar aus der griechischen Kirche aus Katenhandschriften gesammelt*
TA	Thomas Aquinas, *Commentary on the First Epistle to the Corinthians*
VPF	Victor Paul Furnish, *The Theology of the First Letter to the Corinthians*

1 Corinthians 1

Called to Differentiated Unity

¹Paul, called to be an apostle of Christ Jesus by the will of God, and our brother Sosthenes . . .

In the very first line of Paul's epistle to the Corinthians we hear the opening note of a theme that will resound throughout the Apostle's letter: to be in Christ is to be characterized by the practice of naming without boasting. As Paul will soon elaborate in greater detail, this naming of both oneself and others proceeds very differently than the naming that has fueled the factionalization of the Corinthian church. In a move that we will discover to be characteristic of his apostolate, Paul opens his letter by immediately exemplifying that to which he will later (in 3:5–9) explicitly call the Corinthians: a form of church unity characterized by equality in differentiated cooperation. Accordingly, we must recognize that in presenting himself as writing *with* **our brother Sosthenes** Paul cannot be drawing attention to status differentials. Whether Sosthenes took Paul's dictation or discussed the letter with him,[1] such a subordinate figure would easily have been ignored in a greeting. Yet, by explicitly naming him, Paul affirms Sosthenes not as a servant but as a co-worker, a co-producer of this letter.

Commentators modern and ancient have tended to portray this act of inclusion as one of "political tact"[2] toward the wayward Corinthians—Paul hoped to "be more successful with the name of Sosthenes in the prescript of his letter" because "the appearance of that name . . . would give his argument more persuasive force and reliability in the eyes of the Corinthians."[3]

---

1. The practicalities of this secretarial relationship, which was widespread in an age in which writing with quill on papyrus was a more labor-intensive process, are helpfully explained in Longenecker, "Ancient Amanuenses," 281–97, and Richards, *The Secretary in the Letters of Paul*.

2. Richard Hays' phrase (RBH, 16).

3. Verhoef, "Senders of the Letters," 421, quoted in Murphy-O'Connor, JMO, 10. Compare Theodoret: "Since he is about to criticize them, the apostle first soothes the ears of his audience so that they will accept his medicine" (*Commentary*, PG 82:229–32, quoted in JK, 18).

For reasons intrinsic to the theological logic Paul will soon be developing about the appropriate rhetorical stance of the preacher and apostle, we prefer to read the mention of Sosthenes not as a mollifying gesture but as a genuine pastoral act, one marked by its very form as a word from two *brothers*, so exemplifying the type of unity to which Paul will soon exhort the Corinthian believers.

This extension of Paul's authorship by linking it with his Christian brother does not, however, amount to an extension of his apostolate. How then to read Paul's opening self-presentation as an apostle? Perhaps Paul is mentioning his apostolate as one offers a credential to signal the rights of authority, as the later threat to "come with a rod" (4:21) seems to corroborate?

Historical research has suggested that such a gesture of "waving one's credentials" was as familiar in the ancient world as it is in ours. In both contexts it is one of the power moves available to a speaker who wishes to claim an elite vantage point in order to legitimate the correction of those now established as inferiors, a claim typically shored up by some claim to possess exclusive knowledge or expertise. We understand Paul to be making a very different gesture, reminding the Corinthians that as an apostle his purpose is very different: it is his God-given vocation to set both himself and the Corinthians under one and the same Lord. The naming of the will of God as the *source* of his apostolicity is thus to be understood as of special importance because of the claim it will lay on the *form* his apostolate takes. For Paul, any invocation of God's will cannot avoid an implied reference to the well-known overthrow of his own will in his conversion.[4] In a memorable act of divine irony, God has inverted Paul's publicly expressed will to *undermine* churches by turning it into the very public and visible activity of *building them up*. By emphasizing from the start the role of God's will in his life, Paul signals that he does not understand his epistle as the intervention of an apostle determined to overcome what he sees as the stubborn and perverse wills of the Corinthians. Rather, with this salutation Paul signals that his letter will be a move within God's gracious action to overcome the stubborn wills of *both* Paul and the people.

We can thus gloss Paul's self-presentation in this opening line as follows: "You may will to establish all sorts of other authorities, and I may even will to escape becoming embroiled in this conflict, but God has set us into this relationship of church and apostle, and situated all our human wills within one unifying divine will." It is instinctive for us modern Westerners to position Paul's relationship to the Corinthians in terms of a clash of wills, shaped as our sensibilities are by the ideas of Weber and Nietzsche. In a

---

4. Taylor, "Conflict as Context," 915–45.

mirror image contrasting starkly with the divine irony of Paul's conversion, such a reading recapitulates a core component of the problem that besets the Corinthians: it obscures Paul's attention to the dynamics of God's chosen way of overcoming the antagonism caused by all human willfulness—a willfulness from which no one is exempt, even an apostle.

It is on these grounds that we read the invocation of Paul's apostleship as his first pastoral act toward the Corinthian believers, his first compressed and exemplary articulation of the truth that the operative agency governing their situation is God's. God's will stands over, contradicting and so claiming and reformulating all these human wills. That Paul was **called** by the **will of God** is a further specification of what he is indicating when he speaks of God's will. Not only do human agents only properly understand themselves when aware that they exist within the superior realm of God's action, but, more importantly, they must recognize that divine action has already been concretized in their very existence. To speak of one's self as called is to indicate that God's willing has been embodied in specific claims on human lives, paradigmatically displayed here in the bond with which God has bound Paul to the Corinthian believers (4:8-9). Though Paul may not always be happy about having been given this role, he embraces the fatherly authority that has been laid upon him. In a move similar to his inclusion of Sosthenes, Paul extends his own identity in verse 1 as **called** (κλητὸς/ *klētos*) to the members of the Corinthian church in verse 2. This unity in vocation prepares the ground for Paul's paraenesis to follow, a specific and often repeated form of address to the **brothers** (ἀδελφοί/*adelphoi*) (v. 10).[5]

Paul as Apostle, Parent, and Midwife

> ²To the church of God that is in Corinth, to those who are sanctified in Christ Jesus, called to be saints, together with all those who in every place call on the name of our Lord Jesus Christ, both their Lord and ours:
> ³Grace to you and peace from God our Father and the Lord Jesus Christ.

Having presented himself as "one of the called," Paul now turns to name his addressees, clarifying the sense in which he and the Corinthians share a single calling—they stand with **all those who in every place call on the name of our Lord Jesus Christ, both their Lord and ours.** The middle/passive participle construction **sanctified in Christ Jesus** (ἡγιασμένοις/

---

5. For an exegetical and theological discussion of this formula, see Wannenwetsch, "'Members of One Another,'" 200-204.

hēgiasmenois) emphasizes that the term *sanctification* does not refer to moral faultlessness but to a state of living within and under continual divine refashioning. To address the faithful as those who are **called to be saints** is therefore a gesture aimed at heightening their awareness of the sanctifying work of God that is already underway. The Apostle's highly qualified use of the language of sanctification thus offers us a compressed introduction to the content of verses 4–9 as they relate to verses 11ff. We cannot appreciate the theological force of this chapter if we fail to note the striking fact that it is precisely a community shot through with factions and immorality that Paul addresses as **sanctified in Christ Jesus**. How are we to take such an apparent "misnaming" of his recipients? We will only grasp the implications of Paul's naming precisely these believers "sanctified" if we continue on to his further specification that they are such a community together **with all those who in every place call on the name of our Lord Jesus Christ**.

With this formulation Paul simultaneously points to that which threatens the church's sanctification and invokes the power that overcomes this threat. The Corinthian believers are undermining their sanctification in a variety of ways, but the forms these individual threats take in reality share one single grammar. Though the immediate issues in Corinth are factionalism and immoral behavior, Paul is already tracing the link that will recur in many of his responses to individual problems: the issues that plague the local church in Corinth cannot be properly resolved without becoming aware of how they inevitably affect all the other churches, **in every place**. The Corinthians must not think that their local conflicts and arguably immoral behavior can be addressed in separation from the problem of church unity. There are ways for local communities to seek holiness and define right action that can corrode the essential ligatures that bind the whole together. We are therefore warranted in thinking of Paul's move here as enacting what we might anachronistically label an anti-Donatist presupposition.[6] The fourth-century Donatists were distinctive in the seriousness with which they took the life-witness of Christians. From the perspective of the church catholic, however, they slipped into the sin of pride in being prepared to sacrifice shared community in favor of achieving what they understood as moral purity.[7] We will have several more occasions in later chapters to refer to such proto-anti-Donatist emphases, which we discover to be characteristic of the Apostle. Early on in his letter Paul is locating the Corinthian church within

---

6. "These Corinthians were like the Novotianists and the Donatists of today, who claim baptism for themselves and do not recognize anybody else's. Those who are so baptized glory in the names of Novatian and Donatus, having been deprived of the name of Christ" (Ambrosiaster, *Commentary on Paul's Epistles*, quoted in GB, 11).

7. Wannenwetsch, "Ecclesiology and Ethics," 64–71.

the *una sancta* in order to root out any belief that the local church has a right to independently legislate theological or moral questions. The Apostle is thus to be understood as present to them as a living emissary, sign, and servant of this wider community.

Given this role, it is important to note that Paul's letter does not arrive like an instruction of a distant federal governor who does not care how his decree is received so long as it is heard. The Apostle's interest in *presence* is a constitutive component of his understanding and discharge of authority, but what we mean by speaking of presence by means of the epistolary medium must be carefully specified. This will prepare us in what follows to pay attention to the way in which the different emphases of his presence with the Corinthians—fatherly and apostolic—are enacted in a peculiar and intertwining manner. Apostolic authority, on the one hand, is representative of the ecumenical church, and its prime concern is for truth to be sustained. Fatherly authority, on the other hand, is representative of the local community, primarily aiming at and growing from love. Paul's authority over the Corinthians reflects both types, but this letter shows why one must not be reduced to or mixed with the other. Rather, his apostolic authority is brought to bear on their relationship at points where it is necessary to prevent misleading conclusions that might be drawn from his fatherly authority, whereas this fatherly authority provides the basic tone of his relationship to the Corinthian church that he has begotten and through which his wider apostolate is actualized.

Yet it is precisely the embodied nature of Paul's apostolic authority that allows misunderstandings to arise of the type we see very plainly in the community at Corinth. Only because Paul was once physically present with them could he be perceived by some as all too average (4:10–12), allowing his divinely given role to become obscured to some parties. Nevertheless, Paul's understanding of his ministry compels him to be present with the community irrespective of the danger of misunderstanding—present as a mere human instead of the more unassailable role he might take up as a representative of gnomic truths and an awe-inspiring totem of God's irresistible will.

It is an artifact of the humanity of his apostolate that Paul must negotiate being prevented from being physically present in this case, and so finds himself *writing*. The Apostle is known as a powerful writer, as the evidence of his circulated letters attests: "For they say, 'His letters are weighty and strong, but his bodily presence is weak, and his speech contemptible'" (2 Cor 10:10). If his personal presence is susceptible to being underwhelming, his writing faces the opposite danger, of being received as an oracular utterance. Thus neither his presence nor his absence, it seems, has the power to ensure the Corinthians' comprehension. No single intervention can be counted on to resolve the situation. When he is present, the human is seen, and when he is absent, his ideas take on the sense of abstractly valid principles that can be cut loose from the united body, as in fact his past teachings had been misunderstood and used by some to shore up their factionalist positions.

Paul's response to this dilemma is theologically illuminating in that it suggests that what matters is not this or that *type* of authority—whether apostolic or fatherly—but its *manner of discharge*. Ever alert to misconstrual, Paul subversively qualifies his fatherly authority by drawing out the feminine nurturing that is also intrinsic to his apostolate. He is not only a carer for and feeder of the Corinthians,[8] but precisely in this activity is also a midwife to them. Such midwifery aims to bring to birth[9] within the congregation an ethos of *love in truth* and *truth in love*. Amidst the mutual recriminations and the temptation to resolve them through formal means of governance—perhaps by separating the warring factions or tamping down the conflict by banning discussion of the contested issues—an authority of a different type appears in the person of Paul, who now recalls his past physical presence and care in order to qualify his words coming to them through the medium of writing. In either form of presence the Apostle is always careful to counteract the misunderstandings inextricably associated with his every appearance in order to direct the church's attention to the name and work of the one Lord Jesus Christ on whom they all call.

The conjunction of the difficulties faced in resolving the multilayered Corinthian disputes, combined with the complex range of misunderstandings that accompany Paul's every attempt to intervene, bring a point of fundamental importance into view: authority can only be fully recognized within dispute.[10] Paul's presence, whether in person or in writing, is not the arrival of an authority that proffers a formula or technique that will break the Corinthian deadlock. Rather, this authority *emerges* only *from within* such bewildering conflicts, and it is in such moments that Paul's authority is increasingly recognizable as of the Lord. There are many who *claim* authority, but only the Apostle is established in power—through the exposure,

---

8. As Ambrosiaster remarks, Paul's year and a half with the Corinthians grounds his motherly solicitude toward them: "This is why he shows great confidence and affection in his dealings with them, sometimes advising, sometimes admonishing, sometimes coaxing them as if they were his children" (*Commentary*, CSEL 81/2, 3–4, quoted in JK, 8).

9. Etymologically, "authority" is derived from the Latin *auctoritas*, literally "authorship," the capacity to bring to life.

10. We draw here on Arendt's definition of political power. See *Human Condition*, 199–207.

weakness, and vindication intrinsic to the authority that lives by witnessing to a promised arrival.

These suggestions help us see the point in the startling assertion in 11:19 that "there have to be factions among you, for only so will it become clear who among you are genuine." Paul flatly states that in the church there *must be* divisions; splits do not thwart but, paradoxically, serve God's providential scheme. This sheds a very different light on the rise and role of authority within the church, intimating that ecclesial authority must be *revealed* rather than *imposed*. Paul's authority is set out as the continuance of his conversion in which God's will was first revealed to him. In the Corinthian dispute we rediscover what it means that the work of God in *calling* Paul to be an apostle is now concretely *established* through the creation of an extended relation to a given community. The Damascus road experience only prepared Paul for apostleship; the conflicts among the Corinthian believers were God's preparing of them so that Paul's embrace of his divinely given role could bloom into an actualized apostolic relationship. Knowing that he has been called to apostleship Paul must nevertheless wait and court the Corinthians as an acknowledgment that the community's free recognition is one of the constituent components of his apostolate. "1. He experiences their having-become. 2. He experiences, that they have a knowledge of their having become," observes Martin Heidegger, adding, "That means their having-become is also Paul's having-become. And Paul is co-affected by their having become."[11] As Paul will later explain, this also puts him in the awkward position of having to "waive" the rights he legitimately held in relation to the Corinthians (4:9–16). He knows only too well that God alone establishes both the calling and the situation in which authority becomes actual. Hence he can only offer his credentials as apostle as an embarrassing concession of his love for the Corinthians.

In 1 Thessalonians 2:3–13 we see that Paul can take a much different approach when setting out his authority without the distorting effects produced by the Corinthian community's coercive demand for him to produce worldly credentials. It is an instructive comparison because it reveals that the Paul who calmly expounded his account of apostolic authority to the Thessalonians refuses to add new blandishments or more compelling or extensive explication when confronted with the skepticism of the Corinthians. He flatly refuses to defend his position beyond or aside from the "invisible" establishment of his apostolicity by God. With this refusal to mount a more compelling appeal the Apostle is prepared to risk the very authority that is under threat in order to win it again. We do not think we are straining our

---

11. Heidegger, *Phenomenology of Religious Life*, 65.

distinction between two types of authority to suggest that it was the special gift of his fatherly relationship with the Corinthians that positioned Paul to react in such a nuanced way to their questioning of his apostolic authority. The peculiarly affective bond that develops within parental relationships uniquely qualifies a parent to bear the embarrassment and empathetic pain that inevitably accompanies the maturing of a child. We will need to pay due attention to the fatherly discharge of his apostolic authority if we are to make sense of several of Paul's later moves in the epistle.

At least in theory Paul could have come with a rod; he could have ruled by decree or at least used rhetorical force (as distinct from forceful rhetoric) to bring the congregation back into line. As he will explain later in the chapter, however, and as he will model in his approach to correcting the Corinthians, Paul rejects any rule by decree or manipulative force of speech. This point is explicitly stated in 4:20–21: the kingdom does not come through the machinations of speech, whether it be eloquent seduction or authoritarian demand. No mere rhetoric could possibly establish God's reign. The judging rod of authority is thus no real solution to the Corinthians' problems. Any church community devoid of the kingdom in its genuine power will find itself facing a rod, though not the rod of human coercion but that of divine judgment. Paul's presence is thus, properly understood, a sign of Jonah (Matt 16:4) among the Corinthians, at once a living invitation to repent and be remade and at the same time the concrete presence of the will of the final Judge.

Verse 3 ends with a conventional form of greeting: **Grace to you and peace from God our Father and the Lord Jesus Christ.** This greeting commends God's specific christoform grace to the Corinthians, and in so doing draws attention to its taking form in Paul's own apostolic intervention. Their ecclesial existence as an artifact of a grace in which they are already bathed is thus again highlighted. While it is clear that at the level of literary convention the verse belongs with 1–2, the verbal resonances Paul creates between verses 3 and 4 (**I give thanks to my God always for you because of the *grace of God* that has been *given you* in *Christ Jesus***) suggest that he is playing on the traditional literary forms of ancient letters to make a theological point that, we will soon discover, will be the main material theme of the letter. As he undertakes the tasks demanded by the epistolary form—from an opening self-presentation to initial acknowledgment of his recipients—Paul has already found several occasions to stress his main point: because he and the Corinthians are bound and given distinct form by the ligatures of grace they must become responsive to the permeation of their activities by the activity of a superior third party.

Fostering Doxological Perception

> ⁴I give thanks to my God always for you because of the grace of God that has been given you in Christ Jesus, ⁵for in every way you have been enriched in him, in speech and knowledge of every kind—⁶just as the testimony of Christ has been strengthened among you—⁷so that you are not lacking in any spiritual gift as you wait for the revealing of our Lord Jesus Christ. ⁸He will also strengthen you to the end, so that you may be blameless on the day of our Lord Jesus Christ. ⁹God is faithful; by him you were called into the fellowship of his Son, Jesus Christ our Lord.

Now that the author and recipients of the letter have been named, the letter moves into its material treatment of the community. The first two verses are linked to the doxology of verses 4–9 by verse 3, in which Paul gives notice that he will draw attention to the "new order of things, an order of grace and peace,"¹² which the name of **Jesus Christ** brings into existence. This name occurs in every line of verses 3–9, and so again Paul models a form of address perfectly matched with the message he will soon address to Corinthian factions gathering around various other names. With this ostentatious repetition of the name of Jesus Christ, Paul thus plays with and counters the Corinthians' habit of "calling on names" in order to emphasize the one authority that is above every name.

Beginning with a move that may jar many Protestant ears, Paul presumes that the Corinthians have not been called into a direct, individual "personal relationship" with God, but into **the fellowship of his Son**. To know Christ is to be made a part of his body. Paul is unambiguous that this body is not a loose aggregate of individual relationships but κοινωνία (*koinōnia*)—an entity that is fundamentally communal. **By him you were called into this fellowship**. This is a crucial point easily obscured by our modern individualist sensibilities, as exemplified by Stephen Barton's reading of this verse: "Their call is not to apostleship but to be 'saints' (*hagioi*), individuals set apart by union with Christ—'sanctified (*hēgiasmenois*) in Christ Jesus'—who together make up a single body in one place."¹³ Like Schleiermacher's account of faith as having an innate tendency to

---

12. Barton, "1 Corinthians," 1317.
13. Ibid., 1316. Hays takes a very similar line. "Those who participate in the covenant community are the recipients of God's freely given mercy, and they therefore stand within the sphere of God's peace, a peace that should extend to their relationships with one another" (RBH, 17).

congregate,[14] such readings recapitulate the very misunderstanding that bedevils the Corinthians: that the "community" is assumed to be an agglomeration of enlightened individuals and is therefore in principle not an essential part of Christ-following—a matter not of the *esse* of faith, but of its *bene esse* at best. The problem, then, is that the Corinthians conceive *koinonia* as the mere proximity of vertical relationships, but in so doing they drain the immediacy from the gospel's ineradicably social thrust, a thrust captured nicely by Origen: "You were called for no other purpose than to be one with us in him."[15]

Because Paul speaks out of a clear awareness of his place in the fellowship of the saints, it is entirely appropriate that he composes a song of praise to God for the Corinthian community in verses 3-9. **I give thanks to my God always for you** (pl.). Modern commentaries often rest content by simply noting the formulaic structure of this expression and indicating that it seems to be a greeting formula or thanksgiving.[16] Be that as it may, what is striking about *this* greeting is its jarring dissonance with the situation Paul addresses in the rest of the letter. In other words, we would never know from this doxology that the Corinthian community is in disarray. Rather than meeting this disorder with correction, Paul praises God for the Corinthian church, and apparently without reservation when he says, **in every way you have been enriched in him, in speech and knowledge of every kind**—when they are actually fighting and teaching falsely. Paul even takes them to be **not lacking in any spiritual gift**, and to be a community **he will also strengthen . . . to the end**. Such certainty about the blessedness of the Corinthian church appears suspiciously close to ironic hyperbole, if not an outright contradiction to the rest of the letter. How are we to interpret the stubborn fact that this formula flies in the face of the state of affairs described in the body of the letter? Do we have here perhaps an example of a particularly free-handed redaction?

A prominent interpretative strand in patristic commentaries answers this question by reference to distinct saved and damned populations that they assume to exist within the Corinthian church.[17] On this reading some

---

14. Schleiermacher, "Fourth Speech—Association in Religion, or Church and Priesthood," in *On Religion*, 147-209.

15. Origen, *Commentary on 1 Corinthians* 1.3, quoted in GB, 8.

16. Hans Conzelmann is representative (*1 Corinthians*, 25-26).

17. Origen: "These remarks of Paul are not appropriate for sinners, nor are the later remarks appropriate for the righteous" (*Homilies on 1 Corinthians*, 232-34). Ambrosiaster: "Paul addresses two populations in such a way that when he criticizes, those who behave badly should know that it is written to them, and likewise, when he praises, those who stick steadfastly to the rule should know that this is said to them" (*Commentary*,

passages in the letter are directed to a remnant of individuals assumed to have been protected undefiled in the midst of a false group that is sowing discord. The latter are the intended recipients of the epistle's corrective portions to come, indicating that the present doxology should be understood to be praising only those within the Corinthian church who have remained "pure." The theological problem created by this line of interpretation is that it introduces a fundamental divide between verses 4–10 and the rest of the letter. This is to position the bulk of the letter as a disciplinary and pedagogical intervention that will allow the flagrant sinners in the church to rejoin the elect who receive the praise here. The overall effect is to read the epistle as offering only a few verses of gospel before being devoted predominantly to pedagogical law.

This theological partitioning of the book into discrete and essentially separate addresses is structurally parallel to the tendency in modern historical scholarship to assume that ancient texts have almost inevitably been constructed from several different source documents. While in the course of this commentary we will take seriously and often find rich theological material in the text-critical and lexical disputes that have been raised by modern scholarship in the course of arguments for and against the unity of this letter, we begin with the presumption of theological and textual unity. We will do so in hopes of discovering a more complex unity of the epistle than we would expect were we to begin with the presumption that textual problems can be solved by invoking partition hypotheses. Reading the epistle as a unity, addressed as a whole to one and the same body, allows each of its parts to be understood as both good news and judgment, an evangelical instruction aimed to unfold the concrete implications of the hopeful reality that verses 4–7 depict. The whole passage is consistently held in the aorist tense, denoting a state of affairs once begun but still ongoing: **Thanks to my God always for you because of the grace of God that *has been* given you in Christ Jesus**. Here the interesting point is the mode of referring to grace: ἐπὶ τῇ χάριτι (*epi tē chariti*), best rendered as "according to grace."[18] With this formulation Paul signals that he is looking at the community with the eyes of gratitude, in the midst of all their sinfulness, but "according to" the grace of God.[19] The translators of the NRSV were hence right to update the

---

CSEL 81/2:6–8, quoted in JK, 16). Origen famously deployed a three-tier scheme to partition humankind and a two-tier scheme to grade the ontological state of Christians, a scheme allowing him to read texts such as the Corinthian correspondence as separate addresses to two communities that happen to reside in the same locale.

18. Here ἐπὶ is followed by a dative.

19. As Dietrich Bonhoeffer realized, in so seeing the community Paul models the appropriate stance of all Christians toward their local church community. "If we do not

RSV's "in every way you [the Corinthians] *were* enriched in [Jesus Christ]," with **in every way you *have been* enriched in him.**

These grammatical considerations indicate why it is impossible to read this opening to be suggesting that the Corinthians were once given grace that has now been lost, with the Apostle's prayer expressing a hope for its recovery. On our reading Paul takes seriously the ongoing reality of grace in the church, which the local community needs to recognize as present and real. The main reason for Paul's confidence on this point is flatly stated: **God is faithful.** Because Paul understands God's faithfulness as the determining environment of the church, and hence also of his relationship with it, the disputes among the believers that are so obviously visible to the observer's eye are revealed as illusory on the ontological level. These disputes are not the environment that determines the situation at its heart. Not allowing his gaze to be fixated on the empirical surface of events, Paul is determined to bring into view what we might call a divine aesthetic so that the Corinthians will begin to be able to perceive the situation in light of God's providential care for all involved. From this vantage point even the church's factionalism must appear as a means through which God's intervening grace will eventually be revealed, providing, as it does, the very occasion for this letter.

This reading stands in contrast to an interpretative line popular since Bultmann, in which the apparent conflict between Paul's praise for the Corinthian believers and their parlous state, as he will soon describe it, is parsed using another partitioning theory, the famous indicative/imperative scheme.[20] Richard Hays draws on this rationale in commenting that the contrast between the doxology and the rest of the letter implies that "to be God's people entails certain obligations of obedience ... If the church is to represent God rightly ... certain norms and standards must be kept."[21] On our reading, however, Paul is not exhorting the Corinthians to "be what you are" but rather inviting them to "become what you have been given to become." This subtle but crucial distinction will help us understand better what Paul is doing in this letter when he constantly directs the Corinthians' attention to their transformation into an *ekklēsia*, a life that has *already* begun. Paul can thus affirm that the Corinthians are not lacking in gifts

---

give thanks for the Christian community in which we have been placed, even when there are no great experiences, no noticeable riches, but much weakness, difficulty, and little faith—and if, on the contrary, we only keep complaining to God that everything is so miserable and so insignificant and does not at all live up to our expectations—then we hinder God from letting our community grow according to the measure and riches that are there for us all in Jesus Christ." Bonhoeffer, *Life Together* (DBWE 5), 37.

20. Bultmann, *Theology of the New Testament*, 1:332–33.

21. Hays, RBH, 16.

even as they deploy them to create factions. In this situation Paul hints at the redirection he will be seeking by praising God for strengthening the Corinthians to the end even in the midst of their dissension. He thus boldly commends them precisely at the points where the controversies lie.[22]

Again the contrast with the doxology addressed to the Thessalonians is illuminating. The latter makes very specific and straightforward reference to what Paul experienced when he was bodily present with them as the basis for his gratitude. Recalling Thessalonica Paul can praise God for his particular works in their midst, comforted by the assurance of their assent to this rendition of events. It would seem to be highly risky for the Apostle to assume any such shared perspective in his address to the Corinthian community. Given the difficulties that will be involved in Paul and the Corinthians reaching a shared description of their current situation, we might have expected the Apostle to get the ball rolling with a more generic and therefore less contentious doxological formula, putting off the rebukes he has in mind by initially and tactfully delaying any reference to the disputes currently raging in the church. Instead, he immediately dives into the fray with a precisely targeted doxological formulation proclaiming his gratitude to God at exactly the points—their gifts, speech, and knowledge—over which the community is in conflict.

The complex subtlety of the terms Paul chooses is often breathtaking—as, for instance, in his use of the term *gnosis* in the expression **knowledge of every kind** (1:5). This initial resonance would be subtly polemical in insinuating the question, "Since you've been given genuine *gnosis*, why the interest in Hellenistic-style substitutes?" The expansive description **of every kind** is followed by a hint in 1:6 that in the Corinthian church this proper knowledge is mixed up with a variety of presumptuous forms of knowledge. Paul is deftly positioning the Corinthians to understand that the sort of *gnosis* they really need is that which is spelled out in the **testimony**, the μαρτύριον (*martyrion*) **of Christ** (1:6). Already here, by juxtaposing their knowledge and the *martyrion* of Christ, Paul hints at the point that the folly of the cross is the true *gnosis* that alone can satisfy and unify the Corinthians.

Everything hinges on the reader noticing that Paul is alluding directly to their specific problems *in the mode of doxology*.[23] He is not, then, delaying correction, but as prologue to his more candid discussion of the church's predicament, he is from the outset correcting them in a highly theologized

---

22. Garland notes that "Paul is not being sarcastic but is genuinely affirming the particular gifts from God that [the Corinthians] prize the most" (*1 Corinthians*, 34). He does so, we would like to add, by way of qualification, however, not simply to reaffirm, but to reconfigure their understanding of the gifts that they do indeed possess.

23. Heil, *The Letters of Paul*.

manner. He praises them before the Father precisely in their weaknesses by naming that which they need most and which God has already provided. The Apostle's praise is formulated succinctly because he seeks in the first instance not to *uncover* the Corinthians' sins in a kind of inquisition, but to discover with them the fullness of what Christ has given this particular community to *cover* the multitude of their sins.[24] This is why Paul first sets out a doxological counter-view of the contested issues in the teeth of the empirical situation. We may paraphrase the implied statement this passage makes to the Corinthians thus: "I thank God that he has given you all you need, even in this seemingly chaotic situation and despite your delusionary self-satisfaction." Described in more fundamental terms, Paul's opening gesture meets the problem of not being able to trust that he and the Corinthians have a shared narrative of the situation by *redirecting attention to the cross*. The Apostle is only content to draw on the various theological and ethical themes that the rest of his letter will address after making sure that all parties involved have their eyes fixed on the same divine agent who has been revealed most fully in the cross as the supreme act of divine love.

Such an opening is thus best understood as a solicitous preparation for Paul's readers to grasp his mode of speaking in the remainder of the letter. What follows is Paul's attempt to be of service to the community by helping them catch up with the wonderful gifts they have already received. All the forms of belief and behavior he will go on to censure are thus demarcated from the outset as the congregation's foolish preoccupation with lesser goods or even patent evils rather than the gifts that are already present and tangible. Their boasting speech and the spiritual gifts they demonstrate or want to see in Paul are but tragicomic parodies of what is already being given to them in the word of the cross.

Paul's firm hope is that this tragicomedy will be satisfactorily resolved: **He will also strengthen you *to the end*, so that you may be blameless on the day of the Lord Jesus Christ. God is faithful; by him you were called into the fellowship of his Son, Jesus Christ our Lord** (1:8–9). That Paul's confidence is sustained by God's faithfulness alone has direct implications for how he desires the Corinthians to understand their spiritual gifts. They are not lacking in spiritual gifts, Paul instructs them, but only insofar as they wait **for the revealing of our Lord** (v. 7). The participle ἀπεκδεχομένους (*apekdechomenous*) means "waiting for" but can also be rendered as "accepting." To receive a spiritual gift is to be put in a position of passionate waiting for the revealing of the Lord. It would therefore be misguided to read Paul's assurance that the Lord will **strengthen** the Corinthians **to the**

---

24. See Kierkegaard, *Works of Love*, 292–93.

end solely as a reference to their being saved in the final judgment; Paul's formulation nurtures in real time the passionate longing of those who wait. As Luther similarly counsels, "You have all you need for the future; there is nothing wanting, there is no lack of any gift necessary for that future. We need but one thing—that the Lord comes, and we await his coming. This is our lack, nothing else."[25] This emphasis on waiting affords an important insight into the spiritual character of the gifts. When Christians no longer wait (and thus by default assume themselves to be recipients), the Spirit's gifts can only be collapsed into all too human skills, traits or habits that can and must be acquired. This collapse provides the conditions in which an acquisitive posture towards gifts tends to arise that fuels an economy of envy within the church. To forestall this collapse Paul insists that the Corinthians have all that they need only insofar as they live in trust of an appearing Lord. Ceasing to wait leads the *ecclesia* into an arena of competitive power struggle indicative of believers having lost touch with their true gifting.

All the criticisms of the Corinthians that the Apostle will soon set out will be precise pointers to deformations that have descended on the fellowship precisely at those points where they have fallen short of this essential waiting. The contours of our reading here are more sharply visible when contrasted with a reading like Jerome's: "*Although* we lack no gift, *nevertheless* we await the appearance of our Lord Jesus Christ."[26] While Jerome seems to be saying that "*even though* you already have everything, it is *still* appropriate to wait for the Lord," we have preferred a reading stimulated by Luther, which might be paraphrased as "you have everything that you need *so that* you can wait for the Lord Jesus." This latter prioritization ensures that the purpose of the spiritual gifts continues to be sharply defined by reference to what is necessary for the sustenance of the community. What has been given in Christ Jesus is not a gnosis that *ends* the wait for Christ, as though it already united the Corinthians with their divine nature. Rather, what has been given is the *continual* waiting of those **called into fellowship**.

The specific form of the Corinthians' faithlessness has now come to light. They do not just generally lack faith, nor do they repudiate belief in God, but they exhibit an embodied failure to grasp the fact that God has already given this particular community exactly the gifts they need. Their lack of faith is their belief that *God has not kept faith with them*. By Paul's lights, the Corinthians' striving for greater gifts (4:7; 14:12) amounts to a motion of distrust of God as the giver of all good things. They have enacted

---

25. Luther, *Epistel-Auslegung*, 2:14. All quotations from this commentary are translated by the authors.

26. Jerome, *Against the Pelagians* 2.8, quoted in GB, 7; emphasis added.

a faith that is oriented by the assumption that grace is something that can be appropriated and accumulated, and the social conflict this fuels is just an unsurprising byproduct. The Corinthians have not recognized God's real gifts because they have been striving to claim spiritual ecstasy and dominance now—an attitude ironically exposed as a fall from the state of patient confidence in this particular grace.

Paul's doxology thus both reveals the Corinthians' anti-doxology and offers them its precise antidote. If they were to take up the doxology he offers them, their problems would be resolved. Were they able to be united in singing 1:4–9, and with integrity, the rest of the letter would be unnecessary. Thus, *we most fruitfully read the rest of the epistle not as a moralistic pedagogy, but as an invitation designed to bring them to the performance of their appropriate unity in the real grace that is being bestowed on them.* Though by offering this doxology Paul has in principle offered the spiritual meal the starving Corinthians need, he cannot stop here, because he knows they cannot yet effectively digest it. For now the Corinthians will still need to be spoon-fed the component moves that must be learned in order to be united in this doxology (3:2). It displays Paul's parental love for the Corinthians that he will devote the rest of the letter to spoon-feeding them the very same food he is already offering them here but at the much greater length necessary for their immature gums. This graceful expansion of an initial tersely expressed truth in order to meet the capacities of sinful ears is not without precedent in scripture. It echoes, for example, the way the first commandment of the Decalogue is unfolded in the nine other commandments that make its meaning plain. And the Decalogue is itself part of the expansion of the first simple command given to Adam and Eve in the garden which Israel called the Torah.[27] In the same way, the remainder of this letter should be understood as a detailed recapitulation of the introit doxology, a necessary elaboration calling a sinful community back to the song of praise for which they were redeemed.

Ecclesial Unity and the Proximity of Grace

> [10]Now I appeal to you, brothers and sisters, by the name of our Lord Jesus Christ, that all of you be in agreement and that there be no divisions among you, but that you be united in the same mind and the same purpose.

---

27. Luther, *Lectures on Genesis Chapters 1–5* (1535), in LW 1:108–9.

The judgment that it is this precise doxological food that the Corinthians need displays the essence of Paul's fatherly relationship to the church that he founded in this place; verse 1:10 makes it clear that we are now turning to the baby food. Four times Paul must reiterate his point to those who cannot suppress the question, "What do you mean by 'unity'?" "By unity," we overhear Paul replying, "I mean you should **be in agreement**, you should have **no divisions**, and you should be **united in the same mind and the same purpose**." The expression **that all of you agree** (τὸ αὐτὸ λέγητε πάντες/*to auto legēte pantes*) would be literally translated "that you speak the same"; it is unity of shared confession.

Had the Corinthians grasped their given oneness in their **Lord Jesus Christ** (1:9) it would have been unnecessary to develop such a detailed definition of unity as oneness of mind, speech, purpose, and opinion. The liminal position of 1:10 between Paul's doxology and his more detailed comment on the community's problems is theologically significant because it foregrounds Paul's intentional setting of his appeals to *koinonia* under the **name** that indicates the presence of the particular sphere of power in which the ecumenical church exists. The formulation is significant because the admonition that follows to **unity** and **agreement** will be qualified as agreement that is consistent with calling on the name of Christ and on no other basis, whether methods of consensus building or redefinitions that artificially create apparent unities, such as when the scope of agreement is narrowed to the lowest common denominator.

The tailored exhortation to the Corinthians now begins in earnest and will not let up until the conclusion of the letter. In the name of a reality that precedes them, Paul will try to entice them from a number of angles to "look" at that which is already present. **Brothers and sisters** is an address referring to the *koinonia* in the preceding verse. The agreement with each other that Paul desires for the Corinthians is already contained in the story of the progress of grace amidst their very own community that he has just sung for them, and it is by joining him in this worshipful description of their situation that they will discover their unity of mind and purpose. It is a concrete and realized unity that will reach far beyond the mere collective assent to a general account of Christ's work. Their divisions will only be resolved as this community is drawn into a shared understanding of God's *particular* work among *this* community: **By him *you* were called into the fellowship of his Son**.

There are, of course, alternatives to our proposal in which Paul is understood to be suggesting that the problem of Corinthian unity cannot be resolved through efforts to ensure that their descriptions of God are more aligned in a conceptual sense but will depend on their coming to make a better confession together of what Christ has done *for them*. Hays, for example, targets the perennial temptation of the church to collapse God's work for local churches into parochial self-absorption by reading this passage in the opposite direction:

> We are apt to think of the church's life and mission on a small, even trivial, scale. We tend to locate the identity of our communities within some denominational program, or within local politics, or within recent history. But Paul urges us instead to understand the church in a cosmic frame of reference that points toward the final triumph of God's righteousness, the setting right of all things in Jesus Christ. When we understand ourselves as actors in that drama, we undergo a crucial shift of perspective.[28]

Our reading has suggested that already in verse 2 Paul has done the work of contextualizing the Corinthians within the cosmic story of Christ's work. Now he moves beyond his admonishment to acknowledge that they are not a parochial enclave and begins to teach them what it means to be properly aware of the sheer locality of the reconciliation wrought by Jesus Christ's singular cosmic work.

Rivalry vs. *Oikodome*

> [11] For it has been reported to me by Chloe's people that there are quarrels among you, my brothers and sisters. [12] What I mean is that each of you says, "I belong to Paul," or "I belong to Apollos," or "I belong to Cephas," or "I belong to Christ."

As Paul begins to unfold his more detailed discussion he opens by remarking that **it has been reported to me by Chloe's people that there are quarrels among you**. The suggestion here is not that there is a general problem with quarreling in the community that needs to be addressed. The Apostle's target is a specific type of quarrelling about the place of the community in Christ's work: **What I mean is that each of you says, "I belong to Paul," or "I belong to Apollos," or "I belong to Cephas," or "I belong to Christ."** There is no hint here that Paul believes the church should be a place without dissension, some kind of non-conflictual utopia. Nor is his concern the promotion of the *image* of unity, the church's "good face" it naturally seeks to protect. Paul is sharply focused on confronting the one form of

---

28. Hays, RBH, 20.

disunity that is genuinely dividing. There are types of dispute and conflict in the church that may well be appropriate and even worth having within the fundamental unity brought about by Jesus Christ. Such a unity will in fact be strengthened rather than weakened by conflicts reflecting a community's joint commitment to truth and love, and therefore differ in kind from the sorts of unity that can, for a time, arise in communities that are unified only by some form of idolatrous doxology or common enemy.

The account of unity Paul offers is the inverse of the Roman principle *divide et impera*: divide and conquer. The Romans meticulously developed theories and techniques such as bribing factions and sowing rumors before commencing more direct military attacks. Surface solidarities, they understood, must be broken up to expose their underlying fissures and antagonisms. The Romans would then attack with legions whose power was achieved by standardizing human behavior more thoroughly than the world had ever seen.

Because today we live in highly developed societies in which it appears self-evident that greater uniformity generates greater efficiency and therefore power, we are strongly tempted to read Paul as advocating the sociological principle that the tighter and more uniform the social unit, the fitter it will be. Yet Paul is not to be squeezed into this Procrustean bed. He is not propounding the unity associated with religious cults or political sects in which dissenting voices are expelled or manipulatively silenced, tightening up the ranks. His is no militant logic of generating power by manipulating lockstep social uniformity.

What I mean, Paul says in verse 12, is that true unity is broken up in any Christian self-understanding that conceives faith as an essentially vertical relationship with Christ. The expression **what I mean** is directed to "each of you, who *individually* say [ἕκαστος/*hekastos*] that you belong to this or the other leader." Paul's initial target is not their clustering into parties but every individual's claim that he or she belongs to this or that teacher. We can now see that the Apostle is setting out an important qualification of the agreement that is the theme of 1:10: there are many types of disunity or division, but Paul is concerned with this one specific type of disunity because it is threatening the church's very identity, their fellowship in this one Christ. The calling into this unity of fellowship is the climactic purpose of Christ's gifts (1:9), and if *this* is threatened it is more serious than the threat to other gifting, speech, and knowledge (1:5–7). "By claiming these latter gifts through acquisitive logic you destroy your actual unity," we hear Paul suggesting, "which is the organic connection of what is given with the highest of these gifts, that is, your calling to fellowship. You cannot see this connection because you are taking these gifts as itemized objects to be listed and collected by individuals." The evidence of this conceptual misunderstanding is plain: the observable fact that the Corinthians are breaking up into factions organized around founding figures is driven by the logic of the individuality of gifts—as evidenced by their arguments over who baptized them.

The Corinthians have thus translated the Christian faith into a mystagogical cult, Paul suggests, one in which the master teacher initiates seekers into a mechanism that allows each individually to receive the substance called divine wisdom. Because Apollos, for example, is a powerful rhetorician, what matters for that faction is the power of speech. Other factions' adherence to leaders possessing other gifts reflects an idolization of different skills. In every case this elevation of any given gift must happen at the expense of others, which rival groups praise. Paul's core point is to emphasize *oikodome*, the gift of upbuilding the body, which contrasts sharply with the Corinthians' idolatrous elevation of various particular gifts. This motif that we detect in the form of a compressed opening presentation here will become the major theme elaborated by the Apostle in chapter 12.

John Chrysostom shows a fine sensitivity to the connections between acquisitiveness and social rifts when he portrays the Corinthian church's divisions as reflections of the opulent and at the same time exploitative Corinthian cultural milieu with its adulation of wealth and wisdom. He suggests that the devil who "sowed division ... used the wealth and wisdom of the inhabitants as the occasion of his attack. The wealthy and the wise had formed groups ... and people were attached to one or the other of these leaders, to some because of their wealth, and to others because of their wisdom."[29] In such a social milieu, the individualist presumptions of pagan philosophy would accelerate a spirit of religious competitiveness. "That is why they were divided into sects, something else they learned from the philosophers, who are constantly competing."[30] Only those who think you can personally "own" wisdom or spiritual gifts will get caught in the trap of exclusionary dissension in assuming a zero-sum competition to always be afoot in which your gain is my loss, and vice versa. Put in simple terms, the Corinthians understand both Christ and the spiritual gifts within the logic of "commodity"—something that can be possessed as an individual "holding" rather than something which is to be ardently pursued (12:31) for the benefit of the whole—as we will elaborate in our comments on chapter

---

29. Chrysostom, *Homilies on 1 Corinthians*, Introductory Summary, PG 61:9–12, quoted in JK, 9.

30. Ibid., 10.

14. Commodities create markets, and markets create inequalities and with them rivalries.

For this reason these rivalries can even extend to squabbles over the rightful title to Paul's own name: **I belong to Paul**. Some, Paul notes, even claim to be a "Christ" party, understood in a structural parallel to these other parties. That Christ himself has become subject to such claims makes this a quarrel, as Chrysostom notes, "not over trivial matters but over something fundamental. Even those who said they were of Christ were at fault, because they were implicitly denying this to others and making Christ the head of a faction rather than the head of the whole church."[31] We might characterize the Corinthians' crucial error as one that claims founding figures in terms of precursors on whom *they* can lay claim, as opposed to fathers who will *themselves* lay claim *on* the community by critically addressing them.[32] When some of them say they are "of Paul" they are in effect claiming Paul's founding act as legitimizing their present claims. By referring to himself as their "father" Paul implicitly rejects this logic in order to prepare the way for his very different account of relationships of belonging, power, and authority, which he has already begun to display in this chapter.[33]

Butchering Christ's Body

> [13] **Has Christ been divided? Was Paul crucified for you? Or were you baptized in the name of Paul?** [14] **I thank God that I baptized none of you except Crispus and Gaius,** [15] **so that no one can say that you were baptized in my name.** [16] **(I did baptize also the household of Stephanas; beyond that, I do not know whether I baptized anyone else.)**

Just as he undermines the possibility of a "Christ party" by asking, "**Has Christ been divided?**" Paul also undermines the idea of a Pauline party that would claim him as its representative by reference to his baptizing. The

---

31. Chrysostom, *Homilies on the Epistles of Paul to the Corinthians* 3.5, in GB, 10.

32. On the difference between precursors and fathers, see Wannenwetsch, "Conversing with the Saints," 125–36.

33. In stressing the impossibility of a "Christ party" Paul is not engaging the question of whether Christian political parties should be encouraged to exist. But he is certainly casting a critical light on any such endeavor, especially when the establishment or existence of such a party suggests an exclusivist connotation according to which "genuine Christians" would not be supporting other parties. The fact that the most significant parties in Europe that bear the term "Christian" in their official name tend to combine this designator with others such as "social" or "democratic" may be taken as an indication of a theological sensitivity towards this important concern.

language the Apostle uses in 1:13 emphasizes the shocking violence of the separation of Christ's body that has been ongoing in Corinth. The Greek verb μερίζω (*merizō*), translated here as **divided**, is the same term used for a butcher cutting a carcass into pieces. As the grammar does not demand an interrogative here, we could also render verse 13 as a statement to convey the implication that "with this logic you already chop Christ into pieces."[34] The force of Paul's question is the suggestion of the implied negative answer: that Christ (not only should not but) *cannot* be individually claimed. By identifying Christ with Paul *or* Apollos or even with a "partisan Christ" the Corinthians chop up the body of Christ as a butcher does a carcass. The declarative form emphasizes that everyone is individually claiming Christ, and that it is precisely through the making of such individualist claims that the *koinonia* of Christ's body is dismembered. The one chopping up implies the other, though the latter goes a step further than the former, as Chrysostom seems to sense: "You have dismembered Christ and divided up his body."[35] Just as Christ cannot be divided, so, too, must he not be separated from his body.

In a set of notes on 1 Corinthians 3, Dietrich Bonhoeffer suggests that the intention of "Christ's group," to appeal to Christ without the mediation of messengers "in contrast to the apostles," makes it, in fact, "the most dangerous group."[36] The peculiar threat posed by a "Christ party" to the body as a whole in its denial of mediation is, however, no less dangerous than making the (apostolic) mediator himself the center around which the community organizes itself. For the Apostle, it is ludicrous to suggest that a party might form around Paul, because **Paul has not been crucified for you**. He then adds a **thanks to God** that baptism has never been his focus, as this might be seen to lend credibility to what he takes to be the patently silly suggestion of the "paulinists."

"But wait a second," we can hear Sosthenes piping up from his scribal desk, "you did baptize **Crispus,** didn't you? And how about . . ." This imagined riposte presses us to clarify how we understand ourselves correctly to listen to holy writ when it contains a course correction of this type. Our suggestion is that the sort of aside or correction represented by **I did baptize also the household of Stephanas; beyond that, I do not know whether I baptized anyone else** reveals in its own way a central feature of Paul's understating of his own work as one that is to leave space for the work of the

---

34. Patristic commentators often took verse 13 as a statement: "Christ *is* divided." Ambrosiaster, *Commentary*, CSEL 81/2, 10–13, quoted in JK, 21.

35. Chrysostom, *Homily 3*, PG 61:21–28, quoted in JK, 20.

36. Bonhoeffer, "Sketch of a Bible Study on 1 Corinthians 3, May 1940," in *Conspiracy and Imprisonment, 1940–1945* (DBWE 16), 484.

Spirit, or indeed, the folly of the cross. What we can say with certainty is that the final text retains in these traces evidence of an apostolic refusal to make balance, proportion, and polish an overriding concern in the process of composition. This is particularly remarkable in the face of Paul's reputation as the theologically heavyweight author among the apostles. Paul dictates a letter, which is evidently well organized with a clear structure. And as he presents his case we can imagine him thinking carefully about what he is to say, pausing to think, and then concentrating on properly composing and sharply qualifying his claims. And yet in the canonical epistle there remains an element of disinterest in achieving a flawless fair copy. In many explicit statements elsewhere in his writings, we notice the same strong concern of Paul's to keep open a space for the Spirit to work (Rom 7:6; 8:12–15; Gal 5:18). On the basis of these statements we are inclined to read this bit of "sloppy" text as a mark of eschatological and pneumatological openness rather than as a mere oversight or infelicity.

The Consolations of Kenotic Preaching and Wisdom

> **17 For Christ did not send me to baptize but to proclaim the gospel, and not with eloquent wisdom, so that the cross of Christ might not be emptied of its power.**

Paul now moves to clarify the senses in which the power he has in mind differs from the power claims that formed the basis of the factions in Corinth. His preaching, he will demonstrate, does not aim to found or validate any claim by its recipients to possess his mantle by right. His preaching cannot be "owned" because it proceeds from a gospel in which neither baptism nor powerful speech but the cross stands as its sole criterion of truth. That proclamation is constitutive of his apostolate is stressed by Paul's use of the term ἀπέστειλέν (*apesteilen*) in the expression **did not send me to baptize**. He then qualifies what he means by preaching, indicating that his is not the preaching of the sophist, with **eloquent wisdom** (ἐν σοφίᾳ λόγου/*en sophia logou*—literally "in the wisdom of the word"), **so that the cross might not be emptied of its power**. Here Paul directly targets the rhetorical tradition in which the skills of rhetoric were explicitly understood as disciplines to be learned so that words could be used to move people and gain political power.[37] What is only hinted at here—the setting aside of the toolkit of formal rhetoric—is materially carried out by Paul in 1 Thessalonians 2:5 in which he deliberately eschews the terminology of the educated rhetorician.

37. Garver, *Aristotle's "Rhetoric"*, ch 1.

The specific features of apostolic proclamation that Paul highlights in this context find their point of unity in one purpose: that the cross of Christ **might not be emptied**. The word used for "emptied" is κενωθῇ (*kenōthē*), the verbal form of the doctrinally suggestive concept of *kenosis*. For the strongest of theological reasons Paul seeks a way of preaching that empties his speech of all manipulative power; he desires, for the *manner* in which he represents the self-emptying of Christ to be true to its *content*, the folly of the cross. Frustrating those who expect the Apostle to demonstrate his power through mighty rhetoric, Paul knows that he needs to eschew precisely this demand if **the cross** is not going to **be emptied**. The Apostle thus keeps himself in a deliberate position of dependency—waiting for God's own authorization of his work, the proof from divine power.

The NRSV translation makes an unnecessary addition to the original wording: **so that the cross of Christ might not be emptied** *of its power*. The last three words are unnecessary because the wisdom of the cross *is* an emptying of human machination that systematically opens itself for the appearance of divine power. Despite his great reputation, John Chrysostom (which translates as "golden mouth," indicating his fame as a preacher) was an aspirant to such kenotic preaching. In one sermon he relates overhearing a story of an immature Christian debating whether Paul or Plato was the better philosopher. Chrysostom's judgment was that this Christian had already defeated himself by putting the question in these terms. To set oneself up as a contestant in the race to be most learned and eloquent is already to have given up any interest in the divine power that accompanies the wisdom of the cross.[38]

For Paul the folly of the cross is not some counterintuitive or paradoxical quality that gives him license to execute previously unthinkable pirouettes of thought. It is the much more earthy, ecclesial wisdom that discerns and resists all human power claims that undermine the church's unity in the truth. The folly of the cross is thus not correctly understood as a higher wisdom able to see something that others cannot see, a privileged epistemic vantage point in relation to natural human wisdom. It is rather a focused form of that wisdom that upbuilds *koinonia*, the community of those gathered around the truth that is Christ. Within the logic of gnosis, religion is the search for knowledge above and beyond the world; the wisdom of the cross, on the other hand, serves the material coalescence of *oikodome*, the wisdom to live as God's people and so as reconciled creatures.

Whereas the Corinthians might have considered the factionalism of their community as at worst merely embarrassing, Paul considers it the

---

38. Chrysostom, *Homily 3*, PG 61:21–28, quoted in JK, 20.

alarming yet logical extension of the form of wisdom they seek. We misunderstand the genesis of the factions if we read them as having formed as a result of the sociologically describable natural tendency among larger groups to form small subunits in which everyone can know one another. For the Corinthians, the license to form factions is directly related to their desire for knowledge as privileged epistemic insight, the insatiable craving for knowledge pressing beyond proper apprehension of the ways of God in his church and world. Ironically, Paul might have found some agreement among the gnostics in Corinth about his startling claim that "there must be divisions among you" (11:19). The "gnostics,"[39] however, would understand these divisions in terms of rungs in a ladder of progress which designate those who are worthy to belong to a particular group, the higher unity that promises to lift the individual over others.[40] The difference is that the gnostics would see both their divisions and partisan unity as inevitable entailments of their interest in escaping from the earth and with it the unenlightened, whereas Paul assumes that in God's providential care, divisions are permitted to arise only in order to generate the genuine unity of the ecclesia in Christ to which Christians can aspire within the postlapsarian world.

Again, 11:19 illumines Paul's central moves already animating this first chapter: "Indeed, there have to be factions among you, for only so will it become clear who among you are genuine." Why must this be the case? Δεῖ γὰρ καὶ αἱρέσεις (*dei gar kai haireseis*): because resurrection (here: the overcoming of division) will arrive only by way of crucifixion and dying with Christ (here: the community having to learn appropriately to mourn the painful disarticulation of Christ's body). God's way of working with the fragmented forms of human community is through crucifixion and resurrection, not by lifting believers out of history to be with the cosmic Christ. The pivotal transformation is not available through cheaper means.

Because he is working within this cruciform logic, Paul is not satisfied to pronounce a simple command to "seek unity" in 1:10. Instead of simply appealing to unity, the Apostle is committed to work with the Corinthians through the messy materiality of the manifold conflicts that compromise their unity. It is for this reason that he suggests in 11:19 that such divisions are to be the "material" of the *usus gratiae*: the mundane stuff in, with, and under which grace works its transformation. As he then goes on to elaborate

39. For more detailed discussion of this term, see our comments on 2:6-8.

40. As Stephen Barton puts it, "In consequence, wisdom in both its aspects—content and practice—tends to be hierarchical and discriminatory. It divides those who have the upbringing, learning, and leisure to pursue it from those who do not, and it divides those who follow one sophist or sage from those who follow another" ("1 Corinthians," 1318).

in chapter 12, grace aims at a union that does not simply negate division (perhaps by taking sides with the strong and expelling the weak or unenlightened) but allows for differences and creative tension in a communion whose participants are "members of one another," as Paul characterizes the principle of divine *oikodome* in Romans 12:5.[41] In his opening of 2 Corinthians, 1:3–7, Paul blesses the Father of Jesus Christ, "who consoles us in all our affliction, so that we may be able to console those who are in any affliction with the consolation with which we ourselves are consoled by God." This emphasis on consolation, however, is explicitly defined as being "through Christ," who is the meeting point of the suffering of the church and Paul: "For just as the sufferings of Christ are abundant for us, so also our consolation is abundant through Christ. If we are being afflicted, it is for your consolation and salvation; if we are being consoled, it is for your consolation, which you experience when you patiently endure the same sufferings that we are also suffering." Only on the grounds of the work of a suffering and active Christ can Paul have hope that the suffering of division will end in unity: "Our hope for you is unshaken; for we know that as you share in our sufferings, so also you share in our consolation"—that is, the Christ of crucifixion and resurrection.

We have now found the decisive clue to the linkage of the doxology of 1:4–9 to the remainder of the letter with its sharp and direct criticisms of the Corinthian community. Because he is putting his trust in and finding his consolation (meanings that coincide, interestingly, in the German translation *Trost*) in God's own deployment of specific grace (the *usus gratiae*), Paul can rest content that God has given grace in the past and so can be trusted to be working now, if even in a hidden way, to bring his church into fellowship again. Paul's central appeal must thus be understood as an invitation: he is inviting his readers into the consolation he receives in this crucified Christ. The only true consolation available to the Corinthians can never be secured through their various quests to secure special insights. Rather, by sharing in Paul's afflictions they must learn to mourn the situation as he mourns it. The problem that has prompted the Apostle to write this letter has been revealed to be, at the most fundamental level, the Corinthians' incapacity to mourn their true divisions. Their chasing after the illusory figment of a higher wisdom has locked them into the grotesque foreshortenings of the gospel that such quests tend to accord to "charismatic" leaders. It is this epistemic rupture that Paul meets with his opening stress on the antidote to all quests for higher wisdom: the folly of the cross.

---

41. See Wannenwetsch, "'Members of One Another,'" especially 204–9.

Praising the Folly of the Cross

> ¹⁸For the message about the cross is foolishness to those who are perishing, but to us who are being saved it is the power of God. ¹⁹For it is written, "I will destroy the wisdom of the wise, and the discernment of the discerning I will thwart." ²⁰Where is the one who is wise? Where is the scribe? Where is the debater of this age? Has not God made foolish the wisdom of the world?

As should be clear by this point, it would be a fatal misreading to hear these verses as an invitation to join the ranks of the initiated, an epistemologically "inside group." The allure of privileged wisdom is the main draw of gnostic cults that would have typically articulated their offer as follows: "Because you are not or not yet a *pneumatikos*, you cannot expect to understand what we are saying and will find our wisdom incomprehensible as you are perishing." This is not the wisdom of the cross. Yet another misreading hears: "Those who take the message of the cross as folly are perishing."[42] While this latter misreading resists the gnostic rationality of exclusive possession it does so only by inverting its presuppositions. Such readings also tend to come uncomfortably close to expressing a cause-and-effect logic set up in a temporal sequence in which the non-recognition of the wisdom of the cross is seen as the cause of the perishing that results from it.

What we think Paul is actually expressing here is this: the foolishness of the cross is the crucible of both human power and perishing. The Greek keeps us in the present participle tense: a message is announced that is addressed to **those who are perishing** (ἀπολλυμένοις/*apollymenois*) and those who **are being saved** (σῳζομένοις/*sōzomenois*). The ongoing force of the grammar suggests that the NRSV's translation **message about the cross** (λόγος τοῦ [of] σταυροῦ [the cross]), while being technically possible, is theologically misleading in suggesting that the cross is a sort of subject matter about which preaching must inform its hearers. Paul's point is rather that the cross's foolishness determines both the form and content of the message and is therefore literally present before them in his own person and communication. The kenotic form of the Apostle's preaching is a living demonstration of why the "message of the cross" is not to be understood as being *about* the cross, but rather *of* the cross, a cruciform message. In other

---

42 A typical example: "All the hearers of the gospel are divided into two classes. To the one, the doctrine of salvation through a crucified Redeemer appears absurd. They are called 'the lost,' not only because they are certainly to perish, but also because they are in a lost state while out of Christ. . . . To the other, this doctrine is divinely efficacious in producing peace and holiness." Hodge, *Commentary on 1 & 2 Corinthians*, 19.

words, the *performative mode* of the preaching of the cross, its "how," cannot be separated from the "what" to which it witnesses, because the foolishness that is the cross is so all-encompassing that it is impossible to have a disengaged opinion "about" it.

Since this **message** is from God, the foolishness it displays is not one that makes a fool of God (perhaps by enacting a logical contradiction such as an eternal God becoming flesh) but comes across as foolishness *to humans*, who, in their adherence to all sorts of presumptuous forms of wisdom, cannot but see it as ridiculously underwhelming. The **power of God** is displayed in the divine overcoming of these evasions by revealing in the work of the cross the one genuine wisdom that includes rather than brackets out the overcoming of human social and interpersonal antagonisms. On the surface 1:18 reads in binary terms, as if the divine message is foolish to individuals who are perishing but functions as wisdom and power to those who are being saved (as in 2 Cor 2:15). But it is also possible, and we think advisable, to read the polarization in terms of a set of conflicting impulses and behaviors *within each believer*. In the light of Paul's stern warnings to the Corinthians that they are not to treat knowledge of Christ as a possession that can be held, as elite and secure knowledge, it seems problematic for *any* believer to think they have arrived at complete knowledge. To be a believer means to be set on the path of sanctification, as opposed to being completely sanctified, as the disputes among the Corinthians amply illustrate. Having already explained that the basic problem among the Corinthian believers is their losing touch with the divine gifts and thereby with their unity in Christ, Paul is now clarifying that Christians must simultaneously affirm their inclusion in Christ's sacrifice as well as their remaining need still to take up their cross. They can and must be exerted in this duplex fashion because the Apostle considers them to be whole in the register of God's eternal wisdom, and yet heterogeneous in the register of their realization of this determination.

Acknowledging the heterogeneity of believers as *simul iustus et peccator*, Paul expresses his fatherly love for the Corinthians by repeatedly affirming the moments of truth held by his interlocutors. He repeatedly takes up and affirms their favorite ideas while making qualifications that will eventually overturn them. Entering realms of meaning opened by the Corinthians' own self-descriptions, the Apostle deftly evades entrapment in them. In this particular case Paul has explicitly offered a better gnosis to the Corinthians. But he has done so in a manner that explodes the logic of the gnostic cults of his day and exposes those Christian teachers who were offering a Christianity contoured by gnostic presuppositions. This is why Paul's theological engagement with the *manner* in which the gospel is presented is so important in contrasting so starkly with the message of the Gnostics, entirely centered as it is on *content*. For the Gnostics, what counts is the enlightenment that comes with access to ideas themselves, not the linguistic or communicative medium in which these are conveyed. For them, communication is a conveyor belt, a means to an end; but for Paul, *how* the ideas are communicated lies at the heart of the matter, since the Christ Paul serves does not offer an escape from human relations but invites humans into a completely new form of inter-human relationality.

There is a warning here for every generation of Christians: how easy it is to assume that we have already been fully incorporated into the foolishness of the cross. But who among us has been entirely freed from admiration of worldly wisdom in one domain or another? Paul addresses believers who have already literally rubbed shoulders with the foolishness that Paul embodies. And yet these same believers have not yet been fully incorporated into this foolishness and thus, in those areas of their existence where the cross is scorned as silly by their superior self-regard, they show themselves among those perishing. Paul's fatherly role is to name their perishing and thereby bring to them what he has promised, Jesus Christ alone, and him crucified (2:2). This is to read the language the Apostle is using here of perishing and salvation not in terms of their eschatological outcome, but as real-time present operation. We are arguing that "perishing" not be read through binary logic, in which the whole individual is either captive or not to the foolishness of the cross. Rather, we suggest "perishing" should be read with a more gradualist sensibility. Just as the presence of cancer in a body could be called a "living death," worldly wisdom is like a metastasis that, if it is not undergoing a counterprocess of eradication, threatens the organism as a whole. "You *are* perishing" today, though the eschatological horizon of hope is already before your eyes and, through Paul's letter, rings in your ears (1:8).

Relating Creaturely and Divine Wisdom

²¹For since, in the wisdom of God, the world did not know God through wisdom, God decided, through the foolishness of our proclamation, to save those who believe.

In the wisdom of God, the world did not know God through wisdom. Paul's opening and closing this sentence with "wisdom" raises the question of how we are to understand the relationship between worldly wisdom and God's wisdom. The Apostle's central interest here is not in establishing the claim he has often been taken to be defending, that worldly wisdom can never understand anything of God. He emphasizes, rather, that the relatedness of creaturely and divine wisdom is discovered only in the fear of the Lord.

Within the orbit of God's creative work we will find no simple juxtaposition of the wisdom of the cross with the wisdom of the world. Truthful existence, real creaturely *sophia*, can be affirmed only in awareness of the drama of God's relations with the world. This makes crucial the question whether any given enquirer into wisdom is oriented by the desire to understand God speaking through his creation. By taking our interpretation in this direction we suggest that this verse is best understood as echoing the thought expressed in Romans 1:20 that "since the beginning of the world his invisible nature . . . has been clearly perceived in the things that have been made." It is an expression of God's eternal wisdom that there is a witness *of* creation *through* creation, as Hamann so eloquently observed.[43] Scripture depicts all creation as singing praises to its Creator, especially in the psalms (see Ps 19:1–3). But Israel wrote and spoke of this wisdom not because their experiences of the world were different but because they had come to know the wisdom of the Creator as those having been rescued, revealed, and formed into a community of praise. To have been initiated into praise means to have had one's senses opened to the praise that is constantly uttered by God's good creation.[44] Put concisely (in the words of Rush Rhees), "It is not that I praise *because* he is Creator. To say 'Creator' is already to praise. And already music."[45]

These points follow from the observation that Paul's opening of the discussion of wisdom does not immediately draw attention to the points of conflict between worldly wisdom and the wisdom of the cross. To do so would risk fueling the misunderstanding that there must be an ineradicable clash between these two wisdoms and that one can only embrace either the one or the other. Our understanding is that the Apostle implicitly but firmly affirms a genuine convergence between human and divine wisdom while at the same time resisting putting this in a manner that would obscure the genuine antipathy of the wisdom of the world and the cross. Thus the way in which Paul affirms human wisdom gives us the clue we need to appreciate the peculiar nature of that subset of worldly wisdom that does in fact clash

---

43. "Speak, that I may see you!—This wish was fulfilled by creation, which is a speech to creatures through creatures; for day unto day utters speech, and night unto night shows knowledge [Ps 19:2]." Hamann, "Aesthetica in Nuce," in *Writings on Philosophy and Language*, 65. See the discussion of this point in Bayer, *Contemporary in Dissent*, 67–86.

44. Barth, *Church Dogmatics*, 3/1:388–414.

45. Rhees, *Rush Rhees on Religion and Philosophy*, 50.

with that of the cross. In 1:21 Paul is indicating with precision the specific insufficiency of the wisdom of the world. While sufficient as a guide in and for many activities (and this is what makes it perennially attractive), it has lost its grasp on the world as a *creaturely* reality and thus has come to desire divine wisdom *without mediation*. This wisdom characterizes those creatures that have fallen into engaging the creation without praise, becoming instead detached observers and so exploiters (Rom 1:28).

Because human understanding has hopelessly fallen from this state of creaturely sensitivity to the Creator's activity (paradigmatically in the resistance to God that is the cross), Paul depicts the prime characteristic of worldly wisdom as its loss of the ability to perceive the divine gift of *koinonia*. By focusing the ensuing discussion with the Corinthians on the human antagonisms that are so visible to them, he will inevitably be emphasizing the manifold ways in which human wisdom remains in sharp conflict with the wisdom of the cross. It is through the address of love within *this* conflict that Paul intends **to save those who believe**. All of Paul's further elaborations of the clash between worldly wisdom and the wisdom of the cross draw attention to the manner in which the factionalists constantly try to transcend their creaturely location by refusing to suffer the reconciliation of their divisions in the body. Their wisdom demands reading some community members out of the picture because the peace they seek hovers above time or imagines a church existing invisibly beyond agonistic relationships.

The Crucifixion of Pragmatic and Rationalist Christianities

> [22] **For Jews demand signs and Greeks desire wisdom, [23] but we proclaim Christ crucified, a stumbling block to Jews and foolishness to Gentiles, [24] but to those who are the called, both Jews and Greeks, Christ the power of God and the wisdom of God. [25] For God's foolishness is wiser than human wisdom, and God's weakness is stronger than human strength.**
>
> [26] **Consider your own call, brothers and sisters: not many of you were wise by human standards, not many were powerful, not many were of noble birth. [27] But God chose what is foolish in the world to shame the wise; God chose what is weak in the world to shame the strong ...**

The expression **stumbling block** echoes an older Greek usage in which σκάνδαλον (*skandalon*) denotes the stick that holds open a falling trap. Knocking this stick away drops the trap over the unsuspecting victim. One German translation of *skandalon* helpfully speaks of **Christ** as the *Fallholz*, the stick demarcating the border between freedom and entrapment. Whether or not Paul is explicitly drawing on this ancient Greek usage, it illumines his point here. It is as if he is saying, "You factionalists treat the crucified one as an obstacle on your path to enlightenment, but when you kick him away you are entrapped in your own narrow conceptions that cut you off from the very environment of Christ's body in which you may flourish." It is the person of **Christ crucified**, therefore, whom Paul wishes to highlight before the Corinthians. Only such a Christ is **the power and wisdom of God**.

To draw attention to the fact that there are indeed other "Christs" being sought by the Corinthian believers, Paul begins by pointing to two other religious communities: the **Jews**, who he says desire visible **signs**, empirical exercises of power (σημεῖα/*sēmeia*), and the **Greeks**, who look for **wisdom**, timeless conceptual truths (σοφία/*sophia*). In each case, the Apostle's interest is in highlighting the ways preconceived notions will define what counts as a reasonable claim about God. This wisdom of the world is not wrong in its being merely human but in its principled assumption of human self-sufficiency. Such thought schemes not only presume to offer humanity everything they need but also function as arbiters of who God is allowed to be. That such presumptions are illegitimately grasping and therefore contrast with the properly Christian stance is clearly signaled by the verbs Paul uses here: the Jews **demand**, the Greeks **desire**, but **we** (collectively under Christ) **proclaim**. Because it is captured by Christ, Christian speech is an expression of reliance on Christ, who will always have to be *proclaimed* and *awaited* because he is not imprisoned by human grasping or the shape of our desiring.

Verse 27 explicitly states the sharp contrast between God's wisdom and the wisdom of the world that Paul now introduces within an implied dramatic narrative: God actively **chose what is foolish in the world to shame the wise; God chose what is weak in the world to shame the strong**. The irony of this implied dramatic narrative is that a God who takes pleasure in upending humanity's smooth self-mastery appears anthropomorphic and passionate, all the things Greek philosophy could not stomach in a god. Paul's God simply refuses to conform to the image that most tempted the early church, the timeless and passionless deity.

Paul's formulation also sheds light on similar straightjackets for God that tempt modern Christians. Perhaps the renaissance of the ironic pragmatism that is late-modernity can be understood as readopting the "Jewish" end of the spectrum now that the relentless mining of its "Greek" pole by the founders of early modernity has reached exhaustion. If the return of Greek pride and certainty in possessing the "one" truth above all people is the sign of the modern, the late-modern is marked by an ironic stance toward the truth claims and traditions of modernity (and the Christianity that took on its foundationalist form). To be postmodern is not to reject but also not to embrace anything for longer than a moment. While ironic observers are regularly entertaining, they must constantly defer final judgments. They have settled comfortably in the assumption that whatever we have in view, we will always be enriched by hearing another perspective. Like the philosophically minded respondents to Paul in the Areopagus in Acts 17, the late- or postmodern will therefore agree to hear anything that sounds novel (17:21), though not for too long (17:32).

In putting things this way we have risked a transposition that has proved dangerous in the history of Christian theology, that is, designating **the Jews** in a manner that risks reducing the textured phenomena of Israel and present Jewry to a specific conceptual error embedded in an identifiable regime of discourse.[46] Christian theology must not lapse in its attentiveness to the people of the first covenant or indeed the living Israel as it currently exists and speaks.[47] Nevertheless, the Jewish Paul himself leads us into the risky territory of schematization by deploying a concept of "the Jews" that only accidentally touches on his local context. Paul has no interest (at this point) in describing the Jews in a particular topographical location. His concern is rather with the perishing state of those who pursue religion so long as it proves effective, and therefore not finally with diagnosing Jewish belief, but with a posture that is aptly described as *pragmatic Christianity*. The same analysis applies to his use of **the Greeks**, those who are perishing insofar as their quest for religion is tied to what makes intellectual sense—*rationalist Christianity*.

By stressing this polarity between pragmatic and rationalist Christianity we understand Paul to be placing Christians of every age before a theological crux of perennial significance: is the work of Jesus Christ authoritative because it works or because it makes sense? Paul's first-century depiction of two manners of rejecting Christ suggests that these same dynamics remain at work within the ranks of those who confess Christ, perhaps even within the same individual. These verses therefore invite reflection as to whether and where we today are caught up in a Christianity that conforms to one or the other of these rationalities at different points and in variegated ways. We would be foolhardy to deny we are beyond acting like the "Christ party" and would never look for a Jesus who "works for us." To do so would be

---

46. The latter phrase is Alain Badiou's. "When theorizing about the Jew and Greek, Paul is in fact presenting us with a schema of discourses. And this schema is designed to position a third discourse, his own, in such a way as to render its complete originality apparent" (*Saint Paul*, 41).

47. Givens, *We the People*.

tantamount to claiming to wholly inhabit the wisdom of the cross without remainder.

To confess that we have not yet achieved this perfection, we suggest, would go some way toward defusing a good number of the quarrels that beset the contemporary Western church. For example, the debates surrounding managerialist and consumerist trends in Western Christianity are amply and aptly illumed by the perspective Paul has afforded us. The explicitly pragmatic religion proposed by the likes of William James[48] is probably less responsible for contemporary church conflicts than the inexplicit economic and management-led pragmatism so widespread in the contemporary Western church. Churches that explicitly orient themselves around strategies that feed on the consumerist attitude of the people and their tendency to embrace whatever is on offer as long as it "works" are aptly labeled managerial Christianity.[49] A church that allows its policymaking to be driven by the rationality of consumerist pragmatism is easily inclined to understand itself as offering services or ministries targeted to the many different types of "clients" generated by an atomizing society. Their accommodating the rationality of religion as something that is proved in "working" therefore commits such churches to factionalism: special services for the divorced, whose problems differ from those of the married, and also for the youth, whose tastes diverge from those of older congregants, and so on—with each group needing to vie for relative growth and a proportionate share of ministerial "investment."

This observation is not meant to suggest that every attempt by churches to accommodate worship must end in the sort of factionalism depicted in Corinth. We are rather examining how Paul's approach to the Corinthians reveals the normative grammar for making any such accommodation if real unity is to be pursued by it. Pragmatist and rationalist Christianities are most obviously problematic when marked by a lack of hope for genuine togetherness of believers under Christ. The resistance of a church that does not want to perish from pragmatist or rationalist Christianity must come to the point of discovering the unity in Christ that is displaced when rival models of unity are pursued. And when the church discovers its unity in

---

48. See James, *The Varieties of Religious Experience*.

49. Cyril of Alexandria somehow sensed the associated connection made in the gospel narratives between pragmatism and commodification of religion as tagged by the term "the Jews": "When Christ was driving the sellers of sheep, cattle, pigeons, and doves out of the sacred precincts, and said, *Stop making my Father's house a marketplace* (John 2:16), [the Jews] opposed him, asking *What sign can you show us for doing this?* (John 2:18) and *Who gave you this authority?* (Matt 21:23)." *Commentary*, in Pusey, 253–55, quoted in JK, 25.

Christ, the event will be marked by wholesale repentance, as depicted in Acts 19:18–19.

Only from within the wisdom of the cross are we in a position to see how these two religious grammars can have wended their way down through history. The history of the West amply attests that the question, "Is it authoritative because it works or because it makes sense?" has to a limited degree been a *conceptually* fruitful one to ask, insofar as defenders of each position have been effective in pushing their respective opponents on to deeper insights. Again today the modernist says to the postmodernist, "To say that it is true because it works is to throw away any conception of truth." The modernist is questioned in turn: "But how can this be true if it is not embodied?" While Paul might be willing to admit that each side has a point, he would nevertheless insist that this back-and-forth dialectic has no power to ratchet itself up to the wisdom of the cross. Wisdom is an embodied person, Logos incarnate. Jesus Christ makes sense *and* works, but only when the quests for effectiveness or truthfulness are crucified as pursuits assumed to be separable from the person in which they are one. This is to affirm both Jews and Greeks in their proper place. Christians do, in fact, need power and wisdom. The cross negates neither, but properly *unites* the two. In the cross, Christ accomplishes this unification in a manner that cannot be achieved in abstraction from the reconciliation of local communities in truth and love, wisdom and power.

This discourse on wisdom and folly is, therefore, properly understood only if we grasp how Paul has married it to the division-and-unity discourse that precedes it. The fathers saw this clearly, Gerald Bray notes, because they read these passages amidst the schismatic movements and heresies of their own day. They were "well aware that [social] unity and truth went together, and they constantly emphasized this link in their commentaries on these epistles."[50] In the face of contentious relationships, Paul insistently directs the Corinthians' attention to what God has done in and between them. **Not many of you were wise by human standards, not many were powerful, not many were of noble birth**. The **you** here is plural, continuing the **we** of 1:23. Again Paul's mode of address begins with, and scrupulously stays within, the ecclesiological discourse.

Conceptually speaking, for the Apostle, the discourse of church division and unity is always framing the discourse of wisdom and folly. It is thus that the Apostle can name and resist the Corinthians' temptation to buffer Christianity with methods of social engineering, mechanisms of worldly

---

50. Bray, GB, xviii.

wisdom about melding diversity into unity.[51] Yet the way Paul ties together the two discourses is designed to point them to new ways of life rather than simply condemn them for what is going on in their midst. Taken on its own, the ecclesiology discourse would easily seem like bestowing unmediated judgment on the Corinthians. If everything is framed by reference to community, it is next to impossible to escape the barren alternative of either appealing to unity at the expense of diversity or sacrificing unity at the expense of an even higher good such as individual wisdom or even truth. Had Paul portrayed his call for unity in these terms, it would have come down to them as a sheer demand, as if he had said, "There are factions, so sort them out; be unified." The same is true of the wisdom-folly discourse. Detached from the ecclesiological discourse, the quest for wisdom becomes a threatening law to the extent that the folly of the cross is turned into a principle, an epistemological or metaphysical claim. Only Paul's stress on embodiment can anchor the wisdom-folly discourse in the materiality of the local church, a rhetorical cross-tensioning that allows Paul to escape the pull of both discourses toward a collapse into law.

It must be seen as an instance of divine irony that it was one of Christianity's most forceful modern foes who brought Paul's wisdom of the cross back onto the theological agenda in a time obsessed with its own advances. Friedrich Nietzsche was capable of grasping the grammar of the gospel's life-forming power and saw the attraction of a church that truly lives by the "proof from power" alone. This recognition made him a wicked satirist of a church that has given in to the pragmatist temptations of modernity. Such Christianity, he suggests, is happily dispensing with the cross:

> Today we find, as a sign of the extent to which Christianity has lost its fecundity, that other attempt to justify its existence, the idea that even if it [the Christian faith] was an error, it would still be a lifelong advantage to hang on to this error. It seems this faith is retained precisely because of its comforting effect. . . . This hedonistic turn, a justification from desire, is a symptom of decline: it replaces the proof from power, the disturbing aspect of the Christian idea, with the proof from fear. As a matter of fact, by this redefinition of itself, Christianity is only hastening its own exhaustion. One contents oneself with an opiate Christianity since one does not have the energy either to seek, to fight, to risk, or to be left standing alone. . . . Nevertheless, a Christianity that mainly serves to sedate ill nerves no longer depends on the terrible solution of a "crucified god": which is

---

51. Kim, *Christ's Body in Corinth*, ch. 2.

why Buddhism is making its way into all of Europe with quiet confidence.⁵²

Jesus Christ, the Substance of the Virtues

> ²⁸**God chose what is low and despised in the world, things that are not, to reduce to nothing things that are, ²⁹so that no one might boast in the presence of God. ³⁰He is the source of your life in Christ Jesus, who became for us wisdom from God, and righteousness and sanctification and redemption, ³¹in order that, as it is written, "Let the one who boasts, boast in the Lord."**

Paul continues on in his pastoral willingness to frame his presentation as the qualification of terms that are common currency within the Corinthian community. In this section, he gladly takes up and affirms concepts around which conflict is swirling: **wisdom, righteousness, sanctification,** and **redemption**. With each of his qualifications, however, he shifts the content these terms convey toward the cruciform: **God chose what is low and despised in the world**. We can do no better in summarizing the force of this qualification than Maximus the Confessor, who neatly ties together all the interconnections Paul has set out in this chapter, keeping their cruciform character in the foreground, by linking them with the "I am" sayings of the gospels. In doing so he understands these verses in a predicative rather than an attributive sense, refusing all attempts to define wisdom and only then to fit Christ into this definition. Rather, for him, Jesus Christ is the one person in whom the justice and wisdom that we do not yet know are to be found:

> The Word of God is the substance of the virtue that each person possesses. For our Lord Jesus Christ is himself the substance of all the virtues, as it is written: whom God made our wisdom, our righteousness and sanctification and redemption. . . . These words apply to him in an absolute sense . . . [and] are not merely attributed to him, as they are in our case, as for example, when one speaks of a "wise person" or a "just person."⁵³

---

52. Nietzsche, *Werke in drei Bänden*, vol. 3, 488, translation ours. Nowhere are the presuppositions of therapeutic Christianity more clearly on view than in the literature on the healing properties of prayer. See Shuman and Meador, *Heal Thyself.*

53. Maximus the Confessor, *Ambiguum 7*, PG 91:1081-84, quoted in JK, 31. An ecclesial inflection of Origen's point reappears in Stanley Hauerwas's commentary on Matthew. "Virtue may be its own reward, but for Christians the virtues, the kind of virtues suggested by the Beatitudes, are names for the shared life made possible through Christ" (*Matthew*, 65).

Throughout this letter Paul will never deviate from this dual interest in Christ as the substance of all the virtues, and in the church as their instantiation. This observation about the Apostle's positioning of virtue calls into question several dominant frameworks for interpreting his theology, such as Bultmann's famous indicative-imperative scheme[54] as well as narrowly forensic accountings of the relation of justification to sanctification.[55] In doing so it focuses any genuinely Christian account of virtue on questions of moral psychology and agency, but in a manner that is not to be confused with later traditions of Christian virtue ethics that came to be associated with the casuistic moral reasoning of Roman Catholic scholasticism.

The work of the Holy Spirit is both to *create* and to *reveal* an entity that does not "naturally" exist in a fallen world: the church. Human beings have been created for ecclesial being, to live their lives as circuits in the rich ecology of exchanged spiritual gifts that is the church (>ch. 12). This ecclesial being is born as the Spirit brings fallen humans to voice praise of the Trinitarian God whose works are known through scripture. Praise is thus simultaneously the evidence of the dawning of the new creation and a call to embrace an ever deeper transformation. Paul's formulations are thus consciously constructed both to display and to invite the Corinthians (and with them, us) to receive this doxological being, this "becoming what has been given to us to become." His call has a heuristic function in directing believers' attention to the ongoing work of the Spirit of softening hearts and fostering repentance, and in this way catalyzing works of love and service. This activity is the reality that matters, Paul constantly reiterates: "It is already going on. Let it change you." This call into a dynamic form of life with God and the neighbor will animate his approach to a wide range of topics in this letter (e.g., >1:27; 2:2; 3:23; 5:7; 6:19).

---

54. Engberg-Pederson, "Paul, Virtues, and Vices," 608–33.
55. Miller, *Practice of the Body of Christ*, chs. 1–2.

1 Corinthians 2

Human Knowledge That Demonstrates God's Power

> ¹When I came to you, brothers and sisters, I did not come proclaiming the mystery of God to you in lofty words or wisdom. ²For I decided to know nothing among you except Jesus Christ, and him crucified. ³And I came to you in weakness and in fear and in much trembling. ⁴My speech and my proclamation were not with plausible words of wisdom, but with a demonstration of the Spirit and of power, ⁵so that your faith might rest not on human wisdom but on the power of God.

Paul opens this second chapter with a negation: **I did not come proclaiming the mystery of God to you in lofty words or wisdom**. This refusal declares his opposition to any rendering of Christianity as a **mystery** religion. And he emphasizes that this resistance is nonnegotiable, whether we translate ἔκρινά (*ekrina*) as "**I decided**" or "I resolved." We are left asking how this resistance is to be understood, which raises the additional question of what type of communicative strategy this opening represents. We have already understood the Apostle to be unfolding his previously stated commitment to self-consciously disarming himself. He refuses to "fix" what he sees as wrong in the Corinthian church through the vigorous deployment of some preconceived conflict management strategy. Chapter one made it clear why we think the pivotal passage here is verse 2: **For I decided to know nothing among you except Jesus Christ, and him crucified**.

A proper grasp of this sentence depends on glimpsing its dramatic structure and the relation of the subclauses within. The Apostle is communicating in what appears to be a carefully sequenced progression in order to address the specific misunderstandings that he has discerned among the Corinthian Christians. To **know nothing** except Jesus Christ does not mean to know *only* Jesus; instead, **among you** must be understood as bearing its own weight. This suggests that the sentence is properly read, "nothing among you," pause, "except Jesus Christ," another pause, "and him crucified."

The emphasis Paul lays here on **knowing nothing except** is easily (mis-)heard by us inheritors of the Cartesian tradition as a variant of that "doubting everything" that Descartes turned into a method. To read Paul's statement in this direction would lead to the privileging of rational methods of critical access to knowledge over routes such as the prophetic or spiritual. If anything, the Pauline "knowing nothing except" is closer to the apophatic traditions of Christian mysticism in which self-emptying is understood as a form of positive recognition of the divine work being done on the subject. Because this divine working may only incipiently be recognized, an explicit decision must be taken to let go of previous knowledge in order properly to embrace the knowledge that is bequeathed by divine gifting. This quasi-mystical account of knowledge is indicated by the prominence of the language of being emptied (**I came to you in weakness**) and filled (**demonstration of the Spirit and of power**). Ultimately, Paul can only draw attention to the "nothing" that he knows because he affirms it as an artifact of the plenitude and activity of **Jesus Christ**. The Apostle's "nothing" is, then, neither a methodological privileging of the human processes of rational criticism nor a serene and vacuous Zen-like emptiness—let alone a claim that he knows nothing of what is happening on the ground in the Corinthian church.

In short: Paul's concern is to illuminate what it means to let go of any knowledge that is *abstracted* from the person of Jesus Christ.[1] The notion of "nothing" is placed *between* "knowledge" and "Jesus Christ" not in order to suggest that any procedure of subtracting is capable of yielding an overall gain in knowledge, but to indicate that Jesus Christ is the origin and end of *all* knowledge. This is why the Apostle refuses to press Jesus Christ into any pre-existing account of knowledge.[2] Such a reading takes seriously the connections made in Paul's opening, between the **when I came to you** of 2:1, and **for I decided to know nothing but Jesus Christ** in 2:2. His resolve to know nothing except Jesus Christ provides the grammar of his dealings

---

1. See Bonhoeffer's introduction to his Christology lectures, in *Berlin, 1932–1933* (DBWE 12), 300–308, and the chapter "Ethics as Formation," in *Ethics* (DBWE 6), 76–102.

2. We draw here on Luther's claim that Christ's resurrection, and the christological grammar it reveals, must be understood as affecting every conceivable term known to human language. As the Reformer famously put it, this is the case because the "new grammar of the resurrection" transforms the way in which we conceive the very condition of human existence: the life and death of the body. Paul's metaphor in 1 Corinthians 15 of the body as the "seed" of eternal life indicates that death is but a state of transition and the human body in all its present frailty (the infamous "bag of maggots") a thing destined for future glory. See Wiemer, *"Mein Trost, Kampf und Sieg ist Christus"*, 129–31.

with the Corinthians, how he will be **among** them. This Christ makes demands all around, limiting the rhetoric Paul can deploy as well as the self-definitions of the Corinthian believers. Paul meets the people where they are, but precisely by refusing to meet them where they think they are, or where they want to be met.

Even if Paul and the Corinthians can agree that Christian knowledge is to be "christoform" in some sense, misunderstandings continue to lurk. Here the linkage of the previous two phrases with a third is especially illuminating: Paul is indeed giving up some of his knowledge to accommodate himself to the Corinthians, but he does so in order to meet them *in* Jesus Christ, a meeting that demands they all inhabit a *crucified* Christ. The further clarification Paul offers is therefore crucial: **and him crucified**. Christian knowledge is to be not only *christoform* but also *cruciform*. The three strata of this presentation yield a characterization of genuine Christian knowledge as knowledge that is at once kenotic (**nothing**), christoform (**Jesus Christ**), and cruciform (**and him crucified**).

The three terms are not to be understood as sequentially related, as if we need to proceed up a ladder of ascent. Rather, they set up a mutually explanatory grammatical field in which a dramatic reading best evokes the unified and multipolar organization of the sentence. The term **crucified** must be understood as defining the term **nothing**. This was the ground for our claim above that Paul's **nothing** cannot be read as a *nihil* because it reflects the cross rather than the capacity of the human mind for self-emptying. This is why the Apostle cannot be seen as suggesting a method yielding knowledge to those who follow the steps from kenoticism through to cruciformity. Instead, he describes a cycle of knowledge in which believers are interwoven into God's grace in a manner that leads them to expect that the intricacies of their knowledge can continually be understood at greater depth through illumined examination. Paul's careful qualification of the concept of knowledge thus begins chapter 2 by affirming his audience's quest for knowledge but shifting it into an entirely different register—he takes away their "unspiritual knowledge" in order to offer them what he calls "spiritual" understanding.

And I came to you in weakness. The Greek ἐγενόμην πρὸς ὑμᾶς (*egenomēn pros hymas*) in 2:3 indicates both the tenor of Paul's arrival in the Corinthian community as well as the manner of his ongoing presence. On our reading his self-characterization in terms of **weakness, fear,** and **trembling** is to be taken literally. We should not minimize this self-description by presuming it to be only an assumed pedagogical stance or an expression of a passing psychological low point in Paul's movement along the path from initial weakness to eventual strength. This reading makes sense when we understand Paul in 2:4 to be laying out his understanding of his missionary relationship with the Corinthians in yet another three-tiered argument.

The first and most obvious move is a refusal to employ the methods of rhetorical strategy (**plausible words of wisdom**[3]). While scholars have interpreted this passage as itself a rhetorical gesture since it appears in the letter's opening lines, we read it rather as a *rejection* of any formulaic strategy. Somewhat more appealing are readings that take Paul's approach here as a pastoral adjustment to the specific weakness of the community he is addressing. Both types of approach, however, remain caught in the assumption that the Apostle is not fundamentally changed by his interaction with the Corinthians. Both the rhetorical and pastoral readings of his avowal of fear and trembling are unable to grasp the full scope of what is at stake for Paul in this intervention. In contrast, we understand Paul to be throwing himself right into the middle of the conflicted Corinthian situation, disarming himself and appealing to *nothing* except the power of the Spirit. His honesty about the deliberate weakness of his approach thus prepares the way for the revelatory work of God's Spirit and power.

When Paul states that **My speech and my proclamation were not with plausible words of wisdom,** this introduces a fresh distinction that will allow the Corinthians to appreciate the theological implications of Paul's self-presentation. Only because his speech was not rhetorically powerful could his presence provide a **demonstration** (ἐν ἀποδείξει/*en apodeixei*) **of the Spirit and of power.** Here Paul seems to be playing with the linguistic associations of "words of wisdom" with the art of rhetoric, and with the expression "demonstration of power" as it was commonly used by the Sophists. Beyond simple allusion to the Greek context, though, Paul has introduced these terms in order to subvert them. **Plausible words of wisdom** are sharply juxtaposed with the sort of power demonstration Paul is seeking, that is, a demonstration of Spirit and of power. So while actively engaged in a sort of demonstration, *what* Paul aims to demonstrate is not his own power but God's. It is a posture that can only provoke God to show his own power,[4] and one that assumes a Trinitarian frame of reference that Paul will soon make explicit. It is precisely the cruciformity of Paul's proclamation (its weakness) that invites the intervention of the Spirit to reveal the works of

---

3. In the expression πειθοῖς σοφίας λόγοις (*peithois sophias logois*) Paul employs technical terms for antique rhetoric—the skilled use of language as a means to manipulate audiences—the refusal of which he elaborates and makes even more precise in 1 Thessalonians 2:3–5.

4. This is in keeping with acts of faith such as Elijah's contest with the prophets of Baal (1 Kgs 18) and the Jesus tradition exemplified by his promise of the Spirit to teach his disciples what to say in time of trial (John 14:25).

the eternal Father, as he explicitly states later in the chapter: "For the Spirit searches everything, even the depths of God" (>2:10). Thus, Paul's account rests on the assumption that it is the Spirit who makes the redemption of the Trinitarian God concrete in time and place, making God's redemption public by actualizing it.

The message of the chapter thus far is drawn together in capsule form in 2:5, where Paul states his goal: **that your faith might rest not on human wisdom, but on the power of God.** This consecutive clause describes the central purpose of Paul's apostolic mission, simultaneously explaining and defining the shape it must take. Great emphasis is being laid on two distinctions, the first between faith and human wisdom, and the second a categorical distinction between human wisdom and divine power. Again, these two conceptual contrasts are not set up as points on a summary list, but are reciprocally defining. In order to understand the way in which these two motifs are interrelated we must revisit the expression the NRSV translates as **faith might rest**. Other translations suggest "stand in" faith (KJV) or even "*stützen auf*" ("lean on," *Einheitsübersetzung*). Characteristically, however, there is no verb in the Greek, which also allows the translation, "so that your faith be not *in* human wisdom, but *in* God's power." This apparently more general translation seems theologically more appropriate. The productive polyvalence of the formulation "faith in God's power" draws attention both to the *divine creation* of faith in the believer (originated in and through divine power) and to the *type* of faith created, that is, a human faith characterized by its continual reliance on that power.

We will soon see that this formulation is part of Paul's response to profound misunderstandings within the Corinthian account of knowledge and revelation. The Corinthians were relying on only one of these emphases, the originating sense. For Paul, however, the all-important insight was that this faith that owed itself to God's act of creating would have to prove itself by the self-conscious living of believers that is being continually reshaped in its entrusting itself to divine power. This fuller account throws the specific deficiencies of the Corinthian faith into stark relief. Their faith sought to secure possessed wisdom—of divine origin, to be sure, but not reliant on ongoing divine sustenance. The dual emphasis of our translation is reminiscent of the more expansive formula that gained prominence in Reformation theology, *sola fide numquam sola* (by faith alone, but faith never alone). Although much debated and abused, a robust *sola* conceptuality advances our understanding of Paul's argument by offering us a way into the heart of his "nothing except" formula that is so prominent in verse 2 and that reappears in verse 11.[5]

---

5. Proponents of the "New Perspective(s)" on Paul have resisted this Reformation

Outgrowing the Holy Spirit

> ⁶Yet among the mature we do speak wisdom, though it is not a wisdom of this age or of the rulers of this age, who are doomed to perish. ⁷But we speak God's wisdom, secret and hidden, which God decreed before the ages for our glory. ⁸None of the rulers of this age understood this; for if they had, they would not have crucified the Lord of glory.

The next three verses present readers with a significant problem: the author, whose train of thought we have begun to track, suddenly threatens to alienate us. Having just emphasized spiritual humility he seems abruptly to switch tack in nominating some Corinthians as **the mature** who **speak wisdom**, with all the overtones of elitism, hierarchy, and the presumption of a superior vantage point such terms carry. What the NRSV translates as "mature" is even a softening of the Greek τελείοις (*teleiois*), which is more accurately translated as "complete" or "perfect." Disconcertingly, the further claim in 2:8 to exclusive knowledge—**none of the rulers of this age understood this**—sounds suspiciously like the sort of self-justificatory claim made by members of sectarian movements: "This may sound strange, but you are not yet in a position to understand what I am saying. I tell you this as one who has matured and moved up in the hierarchy of knowledge. Wait until you have cleared stage seven, then you will comprehend the real story." Such claims appear not only to run counter to Paul's self-declared kenotic apostolate but also contradict his stress on the transparency of the Christian proclamation, which invites those who hear his proclamation to "judge for themselves" (>14:29).

If we are to undertake a communicative reading of scripture, that is, a reading in which exposure to the text is understood as a form of preparing ourselves to be addressed, part of the task will be to become aware of our own instinctive and unforeseen reactions to that address. Throughout the Christian exegetical tradition chapter 2 has provoked reflections on the implication of the Christian reader in this text, given its emphasis on the revelatory work of the Spirit (>2:9–10). As a result, it has forced practitioners of modern biblical studies to wrestle with important hermeneutical questions, often to good theological effect.[6] Our interest is in advancing this contemporary inquiry by asking what is happening when we are unsettled

---

formulation, and our line of reasoning suggests why this is to be seen as an entirely plausible, if overstated, reaction to a previous loss of the significance of the *numquam sola*—that faith is never alone.

6. See Stuhlmacher, "Hermeneutical Significance," 328–32. See also Origen, *On First Principles* 4.2.1–4 (Greek), SC 268, 292–312, quoted in JK, 39.

by the sense that we are suddenly meeting "a different Paul." Modern commentators have a range of tools at their disposal for explaining the change of voice in these verses, the most popular being the proposal that Paul is here co-opting and making ironic use of the Corinthians' slogans as a mode of refutation.[7] That we are not the first to be unsettled by these verses is easily detectable in the flowering of speculation one finds in some of the fathers[8] and Reformers,[9] as they struggle to reconcile the Paul of these verses with the Paul of the previous verses. Our communicative reading allows space for this unease, taking our discomfort before certain passages of scripture to be a working site for the Spirit who guides us into all understanding (John 16:13). Theologically interpreted, our discomfort is a provocation critically to reassess the picture we have built up of "our Paul," driving us to admit that he is a more complex figure than we had yet noticed while simultaneously opening alternative readings of the unsettling passage under scrutiny.

As this will not be the last time this letter will press this issue on us, it is important to make explicit what might constitute a theologically appropriate response to such a shift in Paul's tone. Our interest in deepening self-critical reading suggests that at such points we need to bring into view our unarticulated assumptions about who Paul is, allowing our picture of him to grow and deepen, while at the same time learning to articulate the theological reasons why certain passages seem to us to clash with the deep structures of the argument Paul is developing.

This espousal of increasingly self-reflexive reading habits is to be sharply distinguished from the sensitivity to common coinage a reader might gain by being widely familiar with first-century sources. To notice that the tone of Paul's speech has changed is not simply to notice, as a historical

---

7. Hays, for instance, resolves the problem of Paul's shift in tone by proposing an ironic reading that is not in the final analysis ironic, because Paul "trumps their boasting by speaking of a secret hidden wisdom" (RBH, 39). The problem with this approach is that such readings leave Paul apparently agreeing with the Corinthians that Christianity is indeed a quest for individual maturity and wisdom.

8. Origen, for instance, finds this address to those with wisdom to warrant his own complex account of the levels of understanding he believes to constitute a ladder of spiritual maturation. Other patristic commentators take Paul to be commenting on the events of the crucifixion; Cyril of Alexandria, for instance, sees in it a reference to demons who incited the Jews and political authorities to crucify a Jesus whom they did not recognize, and Oecumenius takes the same line to discuss how jealousy blinded Herod and the scribes. See Origen, *On First Principles* 4.2.1–4 (Greek), SC 268, 292–312; Cyril of Alexandria, *Commentary*, Pusey 256–57; and Oecumenius, *Notes on 1 Corinthians*, in Staab, 432, quoted in JK, 38–40.

9. Calvin presents Paul as speaking to a virtual community of the perfect precisely because he wishes to "reproach those who had no liking for his preaching, and points out that it was their own fault" (JC, 52).

scholar might, that the terminology being used appears in other historically contemporaneous sources. Paul uses common coinage *both* non-ironically (2:1, "mysteries of God," and 2:4, "*apodeixis*," to take two examples) and ironically. It is not, therefore, the historical horizon of first-century usage that definitively alerts us that Paul is being ironic, but a theological horizon. We detect the type and scope of the Apostle's irony in 2:6–8 not on the grounds that he is deploying common coinage, but on the basis of the role played by the prominent **but** of 2:9. The contrast this conjunction sets up between the content of 2:6–8 and 2:9–12 suggests reading the whole of the former as an instance of Paul appropriating the complex of claims on which the prevailing Corinthian misunderstandings rest. As we have seen, the Corinthian account of mature knowledge is in essence deist in reducing God to one who gives initial faith while denying any ongoing reliance on God's powerful intervention to sustain this faith. Thus the claims to maturity the Apostle has just uttered would fit perfectly in the mouths of all the Corinthian factions, despite their apparent rivalry.

These considerations lead us to understand Paul to be exposing the Corinthians' self-understanding as based on the supposed possession of a **secret wisdom**. They each claim what has been revealed in order to name themselves as **mature**, indeed, as perfect. From the vantage they have gained in setting themselves above the **rulers of this age** they can announce, in a derisive tone, that **had they understood** (what we know), **they would not have crucified the Lord** (2:8). Paul does not deny that the Corinthians have welcomed the revelation of Christ but is showing them that they have not received it deeply enough and have appropriated it in the wrong way. They have turned the message of Christ into *gnosis* wrapped in the self-aggrandizement that "puffs up" (>4:6).

Such a construal of the knowledge of Christ cannot but elevate the Corinthians in their own estimation, yielding the perception that they are superior to the "crucifiers."[10] Their implicit assumption that "we are not crucifiers" is thus a barrier that prevents them from inhabiting a truly cruciform self-understanding. Because their knowledge is not self-perception under the cross, the Corinthians appropriate Jesus Christ in order to "power boost" the knowledge they brought to the table when they were first converted. They resist the living claim of Jesus Christ through the Spirit in assuming that they have outlived the life-form of a student. The Corinthians

---

10. Having explained why we reject this assumption and therefore the readings of many of the church fathers who are attracted to various conceptions of elite knowledge, the reasons are now plain why we cannot support the minor comeback this idea is having today, typically in the form of a recovery of the patristic idea of *disciplina arcani*. See Malesic, *Secret Faith in the Public Square*, ch 8.

thus lay claim to a type of knowledge that is opposed to learning, an account of revelation defined by a framework of the "hidden" that has become possessively *known* in opposition to continually awaiting revelation understood as a process of being taught by the Holy Spirit. Instead of "wisdomizing Christ," Paul says, they should seek the perpetual tutelage that is "cruciform knowledge." In uncovering the grammar of Paul's argument here, we can see why it is theologically unnecessary to soften Paul's opening from one that addresses the "perfect" to one addressed to the "wise." The NRSV imagines that we can understand ourselves as wise, but not as perfect. But Paul seems to assume that it is appropriate to speak non-ironically to Christians as perfect, as long as we understand that the only perfection Paul recognizes is the one that the crucified Jesus Christ himself taught: "Be perfect, therefore, as your Father is perfect" (Matt 5:48).

It is important for our reading to take seriously not only *who* Paul is addressing (the Corinthians who inhabit a specific sociocultural context) but also *what* he is addressing, that is, their attitudes as Paul is depicting them. It is his portrayal of their foibles and misunderstandings that establishes the connection through which the Apostle addresses us as contemporary readers. The importance of this latter point of emphasis is illustrated by attending to the question of the "gnostics" in Corinth. Gnosticism as a formal movement did not arise until the second century,[11] and so when we speak of "Corinthian gnostics" it is easy to hear us referring, anachronistically, to a developed and recognizable belief system and cult.[12] But although Paul uses the term *gnosis* frequently in his correspondence with the Corinthians, we consider attempts to go behind his depiction in order to figure out if there really were any gnostics in the Corinth of his day a distraction from close attention to his portrayal as it stands. There is certainly value in looking into noncanonical books to try to develop a finer-grained view of the logics that Paul is trying to refute, yet the priority of a theological reading must remain

---

11. Raymond F. Collins offers a concise summary of why earlier modern interpreters posited a more developed first-century Gnostic movement in his *First Corinthians*, 16–17.

12. Murphy-O'Connor comments that the group that believed it possessed knowledge "could be termed 'Gnostics,' and many commentators in fact use this designation. Even though it is justified etymologically, I prefer not to use it because it is susceptible of interpretations that are, to say the least, misleading." In a footnote he adds (quoting Conzelmann), "With regard to Corinthian Gnosticism the most that one can say is that 'There are also isolated traces of the beginnings of what later presented itself as 'Gnosticism,' that is, Gnosticism *in statu nascendi*'" (JMO, 88). The current scholarly consensus on the practices in which the Corinthians may have been involved finds their beliefs to be closer to Jewish Sophia mysticism, with its interest in gaining apocalyptic knowledge. The historical debates can be found in Martinez, *Wisdom and Apocalypticism*, and in Hempel, Lange, and Lichtenberger, *The Wisdom Texts from Qumran*.

Paul's portrayal of what the Corinthians are *doing* that he believes is inappropriate for Christians. Such an investigation can be aided by historical research and observation as long as the insight remains clearly in view that what we are listening to is *Paul as present to us in this text*.

The Spirit Is among You

> ⁹But, as it is written, "What no eye has seen, nor ear heard, nor the human heart conceived, what God has prepared for those who love him"— ¹⁰these things God has revealed to us through the Spirit; for the Spirit searches everything, even the depths of God. ¹¹For what human being knows what is truly human except the human spirit that is within? So also no one comprehends what is truly God's except the Spirit of God. ¹²Now we have received not the spirit of the world, but the Spirit that is from God, so that we may understand the gifts bestowed on us by God.

Paul introduces his alternative positive account of the knowledge Christians ought to seek in a manner designed to bring it to bear as sharply as possible on the themes to which he has just drawn attention. The Corinthians desire a higher wisdom than their contemporaries by partaking of a formerly hidden knowledge that they understand now to be available to those in the know. The Apostle opposes this supposition by introducing an alternative set of contrasts: between receiving and appropriating; between being taught and knowing; and ultimately, between spiritual and unspiritual knowledge. The quotation from the prophetic vision in Isaiah 64:4 allows the Apostle to complexify his retort by drawing on its threefold description of the appropriation of knowledge through the human faculties via the **eye**, **ear**, and **heart**. The visual sense allows screening and surveying, the auditory sense makes present what comes in temporal sequence, and in biblical anthropology, the heart conceptualizes and orients all other forms of perception—as implied by the parallel summation that the **heart conceived**. If we remain bound to the flow of the Old Testament passage that underlies Paul's wording here, it becomes obvious to us that Paul responds to the first lines of the citation (**What no eye has seen . . .**) with an alternative, that is, **what God has prepared for those who love him.**[13] The central thrust of the quotation is therefore that "God has prepared exactly that which no eye can have seen, no ear heard, nor heart conceptualized."

---

13. Several early witnesses (A, B, and *Didache*) stress this point by the addition of ὅσα (*hosa*).

On these grounds 2:9 is best understood as undercutting the knowledge that the Corinthians claim to possess in order to clear the ground so that Paul can set out his positive account of Christian knowledge in 2:10–13. This positive account begins by tacitly affirming as entirely appropriate the Corinthians' emphasis on revelation, but only in order to recast it. The Apostle then specifies that what **God has prepared for those who love him** must not be unhitched from the revelation of the Spirit, who **searches everything, even the depths of God**. This pneumatological characterization of the Christian proclamation assumes a Trinitarian interpretation of the mode of "spiritual" understanding corresponding with it. And it is this Trinitarian framework that must firmly be established if the anti-Christian spirit among the Corinthians is going to be effectively resisted. Paul's three-pronged critique can be summarized as follows. First, the Apostle contends that the Corinthians are claiming the Son as their possession, which entails the subsidiary claim to have superior access to knowledge. This is to treat Christ as an intensifier and perfecter of their own wisdom. Second, this type of an appropriation of the Son within foreign frameworks of knowledge presumes an essentially binitarian Christology, insofar as Christ is taken to be the validator of knowledge possessed without reference to any further tutelage of the Spirit. Third, to the degree in which they have lost any sense of the necessary reliance on the ongoing work of the Spirit, the Corinthians have also lost their grip on a truthful account of Christian knowledge, which flows only through a receptive rather than an appropriative faith.

Having more clearly delineated Paul's understanding of the role and work of the Spirit we can now more precisely locate the object of his expression "spiritual understanding" (2:12). We are on safe ground in assuming that the Corinthians in their quest for spiritual knowledge sought to know no less than *God himself*. This makes it particularly striking that Paul deems the object of spiritual knowledge to be **understanding the *gifts bestowed on us by God***. Two aspects of this formulation are particularly noteworthy. First, the Apostle emphasizes understanding the gifts that the Spirit *has already* bestowed, as opposed to those that are still desirable, which he certainly could have, as attested in Galatians 5. Second, Paul's emphasis on *understanding* the fruits already bestowed on *us* we take to point to the corresponding challenge for Christians to use these gifts in the appropriate fashion—that is, as, in, and for the community and to the glory of God. These are gifts that have been bestowed not on "me" but **on *us***. True spiritual knowledge is defined by the ecclesiological imperative of *oikodome*, the upbuilding of the community. The gifts of the Spirit are not individual possessions but gifts for the *us* that is the church. The social character of Christian knowledge that Paul emphasizes in various places contrasts starkly with the solitary knowledge he associates with the proto-Gnostics in Corinth.

This insight allows us to return to 2:2 in a better position to understand a crucial detail in Paul's opening remark, **I decided to know nothing** *among you* **except Jesus Christ.** We understand this **among you** not as a polite acknowledgment of his readers but as every bit as weighty as the other clauses in the sentence. Paul's placing *himself among* them at this early point in the argument draws attention to the hard, on-the-ground work to which Paul is committed. In this he carefully engages the Corinthians on their own linguistic territory in order to lure them away from their solitary knowledge and into the properly social understanding that is the essence of the body of Christ. For Paul all quests for knowledge for its own sake are profoundly antisocial as they remain closed in their own solitary form. Such knowledge will inevitably come to tout the superiority of its possession by creating a two-step movement in which knowledge is first sought for its own sake on the assumption that it can always be readily applied to the concrete life situations its holder might face. The two-step understanding of Christian knowledge that Paul is confronting here by insisting on the sociality of understanding parallels an ancient distinction that resurfaced in high medieval and modern thought between theoretical and practical knowledge, a bifurcation that fostered, among other things, the modern distinction between systematic theology and ethics. It is a bifurcation, however, that hopelessly mangles Paul's later discussions of concrete moral cases in Corinth in demanding that the reader separate his discussions into sections related to "timeless principles" and "mitigating, contingent circumstances."

The solitary knowledge of the supposedly mature may well be deployed to resolve moral disputes, but the sheer diversity of types of knowledge indicates that solitary knowledge can never foster *oikodome*. Any community based on solitary *gnosis*, or rather, an agglomeration of those who possess knowledge of eternal moral principles, can have no sense of *communal* direction, nor can it have any certainty in its concrete moral discernments. That Christian knowledge understood in this way is doomed to run aground in life as it is really lived becomes plain in the widely divergent ways the members of the Corinthian church are living out their bodily lives. Their *gnosis*, with its assumption that the "real subject matter" of faith is purely spiritual, promotes an indifference to the body that can be acted out in radical libertarian directions (the promiscuity of chapter 6) as easily as in radical asceticism (the disparaging of sex as confronted in chapter 7). These comments also hint at some of the reasons why the modern disciplines of systematic theology and Christian ethics face a similar entrapment in the dynamics of knowledge configured as individual *gnosis*.

The Unending Tutelage of the Spirit

> ¹³ And we speak of these things in words not taught by human wisdom but taught by the Spirit, interpreting spiritual things to those who are spiritual.
> ¹⁴ Those who are unspiritual do not receive the gifts of God's Spirit, for they are foolishness to them, and they are unable to understand them because they are spiritually discerned. ¹⁵ Those who are spiritual discern all things, and they are themselves subject to no one else's scrutiny. ¹⁶ "For who has known the mind of the Lord so as to instruct him?" But we have the mind of Christ.

Having elaborated the implications of his insistence on the unending tutelage of the Spirit, Paul is now in the position to offer a tightly formulated extension of his positive account of Christian knowledge and so his riposte to the faulty theology of the Corinthians as summarized in 2:6–8. His next move is to displace the Corinthians' polarization of the mature and the immature with a distinction between being taught by the Spirit and knowledge that is mere human wisdom. By offering **spiritual things to those who are spiritual** (πνευματικοῖς/*pneumatikois*), the Apostle defines as **unspiritual** (ψυχικὸς/*psychikos*) not those who have a certain "air" about them, but very concretely those who **do not receive the gifts of God's Spirit**. After the fall humans can be counted on to be falsely self-assured and so to possess spirit only in the sense of an "air" of trust in self-possessed human reasoning that is by definition hostile to the Holy Spirit. Thus the Corinthians' (gnostic) contrast between maturity and immaturity corresponds with a definition of "maturity" as the state of having passed through, and therefore *beyond*, the status of the disciple or pupil. If the need to be taught demarcates a perennial aspect of the fallen human condition for Paul, the crucial contrast is not between maturity and immaturity, but between being **taught by the Spirit** and being **taught by human wisdom**. Attending to this point sensitizes us to the constant resistance the Apostle puts up to any hermetic construal of revelation, which inevitably generates corresponding elitist conceptions of the individual *and* the community. Such elitist self-perceptions are unable to gain true understanding because spiritual knowledge is by definition outside the powers of human reason, and as a gift of the third person of the Trinity cannot be independently produced or discovered by humans.

Nevertheless, Paul's next phrase strikes our ears as remarkably elitist: **Those who are spiritual discern all things, and they are themselves subject to no one else's scrutiny**. An elitist reading here is inappropriate for two reasons. First, Paul has just insisted that there is no way of getting "beyond teaching" (and the circularity that it involves), because there is no "outside" to the realm of the Spirit's working as Paul has described it. Instead of trying to protect the integrity and purity of an inner group, the Apostle invites everyone in: "Come, learn of this Jesus and his gifts." A moment of exclusion remains implicated in the affirmation that **spiritual things** are interpreted by *only* **those who are spiritual**, but the logic of this exclusion is not one of enclosure and expulsion, but of determination for invitation and experience. Second, Paul has categorically ruled out any claim by human beings to have finished learning and achieved complete knowledge of any sort, secular or sacred. By refusing to be taught by the Spirit one is not thereby freed from being taught but is (consciously or unconsciously) subjecting oneself to other types of **teaching**, of solely and so merely **human wisdom**. The Apostle is insistent that the only vantage point for the creature's access to knowledge is one appropriate to creatures. It is therefore in no way embarrassing or indicative of adherence to a derivative form of knowledge that the knowledge Christians ought to seek is temporal in nature. To the contrary, temporal knowledge is the sole form of knowledge that reflects the notion of the Spirit as a διδάσκαλος (*didaskalos*—a "teacher," 2:13).

To admit that human knowledge of God is inevitably temporal and so contingent is to re-emphasize Paul's shifting the emphasis of the knowledge that is crucial for the Christian life from the type of knowledge that can be put in the form of a noun to knowledge that is describable only with gerunds, as ongoing action. This reorientation is succinctly indicated by Paul's language of **discerning**. Discerning is a form of explicit understanding of **the gifts of God's Spirit** that does not merely deal with the objects of knowledge, but always and at the same time with its contextuality (not unlike what Aristotle called "prudence"). Discernment is an activity that embraces temporality as a constituent aspect of that which needs to be discerned. The result is the realization that just as the tutelage of the Spirit never ceases, discernment is likewise a perennial task that must always be refreshed in the life of the individual believer and that must be learned anew by every successive generation of Christians.

To take this chapter's final verse, **But we have the mind of Christ**, as an ironic trumping of the gnostics' claim to knowledge would undermine the basic continuity we have detected in the chapter's argument. If Paul is here simply beating the Corinthians at their own game, it seems he has overshot the mark by claiming that **we *have*** (ἔχομεν/*echomen*) **the mind of Christ**. This would mean that Paul is not only claiming *access* to the mind of the godhead, as do the gnostics, but indeed, already *owns* that mind himself. We suggest an alternative reading that draws on Paul's elaboration of what it means to be like-minded with Christ in Philippians 2:6–11, in which Christ is depicted as having humbled himself to enter the human state. This reading makes sense of Paul's decision in the opening of the chapter to set his own approach to the Corinthians within the rationality of a cruciform self-emptying: **For I decided to know nothing among you except Jesus Christ, and him crucified.**

Excursus: Paul and Discernment Today; the Genre of Commentary

Right from the outset of this letter Paul has been concerned to convey in rich detail how he is being continually bound to the Corinthians by the grace of Jesus Christ. This raises a question that forces fundamental decisions about how we will read Paul today. To what extent is his address to *them* also an address to *us*? How are Christians today to understand their relationship to Paul as an apostle without collapsing it into or wrongly distancing it from his apostolic relationship to the Corinthians? It is impossible to understand our relation to Paul as our apostle as one that renders the Corinthians in all their historical and embodied particularity irrelevant. As a concrete historical person Paul addressed an equally concrete historical community and did so in writing on parchment that exists, through ancient copies, in our world as an historical artifact. All these features demand that we not lose sight of the fact that when Christians today read 1 Corinthians they are "reading other people's mail." But Paul is also an apostle and, as such, an authority for the church of all ages. Our methodological predicament is that we can *only* hear him speaking to us through his speaking to others.[14] Thus the question cannot be evaded: have later Christians legitimately claimed to be "further" addressees of the letters Paul wrote to churches in other times and places?

Methodologically speaking, modern historicist readings simply bracket this question by assuming what later Christians made of these texts to be extraneous to a proper understanding of them. In so doing they confine the meaning of this letter to whatever Paul intended to convey to his explicitly stated recipients. Once it is assumed that what Paul once wrote to his recipients also exhausts what Paul "meant," this meaning can then best be determined by drawing connections to the ways communication was configured in contemporary literary and social conventions. Investigations of this type have absorbed most of the energies of modern commentators and generated a discussion that has reached a high level of sophistication. Most modern theologians have accepted this framing of the matter, understanding their own theological work as elaborating the "meaning of the

---

14. Dahl, "Particularity of the Pauline Epistles," 261–71.

meaning"—elucidating the theological significance of the historical meaning of the text as analytically described by biblical scholars.

Although there is much to be learned from such investigations, we believe that contemporary Christians should not evade the question of whether or how this Paul, precisely in speaking to the Corinthians, is also able to *address us today*. This is to move one rather large step beyond the hegemonic, modern two-stage account of scriptural application. This account rests on the assumption that scripture must be studied as a historical text to determine first what it meant in its context; only then may the results of this investigation be "applied" in contemporary contexts so as to establish its potential "meaning" for us today.[15] This framing of the exegetical process characterized the formative stages of the development of biblical criticism as well as most subsequent modern theology.

Significant systematic questions are at stake here, which are illuminated by linking them with current debates about the relationship between God's *aseity and immanence*—his being in his triune self—and his *promeity and economy*—his being for us.[16] In our view it is critical to retain a functional role for both aspects of the divine life since a theology that cannot speak of God in himself loses its mooring as descriptive language, and a theology that cannot guide contemporaries to recognize the working of the living God becomes an ideology. Theology must keep both emphases in constant play, and for the same reasons must read the biblical text as objectively fixed—in recounting the frame narrative of God's past and future work that situates all present human action—while at the same time encountering scripture as an active agent revealing itself ever anew as a conduit of the divine economy. These considerations suggest an investigation of scripture with very different contours than we tend to find in the modern academy, the display of which we take to be the core contribution of this commentary. The key theoretical question to be resolved if such an investigation is to be intelligible is this: how does Paul's address to the historical Corinthian church become an address to us today?

A starting point for such an investigation will be to recall the topological rationale that Paul has already set out in 1:22–23: "For Jews demand signs and Greeks desire wisdom, but we proclaim Christ crucified, a stumbling block to Jews and foolishness to Gentiles." Paul can speak not only of

---

15. The reasons for this refusal are discussed in more detail in Brock, *Singing the Ethos of God*, ch. 3.

16. The epistemological significance of the difference between "what" and "who" questions was spelled out by Bonhoeffer in his Christology lectures (*Berlin, 1932–1933* [DBWE 12], 302–15) and in the succinct formulation from his prison correspondence, "Who is Christ actually for us today?" (*Letters and Papers from Prison* [DBWE 8], 362).

"Jewishness" and "Greekness" as types that might characterize the mindset of any believer, but speaks again in this typological manner about Israel in chapter 10:1-12. By reasoning in this manner Paul offers us the crucial clue about how he can be read in a way that hears his direct summons, allowing his face to be turned toward us. When he speaks *to* the Corinthians he is also *describing* a Corinthian church that has clear and specific attitudinal and behavioral characteristics. The *moral* task of a theological reading is to be open to being addressed by looking for ways in which our lives are indeed contiguous with the Corinthians *whom Paul has portrayed*. This pursuit entails a conscious attempt at keeping our distance from the various patterns of immunization against being addressed that go with the modern habit of noticing only the many ways we are inhabitants of a vastly different time and place.

The crucial theological deficiency of the two-step approach is hence also twofold. What concerns us here is not only its assumption that there is a theologically neutral plane called "history" in which the determinative original meaning must be discerned by autonomous rational agents before it can be applied to or freely enacted in contemporary contexts, but also the type of moral distancing that this account demands of us from the outset. On this supposedly neutral plane believer and unbeliever alike are assumed to be able to establish in some methodologically agreed manner which historical, cultural, and textual data can be used to establish "the" meaning of the biblical text as an approximation to Paul's most likely original intent of speech. To be drawn into the praise of Jesus Christ as Lord is precisely to have this illusion about the neutrality of history destroyed.[17]

What happens in what we call "history" will be understood very differently by the believer and the unbeliever, especially when the works of the living God are not excluded from the range of phenomena under discussion. As Franz Rosenzweig has noted, the Jewish people are a paradigm instance of how a genuinely living humanity is constituted by God's call: "There is no *essence*—that would be a 'concept' of Judaism. There is only 'Hear, O Israel.'"[18] That this people is constituted by this call not only means that Jewish life is played out outside the frame of a "universal history," but thrusts the Jewish people into a specific unsettling role within what is taken to be a larger universal story of world history. The destiny of the Jews, Rosenzweig

---

17. J. Louis Martyn has nicely encapsulated the reasons why all such approaches necessarily truncate the dense reality description Paul is offering ("De-apocalypticizing Paul," 61-102).

18. Rosenzweig, *Der Mensch und sein Werk*, 3:601, translated in Santner, *Psychotheology of Everyday Life*, 112. This connection is developed in detail in Rosenzweig, *Star of Redemption*, 403-8.

insists, is neither *historical* (playing characters in the one story of humanity) nor *ahistorical* (being above the rhythms of publicly acknowledged historical events) but *meta-historical*—Jewish history is always a history of the remnant, of those who have been "called out" but who have inhabited and so taken up the histories of the times and places in which their elected lives have unfolded.[19]

By attending to the reality of the church that Paul is both describing and censuring we open ourselves to what we take to be the crucial feature of his apostolicity: that he offers us an invitation into the meta-historical reality that is the reign of Jesus Christ. The moral task this invitation lays on us is not one of mapping and then synchronizing the respective logics of the Corinthian church and our own age; nor is it the task of finding points of conceptual or practical overlap between our lives and theirs, a project that assumes we must first master all the salient historical features of a past age while also having a culturally developed understanding of our own. This would be to grant a supposed "universal history" a salvific role explicitly contradicted by the counterhistorical narrative that is scripture.

We thus need the Apostle because it is through his address that the Spirit can "locate" us, speaking in ways that illumine our true narratival location as we negotiate our contemporary world. What is sought in such a reading of the Apostle are moments in which our more or less hidden identity *with* the Corinthians is illuminated, and by this light we discover our place in the meta-historical narrative of Israel and the church. This is precisely what is meant when Christians call Paul an apostle. We confess that he has been given a special role in the divine economy in mediating the living voice of the Spirit. Because this voice remains bound to the apostolic person, it must perpetually be *sent* toward us out of a highly contingent text and claim us in our present milieu. Through Paul's addressing of the Corinthians, the Spirit convicts us today of the various ways in which we too are Corinthians.

Our proposal then, in short, is to *learn to discern from Paul*, instead of merely *discerning Paul as a historical subject*. By tracing the performance of his missionary activity toward the Corinthians in its connections with the philosophical presuppositions he deploys to explain it, we have discovered that these two aspects of his work are reciprocally reinforcing and seamlessly interwoven. Only because they are can Paul later invite the Corinthians to imitate him. This imitation is not a matter of duplicating his first-century

---

19. Susan Handelman, in *Fragments of Redemption*, explains the reasons for this attack on late Enlightenment (Hegelian) accounts of history among Jewish-German philosophers between the two world wars.

habits but of learning to see what he sees, to discern as he discerns as one who commends the unending tutelage of the one Spirit.

It is with this discerning mode of knowing in mind that we understand the Apostle's discussion of rival types of knowledge (2:6–8) not only as countering one historically specific form of hermetic knowledge but as helping us detect Gnostic types of knowledge whenever they appear. In this way the "dead" Paul, this Paul trapped in textual form, becomes the one who teaches us that the dead can still speak (Heb 11:4). This Apostle teaches us ever anew that we are allowed to be weak in order to be strong. If we press him hard, he surprises us with a swift jab, like a cornered boxer. Trusting that Paul's voice has not been silenced despite its having been "frozen" in a "mere text" allows us the methodological and spiritual room to admit that this or that passage in his writings makes us uneasy. We can genuinely air this unease, and as we do so, it can be rendered fruitful—if we are prepared to admit that this self-exposure is not extraneous to hearing Paul but is a constituent part of our listening intently for his living voice. This admission has critical power in forestalling our evasive and repressive reflexes, as we all too readily reach for easy ways to explain away confusing, difficult, or theologically unsettling passages.

Paul's apostolate really only comes into its own amidst the conflictual life of the community. Our suggestion is that this remains as true today as it did in the first century. To hear Paul's voice we therefore have again *today* to become the Corinthians Paul was addressing *back then*. As an actor in history, it was only as Paul took the risk of sacrificing himself into the agonizing conflicts of the Corinthian body that his decision to know **nothing but Jesus Christ** could be actualized as concrete discernment and so wisdom. His willingness to have everything else he once took to be knowledge stripped from him was part and parcel of his desire to know nothing but God's **Spirit and power**. To take this Paul at his word is to allow him in his weakness to press into our lack of discernment, to expose the hollowness of our false pretensions to eternal knowledge. This is why knowing his Christ in the power of the Spirit demands that we identify ourselves with the Corinthians, sit down beside them as recipients of this apostolic intervention and learn to embrace our being rebuked and instructed along with them.

The summons to "become Corinthians" as our necessary pathway into understanding Paul's epistle to this congregation keeps in play two interrelated moments of recognition: of the inappropriateness of our natural instinct to "side" with Paul in his conflict with that community, on the one hand, and of the power of the apostolic voice to convict us of our spiritual commonalities with the Corinthians, on the other hand. And all such recognitions are internally linked to the formula "the living voice of Paul." This is to confess that the Apostle transmits the voice of the Spirit who, emerging from the depths of God, has bound himself to scripture and so is both mediated by and directed toward the church.

That Paul's voice is heard in its apostolic immediacy only through meditation on scripture means that the church cannot judge it; it is given as read. We must be prepared in the process of such reading to face our own resistance to his authority. There are plenty of "hard sayings" in the Apostle's writings because the Paul we encounter is often at odds with our own cultural or moral instincts.[20] In this chapter, for example, we felt it difficult to not perceive moments of a Pauline brand of elitism, and we easily imagine further along the track meeting, say, the patriarchal Paul, the moody apostle, the manipulative rhetorician, and other similarly unsettling characters. A fruitful hearing of scripture grows from the admission that we cannot finally suppress our resistance to Paul. Speaking our resistance before and with those Christians who have read him before us is, we think, preferable to taking the easy escape routes of expecting that Paul must be mistaken, a victim of textual corruption, or is addressing problems (like eating food sacrificed to idols) that no longer affect us. Our contention is that owning up to and seeking to explicitly articulate our resistance in this manner is intrinsic to the work of receiving him *as an apostle*. To emphasize that Christian readers must "become Corinthians" is to retain a substantial place for spiritual conviction in contemporary theological exegesis. No genuinely theological exegesis is finally sustainable without experiencing instances of illumination and conviction in which we find ourselves alongside the Corinthians, whose questioning of Paul invites the Apostle to respond, clarify misunderstandings, correct, and instruct.

To press or "corner" Paul in the attempt to draw a response from him is not a form of judging him but a way of admitting into our reading the reality that, both morally and intellectually, we *can never escape* assessing, resisting, or embracing the voice of the one we think we hear speaking through a given text.[21] It is a characteristic of fundamentalist hermeneutics, in distinction to the rich exegetical tradition of Christianity, that it seeks to suppress these evaluative impulses. The task is to get beyond our pharisaic impulse to justify ourselves before Paul by not only admitting to but explicitly work-

---

20. See Fowl and Jones, *Reading in Communion*, 57–61.

21. "We often have the impression when we read ancient authors that they write badly, that the sequence of ideas lacks coherence and connection. But it is precisely because the true figure escapes us that we do not perceive the form that renders all the details necessary.... Once discovered, the hidden form will make necessary all of the details that one often believed arbitrary or without importance." Hadot, *Philosophy as a Way of Life*, 8.

ing to discover the ways in which we actually are resisting his words. Only so can we actively receive Paul and, in him, Jesus Christ. We say this in full awareness that modern readers inevitably harbor historical sensibilities about the historical distance between "us" today and "them" in the past, which rather than dismissing we have aimed theologically to situate.

In chapter 3 Paul will explain to the Corinthians why they are wrong to think of themselves within a merely local horizon and encourage them to understand themselves more integrally as members of the universal church. It is our conviction that in this well-developed rebuke to the Corinthians we need also hear a rebuke of a central assumption of our own age: our tendency to be so aware of our cultural and temporal *distance* from the Corinthians that we are at a loss to articulate the way in which Paul's address to them sets us *beside* them, drawing us into *identity* with them as members of ourselves. Our initial distancing from the Corinthians by way of the historical reading has thus, unwittingly, turned into an inverted version of their parochialism; by disclaiming our common apostolic authority, we invoke the name of Jesus Christ to go our own ways very much in the manner of the Corinthian church.

Our fundamental conviction is that to talk about how Paul is dealing with the Corinthians is to attempt to listen to a God who has dared to make his ways known not beyond but in the middle of dealing with a people ever in need of correction. This is why theological and moral attention to Paul as he responds to the problems of the Corinthians has to transcend simple historical reconstruction or a cataloging of the theological claims we see him deploy in order to "fix" those problems—on the assumption that such problems may recur and can be fixed with the same recipe. As fraught as they clearly were, the interactions between Paul and the Corinthians remain a privileged moment in salvation history; they remain of central importance for our churches today, characterized as they are by such obvious puzzlement about how to negotiate their own brokenness. The reading we propose is best understood as formed by the confidence that the same God who revealed himself by confronting the various confusions and estrangements of the Corinthians remains present to the universal body of Christ through the living voice of the Apostle, as it can be heard by reading his letters in faithful alertness.

The deep-seated sense of historical distance that is foundational for modern hermeneutics will remain a persistent barrier to the sort of listening we are espousing. Our historical knowledge of gnosticism "back then," in the first (or second) century, while of indubitable instrumental value, can make it more difficult to "become Corinthians" to the extent that Paul's rebuke "has teeth" for us. The more we know about gnostic sensibilities in their native historical-social setting the easier it will be to summarize and encapsulate them in a manner that makes us feel that we "understand" what is at stake in Paul's criticism without ever querying our own contemporary patterns of gnostic temptation. It would be facile for any modern theologian to claim that they do not face this temptation and, further, that any of us can have a genuinely accurate sense of the extent to which our historical sensibilities are temptations or assets. This is why we understand it to be a temptation rather than a silver bullet for contemporary theologians to try to skirt this problem by attempting to go back to scripture "naively"—as if our historical distance from the authors of scripture and our traditioning as moderns, with modern historical sensibilities, could simply be ignored. The critical approach we have suggested proposes that we *admit* that we cannot escape modern historical sensibilities, an admission that we make in order to allow Paul to *situate*, to *sift* and *judge* this knowledge in its nature as either acceptance of him or resistance to him.

One other Corinthian temptation has lost none of its luster today, namely, the gnostics' certitude that we can point to others as "*those* who crucified Christ," a temptation to which even Jesus's disciples succumbed ("*I* would never forsake you Lord" [Matt 26:22, 33]). To the degree that modern readers assume a superior vantage point on the past, they effectively step into line with the Corinthians by understanding themselves as those who have surmounted others' "lesser wisdom."

Seen from this vantage point, much of the energy devoted in biblical studies to the reconstruction of the beliefs of Paul's historical opponents can appear as the self-protective evasion of investigators who wish to remain un-convicted by Paul. The Apostle's emphasis in this chapter on the church's practices of discernment thus invites further reflection on the theological and ecclesial import of the way we draw on historical knowledge in contemporary scriptural exegesis. One essential aspect of any such reflection is the refusal to reduce theological thought to critical thought. Rather, as Peter Stuhlmacher comments,

> theological thought is in the first instance listening thought, and only then critical thought. It proceeds from faith, and is pleased to be set before a biblical testimony, whose external clarity can be examined with all the appropriate scholarly exegetical tools, but whose internal clarity is not open to such critical analysis.[22]

Rather than rejecting criticism, such a stance reconfigures it by shifting it away from the more popular interest in "detoxifying" and updating the

---

22. Stuhlmacher, "Hermeneutical Significance," 342.

traditions built on these passages toward the more difficult task of becoming aware of our own modes of resistance to scripture. Such an affirmation is only possible for those who have become aware of how the historian's eye incipiently, and in far too many cases actually, becomes a gnostic eye.

These observations also shed methodologically illuminating light on the modern form of biblical commentary. Consider the apparently piecemeal and uneven nature of most patristic commentaries. To contemporary sensibilities the fathers' tendency to comment more fulsomely only on a selection of passages within a book appears as *unwissenschaftlich* incompleteness or methodological sloppiness. As modern interpreters we instinctively presume the superiority of complete and even coverage. But reading scripture with the fathers can become a liberating experience that inverts this modern presupposition if we realize that selective reading has a positive purpose when the commentator is expressing a response to texts that *speak*. What the fathers seek in scripture is a living *voice*. This is why they do not feel compelled to produce an even spread of commentary. In their refusal to apologize for being more interested in commenting on selected passages the fathers show us that selective and uneven reading is not, as we have been taught to expect, uncritical reading but an intrinsic feature of spiritual reading. Modern readers benefit from reading patristic exegesis not simply as an exercise in scratching our encyclopedic itch or as a spur for interpretations or insights that may not have crossed our minds. Their subtle invitation to emulate them by letting the voice of scripture question and address us in our own time as they allowed it to do in theirs may be the most important lesson they hold out for us today.

Only once we have acknowledged the theological significance of the selective interpretation that is typical for patristic readers are we prepared to take on board the insistence on complete coverage typical of modern commentators. Theologically understood, complete coverage makes sense only on the basis of a *theological* aim: such coverage forces us to submit to the discipline of facing our resistance to unpalatable passages we would rather skip. It is precisely these texts that expose not only our resistances but also the procrustean limits of our theologies. If the scripture is to become a pool of vivifying water to us, we must both expect specific passages to draw us in by offering us water to drink *and* be prepared to encounter stones that tempt us to try to open them up by striking them with the stick of method. To submit to "dead" letters is an integral part of discovering, in new ways and places, scripture as a living Word.

To use the language of "dead letters" is in no way to endorse judgmental attitudes towards individual biblical passages or books—as found, for example, in Luther's famous judgment that the Epistle of James was a "straw epistle" so dry that an eternity of chewing would yield little sustenance. By insisting that this text continue to be identified as "scripture" we confess that all scripture can only be received, whether we comprehend its meaning or not. No letter is dead in the sense of lacking the potential to become God's vivifying word to us. No letter in a canonical text is dead. But letters can certainly be dead to specific *readers*, and if a letter seems to be dead to us, our assumption is that this must be so because it offers an aspect of the plenitude of Jesus Christ that we cannot yet comprehend or embrace. It is in this sense that scriptural passages should be understood as speaking at times, while at other times keeping silence or, worse, uttering words that we find repugnant.

We have developed these reflections in the course of our laboring to read First Corinthians, and we believe our experiences are far from idiosyncratic. To interpret scripture is to discover not only the voice of a particular biblical author, such as Paul, but at the same time the vocation of biblical interpretation. The responsibility of biblical interpretation is *first* to act on what we hear by acknowledging the resistance the text puts in *our* way, which we need to allow and to work through. When these barriers are prayerfully and vigorously acknowledged we are positioned to discover how the presumed "dead letter" does offer Christ to us, and along with us to the church with whom we read scripture. These affirmations free us from a simple polarized choice between whether any given utterance of Paul is commendable or not and empower us to ask about which *types* of criticism might be levied at any one of his statements. Our discovery has been that any appropriate criticism of Paul entails a self-criticism that cannot be completely formulated before we begin to engage him, but which can only be carried out in the midst of our opening ourselves to hearing by taking seriously what we realize the dead letter is uncomfortably forcing upon us.

1 Corinthians 3

Factionalism as Immaturity and Starvation

> ¹And so, brothers and sisters, I could not speak to you as spiritual people, but rather as people of the flesh, as infants in Christ. ²I fed you with milk, not solid food, for you were not ready for solid food. Even now you are still not ready, ³for you are still of the flesh. For as long as there is jealousy and quarreling among you, are you not of the flesh, and behaving according to human inclinations? ⁴For when one says, "I belong to Paul," and another, "I belong to Apollos," are you not merely human?

Paul begins to turn up the heat on the Corinthians by making it unmistakably clear that all his allusions and references in chapter 2 are not mere generalities: **brothers and sisters,** the Apostle **speaks to you.** In addressing them as **infants in Christ** Paul is not assuming a patronizing tone but expressing an apostolic discernment: "You who present yourselves as spiritually mature are really just infants; you could not keep down solid food even if you were given it." He identifies his recipients' immaturity as an entrapment in fleshly **human inclinations**. By then adding the description of the infant-like manners of the Corinthians as characterized by **jealousy and quarreling** Paul reiterates his point that the practical realities of Corinthian life are more deserving of the attention that the believers are investing in chasing the theoretical knowledge they so obviously crave. Whereas the Corinthians claim maturity as a way of legitimizing the factions in the community, the Apostle takes the existence of the factions as proof of a lack of maturity.

Though he would rather offer them **solid food**, Paul hands this confused community the **milk** that they need. Notice that these are not opposing but complementary types of food. One who still breastfeeds is meant for something more solid, the appropriate progression being from heeding simple teaching toward the developed capacity to ingest more complex teaching and so to become one who can, in turn, provide nourishment for the communal body.[1] Paul only hints at this progression here; he will bring it to the fore in his discussion of the communal nature of eating in chapter 11. There he will censure the Corinthians for betraying the social body by partaking of the Eucharist as if they are all eating individual meals: "For all who eat and drink without discerning the body, eat and drink judgment against themselves" (11:29). Reference to chapter 11 is appropriate at this point in that neither chapter makes sense if we fail to notice the pivotal role discerning the body plays in sustaining community. Only by keeping in view Paul's overriding concern with *oikodome* (the upbuilding of the communal body) are we afforded the line of sight in which the various pieces of his argument appear as a unified whole.

By the fourth century it had become common for the church fathers to cast the salvific work of Christ as an offer of medicine to sick souls, and it served as the primary metaphor for salvation in the so-called Alexandrian School (Ignatius of Antioch, Clement of Alexandria, Origen).[2] As a result, many church fathers read this letter as Paul's offer of medicine to a sick community. We have preferred to remain within what we take to be Paul's root metaphorical configuration, on the understanding that the food of doxology is the appropriate and unending sustenance of human life (>1:4–9; 13:1–13).[3] In praise human beings both recognize and enact the new life being given to them as "gospel," as nourishing and enlivening. This is why Paul must teach the community the importance of praise of the works of God and must model how it is done so that the gospel can genuinely be comprehended. Medicine is ingested or applied to salve a wound so that the body can heal itself (if it will), the metaphor assuming an end to the necessity of treatment when the body regains its proper vigor. Food, however, as something consistently required for the invigoration of the body, can be metaphorically deployed to remind the reader that believers immediately wither if not fed by grace and so cannot exist without the continual sustenance of an active Spirit. This insight allows us to read this letter not only as a treatment for illness but also as an enlivening and sustaining offer to those who are starving because attempting the impossible task of living by taking idolatrous praises on their lips.

---

1. See Luther's comment on Ps 1:3 in "Psalms 1 and 2," LW 14:298–305.
2. Dysinger, *Psalmody and Prayer*, ch. 4.
3. See Brock, *Singing the Ethos of God*, 315–16, 338–47.

Factionalism as Façade

> [5] What then is Apollos? What is Paul? Servants through whom you came to believe, as the Lord assigned to each. [6] I planted, Apollos watered, but God gave the growth. [7] So neither the one who plants nor the one who waters is anything, but only God who gives the growth. [8] The one who plants and the one who waters have a common purpose, and each will receive wages according to the labor of each. [9] For we are God's servants, working together; you are God's field, God's building.
>
> [10] According to the grace given to me, like a skilled master builder I laid a foundation, and someone else is building on it. Each builder must choose with care how to build on it. [11] For no one can lay any foundation other than the one that has been laid; that foundation is Jesus Christ. [12] Now if anyone builds on the foundation with gold, silver, precious stones, wood, hay, straw— [13] the work of each builder will become visible, for the Day will disclose it, because it will be revealed with fire, and the fire will test what sort of work each has done. [14] If what has been built on the foundation survives, the builder will receive a reward. [15] If the work is burned up, the builder will suffer loss; the builder will be saved, but only as through fire.

The backbone of the argument presented in 3:5–15 may at first strike us as a long diversion. It would certainly have made sense for Paul to have moved directly from the question, **For when one says, "I belong to Paul," and another, "I belong to Apollos," are you not merely human?** to the moral judgment on their behavior in 3:17, that is, **If anyone destroys God's temple, God will destroy that person.** Why then this more roundabout argument? Our suggestion is that these verses seek to preempt an overly hasty and shallow attempt by the Corinthians to resolve their quarreling without addressing its root causes. The "detour" Paul takes in these verses thus prepares the recipients of his letter to appreciate the precise meaning and gravity of his warning in 3:17 that the Corinthian factionalism is destroying God's temple. Their contentiousness is not a minor affair that can be fixed with positive thinking, group solidarity, and the will to stop fighting, but is in fact a desecrating sacrilege to which, as Paul indicates in 3:18–19, they are utterly blind.

The Apostle's first move is to confront the Corinthian factions by deflating their emulative relation to their leading figures. Paul and Apollos are, he curtly insists, mere **servants through whom you came to believe**.

Paul challenges the Corinthians' tendency to quarrel over the comparative importance of leading figures by drawing attention to the fundamental role played by God's work in the growth of the church: **but *God* gave the growth**. He thus exposes the Corinthian factions as an enfleshed denial of the Apostle's ecclesial vision rooted in their evident presumption that the church is an artifact of human rather than divine efforts. The factions defile the character of the apostolic mission in attributing each apostle's work to their individual agenda in diametrical opposition to Paul's characterization of their mission as **co-workers** (συνεργοί/*synergoi*) **of God**. Here the genitive construction allows for two readings that should not be taken as mutually exclusive. **Of God** could refer to those who co-operate *with* God in his mission, and it can also refer to those who co-operate *under* God, according to *God's* mission. That this dual meaning is not accidental is suggested by Paul's word choice in 3:8, where he describes those who plant and those who water as being ἕν (*hen*), one, having been rendered co-workers by God's work through them. The NRSV translation of *hen* as "having a common purpose" is misleading in suggesting that the unity or oneness of the church is essentially a type of agreement between the workers, a shared feeling that they have a "common project." But Paul's linkage of the term *hen* with *synergoi* suggests that the oneness of those who work together is not constituted by *their* shared purpose, but rather by their common subjection to the one purpose of *God* to build up his church.

This contrasting of God's work and co-opted human efforts provides the linkage between the agricultural metaphor of 3:6–8 and the architectural metaphor deployed in 3:10–12, as Paul indicates in 3:9: **For we are God's servants, working together; you are God's field, God's building**. The architectural metaphor explores the manner in which the shape of a foundation demands a precise congruence from the building that rests on it. The passive construction in 3:11, **no one can lay any foundation other than the one that has been laid**, parallels Paul's emphasis on God's giving the growth in the agricultural metaphor. That this foundation has been laid is indubitably a case of *passivum divinum*, of a divine work to which humans can only respond. On first sight this *passivum divinum* seems to contradict Paul's claim in the preceding verse, **I laid a foundation**, but the emphasis placed here on his activity must not overwhelm his own preface to the phrase, that his work is **according to the grace of God given to me**. This formulation carefully sets Paul's emphasis on his own agency within the claim that God's grace is never just a mere "something" that accompanies or endorses human activity, but is always the work of a divine agent. The divine agent's work is foundational in the sense of strongly constraining what can be built upon it by human agency and in the way that the integrity of a building is intrinsically related to the quality of its foundation and the building's congruence with it. Paul does not imagine divine agency competing with human agency. So when Paul says **like a skilled master builder I laid a foundation** he draws attention not to his own skills but to the location and form of his work as wholly congruent with and claimed by the one foundation that is Christ.

A third metaphor allows Paul to develop the implications of this criterion of congruence. The congruence of good work with its foundation can be tested, which Paul asserts will happen on the **day of judgment** by the fire that **will test what sort of work each has done**. God's judgment alone will eventually disclose the quality of the construction of any respective builder, which is impossible to easily read off of surface appearances. The visible outward layer—whether appealingly covered with costly materials such as **gold, silver**, and **precious stones,** or with more mundane materials such as **wood, hay,** and **straw**—is presented as nothing more than a tempting distraction in masking the more important structures holding the building up.

What is needed is a penetrating discernment of what has been built in accordance with the foundation in distinction to that which is merely adornment. "Knowledge puffs up, but love builds up" (8:1). The Corinthians' mistake is to have been fixated on superficial materials, that which is "puffed up," rather than discerning what truly "builds up" in both senses— up from the foundation of Jesus Christ, and up from the childlike beginning to genuine maturity of faith. This is why the Corinthians can see Paul as merely a historical founding figure, Peter to be providing a link with the mother community in Jerusalem, and Apollos as the stunning rhetorician. In their preoccupation with the superficial, the Corinthians are in dire need of the discernment that grasps which structures in fact support the church. The Apostle reinforces this point by emphasizing endurance as the mark of good work: **what has been built on the foundation survives**. Notice that Paul does not depict the work of fire as purgative but as wholly destroying what is not congruent with the foundation: everything that is "all surface" must go. It might help us grasp Paul's point if we call to mind the way that earthquakes, like fire, reveal the value of the work of builders. In emphasizing congruity as the criterion of good work, Paul indicates that this criterion not only provides a standard for judging finished work, but is a standard that ought to orient work as it happens: **each builder must choose with care how to build on it.**

From the time of the church fathers there has been dispute about the proper interpretation of 3:8, **each will receive wages according to the labor of each**; some argue that God will judge the diligence of our efforts (motive),⁴ others that God will judge only outward actions and not our beliefs (objective results).⁵ On our reading this debate might be better resolved by noting that the plain sense of the passage does not emphasize the problem of measuring the metric whereby future reward will be meted out. Instead, the metaphor presupposes that human laborers will in fact be paid in this life for the time they put in, but that this pay is not a measure of the real quality of what they have done. Only time or the acceleration of decaying processes through fire can reveal the true quality of what human labor has achieved in a building. The fault Paul finds with the Corinthians is that they have been preempting the Lord's judgment by having judged the worth of their leaders' works according to the form of their labor, and not according to its actual value as a work built on the one foundation. Because only God has the ability to judge the real product and essence of human work, human beings can only assess those involved in building the church on the basis of what meets the eye of the immediate observer—the oratorical polish of Apollos, for instance, or the numerical growth of the church under Paul. Like all people, Christians then and now are all too easily trapped in surface appearances, being quickly satisfied that "the church is full, the youth are active," as Bonhoeffer puts it, adding the crucial warning, "but nevertheless, [there is] no lasting stability."⁶

It is worth pausing at this point to note how easily passages this rich in metaphor tempt readers into distracting speculations that obscure the overarching message. By drawing together quite different metaphors with all sorts of divergent implications (as growing and building clearly do), Paul signals that he is not setting out a technical treatise on the relation between divine and human action (entering the debates about synergism, congruence, etc.) but is rather stressing, in a supple and suggestive way, the precedence of divine work and its role in defining appropriate human action.⁷ This insight spares us a whole range of potential dead-end enquiries. For instance, the notion of the work each has done being tested by fire can all too easily provoke self-referential reflections on our own individual future before the judgment seat: "What is Paul suggesting this will mean for my

---

4. Theodoret, *Commentary,* PG 82:248, quoted in JK, 55.

5. Chrysostom, *Homily 9,* PG 61:75–80, quoted in JK, 60.

6. Bonhoeffer, "Sketch of a Bible Study," in *Conspiracy and Imprisonment, 1940–1945* (DBWE 16), 486.

7. Paul is not as entrapped by a zero-sum understanding of human and divine agency as the acrimonious debates in Pauline studies tend to imply (focused as contemporary debates are on his Epistle to the Romans and questions about appropriate atonement metaphors). See Miller's summary of the issues at stake in his *Practice of the Body of Christ,* 39–60.

own works when judged and presented back to me at the end of time?" This line of inquiry, however, dissipates the ecclesial focus Paul has been pressing on the Corinthian church torn by their illegitimate adherence to commanding figures. Paul is not offering here a formal or general account of the divine mechanisms for purifying individual lives of sin either in this life or after death. Rather, he has developed this line of argument to confront a specific set of idolatries in Corinth so that the Corinthians can begin to discern what in their own lives and thinking lies under threat of that this-worldly judgment. While God's work of judging and rewarding human activity in this world is not different in kind or detachable from the ways of God's final judgments, it remains true that the final judgment is not Paul's main interest in this particular discussion, as he tries to enliven the Corinthians to the dynamics of God's historical activity of judging the church.

Only by keeping in mind the local focus of Paul's argument as an address to this particular ecclesial body are we positioned to follow his next movement into the stern language of the destruction of God's temple. Victims of buildings that collapse in catastrophic earthquakes or hurricanes learn, to their horror, that they had been living in buildings built with dubious integrity. The immediate and total collapse of their houses on the day of disaster reveals two things to them: the nature of the builders' work as shot through with poor judgments about the quality of construction, materials, and design, on the one hand, and the betrayal of government inspectors responsible for approving the work, on the other. The metaphor brings home the fact that the poor work of builders is never just *their* problem; it is always also *ours*. While today builders usually do not live in the houses they build, Paul's metaphor presupposes that builders are also inhabiting what they are building. These observations draw attention to the ecclesial frame in which Paul's concluding remark is couched: **If the work is burned up, the builder will suffer loss; the builder will be saved, but only as through fire**. In comparing the church to a building, Paul is subtly but sweepingly modifying the mechanics of the metaphor itself. Though a builder can live outside of a building he builds, no such externality is possible for ministers of the Christian gospel. Thus, the fire that will sweep away the work of the factional figureheads is exceedingly dangerous not only to them but to the believers who have gathered around them.

As he reflected on the disastrous capitulation of many churches in Germany to the ideology of National Socialism, Dietrich Bonhoeffer found himself meditating on the theme of what it takes to "stand fast." It had become all too obvious to him that the disaster was not the fire of destructive political conflagrations but what such conflagrations reveal about the disposition of people. Reflecting on the failures of the highest moralities of his day, which he compares with "rusty swords," Bonhoeffer considers how common moral attitudes that were sufficiently present within the German people, such as "reasonableness," "purity of principle," "being a person of conscience," "private virtue," and "duty," were nevertheless shoddy constructions, in the terms of Paul's architectural metaphor—not sturdy enough to withstand the firestorm of Nazi ideologies and politics.[8] Because not founded on Christ alone, Christians in Germany found themselves relying on a morality too flimsy to withstand the winds of political and ideological change and allowed their high moral ideas to be claimed by, and effectively enlisted to serve, a regime of inhumanity.

Paul's discussion of the fire testing the foundation suggests that it is a fate that can befall the church in every age. Neither Bonhoeffer nor Paul is making a slippery slope argument here, as if every little compromise—whether controversial sexual lifestyles, seeker-sensitive liturgical revisions, or women's ordination, to take a few common nominees—is the little flame that, left unfought, will burn the church down. There are debates that we need to have and temptations that need to be resisted, but the fire is an abyss that opens up beyond discourse, a *fait accompli* that swallows every sort of resistance. In such moments of judgment, the congruence of the church's work with its foundation will become startlingly apparent.

Factionalism as the Abominating Sacrilege

> [16] Do you not know that you are God's temple and that God's Spirit dwells in you? [17] If anyone destroys God's temple, God will destroy that person. For God's temple is holy, and you are that temple.

Paul has built anticipation in his addressees for answers to some rather serious questions with this warning that only certain forms of building activity will endure the coming divine judgment. His core claim is pointed: those involved in constructing the church in Corinth are erecting a building in so many diverging directions from the one foundation that they are essentially leveling the building, though this actuality has not yet become fully apparent. By setting up their own assessments (of the hierarchy) of Christian authorities and in making each the leader of a faction, they effectively idolize their leaders, whether their leaders approve of this or not. Hence for Paul the problem at hand is idol worship in the pious guise of adherence to godly figures.

---

8. Bonhoeffer, "After Ten Years," in *Letters and Papers from Prison* (DBWE 8), 38–40.

It is this diagnosis that demands Paul's deployment of the sharpest of language: **If anyone destroys God's temple, God will destroy that person**. Because the temple is the high place of Israel's worship, to worship idols here is to **defile** (as the KJV appropriately translates it) the whole temple and hence **destroy** (NRSV) its fittingness for its original purpose.[9] By invoking the image of the defilement of the temple Paul is drawing on the heart of the biblical story of the golden calf. When the people desire alternative forms of life with their attendant politics they always end up constructing alternative identities for the God who has actually liberated them.[10] Thus to follow rival leaders is not an accidental circumstance that has arisen through inattention or lack of organization in the Corinthian church, but expresses a secret, deeply rooted veneration of a particular *incarnation of power*, whether in the form of rhetorical force, prophetic insight, leadership prowess, or other such magnets of admiration. This is why Paul refuses an analysis of the factions in Corinth that concedes their existence as the result of mere human frailty, as if factionalism has arisen because the Corinthians had succumbed to a natural tendency to cluster in peer groups, for instance. Paul's point is not that there ought to be unity where there are currently factions, but that the factions are highly menacing as embodied politics oriented by idolatrous judgments.

Factionalism as Self-Deception

> [18] Do not deceive yourselves. If you think that you are wise in this age, you should become fools so that you may become wise. [19] For the wisdom of this world is foolishness with God. For it is written, "He catches the wise in their craftiness," [20] and again, "The Lord knows the thoughts of the wise, that they are futile."

The language of self-deception Paul employs in 3:18 is best understood as an extension of what has been said about the inherent idolatry of each faction in its respective judgment that it follows the "real" leader. The self-deception of the Corinthians is not simply that they turn out not to be as wise as they thought they were; the problem runs much deeper. By couching their idolatrous behavior in the language of a higher spirituality, they spawn a competition for the most illustrious shape such a spirituality ought to take

---

9. See, for example, the Assyrian defilement of the temple by the placing of someone else's image in Israel's temple. This constitutes an abominating sacrilege (2 Kgs 16).

10. Wannenwetsch, "Sin as Forgetting," 3–20. See also Lebron, *Wittgenstein's Religious Point of View*, ch. 4.

as it conforms with a particular ideal type (Apollonian, Pauline, Petrine, etc.). Citing Job (5:13) and the Psalms (94:11) Paul reminds the Corinthians of the contingency of human life, drawing on a notion made famous by the poet Qoheleth's meditation on the Hebrew הֶבֶל, which literally means "vapor" or "breath" and is variously translated in the Old Testament with "futility," "vanity," or "absurdity": "'Absurdity of absurdities,' says Qoheleth, 'absurdity of absurdities. Everything is absurd'" (Eccl 1:2).[11] Because of life's sheer impermanence, the efforts of human beings to generate the resources necessary to ensure their own endurance are ultimately **futile**.

Paul's account of what happens to those trapped in self-deception goes beyond the rationality of discovering our psychological blind spots in insisting it be defined in relation to divine judgment. That the true measure of human deception is divine judgment rather than mere psychology is, however, a cause for hope, since the recognition of being under divine judgment is already a form of liberation from the psychological aporia that makes self-deception so otherwise inescapable. This is why we must not miss the hopeful note in Paul's imperative: **If you think that you are wise in this age, you should become fools so that you may become wise.** What is indicated here with the expression "becoming a fool" is not a program to be actively engaged but an acceptance of both human contingency and God's judgment about idolatrous ways, even those we justify with the language of high spirituality.[12] Paul thus offers a breathtaking inversion of his metaphor: as those who are self-deceived, believing ourselves to be free but destroying ourselves, our salvation comes through being driven to the knowledge that we are but contingent creatures who, despite our amazing creaturely powers, nevertheless remain constrained by a remarkably limited vantage point in serious need of constantly being enlightened by the living Spirit of the Creator of all things.

Factionalism as Parochialism

> [21] So let no one boast about human leaders. For all things are yours, [22] whether Paul or Apollos or Cephas or the world or

---

11. Translation that of Atkinson, in *Singing at the Winepress*, 54.

12. Bonhoeffer powerfully elaborates the essence of Paul's warning: "Every human idealized image that is brought into the Christian community is a hindrance to genuine community and must be broken up so that genuine community can survive. Those who love their dream of a Christian community more than the Christian community itself become destroyers of that Christian community even though their personal intentions may be ever so honest, earnest and sacrificial" (*Life Together* [DBWE 5], 36).

> life or death or the present or the future—all belong to you,
> ²³ and you belong to Christ, and Christ belongs to God.

The emphasis on belonging to Christ as trumping personal opinion and preference resonates strongly in 3:21–23. Here the Apostle gives a telling account of the reasons behind the imperative **let no one boast about human leaders**, and in so doing summarizes the central message of the chapter. As his argument comes to a climax, Paul offers a bold and exceedingly positive rationale for abstaining from factional idolatry: **all things are yours**. With this pithy statement Paul exposes the Corinthian claim to wisdom as mere parochialism. Whereas they think they have found the leader and the teaching that elevates them above the crowd, Paul dares to name this very activity as a fateful narrowness of attention, a self-destructive contentment with a fragment of the truth instead of the grand wholeness of Jesus Christ.

The psychology of parochialism remains a problem for the church today, especially when discussing contentious issues. Two of its aspects are particularly worth noting here. The first is one that is portrayed repeatedly in Israel's story—the trap of imagining one's group as small and weak and therefore in need of an alliance with a greater nation that will ensure security. By lusting after a supposedly different and greater power than that which God actually apportions them, they give their allegiance to a golden calf or, worse, a stronger nation that will turn to devour them. The factions at Corinth mirror this shift in their respective individual economies of desire. The second characteristic of parochialism is to grasp for a transnational leader (such as Paul) or an overarching conceptual claim (as presented by a gnostic Christ), to whom one attaches the hope of being drawn up and out of a self-perceived marginal or powerless position. A classic contemporary example is the expression, typically uttered in worried tones, that the church needs to do this or that in order not to "lose touch" with the so-called wider society. Ironically, this concern actually leads churches to self-parochialize, in that they live and speak as if national or local debates are in fact *wider* than their expansive inheritance in the faith. As the Corinthians embrace factional logic as a strategy to overcome a perceived parochial position, Paul insists that it is this strategy itself that is making them parochial in real, cosmic terms. The real church in which they are already involved is one in which all believers are drawn in and together, including every one of the leading figures whom they are so futilely trying to put on special pedestals of honor.

One methodological implication of Paul's argument here springs from his assumption that the "cloud of witnesses" (Heb 12:1) are participants in ecclesial judgments of all types, including exegetical judgments. To exist as the church means that each individual believer is beholden to the whole communal body, because **whether Paul or Apollos or Cephas or the world or life or death or the present or the future—all belong to you**. Paul extends the logic of his local dispute with the Corinthians outward in time and space to suggest that the leaders they line up behind belong to a vast crowd of saints who inhabit all times and places, who are not constrained by death, by being in the past or future, nor to heaven as opposed to earth. By bringing into view the fantastically wide diachronic and synchronic scope of the *communio sanctorum*, Paul introduces a perspective from which the narrowness of claiming to have "just" a Pauline or a Petrine church becomes especially visible.

Within such an argument the cloud of witnesses has a canon-shaping function. This is not to say that it projects one form of saintliness upon the multitude, reifying the kinds of traits the factions worship, but that it sets each saint within a universal church in which the debate over who is greatest is rendered meaningless. Paul reminds the Corinthian saints that they exist within the whole cloud of saints, presuming them to be brothers and sisters who still have something to tell living believers, not just a "past" that must be "explained" today. As fathers and mothers in faith they are not separated from us by a wide and ugly ditch of history, but rather assume a moral, intellectual, and affective equidistance to us as to any other generation of Christians—an equidistance that is the work of the Holy Spirit. Together with us they form what Paul conceived as a communion of discernment (Rom 12:2) that spans all times.[13]

Hence to claim only one or another follower of Jesus Christ as the definitive model of Christian perfection is odd not simply because it generates factionalist quarrels but because it dangerously narrows the horizon of faith. Every saint plays a specific role in inviting every Christian to a more expansive, challenging, and beautiful horizon of faith than they currently possess.[14] The saints, each with his or her own qualities, represent particular aspects of Christian truth with the capacity to expand or correct the particularity of each model held up in specific communities of the faithful in time and space. Just as, with regard to the biblical canon, individual Christians may find they have a preference for, say, the Gospel of John, yet this preference does not constitute warrant for reading this one Gospel at the expense of the others, so we can never claim that one type of Christian life, however impressive it may be, represents the *true* model *over and against* all the others.

---

13. Wannenwetsch, "Conversing with the Saints," 131.
14. Banner, "What We Lost," 175–90.

Paul insists that *his* particularity matters ("in Christ Jesus I became your father" [4:15]) and that in recognizing him the Corinthians have grasped the point that God does call specific persons to specific ministries in his church, with all the individuality each brings to the body. Nevertheless, the fact that like all good gifts the church's teachers come in many different shapes and sizes can also be the occasion for misunderstanding and self-serving appropriations. Against such a backdrop the claim **all are yours** is clearly an explicit negation of the motto of Corinthian partisanship, "I belong to Apollos or Cephas." But it is more than a simple negation. Paul does not suggest that the congregation now be more forceful in asserting the "rights" of the church community to the services of their leaders, which would eventually turn ministers into mere functionaries. The claim that **all things are yours, whether Paul or Apollos or Cephas**, is not the establishment of a kind of "sovereignty of the people" as in modern democracies, where people assume they can legitimately call their representatives to account for their actions at any time. In keeping with his view of the ultimate locus of judgment, Paul does seem to have a relationship of accountability in mind, but he expresses the structure of this belonging in a sequence of modifying clauses. Not stopping at **all belong to you**, he specifies the way in which the community can claim to "possess" their leaders by embedding its rule in a much wider reality of belonging, namely, **you belong to Christ, and Christ belongs to God.**

1 Corinthians 4

Escaping from Human Judgment into Praise

> ¹Think of us in this way, as servants of Christ and stewards of God's mysteries. ²Moreover, it is required of stewards that they be found trustworthy. ³But with me it is a very small thing that I should be judged by you or by any human court. I do not even judge myself. ⁴I am not aware of anything against myself, but I am not thereby acquitted. It is the Lord who judges me. ⁵Therefore do not pronounce judgment before the time, before the Lord comes, who will bring to light the things now hidden in darkness and will disclose the purposes of the heart. Then each one will receive commendation from God.

The discussion Paul opened in 1:11 with "it has been reported . . . that there are quarrels among you" is here drawn together in a first summary statement of the character and function of ecclesiastical ministries and his own ministry in particular. Paul summons his hearers to think of him alongside the other apostles as **servants of Christ and stewards of God's mysteries**, deploying the qualifiers "servants" and "stewards" in a deflationary manner. The lowly status that is undoubtedly true of the servant is also largely true of the οἰκονόμοι (*oikonomoi*—**stewards**), even if the steward is given greater oversight of household affairs. Luther observes that the Corinthians' habit of treating their leading figures with undue deference is a reversal of the more common problem of believers thinking too little of the steward's role in the church.[1] In bestowing their selected leaders with honor in excess of what is due to simple overseers of their Lord's household, the Corinthians in effect elevate them to the proxy role of lords themselves.

By deploying the language of **servants *of Christ*** Paul resists such elevation in a manner that also explicitly rules out treating him and his fellow apostles as if they could be anyone else's servants—servants, for example, of any faction in the community wishing to claim him or anyone else as their particular leader, spokesman, or legitimator. This formulation is best

---

1. Luther, *Epistel-Auslegung*, 2:40–47.

understood as another expression of Paul's "nothing but" rationality (>2:2). Its deployment here sets the stage for the discussion soon to follow of judging and not judging. The emphasis of our interpretation will be on Paul's fundamental insistence that **it is *the Lord* who judges me**, a position that vastly narrows the sorts of claims he believes it would be legitimate for others who wish to be the final guardians of Christian accountability to lay on him. In urging on the Corinthians a differentiation they had not previously grasped between *types* of judgment, Paul is, however, not jettisoning human judgment in all forums. The salutary human judgments made, for example, by the mayor and farmer remain crucial for human life,[2] as do the judgments made by appropriate authorities within and for the sake of the church.[3]

In a compact statement Paul elaborates his notion of servanthood and stewardship by defining both in relation to the task correlative of this status designation: **that they be found trustworthy**. Πιστός (*pistos*), which the NRSV translates "trustworthy," is more accurately and perceptively rendered as "faithful" because faithfulness indicates *what* actions Paul considers to render one worthy of trust. The introduction of this sentence, ὧδε (*hōde*—**therefore**[4]), sets up a strong connection with 3:1 and lends theological *gravitas* to this definition of servanthood as faithfulness. Luther certainly understands this connection as an allusion to Paul's "nothing but" grammar when he renders the construction λοιπὸν ζητεῖται ἐν τοῖς οἰκονόμοις (*loipon zēteitai en tois oikonomois*) as "nothing more is required [of stewards]."[5]

This emphasis on faithfulness as the sufficient and sole requirement for defining the activity of responsible stewardship has a critical edge that bears both on Paul's original addressees and contemporary churches. The Corinthians appeared to expect something more than mere faithfulness

---

2. Ibid., 32-33.

3. "Those entrusted with judging *those inside* are not so foolish as to say, as they judge, 'We are pronouncing the judgment of God.' Rather, they exercise judgment for the sake of the good of the church. If it benefits the church for this person to be excommunicated (1 Cor 5:5), they pronounce this judgment and carry it out. Likewise it is for the good of the church that they commend people; they do not pronounce the judgment of God but only exercise the judgment delegated to them. For we do not 'search hearts,' nor do we know the reasons behind each person's deeds. Those who judge according to the gospel leave *the secret things to the Lord God*, but *the things that are revealed*, as Scripture says, *are for you and your children* (Deut 29:29). They judge whatever comes to their attention and what is known to them. [Here Origen anticipates our discussion of 5:1.] Let us never, then, anticipate the judgment of God and say, 'This man is lost,' or call someone blessed and say, 'That man is saved.'" Origen, *Homilies on 1 Corinthians*, 355-56, quoted in JK, 73.

4. Conzelmann, *1 Corinthians*, 82.

5. Luther's translation: "fordert man nicht mehr."

from their leaders in a manner strangely familiar today. One often hears suggestions that good leadership distinguishes itself by promoting an imaginative and fresh vision, or by being a paragon of best practice, or perhaps by implementing structural reform. Paul confronts such puffed-up expectations and self-images of leadership with a theological sobriety that reminds the Corinthians once again of the oneness and exclusive character of their foundation. The desire for their leaders to exhibit more than faithfulness to the one foundation already laid can only be a recipe for achieving less in the end. In the discussion of judgment that follows, Paul will undertake to illustrate in detail the deformations churches are inviting when they seek to establish leadership marked by "this, *and*" instead of "nothing but." In looking for more than faithfulness the Corinthians give up the genuine freedom that Paul understands to come with allowing the Lord alone to judge. Only the one who freely submits to the one true judge experiences the ensuing liberation from all other standards of judgment and accountability. To say that *God* is our judge, Paul suggests, is primarily a statement that there are no other judgments to fear, for to be a servant of Christ is to be no one else's servant. This freedom is an especially prominent feature of the apostolate—Paul affirms himself not to be accountable to any standard humans can produce, even the ones laid on him by his own conscience.

Recalling the Apostle's discussion of the judging work of fire on the day of the Lord (>3:13), we can now specify that it is precisely the freedom from (any others') judgment that allows one to withstand the raging fire. When Paul says he resolves to know "nothing but" he is jettisoning the ballast of human ideas that make him more susceptible to the judging fire. Drawing on the connection we made between the Day of Judgment and the destructive mechanics of earthquakes, we might say that Paul's resolve to know "nothing but" Christ is the preparation necessary to ride out the tremors shaking the Corinthian community. He does not prepare by adding reinforcements in intellectual terms (so as not be outmaneuvered) or emotional terms (so as not be shaken) but by shedding those attachments that tie his hands as he enters their tumult. This prepares him to become that lighter and more flexible structure that bends with the shaking rather than attempting to remain wholly static—and so being torn to pieces.

Once again it becomes palpable that the freedom that comes with this "nothing but" posture is not gained by simple subtraction. By not being accountable to any standard other than faithfulness, Paul need not, for example, become a great rhetorician, as Apollos was reputed to be. It was sufficient for him to be Paul, faithful Paul, a Paul consigned to conformity with his foundation. The Apostle does not seek freedom from constraint, and indeed, he quotes scripture to the effect that such autonomous freedom is an illusion; he yearns to be caught and known (>3:19–20) by God instead, which is the only way to be liberated from the potentially tempting seductions that are the craftiness, thoughts, and wisdom of the wise.

Commending the faithful patience that waits for God's judgment instead of engaging in prescriptive attempts to anticipate it is possible only on the basis of a hope that the revelation associated with the day of God's judgment will eventually bring liberation. God's judgment, when it comes, **will bring to light the things now hidden in darkness and will disclose the purposes of the heart**, a revealing in which Paul hears a note of hope and cheerful expectation. Unfortunately, the NRSV obscures the hopeful ending of this opening section by rendering the final phrase of 4:5 thus: **Then each one will receive commendation from God**. This translation, in keeping with many other versions, lays the emphasis on what humans can expect to receive from divine judgment. The sparse character of the Greek wording, however, leaves open a very different and theologically more penetrating reading, more literally, "praise will become [real/happening] from God to everyone." We find this reading appropriate because it recalls Paul's opening account of the doxological telos of the human existence (>1:4–9, 31). On this reading God's judgment is not primarily a matter of unleashing deserved punishment, but is a just and merciful procedure of revealing the true and hidden nature of human works, dispensing praise where it is due and cutting away sin to reveal the true form and purpose of each human life.

Paul next warns the Corinthians not to **pronounce judgment . . . before the Lord comes** not in order to *suspend all* activity of judging but to insist that their activity of judging be nothing more than a *following* of God's own revealing of judgment on the grounds that future divine judgments can always be foreshadowed by the present working of God. God's judgment is liberating because it exposes the truths of the human person and so saves people from the tedious, stifling business of having to justify themselves before the myriads of human courts that leave believers too wearied and busy to praise. "Commendation" cannot therefore be read here as a divine ranking procedure that precedes the giving of awards, nor is it a back-patting "good job." It is rather a "look—this here and that there were genuinely human and therefore commendable acts in revealing something of what the divine economy is about."

If we believe that we must justify ourselves in the face of manifold human courts we will find ourselves pressed into alienating doxologies, praising the standards that such forms of accountability presuppose. Those who work in the universities of our day, to take one example, though constantly and increasingly mired in bureaucratic formalities and infighting, still find themselves compelled to sing songs of praise for the system, its standards of accountability and its shining exemplars of "best practice." Hoping to be the recipients of the little praises the system metes out, and to escape its judgments, people are willing to pay the price of singing these alienating doxologies, utterances that are always by definition public. Such doxologies are oppressive precisely because those who sing them do not really believe them but do believe they must accede to singing them. The language of doxology is a reminder that the things we praise and in which we trust claim and orient us as whole beings. And it is as whole beings that Paul invites his readers to give voice to a different song that stills the songs of all other authorities that promise salvation, one that need not, and cannot, be sung as a form of *self*-justification because it can only be received from God.[6]

Scripture as the Limit of Factionalism

> [6]I have applied all this to Apollos and myself for your benefit, brothers and sisters, so that you may learn through us the meaning of the saying, "Nothing beyond what is written," so that none of you will be puffed up in favor of one against another. [7] For who sees anything different in you? What do you have that you did not receive? And if you received it, why do you boast as if it were not a gift?

The memorable formula **"nothing beyond what is written"** has proved perplexing to commentators. If we survey all the biblical passages Paul has cited as authoritative to this point in 1 Corinthians, it seems that the most likely interpretation is that **what is written** refers to the Old Testament as a whole. Each of the phrases in 4:6–7 stresses in various ways the divine nullification of human wisdom and judgment. What Paul wants his **brothers and sisters** to **learn through us** refers back to his exemplary resolution to know nothing except Christ, and him crucified (2:2). Notice that the reason the Corinthians should not go beyond these biblical traditions is **so that none of you will be puffed up in favor of one against another**. To go beyond the scriptures is to rush God's judgment by generating criteria for judging others. On these grounds Paul does not criticize arrogance and self-importance as such, but those who have taken up the stance of self-appointed judges and so are categorizing, separating, and binding into hierarchies the members of the church according to the criteria that make such ranking possible and even incumbent as revealed in their factionalizing behavior. Paul resists this attitude by reminding the Corinthians, **What do you have that you did not**

---

6. See Brock, *Singing the Ethos of God*, 172–79.

receive? What they have received is the crucified Christ, in whom nothing can be found that warrants the sort of distinctions between people that Paul is resisting. The only distinction that really matters, as the Apostle has stressed in 3:5, is between faithfulness and unfaithfulness to the crucified Christ.

Having and Holding Christ's Gifts

> ⁸Already you have all you want! Already you have become rich! Quite apart from us you have become kings! Indeed, I wish that you had become kings, so that we might be kings with you! ⁹For I think that God has exhibited us apostles as last of all, as though sentenced to death, because we have become a spectacle to the world, to angels and to mortals. ¹⁰We are fools for the sake of Christ, but you are wise in Christ. We are weak, but you are strong. You are held in honor, but we in disrepute. ¹¹To the present hour we are hungry and thirsty, we are poorly clothed and beaten and homeless, ¹²and we grow weary from the work of our own hands. When reviled, we bless; when persecuted, we endure; ¹³when slandered, we speak kindly. We have become like the rubbish of the world, the dregs of all things, to this very day.

There is virtually a complete consensus not only today, but stretching right to the beginning of the Christian interpretative tradition,[7] that in 4:8–13 "Paul resorts to irony."[8] Although there are certainly expressions in Paul's letters that suggest he can write in an ironic tone, an ironic understanding of these verses produces three uncomfortable dilemmas. First, it demands reading 4:9, **For I think**, as a "so you think" statement.[9] Second, in 4:8-10, as Conzelmann admits, "Paul notably changes the tone."[10] Whereas an ironic reading understands 4:9-10 to be deploying a sharp ironic edge by setting up contrasts between what happens to Paul and what happens to the Corinthians, in 4:11-13 such a reading assumes Paul to be reverting to plain

---

7. "... speaks in a way designed to shame them" (Chrysostom, *Homily* 12, PG 61:95-98, quoted in JK, 74); "he taunts them" (Aquinas, *Commentary on the First Epistle to the Corinthians*, sec. 208); "bitter irony" (Melanchthon, in Luther, *Epistel-Auslegung*, 2:49); "Now he makes fun . . . speaking ironically" (Calvin, *First Epistle of Paul the Apostle to the Corinthians*, 92); "remarkable harangue" (Barth, *Resurrection of the Dead*, 21).

8. Conzelmann, *1 Corinthians*, 87

9. Aquinas explicitly makes this substitution: "for I think, i.e., you seem to think . . ." (TA, sec. 209).

10. Conzelmann, *1 Corinthians*, 91

speech, in which he simply describes what he has given up in the course of his mission. With this sudden change of tone Paul seems to abandon the ironic posture. At this point we simply observe the obvious difficulty the assumption of irony has in explaining this sudden change of tone and mode of speech. A third problem arises in the ensuing section, when Paul says in 4:14 that he is **not writing this to make you ashamed**. On the irony reading with this statement Paul is understood as shifting into a third mode of speech, a pedagogical strategy, or even worse, changing psychological mood for the third time in seven verses, from biting irony in 4:8-10, to plain speech that could be easily perceived as a lapsing into maudlin self-pity in 4:11-13, followed by backpedaling from both the initial biting irony and the ensuing moment of self-pity to assure the Corinthians that, in the final analysis, they can trust his well-meaning purposes.

Such a reading seems not only overcomplicated and artificial in imagining Paul as a moody, if not incoherent, writer. Furthermore, it is a reading that is hard to reconcile with Paul's claim in 4:13 that **when slandered, we speak kindly**. As a matter of faithfulness to his apostolic mission Paul seems to rule out irony as a bitter or self-protective response to a perceived offense. Here the English translation may hinder theological comprehension. What the NRSV renders as "we speak kindly" is in the Greek, and in Pauline theology, a much more profound concept. Παρακαλοῦμεν (*parakaloumen*) is more suitably translated as providing "consoling exhortation" or "exhorting consolation." The concept of παράκλησις (*paraklēsis*) that Paul develops and deploys prominently in his letters (compare Rom 12:1; 2 Cor 5:20; Philem 8[11]) is an intrinsic part of the fatherly dimension that characterizes his apostolate. This is why in 4:14 Paul summarizes the purpose of his *paraklesis* with a contrast between admonishing his children as **my beloved children** and shaming them. Evoking shame in the Corinthians would be extremely difficult to forestall if this passage was ironic, a shaming that Paul explicitly states he is trying to avoid.

A few modern commentators have picked up the crucial point that the repeated **already** of 4:8 is the language of eschatological presence. C. K. Barrett, for instance, reads 8a as a rebuke to the Corinthians for "behaving as if the age to come were already consummated, as if the saints had already taken over the kingdom (Dan 4:18)."[12] On his reading Paul's wish in 8b that the kingdom the Corinthians hoped for had in fact already arrived is a statement of Paul's genuine yearning for the arrival of Christ's kingdom, which "would indeed be a pleasant change for apostles like Paul."[13]

---

11. See discussion in Wannenwetsch, "'Members of One Another,'" 200-204.
12. Barrett, CKB, 109.
13. Ibid.

Barrett concludes that Paul's complaint is that for the Corinthians, "there is no 'not yet' to qualify the 'already' of realized eschatology."[14] Taking this hint seriously provides a more theologically penetrating starting point for our reading of these verses, one that has the advantage of resolving the problem of Paul's alleged mood swings bequeathed by the ironic reading. It also allows a reading much closer to a unifying plain reading. The main deficit of Barrett's reading, however, is that it resolves the problems of the ironic reading by insisting that Paul is himself still waiting for the kingdom of God to arrive in power, a claim flatly contradicted by Paul's appeal to the "proof from power" (>4:20, >1:26).

The decisive reason for our turning away from a reading of these verses as ironic or as aiming primarily at correcting a Corinthian over-realized eschatology is, however, a positive one: the whole passage makes the most coherent rhetorical and theological sense if read as plain speech throughout. The opening verse that sends most commentators down the "irony" track, **Already you have all you want**, should be read in the closest connection with Paul's earlier emphasis in 3:21 that "all things are yours."[15] Rather than reading this as a quotation of what is assumed to be a boast on the part of the Corinthians, we propose that Paul is instead describing for them an eschatological reality they cannot yet discern. Already all things are theirs: life, death, the present, the future (>3:21), and so **Already you have become rich! Quite apart from us you have become kings!** Paul insists that their royal priesthood does not stand and fall with an allegiance to a quasi-royal supreme figure. They are kings in and only through allegiance to the one king, Christ.

By beginning with **already** the NRSV translation accurately reproduces the order of the Greek syntax, which repeats the term ἤδη (ēdē) to open the first two clauses of 4:8. The effect is to place a heavy emphasis on "already now." It is this strong assertion of a present reality that forces readers to decide whether this passage refers to a present reality that the Corinthians cannot yet discern (our reading), or is an instance of mocking others for thinking they are richer and more important than they actually are. Yet the whole passage is not an unbroken assertion of what already is, but also contains a qualification about the way in which the Corinthians

---

14. Ibid.

15. In his analysis of chapter 3 of this letter, Dietrich Bonhoeffer understands this motto as the center and organizing principle of the whole of the chapter. It is striking to see that Bonhoeffer understands the motto "all things are yours" as a "tremendous *promise*" for a church "during a war," a church "*afflicted*, tyrannized, and muzzled" ("Sketch of a Bible Study," in *Conspiracy and Imprisonment, 1940–1945* [DBWE 16], 482).

are holding or not holding what they already have. Paul in 4:8 reminds his readers that all they "have" has actually been received, and so unless they hold on to what they have (been given), it will not be effective in the way it is *promised* to be.

The terms he uses to note that they already **have** oscillate in a characteristic way between the notions of having and holding. What is entailed in this term is not an "already now, but not yet" rationale, because Paul has previously indicated that they already fully possess the gifts that are theirs. Nor is the grammar one of having without knowing, because their gifts do not find their true flowering if not willingly and actively received. To have the gifts God has bestowed calls for an active perception of faith and a willing embrace that activates what *already* characterizes their situation: hold what you have.[16] The statement in 4:8, **Indeed, I wish that you had become kings, so that we might be kings with you!** is best understood when embedded within these distinctions. Paul says here, in effect, "You want to claim your royalty as a function of your alliance with a human 'royal' figure that you set above you. Yet this is a profound misunderstanding of your own royalty status, which is owed exclusively to your participation in the reign of the one king, Christ. Were your eyes opened to your genuine royalty as it is already established, it would be an invitation to me, your apostle, in turn to simply participate with you in this one kingship."

Having characterized Paul's speech in 4:8–9 as almost terrifyingly direct, we understand 4:10–13 to extend the same direct mode of speech. **You are held in honor, but we in disrepute**. Here Paul marks the contrast between his own suffering and the wellbeing of the Corinthian community not as an ironic expression of regret but as a reiteration of the kenotic character of his apostolate. In keeping with his opening in chapter 1, he again reminds the Corinthians that he upholds them in praise (ἔνδοξοι/*endoxoi*, translated here as **held in honor**) and so honors them as God's works. As he does so, the Apostle is prepared to become weak in uplifting the weak to God so that they may become strong, to become a spectacle in the arena so that they may live and become exhibited as a healthy witness to other Christian communities. He is prepared even to make himself a fool for the sake of Christ so that they become **wise in Christ**. The claim **We are fools for the sake of Christ, but you are wise in Christ** again proves why this passage cannot be understood as ironic speech. An ironic rendering of this

---

16. "Christian community is not an ideal we have to realize, but rather a reality created by God in Christ in which we may participate. The more clearly we learn to recognize that the ground and strength and promise of all our community is in Jesus Christ alone, the more calmly we will learn to think about our community and pray and hope for it." Bonhoeffer, *Life Together* (DBWE 5), 38.

line would be "we are fools for the sake of Christ, but you are wise"—raised and puffed up by human wisdom. Neither here nor anywhere else in Paul's corpus do we find (or expect to find) him debasing the language of being in Christ by uttering it in an ironic tone.

Be Like Your Father

> ¹⁴I am not writing this to make you ashamed, but to admonish you as my beloved children. ¹⁵For though you might have ten thousand guardians in Christ, you do not have many fathers. Indeed, in Christ Jesus I became your father through the gospel. ¹⁶I appeal to you, then, be imitators of me. ¹⁷For this reason I sent you Timothy, who is my beloved and faithful child in the Lord, to remind you of my ways in Christ Jesus, as I teach them everywhere in every church. ¹⁸But some of you, thinking that I am not coming to you, have become arrogant. ¹⁹But I will come to you soon, if the Lord wills, and I will find out not the talk of these arrogant people but their power. ²⁰For the kingdom of God depends not on talk but on power. ²¹What would you prefer? Am I to come to you with a stick, or with love in a spirit of gentleness?

The chapter concludes with an emphasis on the parental relationship that the Apostle enjoys with the Corinthian church. It is Paul's spiritual fatherhood that allows him to address the congregation in the mode of *paraklesis*: **to *admonish* you as my beloved children**—and **to admonish you *as my beloved children***. Verse 15 expressly states this parental warrant: **I became your father**. Note here, however, that Paul mentions his special relationship with the congregation as a father only after having prepared the ground by distancing himself from any suggestion that his claiming a special relationship could be appropriated by anyone else as a claim to superiority within the grammar of rivalry that has ensnared the Corinthians. The point is made with a twofold qualification of his claim to patrimony evident in the phrases *in* **Christ Jesus I became your father**, and *through* **the gospel**.

Taking this reasoning one step further, the language associated with the procreative function (literally, "I begat you" rather than **became your father**) is to be understood as yet another Pauline disassociation from the role of the founder of a political entity. Paul's **laying of the foundation** of the church in Corinth differs from the sorts of activities that political philosophy associated in a prototypical way with the founding of a city such as Rome. Whereas in political foundation the will to found is the foundation itself, parental/procreative language assumes that the coming into being of a new entity (new one) is the result of a mingling of preexisting entities. No one can "found" a family; humans can only enlarge preexisting families whose lineage precedes any given actor and reaches all the way back to the first couple. This emphasis on the secondary and co-operative nature of begetting in distinction from the active will of founding helps us understand what Paul is doing in adding the qualifiers **in Christ Jesus** and **through the gospel** to specify the meaning of his claim **I became your father**.

In 4:15 Paul sets out yet another contrast, this time between the father and the pedagogue, to specify even more precisely the essential grammar of his claim to spiritual fatherhood. On our reading, Paul's summoning of the congregation to **be imitators of me** must be understood within this theological grammar of "begetting" as an exhortation to the sort of imitative emulation of parents that comes naturally to children in the process of their upbringing. In other words, Paul admonishes the Corinthians not to be *his* disciples but to imitate him in becoming disciples *of Christ*. This insight is further reinforced in 4:17 by Paul's specification of what it is that they should imitate, namely, **my ways *in* Christ Jesus**. It may seem to contradict our reading to find that Paul does not present himself in the role of a father but a teacher when we read in verse 17 that he has **sent you Timothy** as a transmitter of what **I teach**. But the only aspect of Paul's teaching that he indicates that Timothy will mediate to them is precisely **my *ways* in Christ Jesus**. That which can be imitated is not equivalent to information that can be apprehended. Rather, Timothy is assumed to be in a position to teach them Paul's ways in Christ only insofar as he, Timothy, has in the first instance become an emulator of these ways himself.

Paul is glad to speak of his teaching only as long as its specific parental character remains in view. The significance of this insistence is revealed in a telling linguistic detail. When Paul speaks of his own teaching, he uses the term *didaskalos* (4:17), which is linked to his fatherly ways with his Corinthian children. The rival teachers in the community, by contrast, are referred to with the term *paidagogos* (4:15). This term usually denotes a hired hand such as a slave or schoolteacher. The *paidagogos* instructs the pupil about things that must be learned. A father, by contrast, teaches in the manner of a *didaskalos*, who teaches not only *about* things but teaches ways of life to be emulated. The point is not that the *didaskalos* is more practical than the *paidagogos*, but that the *didaskalos* teaches with an authority the *paidagogos* can never have.

Using the language of teaching in the context of his apostolic work **everywhere, in every church**, Paul indicates to the Corinthians that his role as the ecumenical apostle rules out any claims of superiority from the church he personally bore in Corinth. No tribalist claims legitimately spring from this intimate special relationship, no claims that could warrant their being closed off from others, or thinking of themselves as especially privileged. It is as though Paul is saying with this qualification, "I am your father, but I am still the Apostle. I am *your* father, since I was instrumental in your founding, but I am also and more importantly your *apostle*, as I would be to any other church I have not myself founded." In his affirmation of the fact that he is *papa* to the Corinthians Paul again is at pains not to bolster their wish to establish a hierarchy among their teachers or even among the apostles whom they thereby render "merely" teachers. Though he could have made his foundational authority a trump card in this game by saying "not Apollos, not Cephas, but Paul," Paul repudiates this strategy by using the leveling formulation **as I teach them everywhere in every church**, which maintains his foundational role in the church but not by claiming superiority to the other apostles.

The rather startling phrases in 4:18, 19, and 21 read much differently when considered as forms of parental, loving admonition. It is only when such threats are read in abstraction from a setting within parental love—as they might sound, for instance, in the mouth of a hired *paidagogos*—that they appear as the "bad" pedagogical moves so distasteful to modern liberal sensibilities.

Excursus: Moral Dimensions of Characterization and Scripture's Plain Sense

Having understood Paul's parental affection for the Corinthian community to define the main contours of the whole of chapter 4, we feel confirmed in rejecting the interpretative strategy that reads 4:8 and following as ironic in tone. Though some intratextual moments do seem to suggest the ironic reading, the difficulties such a reading creates for the chapter's coherence far outweigh the benefits. The rather perplexing fact that the ironic reading remains plausible to the vast majority of interpreters regardless of its manifold inconsistencies invites methodological reflection.

To read a passage as an instance of caustic irony implicitly pushes the reader towards taking up a twofold hermeneutical stance: a stance of superiority toward the initial recipients of the letter, who, the reader presumes, must have struggled to comprehend a mode of speech that the reader has already grasped as ironic; and a stance of assumed intimacy with an author who is taken to be just as capable of encoding his message as the reader is capable of decoding it. As if to protect ourselves from the dreaded charge of naïveté for sticking to the plain or non-ironic reading of these passages, we are willing to turn Paul into a moody and resentful character, not to mention a bad pedagogue. The higher irony in this situation is that such ironic readings hide the Paul who so conspicuously notes in this chapter that it is out of fatherly love that he resists being reduced to a mere pedagogue.

At this point it is helpful to consider an often overlooked point of great significance for our understanding of the task and reality of Christian interpretation of scripture: the inescapable *moral* dimension of our reading strategies. Ignoring this dimension imperils all exegetical efforts. This must be so because when reading scripture we assume that our shared participation in the *communio sanctorum* is a truthful description of our relation to the texts/authors we engage within it. But precisely this acknowledgment raises the question of how we *treat* the authors we engage, in a morally qualified sense. Does sticking to predetermined rules of interpretation (as we usually define properly "scientific" or critical interpretation) really ensure we do justice to an author or text? In reading this chapter we have discovered how much it matters what sort of character we take the author to be, and what sort of interpersonal rapport we establish with him or her.

In our desire to "come to terms" with the text and "make sense" of it, how often and how easily do we employ interpretative accounts in which Paul is forced to play the role of a moody character prone to cringe-worthy pedagogical errors? How aware are we of what we are doing in making such ascriptions, and do we know how such moves affect our relationship with the author? Our suggestion is that by returning again to the assumption inherent in the belief in the *communio sanctorum*—that the biblical authors are guided by the same Spirit that is to guide our interpretative efforts—we also assume that our relation to these writers *must* be grounded in love. We thus cannot rest content with reading strategies that resolve or explain difficult passages at the expense of generating a portrait of an author who is internally inconsistent and whose faith is anything but trustworthy (>4:2). The oft-heard call for "charitable interpretation" requests this much more demanding, larger frame of reference if it is to be meaningfully carried out. Having embraced this assumption we have found ourselves driven toward a preference here for a plain sense reading precisely because this chapter tempts us in an especially strong way to opt for an ironic reading. This temptation illumines how we are prone as readers to recapitulate the very sin Paul is fighting in the Corinthians—by taking up an interpretative stance that claims the freedom to characterize our author in such a way that, in effect, we no longer think of ourselves as "members of each other" (Rom 12:5).

Such an interpretative approach has moral significance, of course, only if we understand authors not as dead bodies but as living voices. One crucial aspect of the process of reading is the generation of an imagined authorial persona as we read. While this imaginative fabrication is in itself inevitable, our interest is in drawing attention to the high moral charge that attends it. As we characterize people in one way or another, we easily flatten them into two-dimensional pictures, which are useful as a rapid communicative shorthand but which also prevent others from getting to know them in their full and often surprising roundedness. This observation about characterization grounds our preference of a "plain sense" reading. Real people must be allowed to characterize themselves. To take someone seriously is to listen closely to what that person is really saying and doing, refusing to allow our stock overlay of what we have heard that someone "is like" to substitute for a close listening to another's own self-articulation. In the same way, a preference for sticking to the plain sense of scripture and growing alertness to the inescapable moral dimensions of characterization are ways of resisting forces that so easily deafen us to the real voices of others.

We have received a counsel to attend to "nothing beyond what is written" (4:6). What then is a "plain sense reading"? It is our contention that the plain sense is rarely obvious since it only becomes obvious to those willing to practice repentant reading. Such reading must be prepared not only to relinquish first impressions but also to curtail speculation. To grasp the plain sense requires going beyond the stance of self-justifying distancing to discover the ways in which *we* are chastened and purified as we pass up interpretative avenues that attract us or offer us an easy rendering of a passage. Refusing to distance itself from the author, a plain sense reading, as we understand it, instead assumes a critical distance from hermeneutical method in order to resist its capacity to foster evasions. The fatal temptation is to allow interpretations to be generated without demanding that those interpretations be spiritually judged and reformed.

One of the besetting exegetical sins of our age is that no one (but fundamentalists) even seeks the *sensus literalis* any longer, because doing so is perceived as merely reading what is "given" and is therefore presumed to be fatally unsophisticated. What results is biblical exegesis turned into a sort of methodological brothel, in which the exegetical methods of the day compete for adherents by offering wild interpretations that demonstrate their capacity to generate exciting "new" readings. There are many who sense this problem, but one of the most common responses to meet the challenge is by "fusing" the horizons associated with well-developed and widely accepted, if seemingly incompatible, hermeneutic approaches. But no such fusion can address the problem that a plain sense reading addresses in beginning from the other end of the problem with the question, how are we to break through all our interpretative grids? How are we to avoid entrapment within the patterns of, say, a psychological or sociological interpretative grid, to take two powerful examples that we so often encounter in our exposition of Paul's letters?

The plain sense is the deepest lineament of the text. But to read for this sense is not to be confused with the assumption that the meaning lies *behind* the words of the text. The plain sense *is* the literal sense. This is to resist the conflation of the surface of the letter with the surface meaning as derived from a specific exegetical method. On the contrary: the material surface of the letter is the surface that *resists* initial readings and explanatory accounts of "what Paul really means" by claiming to be able to go "beyond" or "behind" the letter. Rightly understood, the *sensus literalis* indicates a mode of reading that resists this pulverization of the letter. Plain sense reading is thus a way of resisting the flight into any form of sophistication that alienates us from the author as the living spirit of the letter. Luther's emphasis on the *sensus literalis* rests on the Hebrew sensibility that "not one jot or tittle" will perish from scripture (Matt 5:18 par.), combined with his affirmation of the eternal life of the saints in Christ. The implication is that only the reader who is willing to struggle with the letter will eventually understand the plain sense of scripture, that is, actually *hear* the voice of the Spirit who animates it.

This is why struggling with the letter cannot be reduced to philological work alone. Struggling with the letter means battling our own tendencies to escape from the challenge a literal reading might imply for us. The letter is the sheer given that emerges or remains *only* when we read against the pronouncements of our own instinctive or inherited reading strategies. Thus the literal meaning is not on the surface of the letter any more than a conversation with a person is reducible to a transcript of the words our interlocutor speaks. Paul remains, as chapter 13 will put it, the Apostle who is "hoping all things" for us, and is still being made the Apostle in making us the church. For these reasons we do well to expect coming to terms with the literal sense to take a long time, and to be characterized by much thinking and repentance.

1 Corinthians 5

Taking Pride in Sin

¹It is actually reported that there is sexual immorality among you, and of a kind that is not found even among pagans; for a man is living with his father's wife.

Turning now to a series of moral disputes among the Corinthian believers, Paul's aim in the following sections is persistently to draw his readers' attention to the political dynamics that drive those disputes. This aim becomes immediately apparent if we notice that Paul does not begin directly with the demarcation of a particular moral case (a case of incest, perhaps) but with the remark **It is actually reported**. This opening will set the stage for the Apostle's insistence that what needs to be dealt with in the community is not simply a particular moral transgression. Paul's focus is on the unique challenge that arises because the transgression has become a public matter, thus putting the *doxa* of the community on the line. The circulation of this report threatens the *doxa* of the community both in terms of the church's *public reputation* and its *glory* as a community cleansed through baptism.

There is no textual evidence for speculating that Paul has bypassed the normal means of perception through some mystical insight,[1] or that his interest is that of the tabloid journalist who feels as if he has not gotten to the bottom of the story until he has rooted out the human baseness fueling it;[2] nor finally does he strike the indignant stance of the imperious moralist on hearing a scandalous secret. Such interpretations are plausible only if we ignore his own chosen opening, which begins by setting the discussion of moral problems that follows within an observable development in the political configuration of the church visible to the public eye. It is easy to imagine that up to this point those who were sensitive to the public talk and gossip

---

1. Contra Origen, who compares this presence with Elisha in 2 Kings 5:23–26 (see JK, 85), and Hays: "Paul had strong mystical experiences.... It would not be difficult to imagine that he could think of himself as being transported 'in spirit' from Ephesus (1 Cor 16:8) to Corinth" (RBH, 84).

2. Bonhoeffer, *Letters and Papers from Prison* (DBWE 8), 455.

that predictably arises in cases of presumed sexual immorality in the church may have, with the best of intentions, allowed this case to remain covered up for some time, and may well have been relieved that it at least stayed out of sight, in the private sphere. But this situation no longer obtains.

Because the matter has come out into the open the Apostle's concern is now not only the community's moral integrity, but the integrity of the church's political ethos. By emphasizing the political aspect of the situation we offer a corrective to an all too popular reading in which Paul is imagined to have heard a whispered rumor, **it is actually reported**, and has then undertaken to uncover the "facts" according to which **a man is living with his father's wife**. Paul is presented here in the pharisaical guise of a moral policeman who first detects a vague rumor, in itself considered a premoral phenomenon, and is then prompted to investigate this fog of "just talk" to get at the "hard moral fact" of an actual, substantiated moral failure as the real issue that requires a pastoral response. Such a chain of assumptions about the opening of the chapter bolsters the familiar organizational schema in which chapter 5 and the chapters that follow are understood as the Apostle's untangling of a set of discrete moral case studies. As he takes out the subfolder labeled *incest* we contemporary readers are encouraged by this schema to understand it as another partial installment useful in the construction of a so-called Pauline sexual ethics.

Our reading instead takes this introduction to be an opportunity for the Apostle to foster in his readers an appreciation for several conceptual distinctions he will soon reveal to be his central concern. His comparison of the reported behavior with pagan morality is another aspect of this solicitous approach. To say that his opening represents an act of fatherly solicitude is to allow that this emphasis on the gravity of the moral transgression at stake—**a man is living with his father's wife**—as something **that is not found even among pagans** must be more than simple moral shaming. Though tempting, to read the comparison as an act of public shaming would be to detach the opening rhetorical move from the material issue at hand and to reduce it to a brisk "listen up" gesture that might preface any session of moral upbraiding. But as our reading of the remainder of the chapter will show, one of the core problematic aspects Paul wishes to confront is the escapist manner in which the Corinthians deploy comparisons between the Christian ethos and the ways of the world. His discussion of particular moral questions is therefore best understood as a preparatory work on the way to reaching his actual goal, which is to indicate and foster the genuine new creation of the community as it is meant to be. We read Paul then as aiming from the very first verse of the chapter to foster the gospel's creation of a "new batch" of dough (5:7), that is, to bring to life a community whose political ethos has been renewed by conformity to Christ's body.

It is our suggestion that Paul has introduced a comparative moral standard only in order to set up the crucial point he will soon urge onto his readers in the community of Corinth: that the Christian ethos is in no way a derivative function of any comparisons with the standards of the world, whether in the liberal fashion that intends to soften moral boundaries to better align with supposedly wider or even universal moral standards ("straight but not narrow") or in a conservative fashion that seeks a moral perfection that ostentatiously contrasts with the world ("straight and not queer"). The Christian ethos, in short, is not determined by the need for the church to be a contrast society. This core point is often missed: "Paul knows it is not easy for the community to maintain a sense of its distinctive identity, and to be faithful in observing the boundaries deemed to be appropriate to that identity."[3] The logic Paul is beginning to unfold here does not revolve around setting, protecting, or expanding the boundaries that distinguish the community from others—again, as determined by comparison with the world. Instead, the Apostle is carefully developing a (re-)description of the church whose true moral and spiritual liveliness moves outward from a distinctive center. It is this center that must be understood and actively sought for what it is, if any moral failure among the members of the church is to be appropriately remedied.

Grasping the basic differentiation between these two rationalities—boundary maintenance in contrast to expansion from a distinctive center—will also help us understand why Paul will quickly pivot in 5:2 to address the Corinthians in a sharp tone: **you are arrogant**. What arrogance is Paul fingering here? We can safely assume that, having censured pride and boasting several times in previous chapters as recurrent threats to the life of the church in Corinth, Paul is now making that general accusation more concrete here. As we shall see most clearly articulated in Paul's choice of the yeast metaphor as his central means of addressing the issues under discussion (5:6–7), and also in his exhortation for Christians not to eat with transgressors (5:11), the logic of boundary maintenance will be totally inadequate to explain the themes that emerge as his central concerns. In fact, such boundary grammar is itself susceptible to Paul's diagnosis of Corinthian pride: on one hand, the Corinthians express pride in pushing moral boundaries outward in a progressive expansion; on the other, they exhibit the hubris of a custodian who is puffed up with his success at having kept the moral boundaries inviolate and intact. Acknowledging this challenge

---

3. Furnish, *Theology of the First Letter*, 52.

to the Corinthians' tendency to think within the rationality of boundary maintenance now makes it apparent that Paul regards the arrogance and the boasting that accompanies it as an attack on the generative center of the community's life, the very center that should be animating the outward expansion of the church's distinctive ethos.

The precise nature of the moral case in question has been much debated, whether the expression **his father's wife** is a euphemistic way of naming something too shameful to even be named—that is, the incest of a son with his mother—or whether the relationship is that of a son with his stepmother or his father's concubine (with or without the father still being married or even being still alive).[4] Another indicator that Paul's interest here is not in developing a sexual ethic is that he simply condemns the behavior without giving any reasons for his position (most likely a simple restatement of the Levitical prohibition "You shall not uncover the nakedness of your father's wife" [Lev 18:8]). Our political reading allows that whichever of these situations obtained, the quandaries associated with ascertaining the historical circumstances should not divert us from the decisive question: "In this case, what sort of *boasting* by the community is Paul censuring?" Although it cannot be completely ruled out that the most radically spiritualist group in Corinth might have directly applauded the man for demonstrating how devoid of boundaries the freedom of a Christian can be as regards the carnal side of human existence ("anything goes, *pneumatikos*"), the more likely scenario to which Paul's charge of "boasting" applies is this: those boasting acknowledge the activity as morally impermissible and yet take pride in demonstrating a tolerant attitude toward it—"it's their business, after all."

Adopting a standpoint from which church and world can be compared in order to declare a case to be not as embarrassing as it seems is a favorite maneuver of the pride that expresses itself in the mode of ethical justification. Always prone to feeling a hint of superiority toward the overly rigid morals of the Hebrew Scriptures, Christians easily fall into a stance that sits quite comfortably with a very different contemporary sense of superiority to the evidently lax morals of the people of Corinth, among whom living with one's stepmother might remain an excusable moral offense (the scenario that we think, on balance, is the most historically likely).

Grief over the Fractured Body

> [2] And you are arrogant! Should you not rather have mourned, so that he who has done this would have been removed from among you?

---

4. The debates are summarized in Fitzmyer, *First Corinthians*, 233–35.

It might come as a surprise that Paul now proposes an alternative to the arrogance of the community that sounds more emotional than procedural: **Should you not rather have mourned**? It would be easier to imagine him, for example, shaking his head that the Corinthians are not appalled at what is going on or confronting them for their failure to confront the offender. The first option would have been the moralized response ("we" should have distanced ourselves morally from "them"), while the second, to be more proactive in confronting the offender, would have amounted to a call for moral courage. Counterintuitively to modern sensibilities, Paul instead proposes mourning as the appropriate response, thus reframing the issue to highlight an affective acknowledgment that fellowship has been damaged.[5] Mourning in the face of a fellow believer's moral debasement reveals a deeper fellowship than either stances of tolerance or pedagogical instruction. The horizon of ecclesial fellowship at work here indicates why the grief that Paul is commending must be understood as grief over the state of the fellowship with the fallen brother *and* the fellowship of the body as a whole, since the whole body is affected where one member is affected. Such mourning is not simply an affective state but is a trans-subjective extension of lament that necessarily encompasses a public and communal task.

This lamentation, Paul clearly assumes, must be learned, a theme Augustine later develops in a direction that illumines the christological and eucharistic grammar we see underlying Paul's argument in this chapter. In his meditations on the Psalter, Augustine comes to appreciate the *oikodomic* aspect of Christ's passion. Christ's true sorrow on the cross was not a response primarily to the physical pain he suffered, nor even his painful severing of communion with the Father, but that those followers who grieved for him did so for carnal reasons. Having not understood his hints that he was to be resurrected,[6] they were caught up in lamenting his physical suffering and loss of earthly life on the cross. As Augustine preaches,

> Their pity would have been better spent on those blind people who killed their physician, on the wildly delirious patients who attacked the one who had come to bring them health. He willed to cure them, but they thrashed about savagely; and this was the source of sorrow to the doctor. Now ask yourselves, whether he found any companion to share this sorrow of his. The psalm

---

5. Ezra mourned over what happened to Israel in its exile (10:6), which the translators of the Septuagint describe using the same word Paul uses here (Hays, RBH, 82).

6. The following quotations are from *Expositions of the Psalms*, in The Works of Saint Augustine, but references to Augustine's *Enarrationes in Psalmos* (hereafter *Enarr.*) will in what follows be noted using the standard reference numbers, in this case, *Enarr.*, 68 (1).19.

> does not say, "I looked for someone to grieve, but there was no one"; it says, *For someone to grieve together with me* (that is, someone to grieve for the same reason that I grieve myself), *and I found no one* [Ps 69:20].[7]

Augustine finds a strong doctrine of the unity of Christ with his ecclesial body to illumine here the true nature of the believers' lament. What this account of unity implies is that this one lament of Christ in his passion is, properly speaking, the one lament of Christ's body in all times and places.

The effect of this reading of Christ's passion is to transform lament into a fundamentally communal activity. The apostles are to be emulated by Christians because they display what it means to understand and inhabit scripture, to preach it and in so doing to discern and respond to the actual sin and decay that destroys the believing community. The apostles are thus the supporting "bones" of the body that "stiffen" its more fleshly parts, and their fervor and persevering pastoral activity should be understood as a direct outflowing of love for Christ's body:

> If any member is scandalized and imperiled in spirit, the bone is roasted [Ps 102:3] with an intensity in proportion to its love. ... Let charity prevail, and then, if it is true that whenever one member suffers, another suffers in sympathy, how fiercely must the bones be heated—the bones that support the whole bodily frame?[8]

It is *this oikodomic* suffering that generates the lament of the righteous, and therefore Augustine can make the bold claim that, as the body is made up of the strong and weak, although it is supported by the strong (Rom 15:1), so too is it held together by such righteous lament.[9] Echoing the core motto that Paul develops in Romans 12 and 2 Corinthians 11:29, mourning is the attitude that most radiantly displays an understanding of the church as "members of one another." The amplitude and focus of Christian lament is a function of the believer's love for Christ's body and as such is an indicator of the depth of the believer's identification with Christ (>12:21–26).[10]

---

7. *Enarr.*, 68 (2).5.
8. *Enarr.*, 101 (1).4.
9. *Enarr.*, 101 (1).6.
10. *Enarr.*, 21 (2).1; 68 (1).1; 85.19. For a more extensive discussion, see Brock, "Augustine's Incitement to Lament," 183–202.

Empirical Knowledge and Moral Discernment

> ³For though absent in body, I am present in spirit; and as if present I have already pronounced judgment ⁴in the name of the Lord Jesus on the man who has done such a thing. When you are assembled, and my spirit is present with the power of our Lord Jesus, ⁵you are to hand this man over to Satan for the destruction of the flesh, so that his spirit may be saved in the day of the Lord.

Mourning a brother's fall indicates engaged presence with one another. Paul claims just this affective engagement with the Corinthian body in 5:3, from which he derives his authority to pronounce judgment: **For though absent in body, I am present in spirit; and as if present I have already pronounced judgment.** Such a claim positions Paul to deflect an obvious objection: How can you who are far away dare to venture judgment on an affair about which you know very little, and into which you can have little meaningful insight? Paul seems to agree that on a purely human plane judgment from outside cannot rise above armchair punditry. But the insight Paul claims **in the spirit** is more intimate than even physical proximity can ensure. The background narrative and the loving care that have characterized his apostolate have bound him to the Corinthians and constituted a trans-temporal and trans-spatial proximity that renders the church's members part of him, as he participates in this church's life as members of one another (>12:4–13).

The way in which Paul claims to have spiritual insight and so be in a position to judge thus differs in kind from that of the Corinthians, whose refusal to mourn exposes their disengagement with their fallen brother despite their obvious physical proximity. The contrast is heightened when Paul makes the bold affirmation that **as if present I have already pronounced judgment**, a claim burdened with the bitter irony that it is the physically proximate Corinthians who lack judgment. And Paul goes further than simply denying that the Corinthian church is truly present with the fallen brother; he is indicating that the spiritual proximity he expresses in his judgment and mourning is also the first shoot of *their own* judgment, the proximate and real judgment of the whole body. **When you are assembled, and my spirit is present**: then *you* are to express *my* judgment—the judgment that ought to have already been discerned by them—by expelling the offending brother. In this gesture Paul dissolves the dialectic of judgment and nonjudgment in favor of *common* judgment. This cutting of the Gordian knot of fruitless alternatives rests on the spiritual judgment that is characteristic and foundational of the apostle's unique office. This is not a unilateral power, however; it is not the Apostle—or, in his wake, the bishop—who *does* the work of expelling for the community. Rather, the Apostle leads them in this *communal* work,[11] just as legal codes in the Old Testament indicated the whole community's responsibility to participate in stoning offenders.[12]

The contrast between the "real presence" of Paul and the virtual presence to which the Corinthians have reduced themselves, and proudly so, gives us a fascinating insight into the relationship of empirical knowledge to moral judgment. While the physical presence of the Corinthians with the fallen brother has given rise to the arrogant claim of a superior vantage point for moral judgment grounded in their firsthand historical and empirical knowledge ("only we know all the details of 'what really happened'"), it is the spiritual proximity of the physically distant Paul that has led to actual judgment. The surprising truth that this judgment reveals (that the Corinthians were procrastinating in deferring judgment) is its articulation of a counterclaim that was obviously hidden to the Corinthians themselves. If we assume that moral judgment is nothing more than a function of an empirical discovery we easily slip into an evasive suspension of judgment on the grounds that the facts on the ground have not yet been definitively established.

It will be critical for understanding our approach to the string of ethical discussions soon to follow to understand that we do not consider the case that is really engaging Paul's attention to be a dilemma in sexual ethics (in this case, probably a form of incest). There is no indication of any debate concerning on what grounds the moral issue is to be adjudicated. The Apostle simply presupposes the wrongness of the behavior without seeing the need to discuss it any further. But the reported incident presents him with an occasion to draw attention to and respond to a more deeply rooted problem in the Corinthian church: their allowing certain behaviors to continue that may be morally suspect, thereby consigning any individual believer's misgivings to an allegedly private realm. Paul is trying to show the Corinthians how they are illegitimately constraining their engagement in this situation by letting the domain of "merely" private opinion proliferate. In this particular case Paul is indignant that though the Corinthian

---

11. Church discipline "must be exercised by the elders acting together, and with the consent of the people. And let us also note that this is a remedy for the prevention of tyranny. For there is nothing in greater opposition to the discipline of Christ (*Christi disciplinae*) than tyranny; and the door is wide open to it, if all the power is surrendered to one man" (Calvin, JC 107).

12. Discussed below in relation to the Old Testament usage of "drive out the wicked person from among you" (>5:13).

church seems to hold "correct opinions," they hold them in a way that has no consequences for how they respond to the actions of others in their community. In methodological terms, Paul is not undertaking moral casuistry on the topic of sexual ethics but is dealing with a theologically significant breakdown in the linkages between confessed faith, ecclesial discernment, moral deliberation, and church discipline, a complex problem sure to recur in response to all sorts of moral infraction.

The alternative procedure Paul proposes to provoke the Corinthians to stop delaying and evading a public judgment on the offender (5:5) has drawn so much attention that it has absorbed the bulk of the exegetical energy devoted to the chapter as a whole. The widespread tendency to allow this focus on the material aspects of judgment to be framed in terms of the individual rather than as a political act is doubly deplorable. True, Paul indeed commends a particular "handling" of the transgressing person: **you are to hand this man over to Satan for the destruction of the flesh, so that his spirit may be saved in the day of the Lord**. But what must carefully be distinguished is the different agents that Paul sees involved in this process and their respective responsibilities. The wording is precise in this respect: it is the business of the congregation to expel the transgressor and therefore hand him over to other powers, even though neither the destruction of the flesh nor the salvation of the spirit can be understood as something the congregation actually accomplishes. This does not mean that the act of handing over is nothing more than the exposure of transgression without direction and engagement. To act in service of the transgressor's specifically configured destruction and salvation is an active expression of hope. But hope for what? Here we must come to terms not only with a linguistic problem about the translation of ἐν τῇ ἡμέρᾳ τοῦ κυρίου (*en tē hēmera tou kyriou*) but also with a wider question of how the procedure Paul is recommending is related to the Old Testament parallel from Deuteronomy with which Paul closes the chapter: "**Drive out the wicked person from among you.**"[13]

The question of the aim of excommunicative judgment can be answered by investigating the phrase **so that his spirit may be saved**. A "punctual" reading of the temporal expression **day of the Lord**, as indicating a particular future date on which God's final judgment occurs, would suggest

---

13. The phrase recurs at crucial points in the law codes of Deuteronomy. Chapter 17 verses 7 and 12 provide the most complete description of the appropriate subject of its application, as well as the formal procedures that appropriately accompany its enactment. It does not appear accidental that this fulsome explanation is attached to breaches of the prohibition of idolatry. The many other formulaic deployments of the idea (19:19; 21:21; 22:21, 24; 24:7), like Paul's use here, are used to definitively conclude discussions of the appropriate response to various moral transgressions.

that excommunication or expulsion ought to be understood as a final cut-off point in the communal body's relationship with the transgressor. The excommunicated member is left to whatever mercy he will find in God's eyes at the end of all days, and the judgment of excommunication by the congregation simply hands him over to that later judgment. However, the Greek expression *en te* allows for an alternative that would indicate not a final date but a period of time that could be taken as a gracefully extended time for reconciliation—"towards" the day of the Lord, as it were. In theological terms the two linguistic alternatives are not mutually exclusive, since the day of the Lord is a stock prophetic concept that, according to its origin in the book of Amos,[14] refers to potentially any day on which God brings his judgment over the people—as proleptic of that culminating Day.

Although we cannot base hope for the salvation of the transgressor's spirit on a congregation's desire for a future reconciliation, and although Paul does not use any of the technical terms that came to play central roles in early Christian penitential rituals of readmission to the eucharistic community, his argument does drop a significant hint in this direction. This becomes clearer if we notice the difference it makes to read "the evil" impersonally in contrast to a personal reading. If our reading of Paul's political approach to this moral case has been correct, it should be clear that the evil that, in the Apostle's perception, has affected the community at large—including the undermining of its ethos through the pride of false tolerance—is considerably more comprehensive than what could be eradicated by removing the evil *doer* from their midst. A merely personal reading of "the evil" would hence precisely undermine Paul's political intentions and reduce his strategy to a mere moral level.

A more thorough investigation of the inversion Paul is performing here suggests that the handing over he commends is best understood as an invitation for the Spirit to intervene. Whereas the logic of the Deuteronomic expulsion[15] proposes the eradication of *evil* by eradicating the *evil one* (the community purifying itself), Paul's understanding of expulsion has honed in on the theological core of the Old Testament witness: all such expulsion is not self-purification (of Israel and subsequently the church) but is an action in faith and hope that *aims at the renewal of the communal body.*[16] The **new**

---

14. See Amos 5:18, 20; 8:9–14.

15. "Then all the men of his town shall stone him to death. You must purge the evil from among you. All Israel will hear of it and be afraid" (Deut 21:21).

16. The inner connection of the old and new covenants at this point was already apparent to John Chrysostom: "This [expulsion rather than stoning] is not an innovation, but . . . from the beginning the giver of the law thought it good that such people should be cut off. In the Old Testament this was done with greater severity; here, however,

1 Corinthians 5

dough is always open to further and deeper renewal precisely through the reconciliation with the (formerly) wicked for which the community hopes. Because the community cannot guarantee this reconciliation through any formal procedures, it is appropriate to seek it solely as a gift from God. In the same way the church cannot guarantee the destruction of the flesh by the giving over of the transgressor to his evil ways. If the church *is* an ethos, and does not simply *have* one, then sustained and proud transgression of the law is to be understood more as a process of self-exclusion than as something that the pronouncement of judgment by the body establishes as a completely new state of affairs. Judgment by the congregation properly aims, therefore, to bring to full exposure what has already been inaugurated and accomplished by sustained practices diverging from the ethos of the gospel. At the same time, because both the "sustained" and "proud" are variables in this formula, we see Paul allowing space for ambiguity and time for the judgment to be formulated and accomplished. Judgments may be prematurely made, but the wavering and suspended judgment that characterizes the Corinthian church in this case has begun to subvert the ethos of the whole community because it has allowed the alternative ethos growing within it to reach a critical mass.

These considerations offer us further insight into Paul's use of underdetermined language in 5:11 as he admonishes the believers not to associate with anyone who is immoral but is still **called by the name of brother** or sister. The ambiguity introduced by the participle construction ὀνομαζόμενος (*onomazomenos*) invites the question, who actually is doing the naming here? Is it the one who calls himself brother or sister, or is it others who identify them by this name? However these questions are to be answered regarding the case mentioned in 5:1, Paul is indicating with this expression the ambiguous ecclesial status of the transgressor. No longer simply and fully "brother," and not yet merely "ex-brother," the offender exists as an embodied icon of the confusion of the Corinthian body. Paul's grammar of excommunication, impregnated as it is with the hope for reconciliation, pushes us beyond the alternative of either exclusion ("ex-brother")

---

there is a milder way.... There the adulterer and the murderer are immediately put to death, whereas here, if they are cleansed through repentance, they escape punishment. In the New Testament, nonetheless, one can see examples of more severe punishments and in the Old milder ones, which shows that throughout the two covenants are closely related to each other and come from the same lawgiver.... God is satisfied with repentance alone" (*Homily* 16, PG 61:131, quoted in JK, 90–91). Similar conclusions can be found in contemporary literature as well. "The common descent... shared by the Jewry of the rabbinic period and the nascent Christian church, suggests that the application of an ecclesial word to a Jewish practice, if made with due care, is not illegitimate." Horbury, "Extirpation and Excommunication," 15.

or inclusion ("brother by default") in emphasizing the loving hospitality of the divine judging activity and the church's role in bringing this truth to articulate expression.[17]

Baptism, Eucharist, and Poisonous Tolerance

> [6] **Your boasting is not a good thing. Do you not know that a little yeast leavens the whole batch of dough?** [7] **Clean out the old yeast so that you may be a new batch, as you really are unleavened. For our paschal lamb, Christ, has been sacrificed.** [8] **Therefore, let us celebrate the festival, not with the old yeast, the yeast of malice and evil, but with the unleavened bread of sincerity and truth.**

Our preference for a political reading of this chapter over a reductionist moral reading crystallizes as we negotiate two abrupt shifts of tack presented in these verses—disruptions that unsettle a smooth "moral case" reading. The first comes in 5:6a, **Your boasting is not a good thing**. This interjection is strange and unnecessary on a moral reading, since 6b (**Do you not know that a little yeast leavens the whole batch of dough?**) would follow logically and smoothly from **you are to hand this man over to Satan for the destruction of the flesh, so that his spirit may be saved in the day of the Lord**. Without the comment on boasting in 6a, the meaning would be: "Expel the wicked one, since you'd better bear in mind that a little yeast leavens the whole batch of dough." On such a reading the yeast that needs to be done away with would be the transgressor of the law, but Paul's seemingly unnecessary disruption of this line of reasoning with a comment on boasting takes us in a very different direction. The yeast that needs to be done away with is not merely, or even primarily, the wicked person, but the way in which the community deals with the whole situation; in Paul's view, it is primarily their lack of judgment that in the long run will ruin the dough. Chapters 4–7, to reiterate, do not set out a sequence of discrete and unconnected moral case studies, a string of contested questions for Paul to resolve, perhaps in response to a letter from Corinth (as some have imagined). Throughout the whole sequence of discussions Paul is elaborating a

---

17. "To be punished as a Christian is to be called home so that we may be reunited with the community of forgiven sinners called church and, thus, reconciled with our own life.... Excommunication is a call to come home by helping us locate how we have alienated ourselves from God and those that gather to worship God." Hauerwas, *Performing the Faith*, 199.

single emphasis on the factors that sustain or inhibit true deepening of the communal body's ethos.

While the first disruption of a moralist reading in the direction of a political one deals with the material aspect of Paul's discussion—what or who the yeast represents—the second exposes the theological basis of the argument.[18] A straightforwardly moral imperative is apparently presented in 5:7: **Clean out the old yeast**. Yet even with the inclusion of the political horizon, **so that you may be a new batch**, a Donatist-style reading would not be ruled out. To fend off any suggestion that the community's task is to ensure its moral purity, Paul adds another clause: **as you really are unleavened**. What is often referred to as an indicative-imperative pairing ("be what you are") thus demands a more profound analysis, given the political situation just set out. To call this an indicative-imperative pairing does not in fact answer the question of what Paul wishes to rule out with the addition of this "indicative." The additional clause **as you really are unleavened** draws a baptismal rationale into the dough metaphor. Paul sets before the Corinthian body the reality that the cleansing that Christ's once-for-all sacrifice has brought into being is the new situation of the church (5:7b, **For our paschal lamb, Christ, has been sacrificed**). This baptismal framework ensures that the moral exhortation to **clean out the old yeast** is not understood according to the sociological idea of a necessary self-purification that ideological communities must occasionally undertake in order to stay compact and distinct enough to survive.

This baptismal reference leads Paul into his next move, which begins with a summons: **Therefore, let us celebrate the festival, not with the old yeast, the yeast of malice and evil, but with the unleavened bread of sincerity and truth**. As a matter of fact, every celebration is a fresh acknowledgment of something new. One never celebrates the sheer continuation of something old, such as the past occasion of driving out a disruptive element in order to "spare"[19] both the offender and the community. At the same time, a celebration cannot be a total negation of the past, which is why Paul

---

18. The translation of the term ζύμη (*zymē*), which appears in an identical phrase in Galatians 5:9, is relevant here. David Horrell comments that despite many modern translations (including the NRSV), *zyme* should be rendered "leaven" and not "yeast," because "leaven comprises a portion of previously made dough which enables the raising effect of yeast to be reproduced through the incorporation of a piece of the old dough into a new batch. At the same time as this was a useful technique it was also risky, since any impurities or pollutants in the leaven would be transferred into the new dough, where they would come to permeate and infect the whole" (*Solidarity and Difference*, 143).

19. For Chrysostom, "the purpose of expelling this person is not only to spare him but the others as well" (*Homily* 15, PG 61:124–26, quoted in JK, 85).

can invoke the paschal event in 5:7 to indicate the church's understanding that all its time is festal time.[20] Celebration is linked with the arrival of the unexpected, as marked by the grammar of an intervention from outside. As the connection of verses 7 and 8 makes obvious, what is to be celebrated is genuinely the paschal festival and not the body's own moral integrity—whether in the form of self-congratulation for achieved purity or the pride of complicit tolerance.

Next, Paul develops what we take to be a movement from a baptismal to a eucharistic rationale by turning from a comment on the ontological referent of the celebration to the elements themselves. The dough that metaphorically represented the body up to this point in 5:6–7 now becomes the bread *with which* the body is to celebrate in 5:8; interest in the renewal of the body's ethos is turning into a question of what food sustains this renewal. When it comes to the material basis for a feast, yeast, of course, will not do; bread is essential. The more interesting and complicating issue here is how we are to understand the transition from the baptismal to a eucharistic grammar without losing sight of the theological rationale governing the chapter as a whole. We must find a way to read this transition as theologically enriching and elaborating Paul's argument rather than taking it as simply a logical jump from one metaphor to another, and without positing a disjunction between church discipline and eucharistic exclusion.[21]

The connection we sense here can be made more visible by drawing on eucharistic accounts as they have been developed in early patristic theologies.[22] This early tradition understood the bread with which the body is invited to celebrate the eucharistic feast as simultaneously a material representation of the community as a whole.[23] As the elements of bread and wine are brought forth by the labor and offering of the community, so the lives of

---

20. The phrase is Chrysostom's. See *Homily* 15, PG 61:124–26, quoted in JK, 86.

21. We demur here from the consensus view in biblical studies, here articulated by Hays: "The Passover imagery is not primarily eucharistic; rather, it points to the necessity of community discipline and purity" (Hays, RBH, 87).

22. The theology on which we are drawing was reintroduced to the modern church through the rediscovery and reintegration of the offertory rite in some Western church traditions, inspired by the scholarly work of Gregory Dix, J. Jungmann, and others, but also within the practice of Orthodox theology. See Du Boulay, *Cosmos, Life, and Liturgy*, ch. 5, "Work and Bread."

23. "Each communicant from the bishop to the newly confirmed gave *himself* under the forms of bread and wine to God, as God gives Himself to them under the same forms. In the united oblations of all her members the Body of Christ, the church, gave herself to *become* the Body of Christ, the sacrament, in order that receiving again the symbol of herself now transformed and hallowed, she might be truly that which by nature she is, the Body of Christ, and each of her members members of Christ." Dix, *Shape of the Liturgy*, 117.

all of its members are "baked into" the elements, as it were. Thus the paschal grace that sustained the lives and human activity through which the elements were turned into edible foodstuffs is literally folded into the material basis of the eucharistic meal. And by the same grace that mediates the fruit of Christ's salvific sacrifice that is united with the eucharistic elements, this material basis is opened up again to the transforming power so as to allow the believers in the eucharistic consumption to receive themselves anew as creatures and a renewed community. On a reading along these lines, we could see how Paul is once again treating us to a theologically mediated description of ecclesial coherence or even unity rich enough to provoke much further consideration.

The coherence we detect also allows us to emphasize the continuity of the yeast metaphor running through 5:6–8. In 5:8 Paul characterizes the unleavened bread as **of sincerity and truth**, paralleling it with his characterization of the **old yeast** as one of **malice and evil**. Drawing on our analysis of Paul's argument up to this point allows us to assume that the malice Paul has in mind as the antithesis to sincerity is precisely the pride that comes wearing different guises: on one side as the assurance of having achieved moral purity that is in itself beyond judgment, and on the other as a tolerant refusal of judgment altogether (except, perhaps, of those who are less than tolerant). On this view the opposite of truth would be the suspension of judgment—exactly what the Apostle finds most mournful about the Corinthians' tepid ambivalence about the particular moral issue in front of them.

The Lack That Poisons the Bread of Life

> ⁹I wrote to you in my letter not to associate with sexually immoral persons— ¹⁰not at all meaning the immoral of this world, or the greedy and robbers, or idolaters, since you would then need to go out of the world. ¹¹But now I am writing to you not to associate with anyone who bears the name of brother or sister who is sexually immoral or greedy, or is an idolater, reviler, drunkard, or robber. Do not even eat with such a one. ¹²For what have I to do with judging those outside? Is it not those who are inside that you are to judge? ¹³God will judge those outside. "Drive out the wicked person from among you."

We suggest reading 5:9–11 as Paul's personalized interpretation of the Torah's expulsion formula (discussed above), which he cites in 13b: "**Drive out the wicked person from among you.**" In 5:9–11 Paul clarifies his interpretation of this injunction with the exhortation **not to associate**. Since Paul explicitly refers to a previous letter in which he had already warned the Corinthians not to associate with sexually immoral persons, we can infer that what provoked him to write again on the matter must have been a profound confusion on the Corinthians' part as to how this prohibition of association should be understood. Yet the way in which Paul answers in these verses opens up a number of further questions, giving occasion for further misunderstandings. What, for example, is he driving at with the introduction of a whole list of vices in 5:11 that line up the case under discussion (sexual immorality) alongside other types of immoral behavior? And what are we to make of Paul's yet again drawing on inside-outside (church-world) rhetoric in 5:12 to clarify the sort of judgment he has in mind?

Yet again the very fact that the Apostle sets the one instance of moral transgression that has triggered the whole discussion within a longer list of vices warns us against a case-study approach to this chapter, which would suggest that Paul's interest has been to customize a generic drug for therapeutic application to this specific disease. To read the chapter as offering such a targeted prescription would mean the vice list he now introduces is watering down the advice he has given about a problem of sexual ethics. Paul, by drawing up such a list, sets up for a shock any reader interested in a case-specific therapy for the problem of incest. "How can the apostle put my occasional temptation to greed on the same moral plane as a man openly living with his (step)mother?"

If our analysis has been appropriate so far, however, and the issue Paul is addressing in this chapter actually revolves around his interest in fostering the **new dough** that is threatened by the suspension of judgment, then his widening of the domain in which judgment must not be suspended by adding a list of additional connected vices makes perfect sense. An unwillingness to judge and be judged is a problem that can flare up in relation to all sorts of sin in the church. All of this confirms our suspicion that Paul's concern was never primarily with the specific sin under discussion. His main interest is in addressing a problem that is bound to recur in a church that is not adept at responding to individual sins at the point when they have begun to generate critical levels of political ferment detrimental to the whole community.

The danger of proposing any list of vices or virtues is that it will always touch off debates about ranking and ordering them. Does Paul's treatment not implicitly suggest that sexual immorality is an especially grave type of transgression? If Paul is allowing that the case under discussion has a special gravity because it is **not even found among pagans** (5:1), surely he must be indicating the special gravity of a particular sexual transgression rather than the special gravity of sexual immorality over other types. It is true, as Paul soon makes clear, that he understands sexual immorality to be accompanied by singular risks—"everything you do is outside your body, but sexual immorality is doing harm to your body which has been marked out as the temple of the Holy Spirit" (6:18). But if we bear in mind that in chapter 6 Paul will respond to those who downplay the moral significance of the body, it is probably wise not to see the discussion here as suggesting a special significance in principle for sexual immorality that pushes it to the top of any vice list.[24] One interesting aspect of Paul's introduction of a vice list in this chapter is that all of the other types of sin he names—such as **greed, robbery, idolatry**—can very well be expressed by way of sexual immorality. These vices are mutually permeable. Sex can absorb all these other vices, spawning sexual greed, sexual conquest, and sexual idolatry. In the same way, each of these other vices can also be understood to take hostages from any of the full array of human capacities.

On the basis of this insight into the permeability of vices it is advisable to abstain from any attempt to elevate one particular vice to hegemonic status or downplay it as not terribly relevant. Both mistakes are easily found today—as, for example, when liberal Christians reproduce the attitude associated with the Greeks that downplays sex as really "nothing so special" ("How can we waste time and energy by discussing bedroom antics while there are children starving?"). Paul's treatment in this chapter has amply indicated that the problem here is not in fact sex. The opposite mistake is often made by conservative Christians, who, assuming the puritan equation of sex with concupiscence, elevate all matters sexual to the pedestal of supreme importance. Such elevation is marked by a negative veneration of lust as the highest deity in a perverse pantheon. This secret veneration explains the notorious tendency in such quarters of exhibiting supercharged outrage at sexual misdemeanors, especially when committed by public figures ("How could a Christian ever vote for someone who has done *that*?"), while finding much less energy to notice or complain about, say, suspicious financial dealings.

A final question concerns the phrase **with such a man do not even eat**, by which Paul clarifies in practical terms what he means by his injunction **do not associate**. On the surface this could be understood as discouraging Christians from the sort of social contact with moral transgressors we associate with the domestic communication that table sharing entails. Here a

---

24. This is to resist a recurrent exegetical habit, here displayed by Aquinas: "Therefore, since by the unnatural vices man transgresses that which has been determined by nature with regard to the use of venereal actions, it follows that in this matter this sin is gravest of all" (*Summa Theologiae* II-II.154.12).

translation problem turns out to be decisive. If we follow the NRSV, **do not even eat with such a one**, we must understand Paul to be recommending a clean break with the transgressor up to and including basic social contact. Yet, the Greek μηδὲ (*mēde*) by no means necessitates the translation "even." On our understanding, Luther displays finer sensitivity by rendering it *auch*, or "also": **And *also* do not eat with such a one**. Given the background of Jewish sensitivity about the religious implications of eating, a refusal to adopt an anticlimactic reading such as we find in the NRSV opens up the possibility of a eucharistic understanding of Paul's suggestion. To understand the prohibition to **not eat** as the exclusion of the transgressor from the eucharistic celebration of the body makes perfect sense within the horizon of Paul's discussion of the integrity of the new dough, so that, as suggested in 5:8, to eat with such a one would be to celebrate not with unleavened bread but with the yeast of the old dough.

The eucharistic theology we find here *in nuce* will open up new avenues for our later engagement with chapter 11, in which Paul deals with the contamination of the dough that is the community by the vice of greed, which prompts individual believers to provoke divine judgment by approaching the communion table as a quasi-private dining table. Our discussion here can serve as a useful preparation for this more explicit eucharistic chapter in introducing the theme of yeast that does not nourish but makes people feel bloated, gassy, and dissatisfied. Chapter 11 will bring before us a theological parallel to the case in this chapter, since both chapters are concerned with the corrupting of the body and the courting of divine judgment based on a lack of διακρίνειν (*diakrinein*)—"you do not *discern* the body" (11:29). Chapters 5 and 11 thus mutually illumine one another in their different but intertwined deployments of the eucharistic grammar, which rises more explicitly to the surface in chapter 11 (the moral case being the self-absorption of the rich in dining). Here in chapter 5 the moral case is in the foreground but, as we have argued, the eucharistic basis of Paul's intervention provides the background presupposition that when brought into view prevents the interpretation of his moves in this chapter from sliding into moralizing avenues.

Excursus: The Dynamic Nature of Pauline Reasoning

The relationship we have just noted between the foregrounding of the eucharistic motif in chapter 11 and its important background function in chapter 5 invites a methodological clarification that will help us better understand Paul's typical patterns of argumentation. Contemporary biblical scholars seem almost haunted by the task of dividing up the material in this letter and other books: defining where one argument ends and a new one begins, followed by the attempt to explain how the different pieces hang together.[25] This approach inevitably raises questions about why the subsections are never very symmetrical, often don't seem to flow well from one to the next, and often seem simply out of place and so beg for the label "interpolation."

It should by now have become apparent that the argument of Paul's first letter to the Corinthians does not function in a linear way, progressively building up to important points or descending from them. Instead, the argument in the letter moves back and forth and side to side through a complex web of claims, and in any given chapter one claim is pulled forward only to be returned to the background as the argument progresses and another important consideration is brought to the fore. Unfortunately, when the letter is approached as a long string of discrete logical sequences that are evidently punctuated by jarring and confusing transitions, the structural integrity of Paul's writing as a *theological* performance is easily missed. Our steady presumption has been that it is more true to the letter's own sequential arrangement of topics to take it as a rhetorical performance in which a set of truth claims, theological priorities, and moral insights are skillfully woven together in the tightest connection in order to reveal mutually illuminating facets of each move along the way.

This methodological insight allows us purchase on contemporary debates in both biblical studies and systematic theology. Paul draws explicitly on a recurring phrase from the Pentateuchal law in 5:13, which raises the question of his relation to the Old Testament. How are we to understand the force of this his first direct invocation from the heart of the Torah? What does this quotation assume, and what does it tell us about Paul's understanding of the Law's authority? Of all the passages Paul might have quoted from the Law, given the sin under question, this seems a surprising one to invoke. Yet as we have seen, it does serve to illumine the appropriate ecclesial *response* to the situation created in the community by the sin. Paul evidently understands this facet of the Law to address the reality of the situation in the Corinthian church. He reaches back into the Law to draw out a theological affirmation he detects in its deep background that appears to him to connect directly with his present concern. He thus freely (and without intervening hermeneutic apologies[26]) pulls out this command from the

25. Anthony Thiselton's clunky division of this chapter into two parts is symptomatic of the problem: "The Problem of the Incestuous Relationship (5:1–8)" and "Further Reflection on the Holiness of the Congregation and Allusion to the Previous Letter (5:9–13)," in ACT2, 384–418.

26. Watson, *Paul and the Hermeneutics of Faith*.

Law and as a Christian delves deep into its inner connections with Israel's worship (specifically the Passover celebration).

Paul's overarching aim, then, is to discover how Christ's work, as it incorporates believers into the church through baptism and eucharistic fellowship, yields an ethos that both exposes certain behaviors as counter to Christ's reconciling work and suggests an appropriate response that strengthens the grip of Christ's working on the community. In so doing he challenges the longstanding and understandable habit of Christian interpreters to divide biblical material into moral, theological, or ceremonial passages; this challenge extends by implication to heavy-handed divisions between the Old and New Testaments, and in particular between the forms of worship and church discipline in Israel and the church. The reading of Paul we have attempted to model attempts to let him refute our habits of reading conceptual polarities into his work, which are, on closer inspection, foreign to the logic displayed in his own highly skillful argumentation.

1 Corinthians 6

Courts as Accelerators of Dissension

> ¹When any of you has a grievance against another, do you dare to take it to court before the unrighteous, instead of taking it before the saints? ²Do you not know that the saints will judge the world? And if the world is to be judged by you, are you incompetent to try trivial cases? ³Do you not know that we are to judge angels—to say nothing of ordinary matters? ⁴If you have ordinary cases, then, do you appoint as judges those who have no standing in the church? ⁵I say this to your shame. Can it be that there is no one among you wise enough to decide between one believer and another, ⁶but a believer goes to court against a believer—and before unbelievers at that?

The situation to which Paul responds in the first half of chapter 6—legal disputes among Christians—has proven a particularly difficult exegetical knot to unravel, and a whole number of avenues have been rather inconclusively explored by interpreters ancient and modern.[1] Without immediately engaging the most controversial semantic and interpretative issues in this chapter, it is worth beginning by summarizing what we know. Paul is indubitably drawing the attention of the Corinthians to three areas of concern:

A. Disputes among believers are being taken before pagan courts.

B. The institutions of intra-ecclesial arbitration are in a deplorable state.

C. The existence of lawsuits at all between believers is an indicator of a general disinterest in reconciliation.

Paul begins with an expression of shocked disbelief at the reports he has heard: ***Dare you* go to court before the unrighteous?** The term Paul uses to characterize pagan courts highlights the reasons for his disbelief: the Corinthians are seeking their rights from the unrighteous, ἄδικοι (*adikoi*).

---

1. The many options and textual cruxes presented by 6:1–11 are presented in Garland, DEG, 195–210.

Incredibly, they are seeking justice from the "unjust." Recent scholarship has suggested that, in distinction from the relatively equitable regional criminal courts, the Roman provincial law courts involved in adjudicating civil cases in this time period were notoriously partisan, favoring those of high estate and wealth.[2] More difficult to ascertain is the historical state of affairs with regard to the institution of intra-ecclesial conflict arbitration. It is reasonable to assume that they existed in one form or another in Christian communities attempting to be faithful to the dominical teaching regarding conflict resolution in Matthew 18, and that they would have had various continuities with the practices developed by the Jewish Sanhedrin.

Whether we take Paul's comment in 6:4 as a rhetorical question or a description of the situation (**do you appoint as judges those who have no standing in the church?**), what seems obvious is the Apostle's dismay at the state of the institutions for Christian arbitration in the Corinthian community. Whether the institutions designed to resolve church conflicts have been neglected to the point of virtual nonexistence, or whether the neglect is represented in the actual practice of those they **appoint as judges**, the result in either case is the **shame** of the Corinthian church.

What seems safe to assume is that if the ecclesial institution of arbitration had been in working order in the first place, it would have considerably reduced the temptation for the Corinthian Christians to bring internal conflicts before secular courts. We might also think of Paul as assuming that **trivial** internal conflicts tend to grow if unresolved, a thought that would follow on from the yeast logic deployed in chapter 5. It is easily conceivable that, for instance, a simple interpretative difference about property rights, if not resolved early on, will only nurture much more disturbing dynamics of slander, hatred, and the desire publicly to humiliate.

These observations suggest, second, that the Apostle is convinced that the order of judgment and the order of communal life are vulnerable to simultaneous breakdown. A tale from an Anglican diocese near Washington, DC, provides a more recent and saddening example of this simultaneity. An initial rift over disputes centering on the ordination of homosexual clergy grew to the point that the parties on each side recognized that separation was inevitable. The bishop and a prominent dissenting parish initially agreed to separate amicably in the spirit of Christian charity and fellowship. It was only when the bishop allowed himself to be convinced by lawyers that a lawsuit over property rights ought to at least be threatened that the process of separation was thrown from an amicable one into an us-versus-them battle

---

2. Thiselton, ACT2, 424. That Paul has these civil courts in view is clear from his use of βιωτικά (*biōtika*) in verse 3, designating cases that draw his ire as pertaining to matters of everyday life.

in which neither party was likely to emerge unscathed. This scenario illustrates the way in which seeking one's rights in court only hardens conflicts and, as a result, cements divisions by dividing up the parties into winners and losers—a situation in which any future conciliatory overtures can only appear as condescending.

The Forms of Justice as Reconciliation

> ⁷In fact, to have lawsuits at all with one another is already a defeat for you. Why not rather be wronged? Why not rather be defrauded? ⁸But you yourselves wrong and defraud—and believers at that.

Having addressed the relation between Paul's points A and B, we find the relationship of A+B to C to raise the set of difficult and theologically wide-ranging questions that spin off from Paul's statement in 6:7: **In fact, to have lawsuits at all with one another is already a defeat for you.** We have now arrived at the heart of Paul's message in this chapter: Christians who "have issues" (which better represents the Greek πρᾶγμα ἔχων [*pragma echōn*] than does the NRSV's **has a grievance**) with each other are to resist these "issues" growing into legal cases at all. As we have already seen, Paul is realistic enough to know that the close coexistence and fellowship of the church is bound to entail conflicts or grievances and that these have to be dealt with in some way or other. The interpretative problem that his exhortations entail is how his emphasis in 6:7 that the existence of any lawsuits at all among Christians is already a defeat relates to his discussion of the deplorable state of intra-ecclesial arbitration. From the perspective of the general statement in 6:7, the existence of and care for ecclesial courts would seem to be a mere concession to a reality that the Apostle rather wishes would not exist at all—something not unlike a brothel as a place that exists as an embarrassing concession to an embarrassing state of reality.

With its rather sheepish embrace of arbitration processes, the fourth-century *Apostolic Constitutions* can be seen as attempting a sophisticated solution to the logical problem that makes Paul's argument in these verses seem contradictory:

> It is good for a Christian to have no dispute with anyone; but if . . . a dispute arises . . . although thereby he be obliged to lose somewhat, let it not come before a heathen court . . . as though we had "not one wise to judge between his brothers."[3]

---

3. From the *Apostolic Constitutions* (2:45), attributed to Julian; quoted in Thiselton, ACT2, 430.

Julian (to whom the *Constitutions* have been attributed) grasps the logical and moral priority of Paul's verdict that there should be no lawsuits at all among believers. He is also sensitive to the fact that concerns C (no legal disputes) and B (intra-ecclesial arbitration) cannot be understood in terms of a sequential process. Even if it becomes evident that solution C is impossible in a particular case, this realization will not entitle Christians to then proceed as if solution B had no relation to the reasons why C was given priority in the first place. The above passage makes clear that even in seeking arbitration Christians must not abandon the grammar that grounded Paul's climactic injunction: that disputants be prepared to give up what might be formally due them. Although Julian works constructively with this difficulty, the sense of embarrassment if not outright compromise remains, as reflected in the notion of "obliged to lose *somewhat*." This sounds like an implicit admission that ultimately the two claims are impossible to harmonize: can one really believe in ecclesial arbitration and work to keep its mechanisms in good shape while genuinely believing that it would be better if they were not used at all?

Later in the chapter we will see where the problem in Julian's approach lies. What is worth noting at this point is that he is traveling in good company with representatives of major trains of thought that would later develop in the Western Christian tradition that partitioned the scriptural ethos into two separate spheres: a sphere of "commandments," on the one hand, and one of "counsels," on the other. This two-tier system parallels the modern distinction between moral idealists, who never compromise on a moral point, and realists, who insist that the moral high ground is constituted by a willingness to compromise in order to get along. When this bifurcation is applied to Paul's challenge to endure injustice rather than to grasp for one's own justice, any decision to give up one's rights appears as what came to be called a "supererogatory work," one going beyond what is demanded of ordinary (realist) Christian morality. Within this line of interpretation it could be assumed that the vast majority of lay Christians were to live within the morality of the "permitted," while those who voluntarily relinquished their legitimate claims to justice could be seen as adhering to the "counsels" of a higher morality. Within this framework legal quarrels between Christians not committed to the higher way of the counsels could, without embarrassment, be arbitrated inside the church's own walls (if not even, by extension of this rationale, be brought before civil courts). Yet, as the Reformers emphasized, the distinction used to achieve this solution, between "commandment" and "counsel," comes at the unbearably high price of dividing the church into classes inhabiting different Christian moralities.

If we start over in our analysis of these verses in the light of Paul's line of reasoning to this point in the letter, we can begin to see the problem that the concept of supererogation shares with Julian's attempt to harmonize the last two of Paul's injunctions: both work from the perspective of the individual believer understood as a self-contained moral subject. Here the Reformers' criticism of the high medieval teaching on supererogatory works opens up an alternative avenue of interpretation of these verses. Rather than partitioning ideal and realistic approaches to morality, the logic that Luther employs in his discussion of whether a Christian prince is to take up the sword suggests itself as theologically more congenial. The Reformer draws a distinction between the prince as an individual who is, like all fellow believers, bound by the dominical verdict against resorting to violent means for one's own sake, and the prince as a bearer of responsibility for others whom he is bound to defend for their sake.[4]

This distinction seems helpful in its capacity to also illuminate the scenario of inter-Christian legal quarreling that Paul discusses in this passage, as it allows us to distinguish between the individual Christian with regard to his own sake, and the Christian with regard to his (princelike) responsibility for the wellbeing of his fellow believers and the church as a whole. Working from within the first of these two perspectives, we could say that as an individual and for his own sake, the Christian is the immediate addressee of (and remains bound by) Paul's summons to suffer injustice rather than seeking his own right as an uncompromising characterization of the heart of the Christian ethos in all situations of conflict: **Why not rather be wronged? Why not rather be defrauded?** This approach renders superfluous any searching for a way to soften this injunction at any point, as we saw Julian attempt to do with his moderating "to lose *somewhat*." Approaching Paul's discussion from the angle of Luther's distinction will also allow us to understand and endorse Paul's call for proper maintenance and care for the ecclesial courts of arbitration as equally valid as and congruent with his summons to abstain from seeking one's own individual justice. The Apostle's care for ecclesial arbitration becomes comprehensible in an equally uncompromising manner if understood as addressing the believers with regard to their responsibility for the wellbeing of the *church as a whole*. The overall gain of taking this interpretative line is the restoration of the unity of Christian morality as uncompromising obedience to the divine claim.[5]

Shifting the angle from which ecclesial arbitration is viewed from that of the individual to that of the *ecclesia* has the further advantage of shedding

---

4. Luther, *On Temporal Authority*, in LW 45, 81–129.
5. See Brock, "Supererogation and the Riskyness of Human Vulnerability," 127–39.

light on a dispute over whether the expression καθίζετε (*kathizete*) in verse 4, **do you appoint**, is to be taken as indicative or imperative. If we take the ecclesial body as the center of agency, an imperative reading is ruled out, since there is no longer any theological scope (despite the grammatical possibility) for understanding ecclesial courts as an embarrassing concession to sin. An imperative reading would assume Paul to be making a rather absurd suggestion, one that Barrett nicely characterizes as follows: "If it is absolutely necessary to have suits dealing with everyday affairs, show your contempt for them by singling out the meanest and most despised members of the church and appointing them as judges."[6]

Our line of reasoning has the additional advantage of rendering the remarkable equation in 6:7 of seeking justice with doing injustice entirely comprehensible: **But you yourselves wrong and defraud—and believers at that.** If the Christian standard of justice has an essentially communal orientation, then the *definition* of justice is that which gives the individual what is due by giving the body as a whole what is due. It is this justice that constitutes the social realm that we call the church. In this realm, there is no justice "just for me," or "just for you." The Hebrew term for justice צְדָקָה (*tsedaqah*) entails, as the German translation nicely captures, *Gemeinschaftsgerechtigkeit* (literally, "communal justice"). To maintain working institutions of intra-ecclesial arbitration with good conscience and prudence will certainly imply recognition that what is sought in them cannot be accounted for in terms of the distributive justice with which the pagan courts concern themselves (to *each individual* his own), but must be construed in light of what is *due to the body* as a whole. Another way of putting this same principled difference between pagan and Christian courts would be to say that what Christians seek is the reconciliation of persons instead of the arbitration of rights.[7]

While this line of interpretation will encourage keeping a certain distance from a range of construals and deployments of modern rights language, it is capable of embracing the very impulse to seek justice per se. Our point is to throw into relief Paul's main concern, which is to urge the Corinthians to be intensely focused on the pursuit of interpersonal reconciliation. Having this end firmly in view would enable them to undertake the task that at the moment seems beyond them: to sift and assess all human practices of judgment with an eye for their capacity to foster true reconciliation. There is no suggestion here of any absolute contrasting of reconciliation and adjudicated arbitration, since seeking the reconciliation

---

6. Barrett, CKB, 137.
7. See Wannenwetsch, "'But to *Do* Right,'" 138–46.

of persons might well include the arbitration of individual claims. Yet the former could never be seen as a mere function of the latter. While there is nothing wrong with dispensing justice under the heading of rendering "each his or her due" (*suum cuique*), the principled difficulty lies in the vast distance between what the different parties define as what is due. The crucial distinction, then, is not between these rival accounts of the *cuique*, but between a justice that makes reconciliation rather more difficult and one that keeps the door open for that which no justice procedure can of itself produce: true reconciliation. Because the Christian life is at its core describable as a constant quest for reconciliation to the point even of taking a personal loss in the service of this quest, those who seek justice-as-reconciliation are given an unprecedented inner freedom of movement within the structures of legal judgment of all types.

This theological stress on reconciliation as defining the logic of justice for Christians has direct bearings for how we understand the related ecclesial practice. Church arbitration dispenses a justice that is qualitatively different from that of secular courts, a difference in kind that has not always been well understood in the Christian tradition. Even the lawyer-theologian Calvin is a case in point here. Recognizing the gravity of the loss of an appropriately theological account of rendering justice in the canonical courts of his day, he responds by suggesting that the very existence of canonical courts is simply an interpretative error made by the church:

> It appears from a certain passage in Augustine that this sentence was incorrectly understood by the men of long ago. . . . The bishops were accustomed to sit at specified times to settle disputes; as if the apostle is referring to them in particular in this passage. . . . From that error there afterwards developed the jurisdiction which the officials of the bishops appropriate for themselves in money matters.[8]

Calvin grasps the church's defeat when its courts are able to express judgment only within the secular logic of giving each his or her due. He is also correct in seeing the distortion of the Pauline teaching about justice in cases where church courts with their quasi-independent jurisdiction are used to shield perpetrators of criminal activity from facing prosecution in the secular courts. But he refuses to consider that church courts might function correctly only when dispensing a different *kind* of justice, the justice of reconciliation, a justice outside the remit of secular courts.

---

8. Calvin, JC, 120.

The crucial distinctions for Paul, then, concern *where* Christians are to seek justice (from God) and *what* the true aim of justice is (reconciliation), both of which shape our understanding of how justice is to be sought, recognized, and accepted.

Bearing in mind the emphasis on relationship and reconciliation laid out in Matthew 18, the arbitration of material claims must be understood as a secondary effect of the primary task of finding the reconciliation between persons that must be collectively discovered. While it is certainly legitimate to ask where we can expect to *find* the dispensing of God's justice, and to hope for it to be given in a range of forums inside and outside the church, Paul's main emphasis is on pushing his readers to become engaged in a quite different quest: to begin asking how Christians are to actively *seek* justice. Rather than asking primarily, "How can I secure what is due me?" the question the Apostle presses on Christians then and now is, "How is God's justice to be sought, recognized, and accepted?"

Excursus: Familial Language as Political

There are divergent textual traditions of Matthew 18:15 that offer us an opportune illustration of the difference between perspectives that Paul is concerned with here. One tradition (the older and textually better-attested version) reads, "If your brother *sins*, go and tell him his faults." A significant number of witnesses, however, feature the addition "if your brother sins *against you*." This is no minor difference. The first version sets out a responsibility with broad political implications. In this perspective, every sin a brother may commit is considered a disruption of the common ethos and therefore affecting the whole community. The second version is more concerned with individual morality, in that the addition of "against you" sets up the situation as primarily a dispute between two private individuals. Within the scenario this moral rendering puts before us, a violation would take on political significance only under the condition of not being appropriately dealt with by the two individuals. Were it to become political eventually— that is, an issue to be dealt with by the "whole church" (Matt 18:17)—it could only be construed as a regrettable third-stage development—instead of being understood as an intrinsic aspect of all sin in the church.

However we negotiate these textual variants, Matthew 18 remains an indispensable background component of our account of Paul's purpose in this chapter of 1 Corinthians. It now presses us to consider how we understand disputes between believers to be implicated in "sinning." Paul's approach has suggested that sin, whether against the body as a whole or more specifically against an individual member of the body, is always and immediately disruptive of wider social relations. The way in which those in Corinth seemed to have no qualms about dragging a brother or sister to court was thus already indicative of their lack of an ecclesial conscience. They were obviously happy to present the dispute in impersonal terms—as if a "thing," πρᾶγμα (*pragma* [6:1]), could be taken to court without at the same time dragging a person there as well. The deepest problem that Paul discerns in lawsuits between Christians is that they constitute a denial of the existing relationship constitutive of Christ's body, expressed by the term "brother." Whereas the Corinthians seem to think they can have legal cases that are *merely* legal, Paul in effect reminds them that the involvement of brothers and sisters in those cases cannot but implicate the church.

The familial language employed here by Paul thus serves the purpose of emphasizing the bonds that characterize the Christian body, as Richard Hays comments: "Once again the NRSV's effort to achieve inclusivity by using 'believer,' rather than 'brother,' loses the point that Paul regards the community of faith as God's *family*. The Corinthians are shamefully taking family disputes out into the streets, as it were, thereby bringing the whole family into disrepute."[9] We note, however, that the way Hays emphasizes the role of the individual in making a matter public does not assume that sin is ineradicably political, but ties it again into the rationality of the individual case—the moral failing being an individual one that reflects badly on the community. What is crucial here (and what Hays overlooks) is that the familial language that Paul employs in this context is thoroughly political.[10] The scandal that concerns the Apostle is not a likely public relations disaster, but the breach of communal attachment that underlies it.

Courts (and civil courts especially) make reconciliation more difficult by dividing up contested goods within the logic of winners and losers. Once a particular social space has been declared a site of this kind of contest, reconciliation is rendered a side issue at best, and its achievement becomes ever more unlikely. Within such a setting, any move toward reconciliation will be met with an element of suspicion—whether performed by someone in a legally strong position, when such a move will be seen as condescending, or by those in the weak position, when it will appear as an attempt at face-saving or as driven by some other ulterior motive. But when Christians acknowledge that their priority concern in a dispute is not the material goods under dispute but rather the maintenance of the bond of peace that

---

9. Hays, RBH, 95.

10. For a more detailed discussion of the political significance of familial language in Paul and the Gospel of John, see Wannenwetsch, *Political Worship*, 133–59, and Wannenwetsch, "Political Love," 93–105.

defines the Christian ethos (Eph 2:11–22), they will be prepared to go as far as necessary to retain their mutual fellowship. Such willingness works to renew the Christian ethos and renders any subsequent division of goods a less critical affair that may well be aided by the church's offer of arbitration.

Does this suggestion that the church has good theological reasons to maintain structures for arbitrating disputes imply that Christians are never to be involved in litigation under *any* circumstances? As we draw this discussion to a close we should not lose sight of Paul's initial dismay: **Do you dare to go to court?** Our emphasis on what is to be sought in any such dispute—reconciliation versus our right—is not an assertion that Christians are duty-bound to keep out of litigation. There is a difference between taking the initiative and instituting court proceedings, on the one hand, and being the subject of litigation, on the other. As Calvin notes, "It is therefore wrong to take the initiative. . . . It is in order, however, to come into court and conduct your case, if a charge is made against you."[11] But in what *sense* is it "in order" to conduct one's case in court? Since Calvin was able to assume that all secular government resided within a Christian society, he might have found it easier to negotiate the prohibition of Christians taking their cases before pagans than we are today or than Paul was in his age. That context admitted, Calvin nevertheless seems here to swing open the door a little too wide in proposing that Protestant Christians, having given up canonical courts, ought to be of good conscience in taking litigation against believers into secular courts as long as they take care to be pure in their motives.[12] This justification of the very thing Paul has been concerned to reject looks like an unwarranted harmonization of the text, and Calvin himself senses the tension that the distinction has introduced: "I indeed admit . . . that it is rare to get an example of a good litigant."[13]

Our criticism of Calvin lies with his flattening out of the tension between Paul's three injunctions by deploying a concept of psychological detachment that has no correspondence in Paul's own treatment. Rather than urging the Corinthians to be emotionally *detached* as they go to court, Paul's core concern is for believers to *passionately* seek reconciliation—the specific *type* of justice that comes from God alone. Calvin's emotional stoicism sends us in a very different direction. By urging that, once legal proceedings have begun, Christians are to remain emotionally above the unfolding processes of legal dispute, he effectively suggests leaving the mechanics of the

---

11. Calvin, JC, 118.

12. "If a Christian therefore wants to prosecute his rights in a court of law, without going against God, he must take special care not to come into court with any desire for revenge, any bad feeling, any anger, or in a word any poisonous thing" (ibid., 122–23).

13. Ibid., 123.

dispensing of judgment to lawyers and judges. Such a position encourages Christians to examine their consciences before entering legal proceedings, and then to let the processes run their course.

Compared with Paul's emphasis on the importance of judgment, however, Calvin's suggestion appears to approximate an unwarranted suspension of judgment. No one chooses to go to court just once, because by entering litigation we enter into a course of events that will demand many more judgments. A parallel can be drawn here with the Christian reflection on "just war." According to this tradition, Christians are not only to critically scrutinize the justice of going to war (*ad bellum*), but, should they enter into one, they are to be as vigilant concerning their conduct in waging war (*in bello*). Neither in war nor in securing what may be due to them can Christians ever escape the imperative of reconciliation. What we can embrace from Calvin's treatment of these issues is his awareness that even legitimate quests for justice can be instrumentalized to justify combativeness in a manner that allows it to fester into an expression of various other vices. In this capacity, the combativeness that spurred the Corinthians' going to court against each other echoes what Paul has stated earlier in his discussion of the capacity of sexuality to absorb the whole range of vices available to human beings (>5:11).

Released by Baptism from the Quest for Individual Justice

> ⁹Do you not know that wrongdoers will not inherit the kingdom of God? Do not be deceived! Fornicators, idolaters, adulterers, male prostitutes, sodomites, ¹⁰thieves, the greedy, drunkards, revilers, robbers—none of these will inherit the kingdom of God. ¹¹And this is what some of you used to be. But you were washed, you were sanctified, you were justified in the name of the Lord Jesus Christ and in the Spirit of our God.

When Paul says that **wrongdoers will not inherit the kingdom of God**, he is not suggesting that particular groups of people are being summarily cast out. Rather, their nonparticipation in the kingdom of God is being named as an implication of their refusal to enter the social space that is the divine *tsedaqah* ("justice"). Dragging a brother or sister before *any* court is to exit this sphere of divine justice by undermining the very mode of judgment that characterizes the core feature of this kingdom. It is not Paul's concern here to set out his theological rationale for the existence of a political system that warrants earthly justice, as he does in Romans 13. As Theodoret reminds us, here the Apostle's focus is "the more perfect commandment: to refrain from all lawsuits."[14]

Once again readers find themselves baffled as to why at this juncture Paul introduces another list of those who will not inherit the kingdom. A moralized understanding of the sort of "doing injustice" that Paul has just discussed would be embarrassed at being included in this list, prompting the question, "Why should claiming my rights before a legitimate authority be set alongside these other clearly immoral activities?" Only such a moralized reading would assume that once again Paul, in a rather careless way, is lumping together a number of categorically different vices.

But if we understand the Apostle's main interest to be setting out the centrality of *tsedaqah* that circumscribes and orients the ethos of the body, it will become evident that taking another member to court is as grave as any of these other vices. It will be apparent, then, that the vice lists in both chapters 5 (5:11) and 6 are meant to resist rather than invite extended discussions of the precise meaning and relative relationship of the various vices. They are offered, rather, in order to draw out the relation of the whole mass of sins to the one sin under discussion. It is precisely because Paul wishes forcefully to communicate the centrality of his understanding of communal justice that he insists that very disparate vices can, and indeed must, be drawn together on the same plane of moral severity. Paul is banking on the Corinthians already agreeing that the vices on this list are severe in order to teach them to appreciate the severity of their disinterest in seeking genuine reconciliation.

The expression in 6:11 **you** [pl.] **were washed** echoes the baptismal logic we detected in 5:7. Here not only is the washing of baptism made fully explicit, including its embedding within a Trinitarian baptismal formula, but an additional link is also made with baptism as an expression of the external justification wrought by Christ: **you** [pl.] **were sanctified, you** [pl.] **were justified in the name of the Lord Jesus Christ and in the Spirit of our God**. It is this external work of justification that suggests that the comment **this is what some of you used to be** must apply to those in the church who are seeking justice. It is the reality of their washing in this divine work that both summons and empowers the Corinthians to abstain from seeking either private justice from the courts or private retaliation. The plural "you," emphasized here by being repeated three times, is an indicator that a sacramental logic is at work that unifies this chapter. Christians belong to *the body* of Christ, which is neither a relationship between individuals nor an undifferentiated collectivity. The reminder that they are released from their

---

14. Theodoret, *Commentary*, PG 82:265, quoted in JK, 94.

desire for private justice by the justifying and sanctifying power of Christ links Paul's treatment of this point to the hinge of the verse that follows.

Possessed by Our Possessiveness

> ¹²"All things are lawful for me," but not all things are beneficial. "All things are lawful for me," but I will not be dominated by anything.

Though this verse has almost universally been understood as opening the last section of the chapter,[15] it should have become clear by now that it also summarizes the central concern of Paul's discussion of lawsuits. The whole body benefits when individuals refuse to pursue lawsuits even when they are formally permitted. Modern translations sometimes obscure this relation with an excessively individualist rendering of the second phrase, as in the German *Einheitsübersetzung*, which reads (in the English equivalent) "but not everything is beneficial *to me* ["*mir*"]." It is just this focus on the individual, paraphrased in the Corinthians' motto πάντα μοι (*panta moi*, "all things for me"), that Paul wishes to confront by way of the sharp contrast he sets up in his twofold riposte. On the matter of seeking justice, the problem of the Corinthians is precisely their fighting to preserve justice for themselves *conceived only as individuals*. They would be moving in the right direction were they to take their grievances to church courts, though this is not the solution Paul favors. As we have seen, the justice he is urging them to seek is the justice of the whole, even to the point of giving up their quest for private justice entirely.

The background problem with which Paul is wrestling is how to respond to the Corinthians' lack of traditioning in the covenant logic that holds Israel together as a social aggregate. The Roman definition of justice as "to each what is due" is unambiguously oriented by the rights of "each" individual. But for Paul it is what is due to *the body* that defines the justice that is to be sought by any one individual. This is not to set a collectivist account of justice against an individualist account. Paul works on the theological presupposition (presumably based on Matthew 6:33, "But seek first his kingdom and his righteousness, and all these things shall be yours as well") that the primary pursuit of what is due to the body will not sacrifice or contradict what is due to each individual member of the body. On the contrary, putting the body (as the local instantiation of the kingdom) first

---

15. Less frequently, it is taken as the conclusion to the discussion of lawsuits, as it is, for example, by Aquinas (TA, secs. 289–96).

will fulfill what is due for each member in a manner that would be inaccessible and even inconceivable to any individual pursuit of justice. In contrast to both a proto-communist sacrifice of the individual in the name of the collective and a proto-capitalist promise that the collective is automatically better off when its members follow their individual self-interest, Paul calls for something that is gained only by embracing the suffering of reconciliation. In this embrace, the individual will indeed be in the position of "having" less, but this "less" is simultaneously "more," not measured on the same quantitative scale as what has been given up, but being of a different quality entirely.

It seems best, then, to read 6:12 as a hinge verse that carries momentum from Paul's discussions of litigation forward into a new discussion on dietary and sexual habits, and does so in a manner that allows for a mutual shedding of light on either string of discussion. The urge to be "done justice" can so occupy the individual's economy of desire that they end up engaging in self-referential lawsuits. And by the same token, the desire to "get what I deserve" can just as easily capture people through their bodily functions, as they position themselves through habits of eating and also sexual behavior.

We should not miss Paul's deft sense of irony (if not ironic speech) here: **all things are lawful for me** goes the bold claim of some of the Corinthians, **but I will not be dominated by anything**, he replies. The expression **everything is lawful** (ἔξεστιν/*exestin*, which is of the same root as ἐξουςία/*exousia*) Paul will later use again (10:23), alongside his identical responses to it in his engaging of the idol food problem in that congregation. Scholarly discussion has made much of the question whether this formula, which is known to have had currency in Stoic quarters, is used by the Apostle as a paraphrasing of the Corinthians' mindset (the more likely option) or as a statement of his own. But the question whether this motto is confronted (as in the first case) or qualified (in the second) by what Paul adds to it in the respective half-sentences he uses to complete the statement, strikes us as less indicative than the following observation: the expression ἐξουσιασθήσομαι (*exousiasthēsomai*, "will be dominated") which Paul uses to confront (or qualify) their motto is such a rare and unusual verbal usage in the *futurum passivum* construction[16] that it seems to be an ironic usage foreshadowing his next discussion: those who presume that they possess their bodies are best understood as possessed by an anonymous power they cannot control. The marked contrast of language by which Paul highlights the rift between the expression of self-possessed liberty, on the one hand, and of complete lack of self-governance, on the other, foreshadows his suggestion later in

---

16. Rienecker, *Sprachlicher Schlüssel zum Griechischen Neuen Testament*, 363.

this chapter that those who self-assuredly claim their bodies as their own privately held property are the first to be enslaved by the irresistible force that bodily functions, needs, and drives exert.

Having seen how the desire to wrest individual justice from the courts denudes the social body, we now come to explore the inner relationship of this problematic to corresponding practices that emerge among Christians who mistakenly believe that they own their bodies without reference to the *ecclesia*. In both the desire to go to court and the desire to have untrammeled ownership of one's own body, all sorts of impersonal dominating powers hover in the wings, waiting to possess those who have rendered themselves "individuated," that is, naked subjects with no defenses against the powers.

The Dual Bodiliness of Christian Existence

> [13] "Food is meant for the stomach and the stomach for food," and God will destroy both one and the other. The body is meant not for fornication but for the Lord, and the Lord for the body. [14] And God raised the Lord and will also raise us by his power. [15] Do you not know that your bodies are members of Christ? Should I therefore take the members of Christ and make them members of a prostitute? Never! [16] Do you not know that whoever is united to a prostitute becomes one body with her? For it is said, "The two shall be one flesh." [17] But anyone united to the Lord becomes one spirit with him.

Given the overwhelming modern tendency to understand legal matters as relating to justice, and so "public" morality, the discussion that follows in verses 13–20 inevitably sounds like a reversion to the "private" realm of human sexuality. Such a reading gets us going down the wrong track, however, by leading us to assume that Paul is no longer committed here to discussing the basic implications of the justice necessary to sustain a community that is always vulnerable to division. Instead of embracing this presumption, we are rather prepared to reckon with a continuous grammar running through the whole chapter: whether heading to court or into a prostitute's embrace, the Corinthians are keen to secure something they conceive to be their private due. This is why we see Paul simply continuing his account of justice as a reminder that individual Christians' bodies in fact exist as part of a collective matrix that cannot be shaken off. He wishes the congregation to understand that this divinely sanctioned collective matrix—the ecclesia—is that which each member inevitably drags into every "private" sexual liaison, just as they do into every public court. Paul reinforces this point by insisting on the plural when speaking of individual Christians: **Do you not know that *your* bodies are *members* of Christ? Should I therefore take the *members* of Christ and make them *members* of a prostitute?**

If the communal nature of the church's justice provides him with the rationale for his prohibition of visiting prostitutes, Paul must now move from the discussion of legal disputes to develop a corresponding yet different account of *how* visiting a prostitute undermines the integrity of the body of Christ. This he begins by discussing the relation between the stomach, as a bodily organ, and the sexual organs. Here the Apostle is almost certainly upending some familiar Corinthian slogans. The stomach is introduced in its quality as a univocal organ, its function directly indicating how it should be used: **Food is meant for the stomach and the stomach for food**. Already in this characterizing of the simple stomach-food relation, Paul seems to be hinting at a core difference from human sexuality, where no such univocity can be assumed with regard to the functioning of the sexual organs, the urgings of which confront the person with a much more complex task of response. While the stomach's function as a particular organ in sustaining life is equally limited as the material it draws on for this purpose (**God will destroy both one and the other**), the body as a whole exists for a higher end: **God raised the Lord and will also raise us by his power**. With this move Paul is setting up his readers to understand what is indicated by the clause **the body is meant not for fornication but for the Lord, and the Lord for the body**. The body, as a whole, is not meant for fornication in the way one might (simplistically, as in direct parallel to the stomach) assume genitals are made for, and are therefore owed, regular sexual activity. "Fornication and food are on a different footing," comments Calvin, "for God has not intended the body for fornication, as he intended the belly for food."[17]

The logic of resurrection breaks in on the teleology of the organic. It is according to this eschatological grammar that Paul can insist that the body is not meant for fornication, because the body, as a whole, is **for the Lord**. This claim allows us to resist two common assumptions. First: understanding the body as a totality rather than as a simple aggregation liberates us from the servitude that the functional ends of specific bodily organs is understood to lay on the individual ("I could not miss the opportunity with my neighbor's wife, because I am evolutionarily hardwired to sow my seed"). Second, some emphasis on the whole human being allows one to emancipate oneself from the related body-plus-spirit model. In this account, bodily drives are considered autonomous, potentially tyrannizing, and hence in need of being controlled and curtailed by the higher human

---

17. Calvin, JC, 129.

faculties associated with the "spirit" as representing an altogether distinct and separate plane. This latter bifurcation is evident in claims widespread in popular culture, from Cervantes[18] to *Indecent Proposal*, such as, "If I don't take my *spirit* to the prostitute, she won't have *me*." If human body and spirit are an indissoluble whole by virtue of being **for the Lord**, the nature of such beliefs as making captive those who believe in their "liberating" power is exposed. This is why Luther's statement "no one has the right, for any reason whatsoever, to permit his wife to commit adultery"[19] can be read as an exact flip-side expression to the liberation that comes with Paul's account of the purpose and nature of the body that does not abstract from the resurrection but rather builds from that hope.

It is tempting, though, to read 6:17 as if relying on just this body-spirit account of the human: **But anyone united to the Lord becomes one spirit with him**. To do so, however, would demand a bifurcated anthropology that places the believer's spiritual union with the Lord on a different plane than the fleshly becoming of one body that is the sexual act. But Paul's rationale works precisely the other way around: the Christian ethos is incompatible with prostitution because the body is not a separable aspect of/from the person. Rather, the ensouled body *is* the person. To unite in the sexual act, even with a prostitute, is to unite two ensouled bodies or whole persons. Only from within such a grammar can Paul put the question of 6:15 as he does: **Do you not know that your bodies are members of Christ?** Verse 17 should therefore be read as a restatement of this en-membering through the language of the spirit. No hint can be found here of a doctrine of immaterial spiritual union. To be **one spirit with the Lord** means precisely to be of one spirit with the body, the body of Christ. That Paul makes this point by reference to a eucharistic grammar of being **united to the Lord** (through physically partaking of the elements together) reemphasizes that what is at stake here is also the heart of the eucharistic celebration: a bodily and sensually perceptible unification by which Christ, through eating, is incorporated into believers' bodies so as to permeate their whole being.

We can now describe the inner connections the Apostle has developed in this chapter by explicating how he has interrelated the political, personal, and social dimensions of his argument with remarkable precision. According to the *political dimension*, we see Paul once again to be emphasizing his *oikodome* account of the body. In this light, to visit a prostitute or to go to court against a fellow member is to take the (communal) body to a place that is a non-place, so up-rooting and dis-integrating that body. The

---

18. Cervantes, *Don Quixote*, I.33–35.
19. Luther, *Commentary on 1 Corinthians 7* (1523), in LW 28:34.

second, *personal dimension* of his argument reengages the topics discussed in the political dimension from the perspective of the individual person. Paul elaborates a high theology of the body that is grounded in a theology of the resurrection, as 6:14 emphasizes—God raised not only Christ and with him us, but more strongly, **raised *both* the Lord *and* us**. No higher praise and value can be bestowed on anything or anyone than to be the material element of the resurrected life of Christ, a resurrection that does not supersede but perfects human bodily existence (to be discussed in great detail in chapter 15).

These first two points mutually illuminate one another, with both being necessary in order to make good theological sense of the semantics of **taking** and **uniting**, as Paul describes it in 6:15. On the one hand, illicit erotic encounters mean "taking" a member of Christ and "making him one" with, say, a prostitute. The Greek expression ἄρας (*aras*) points not merely to a functional or logical requirement but envisions "taking" to be understood in political terms as the dislocation or even stealing of a member from the place it belongs, Christ's body. If this political facet of the dismemberment of the individual is not added to the analysis, we will be left with an unsatisfactorily moralized suggestion that sexual immorality must be avoided because it makes Christ filthy, or contaminates him by way of his members' contamination.

Calvin's comments on this passage illustrate the reasons why it is important (and difficult) in theological exegesis to balance the moral and political aspects in view in this discussion. The first point to note is that he helpfully summarizes the high theology of the body that Paul is offering:

> The spiritual union which we have with Christ is not a matter of the soul alone, but of the body also, so that we are flesh of His flesh, etc. (Eph 5:30). The hope of the resurrection would be faint, if our union with him were not complete and total like that.[20]

But because he is missing the political horizon of "uniting" developed by Paul, Calvin falls back on a moralizing account of fornication as contamination:

> The words, "the two shall become one flesh," refer, strictly and properly speaking, only to those who are married. But they are applied to fornicators who come together in a corrupt and unclean union, so that the contamination passes from one to another. ... The union (*coniunctionem*) of Christ with us is closer than that of husband and wife. ... We ought to look on

---

20. Calvin, JC, 130.

fornication with the utmost horror, keeping in mind how very shameful and filthy it is.[21]

By staying close to Paul's spatial explication of the problem of the severing of the body, we have been able to affirm his high theology of the body without framing the problem of sexual immorality in terms that inevitably sully human sexuality.

This brings us, third, to the *socio-physical* dimension of Paul's argument in this chapter. David Horrell indicates this aspect of the argument when noting that "it is clear enough that corporate solidarity, based on a vision of incorporation into Christ, many becoming one, is a basic metanorm in Pauline ethics, an essential foundation for the other aspects of Paul's ethical instruction."[22] When discussing sexual relations Paul assumes the power of bodily encounter to establish relations that, by definition, always go beyond the "merely" physical. The infamous utterance of the embattled politician, "I did not have a sexual relationship with that woman," must be seen to be a contradiction in terms when understood against the background of a Christian theology of the body which insists that there is an inevitable communicative power in bodily intimate encounter. The body is not silent, some mute functionary that can be given any interpretation we please, as though we had a right or the power to coin a private language in which we could define all the terms at will.

Fleeing the Bondage of Generation Porn

> [18] **Shun fornication! Every sin that a person commits is outside the body; but the fornicator sins against the body itself.** [19] **Or do you not know that your body is a temple of the Holy Spirit within you, which you have from God, and that you are not your own?** [20] **For you were bought with a price; therefore glorify God in your body.**

If we continue with the socio-physical reading just set out we are afforded purchase on the enigmatic phrase **Every sin that a person commits is outside the body; but the fornicator sins against the body itself**. To sin against the body is to turn the body into a liar by overriding its own communicative action by means of a supervening interdict ("This has no strings attached/it is off the books"). To sin against the body lies in this perversion of its communicative meaning in the interest of sustaining illicit *social* bonds.

---

21. Ibid., 131.
22. Horrell, *Solidarity and Difference*, 131.

Human beings inevitably and continually communicate with their bodies but have also developed socio-cultural strategies that attempt to circumvent these messages, such as the transient arenas of the "no strings attached" culture of erotic encounter. A circumvention it still is even when, as in the case of prostitution, both parties agree from the outset to deny the meaning of bodily intimacy. The immorality practiced in these forums is training in deception, even when there is mutual consent to the lie by the "consenting partners." The obfuscation, if not outright deception, built into the utterance "I did not have a sexual *relationship* with this woman"—when in fact there was a mutual engagement in the body language of intimacy—is revealed when one party falls into the painful no man's land of wishing to ignore the merely verbal interdict and instead take the body's word seriously. This is because our most basic knowing is bodily, as the philosopher Michel Serres so beautifully puts it:

> This is the first *cogito*, more deeply buried although more visible than the thinking *cogito*. I feel, I have felt; I have seen, heard, tasted, smelt; I have touched; I touch, I enclose myself in my pavilion of skin. . . . The speaking body, flesh filled with language, has little difficulty in remaining focused on speech, whatever happens. Words fill our flesh and anesthetize it . . . . Nothing makes one more insensitive than words.[23]

The fornicator's sin is the denial of the body's peculiar nature as a means of human communion. It represents a self-destructive attempt to control the communicative properties of our outer surfaces by means of some "inner" fiat, as if by speaking we could leap beyond the veil of skin with which we touch and are touched by the world.

This understanding of fornication as a sin against the body allows us to overcome an interpretative embarrassment suffered by many exegetes. As Lietzmann has noted, are not gluttony, drunkenness, self-mutilation, and suicide also crimes against one's body?[24] Barrett presents us with the two main alternative interpretations of this passage that such a line of questioning prompts. The first is an outright excuse: "It is perhaps best to suppose that Paul is writing rather loosely, and not in the manner of a textbook of moral philosophy."[25] The second (which Barrett wrongly assumes is implied in the first) expresses a long-codified theological mistake propounded at least as early as Calvin: "My explanation is that he [Paul] does not completely

---

23. Serres, *Five Senses*, 58–59.
24. As noted in Barrett, CKB, 150.
25. Barrett, CKB, 150.

deny that there are other sins, which also bring dishonor and disgrace upon our bodies, but that he is simply saying that these other sins do not leave anything like the same filthy stain on our bodies as fornication does."[26]

We must take Paul's claim about the sin against one's own body more seriously than these readings allow that excuse it as either fuzzy or hyperbolic. In so doing we hope also to cast aside a long and shameful tradition in which Christian moralists have tried to press home the command to **shun fornication** by way of what we would today call biomechanical accounts. In such accounts the mechanics of biology can be trusted to ensure punishment for sexual sin in and through the body. For masturbation males will inevitably go blind or will use up the one thousand or so ejaculations that they are allotted, while women will become hysterics (or worse): the litany of bogus biological claims seems almost endless.[27] This tradition is shameful on multiple levels: for baptizing biological absurdities; in its tendency to spoil any sense of enjoyment of physical pleasure for believers; and, most grievously, in its perverse inversion of Paul's high theology of the body by bringing it down to the level of his Corinthian interlocutors for whom the body seems to be nothing more than its biological processes. To speak this way is to assume bodies are reducible to the organs that make them up and that we are no more complex than the **stomach for food and food for the stomach**.

What sort of summons, then, do we find in **flee πορνεία (*porneia*)**? It must have been comparatively easy for C. K. Barrett, writing from his professorial desk in the quaint North England town of Durham in the 1960s, to deploy a historicizing view to locate the problem of *porneia* firmly in the past: "Temptations to fornication were so common in Corinth that mere disapproval was likely to be inadequate; strong evasive action would be necessary."[28] Barrett seems to have been on safe ground with his assessment of the temptations available in the Corinth of Paul's day, a sentiment confirmed by contemporary archeologists who believe that the rates of cultic and commercial prostitution were exponentially higher than in any modern Western city. As a port town housing equal numbers of wealthy merchants

---

26. Calvin, JC, 131-32.

27. Aquinas is typical in linking such an account with a hierarchizing of sin that renders sexual sin graver than all others: "Now venereal pleasures above all debauch a man's mind" (ST II-II.153.1); "What matters is how much the interior appetite is affected by that pleasure" (ST II-II.153.2); "When the lower powers are strongly moved towards their objects, the result is that the higher powers are hindered and disordered in their acts.... Consequently, the higher powers, namely the reasons and the will, are most grievously disordered by lust" (ST II-II.153.3).

28. Barrett, CKB, 150.

and artisans as well as a strikingly large population of local and transient slaves and sailors, it is safe to assume that some of the new believers in the Corinthian church were long habituated in the culturally familiar routines of transient erotic contact with strangers. So while Barrett in his own cultural context might have had legitimate reason to feel quite distant from this sex-saturated society, it is just as clear that the cultural changes in motion since Barrett's day give us less warrant to speak in such a detached way. If we are prepared, here it may be easier than we expect to "become Corinthians."

We know, of course, that *porneia* (inappropriate sexual conduct of any type) is more than what we today call pornography, which has become a ubiquitous feature of contemporary culture in developed societies. But given its pervasiveness, pornography almost forces itself on our discussion here as a paradigmatic iteration of the *porneia* Paul summons the Corinthians to flee. With our bodies unable most of the time to walk away from the machinery that links us with the ubiquitous products of the porn industry—always but one keystroke away—and being told by the cultural avant-garde (not least through advertising) that we must eventually learn to embrace our voyeuristic-pornographic selves as part of our sensual liberation, we find ourselves in a situation in which there seems to be no "outside" to which we can flee.[29] On the one hand, this puts us in a privileged interpretative position, as it is precisely we, Generation Porn, who seem best placed to investigate what it is Paul means when he says to "flee." In particular, our situation gives us a vantage point from which we can grasp the *trans-moral* nature of Paul's exhortation here, which points to a level of the demonic that is more powerful and problematic than moral injunctions are equipped to bear and that can only be dealt with by exorcism. On the other hand, it is precisely the ubiquity of porn that puts our generation in the seemingly hopeless, near-hypocritical position of being unable to comprehend Paul's call to flee from *porneia*.

If there literally is no escape route out of the realm controlled by *porneia*, are we then to acknowledge that we have allowed our society to organize itself in such a way that scripture has been rendered unintelligible? This, of course, is a vastly more serious situation than can be captured by a merely moral analysis of the situation. Is it still a mark of responsible parenting, for example, to apply without any further thought the label "bad

---

29. Our account of bodily communication indicates why the most disastrous *theological* judgment made by John Howard Yoder in defense of his sexual exploits was to respond to these modern trends by arguing that what was needed was not flight but a desensitization program to help Christians learn, both in theory and in practice, that transient erotic encounters do not violate the traditional Christian espousal of marital fidelity. See Goossen, "'Defanging the Beast,'" 7–80.

boy" to a teenage son's apparent inability to resist pressing the p-key on his personal computer's keyboard? This is why we understand Paul's summons to "flee *porneia*" as a trans-moral statement; its subject matter is not the capacity to choose between right and wrong, but precisely a situation—our generation's situation—in which it seems impossible to position ourselves in a realm where such a choice does not have to be faced.

This is to suggest that the cultural location of Generation Porn affords us better insight into what was at stake between Paul and the boasters in the Corinthian community. Their boasting consisted precisely in their insistence that every question can eventually be boiled down to a moral choice, sexual (im)morality included, even cases of *porneia* within the Corinthian church (>ch. 5). They obviously felt their combination of disapproval and toleration to be a more noble response than Paul's apparently simplistic call to flee. The Corinthians seem to have committed themselves to translating every situation into a question of moral choice in their resolute self-assertion as sovereign moral subjects impervious to domination by anonymous forces.

For the Corinthian moralists, whether approving or disapproving of specific actions, the higher moral ground was always to extend tolerance, because for them there seemed no powers afoot that must be expelled or which demanded immediate flight. Contemporary liberal sensibilities parallel this pattern—for instance, by encouraging us to look down on parents who say "no TV and Internet in our home" as ruling by force rather than appropriate persuasion. In so doing they deceive us and our children into thinking that there can be and always needs to be a way of "learning to cope" with every temptation. There may be a wisdom to be gained in "learning to cope" that surpasses the simpleton's solution of tearing out the p-key from the keyboard. But the path of this wisdom is one that easily draws others further into the self-delusion that increases the threat of their destruction.

Within a framework of moral discourse it is of course only too appropriate to say "learn to cope." But when it is the theologically appropriate time to say this can never be comprehended without taking a step beyond the moral discourse of making right choices. Paul's summons beyond the moral therefore fosters judgment among Christians by insisting on a more truthful account of reality that takes seriously the existence of forces beyond the moral capacity of human beings. Paul's "flee *porneia*" supposes that sometimes what will be demanded is not moralized exhortation to greater vigilance in doing good, but precisely the distancing from or expulsion of a power that possesses and enslaves. These forces are not particularly or exclusively associated with human sexual drives. But the strength of these forces is often generated from the marriage of powerful human capacities (in this case the sexual drives) with powerful ideologies (in this case the technological imperative embraced in the assumption that certain digital technologies are inescapable means of human communication).

Being members of Generation Porn has, in an ironic way, made Paul's urging more intelligible to us, but at the cost of seeming to render unintelligible or inapplicable his exhortation to flee, as we are members of a society that keeps systematically ferreting out and bolting closed the escape hatches through which we might once have fled. Such a claustrophobic situation is, however, a gift in disguise insofar as it brings the essential theological question into stark relief: must we bow to those cultural evolutions that we cannot escape? It seems clear that to flee cannot simply be equated with outwitting the porn imperative by refusing computers entirely or installing ever more sophisticated "filth-filters" in our machines. Rather, what is necessary is to identify a space in which true freedom is available for us to inhabit. Paul gestures toward this realm of freedom in the preceding verse: **It is said, "The two shall be one flesh." But anyone united to the Lord becomes one spirit with him**. In what sense is Christ alone the "outside" into which we can flee from the realm of *porneia*?

It may give us a jolt to see the same word, κολλώμενος (*kollōmenos*), used to describe uniting with a prostitute and being united with the Lord. How can these two embraces be equated? Our understanding of the ecclesial background of Paul's point is that believers are united with Christ precisely by way of being incorporated into him through the Spirit in eucharistic en-membering. To eat and drink Christ's body and blood is as *bodily* a union with Christ as any carnal embrace. It is here that we encounter the place outside of *porneia* in all its very physical as well as virtual (porn) manifestations. Even in this Internet age Christians do not gather for Eucharist around the keyboard. We do read, write, and (in the case of some) even proclaim and confess our sins on the Internet in the manner we consume porn, but we cannot gather for Eucharist within this virtual connectivity.[30] Because we must gather for Eucharist with the community in the most basic and physical sense, we have access to a community that exists as a firewall against the material vectors of porn.

In other words, it is the materialist nature of the eucharistic gathering that stands as the promise of an "outside" for a porn generation that has been systematically taught that no such outside exists. To communicate here means to eat, materially to incorporate the body and blood of Christ into our material bodies. The communicative power of our bodies, which have their pinnacle expression in the sexual encounter, displays for Paul the complete absorption of the eucharistic embrace that alone can offer the

---

30. Bennett, *Aquinas on the Web?*, ch. 5.

outside that the imperative to flee presupposes. Here no dualist Gnosticism grounds this command to flee but an acknowledgment of the enormous communicative power of bodily existence. To flee *porneia* is not to flee *from*, a mind-over-matter feat undertaken within the logic of sexual immorality as filthy; it is a flight *into* a genuine corporeality that feeds off the communicative power of the body that eucharistic existence offers. "Flee—that can only mean flee to the place where you can experience protection and help, flee to the Crucified one. Alone his image and his presence help."[31] To flee to eucharistic celebration is to flee from a *space*, one in which we roam endlessly and never need to come to rest, into a *place* as belonging, as physical fixity grounded in physical presence. In this flight we do not simply exchange one sphere of influence for another, or simply substitute one set of educative habits for another. There is a structural difference between these two spheres. We flee from the deceptive promise of relief from our physical desires and escapist fantasies in a nonphysical universe (the virtual space of porn) into a sacramental practice that meets and satisfies us by tying us as bodies to a place and truly free relationship.

Paul's ethical point grows from his theological insight that Christians are those who do not even claim self-possession of their own bodies. To be claimed by Christ is to renounce any rights to individualistic self-determination of the body. **Or do you not know that your body is a temple of the Holy Spirit within you, which you have from God, and that you are not your own?** To receive the body as a gift from God, as a temple of the Holy Spirit, is precisely to characterize the Christian ethos as one constituted by the renunciation of the right to claim the body as something that can be put to what and whoever's service the individual sees fit. Christians are to live in any setting not as those who definitively know and possess themselves but as members of Christ. Each communicative encounter is condemned when expressing self-chosen agendas and ways of seeking our individual due or justice. In short, Paul concludes, if Christians are to **glorify God in your body**, this glorification can only occur when Christians understand their conduct in a manner that holds together the political, personal, and interpersonal. The "temple" is a space for *public* worship of the *one* God. When the idea of the temple is reinterpreted in individualist terms it can only designate a shrine that the lustful gods of this world—whether of sexual pleasure or physical prowess, whether of authority or wealth—will soon inhabit.

---

31. Bonhoeffer, "Bible Study on Temptation, Zingst, June 20–25, 1938," in *Theological Education Underground, 1937–1940* (DBWE 15), 405.

1 Corinthians 7

Bodies between Chastity and *Porneia*

> ¹Now concerning the matters about which you wrote: "It is well for a man not to touch a woman." ²But because of cases of sexual immorality, each man should have his own wife and each woman her own husband. ³The husband should give to his wife her conjugal rights, and likewise the wife to her husband. ⁴For the wife does not have authority over her own body, but the husband does; likewise the husband does not have authority over his own body, but the wife does. ⁵Do not deprive one another except perhaps by agreement for a set time, to devote yourselves to prayer, and then come together again, so that Satan may not tempt you because of your lack of self-control. ⁶This I say by way of concession, not of command.

Much of the Christian exegetical tradition from ancient to modern times has operated on the assumption that Paul's claim in 7:1, **It is well for a man not to touch a woman**, primarily articulates the relationship between singleness and the institution of marriage.[1] Though explained in a range of ways over the centuries, the general trend is either to embrace or explain away Paul's opening commendation of the state of celibacy over marriage. A position must be taken, it seems, about whether or not Paul can be legitimately called a champion of Christian monasticism.[2] We will suggest that it is not

---

1. This reception history is little affected by the fact that what we have here is almost certainly a popular maxim or a slogan that the Corinthian Christians embrace. Whether we take Paul to be affirming or denying this slogan will turn on our reading of the chapter as a whole. That the newer consensus view has more recently rejected the earlier consensus by taking this to be a slogan that Paul is contradicting only confirms our observation that the passage has been read as articulating the relation of marriage to the unmarried. Garland surveys the modern consensus in biblical studies (DEG, 247–51).

2. The fathers often read Paul as commending virginity so strongly here that they are forced later, in their commenting on 9:5, to interpret Paul as suggesting that the apostles were unmarried, references to wives being variously interpreted as chaste

necessary to decide whether Paul is responding to Encratite claims—an ancient ascetic movement forbidding marriage—or instead to proponents of Joseph-type marriage in which sexual abstinence within marriage is considered the higher way.³ Several issues raised in the chapter will be more easily accessed if we consider Paul first to be offering a more principled position to set the stage for more detailed questions about what is appropriate when Christians **touch a woman**, including the fiancé and widow. As we hope to demonstrate, though marital and sexual relations figure prominently in this chapter, the Apostle's main interest is not in the various loosely related situations on which it touches, but rather the Christian calling to chastity in *all* circumstances.

The key to our reading of the chapter as a whole is the concession articulated in 7:6: **This I say by way of concession, not of command.** The widespread tendency to understand Paul as commending celibacy over marriage presupposes that this verse is either a concession to *marriage* or to *sex within* marriage. We understand the scope of this concession to be much more narrow, a supposition based on Paul's linking it with the immediately preceding comment via the expression τοῦτο δὲ (*touto de*, "This I say"). Paul's concession is to allow, within limited parameters, special times of prayer to interrupt the regularity of marital intercourse (7:5). Though neither of the alternative readings can be ruled out in principle, we think it will become apparent in our treatment of the remainder of the chapter that we are opening up an approach that allows sense to be gleaned from passages that other readings render intractable.

The apostolic concession for couples to set aside special times to devote to prayer is best understood as a parallel to practices of fasting, which themselves tend to draw on two rationales. The first is an enforced break from routine patterns in order to respond to a situation that requires a higher

---

wives or female assistants. See Tertullian, *On Monogamy* 4.60; Jerome, *Against Jovinian* 1.7; and Augustine, *Work of Monks* 5-6, CSEL 41:538-40, quoted in JK, 147.

3. Garland, providing a detailed summary of the various hypotheses about what the historical conditions in Corinth could have been that motivated Paul's engagement in this question, finds contemporary defenders of no less than twelve possible scenarios (see DEG, 263-66). His conclusion we find appropriate: "Since we must largely rely on guesswork via mirror-reading to identify their motivations, and since the cultural landscape of Corinth permits a mélange of influences, we must allow for a variety of factors that could have influenced their decision [to court or embrace various forms of celibacy or abstinence].... No one view completely explains the Corinthians' motivation. Many interpreters jump to theological conclusions about the causes and neglect the medical, cultural, and even physical circumstances that may have bred the situation. Narrowing it down to one cause or another presumes that we know more than we do. I choose to be vague about identifying the specific impulse that led to the Corinthians' attitude toward sexuality" (ibid., 266).

state of bodily and spiritual alertness. The ability of sexual intimacy to calm and satiate the body is forgone in service of holding on to the keen vigilance required by the urgency of a particular situation. Ritualized abstention is a similar form of fasting through which believers renew their awareness that bodily needs and urges are not a command to be slavishly obeyed. It seems that it is this latter sort of fasting that Paul's concession presumes, a reading that is reinforced when we note its limits: it is only to be pursued **by agreement for a set time**. This apostolic call to limit ascetic abstention is also a reminder that creaturely life is marked by inherent boundaries. Pursuing spiritual discipline of the body must not expand to allow a false sense of mastery to evolve that assumes the "law in our members" (Rom 7:20–23) can be totally vanquished.

On this reading, the warning **that Satan may not tempt you** is not a reference to sexual desire roving outside the marriage but to the overheating of ascetical desires to be in total control of bodily powers. In the Greek this temptation is described as one that comes into being διὰ τὴν ἀκρασίαν (*dia tēn akrasian*). Understanding what is meant by temptation in this context depends on our rendering *dia* (as according to the accusative it prompts in the noun that follows) as "through." What could it mean to be tempted by Satan *through* a lack of abstinence? The NRSV translation **because of your lack of self-control** once again psychologizes Paul's more factual language, thus obscuring the Apostle's all-important move to turn the tables on the Corinthians' linkage of temptation with the *carnal* by linking it with the *spiritual*.[4]

A psychologized reading is bound to sexualizing temptation—a move that corresponds with the "concession" reading we find so misleading. Paul's factual language, speaking simply of a lack of abstinence (*akrasia*), appears to assume that the fall to temptation takes place when a married couple resumes their intimacy earlier than previously agreed. The *desire* to have sex is not the temptation but *how the couple understands it when it takes place* in the context of an agreed period of abstinence. The Apostle is apparently suggesting a situation in which Satan enters to tempt a couple to consider their resumed intimacy an embarrassment because they have not been true to their planned period of abstinence. The temptation is to feel guilty about an activity that is in principle a good thing but given its timing must now be "excused" by way of a concession.

It is not farfetched to detect in the formulation of Paul's advice to limit periods of marital abstention an implicit anthropology which assumes not

---

4. Other translations make the same presumption as the NRSV: ". . . if Satan went on putting you through trials beyond your self-control" (Thiselton, ACT2, 509).

that we *are* our bodies but rather that we *have* our bodies.⁵ Contrasting with contemporary cultural and theological fashion that emphasizes the immediacy of bodily nature ("I'm not a mind *carried* inside a body, I *am* my body!"), Paul seems to believe that it is characteristic of human beings to need to learn how to *respond* to one's bodily urges. At first sight this notion that human beings *have* rather than *are* their bodies seems to contradict what Paul says in 7:4, **For the wife does not have authority over her own body, but the husband does; likewise the husband does not have authority over his own body, but the wife does**. Here Paul obviously envisions a sort of nonproprietary relationship to our own bodies, reflected in the way in which marital relationship, specifically intercourse, is presented as a kind of enhypostatic dwelling, with one's existence "dwelling" in another's (bodily, in this case). We might also refer to this as a non-Cartesian account of having a body, a mode of possession that does not presuppose the prior objectification of the body by which moderns establish their belief that they own their own bodies.⁶

To suggest that Paul is assuming a non-Cartesian ownership of our bodies is therefore to take him to be expecting human beings to exist within a lifelong process of learning to make their bodies their own by acknowledging, appropriating, and embracing that part of themselves that is materially and tangibly present in the world.⁷ That this task is complex and perennial is displayed in a representative way today by the countless tragedies played out in the lives of teenage girls who experience puberty as a deformation of their appearance that can only be fended off by starvation or self-mutilation. These are battles in an epic war raging in the contemporary West for a whole range of people for whom dwelling in their own bodies is experienced as a kind of spiritual homelessness. The promise of surgical relief is often held out to those who suffer from this sense of estrangement, most radically in transgender operations, but also to those who find themselves repelled by the mundane process of bodily aging.⁸

We suggest approaching Paul's ruminations in this passage on marital sexual relations as probing the particularly important question of how

---

5. Spaemann, *Persons: The Difference between "Someone" and "Something"*.

6. "Though the earth, and all inferior creatures, be common to all men, yet every Man has a *property* in his own *person*: this no body has any right to but himself." Locke, *Two Treatises on Government*, II.§27.

7. For a wider theological and philosophical account of the questions the following sections raise (and which follow closely and in part verbally overlap with this article), see Wannenwetsch, "Owning Our Bodies?," 50–65.

8. No one has more precisely captured this contemporary predicament than Elliot, *Better than Well*.

marriage intensifies the general human task of learning to own our bodies in a nonproprietary fashion. The intensification Paul suggests is generated by his call for Christians to give up the ἐξουσία (*exousia*—might or **authority**) over their bodies to the spouse. Only a body that is in some way owned can be given, yet only a body held nonpossessively can be given in a form that is distinguishable from prostitution. Here a critical limit of the discussion needs to be noted. The logic Paul is developing works only if the authority over another's body is nonreciprocal. For Paul to claim that **the wife does not have authority over her own body** is not to establish the right of husbands to demand the use of their wives' bodies at will, which would entail at its furthest reaches a sinister legitimation of marital rape. The key to avoiding such overreading is to take the parenetic nature of Paul's summons seriously. His argument does not establish an ontological claim to ownership like a legal document certifying an owner's rights that comes with the purchase of property; his is an addressee-specific moral exhortation. In exhorting both wife and husband to not assume exclusive property rights over their own bodies the Apostle is thus simultaneously barring spouses from any claiming of property rights over the other's body. The NRSV's misleading translation of ὀφειλὴν (*opheilēn*, "what is owed") as **conjugal rights**, instead of the more appropriate "duties," lends itself to such an ontological misreading. A right can be claimed from another, but a duty to another can only be honored. In common with ancient discussions of sexuality, for Paul the issue is not *ownership* of my body in the sense of defending it against others' legal claims, but the *responsibility* of my use of it.[9]

Every linkage of the language of rights, debts, or duties to the realm of sexual pleasure has become highly suspect in modernity. Yet it remains an open question whether or not this modern unease with the Pauline expressions of duty and debt has really yielded a language in which a richer understanding of sexual life in marriage is conceivable. Only the displacement of the older Christian language of covenant by that of contract in Enlightenment philosophies of marriage could allow Kant to propose, apparently with a straight face, the famous definition of marriage as the lifelong mutual possession of the spouse's sexual properties.[10] With the grain of the romantic revolution against this hyperrationalism being ascendant today,[11] we tend instinctively to shy away from applying any language of duty to intimate marital encounters, preferring instead to valorize spontaneity and simultaneity. In the face of such commonsense accounts of sex

---

9. Deming, *Paul on Marriage and Celibacy*, ch. 2.
10. Kant, *Metaphysics of Morals*, Part I, sec. III.
11. Rees, *Romance of Innocent Sexuality*, ch. 3.

and marriage we need Paul to lead us beyond the polarity between Kantian sexuality, with its deadening emphasis on functional sexual availability, and romantic sexuality, with its deadening disdain for all sexual practice that is not ecstatic. The account Paul offers opens up both constrictions by developing a robust marital eroticism rooted in the nonproprietary ownership of our own bodies that reflects the wholesome claim that, ultimately, we are the possession of the One who gave his life for us.

Our treatment might be considered an expanded gloss on what the Christian tradition has termed *chastity*. In Galatians 5:22 Paul lists *enkrateia* ("chastity") as one of the fruits of the Spirit, so presenting it as an inextricably social virtue with far wider implications than mere sexual abstention. The various themes of human sexuality Paul is addressing in 1 Corinthians 7 are therefore best understood as his outworking of a principled dichotomy between *enkrateia* and *porneia*. This is to understand the individual discussions in this chapter as an apostolic display of *how* chastity situates and explicates various fields of human sexuality such as marital intercourse, religiously mixed marriages, singleness, widowhood, and engagement.

Verse 2 immediately creates problems for any theology of sexuality that reduces the frame of the discussion to the choice between binary vocations, that is, one is either married or (preferably) celibate. If marriage and celibacy are in competition here, then this concession must be understood as directed only to the unmarried: **But because of cases of sexual immorality, each man should have his own wife and each woman her own husband**. Taking this line, however, guts the substantial unity of the chapter in offering little more than a paper-thin thematic unity centering on issues of sexuality, with 7:2 being the single line of advice offered to those who are single. In this interpretation, only the unmarried need to worry about the question of whether or not they are tempted by *porneia*, and if they are, they should enter the state of marriage. Such a reading must then take the rest of the chapter to be offering discrete sets of advice tailored to different subgroups in the Corinthian church that have fallen short of the superior discipline necessary to remain celibate and so need differentiated instructions about how to deal with the problems that have cropped up in their marginal states of life. On our reading, such an approach obscures the rich account of chastity being offered here in which a particular way of learning to live the Christian's overall vocation to chastity is described within a wide variety of circumstances.

Our preferred reading is to take 7:2 as an anticipated conclusion explicating the type of nonpropriety body ownership to which Christians are called in every walk of life. Such ownership is organically related to monogamy in that owning the spouse's body is paralleled with, and integral to, the task of owning the body one has. Another advantage of such a reading is that it also helps us grasp the significance of the formula διὰ δὲ τὰς πορνείας (*dia de tas porneias*), which the German *Einheitsübersetzung* translates "because of the danger of unchastity." The NRSV introduces the notion of "cases" in its rendering **because of cases of immorality**, which Anthony Thistleton defends as a reference backward to the scenarios discussed in chapters 5–6. We take Luther's rendering, "in order to avoid sexual immorality," to be best situated to grasp Paul's account of *principled* opposition between *porneia* and chastity. Chapters 5–7 amply illustrate how both *porneia* and chastity play out in a range of social contexts: just as there are different expressions of *porneia*, so chastity can be lived in marriage both in prayerful abstinence from *and* by the regular practice of sexual intercourse, as it can in the lives of virgins, those who are engaged, and those who lead their lives as celibates. To understand Paul's arguments in chapter 7 as based on a principled opposition between chastity and *porneia* (rather than between celibate and married forms of life) helps us grasp why the Apostle does not consider marital sex a concessionary hedge against *porneia*. Instead, he holds out a vision of sexual chastity in all its forms as the promising, only, and proper rival of *porneia* in all its forms.

Chastity vs. Control, Repression, or Repudiation

> **⁷I wish that all were as I myself am. But each has a particular gift from God, one having one kind and another a different kind.**
>
> **⁸To the unmarried and the widows I say that it is well for them to remain unmarried as I am. ⁹But if they are not practicing self-control, they should marry. For it is better to marry than to be aflame with passion.**

If we take the chastity-*porneia* polarity to be the scarlet thread running through the whole chapter, how then are we to take Paul's suggestion in 7:7, **I wish that all were as I myself am**? Is this not a commendation of his own unmarried state as displaying a life untroubled by the lure of *porneia* and therefore beyond the need for marriage? It is probably wise to resist speculating about the nature and intensity of Paul's libido. On the basis of our discussion of chastity, the invitation to "be like Paul" becomes comprehensible only as a call to learn, as he has, to own one's body in a way that resists the enslavement to the "law in his members" that drives toward *porneia*. But if it is inadvisable to take Paul as a "natural" celibate gifted presumably with low libido, perhaps it is better to think of him as a stoic in these matters?[12]

The way in which most English translations present 7:9 (**it is better to marry than to be aflame with passion**) would seem to make such conclusions inevitable. This impression is further strengthened when the NRSV renders 7:36 as **if his passions are strong** and verse 37 as **having his own desire under control**. The translation of 7:9b as **aflame with passion** only accentuates the inner recoil of modern sensibilities from this stoic Paul who resists sexual passion not because it is *sexual*, but because it is *forceful*. It is no little irony that modern sensitivities that are prone to denouncing marriage in favor of being aflame with vitalistic passion would come to stand in closer proximity to that (stoic) Paul, precisely to the very degree in which he is taken to be making passion and self-control mutually exclusive. This leads to an embrace of what he is understood to call the disease rather than of his proposed therapy. Tellingly, though, in the Greek we find no mention whatsoever of the passions. The expression used is πυροῦσθαι (*pyrousthai*), or simply "burning," with its encompassing context more accurately rendered as "it is better to be in the married state than to burn."[13] The emphasis of this concluding verse is on being consumed or enslaved rather than drawing attention to the hypertrophy of any human faculty—in this case, the libido.

Having already observed stoicizing tendencies in various English translations of this passage, we find our criticism reinforced when noting translators' importation of another idea not present in the Greek, the notion of **self-control** (NRSV), which Thiselton correspondingly renders "power over their passions." Paul himself uses more mundane language, speaking only of those who οὐκ ἐγκρατεύονται (*ouk enkrateuontai*, "cannot keep abstinent"). This importation of a stoic rationale is one of the ways the tradition of reading the concession of 7:6 as allowing *marriage and sex* is shored up in the face of Paul's own interest in addressing the *limits of abstinence* from sex. The stoic reading, in effect, forces marriage to play the role of the fire department arriving to help those who cannot put out the fire of their passion with only the meager buckets of self-discipline at their

12. In the discussion that follows, our use of the language of "Paul the stoic" names a modern moral ideal rather than being a historical ascription. Today the moral ideal that goes with this label names someone who believes that their actions should be unaffected by anything they might feel. As we pointed out in our discussion of historical Gnosticism in 2:6–8, historical scholars remind us that much of the content of Paul's treatment of sexuality in this chapter does draw on ancient stoic thought, as well as that of their opponents, the cynics, though not in a manner that would suggest reading him as simply a representative of either of those ancient philosophies. See Deming, *Paul on Marriage and Celibacy*.

13. Barrett, CKB, 158.

disposal. Our reading, in contrast, assumes that it is not *marriage* as such that is the remedy for burning, but *chastity*. The fact that sexual chastity is livable for many only within the institution of marriage renders marriage not as a *means* by which the fire can be smothered but as a *medium* for a life liberated from enslavement to *porneia*. Paul offers us not a single hint that the institution of marriage works automatically, as if by walking the aisle we can, "abracadabra," end the burning. He offers instead a complex account of the liberation available in marriage growing from his more fundamental understanding of the call of Christians to nonproprietary ownership of their bodies.

The substitution of the language of self-control for Paul's objective and external notion of practical abstinence introduces a gradualist presumption that shapes in turn the reading of the passage as a whole. On the gradualist reading married people are those who were never really good enough at self-discipline and so have rightly chosen to confine their burning to one person who, it is hoped, will help domesticate its destructive effects through the pacifying routines of marriage.[14] Marriage, according to this understanding, does for the passionate what they cannot do for themselves in providing a systemic check on their runaway passions, though one that is intrinsically inferior to the discipline they might have otherwise been expected to muster. In this vein, the stoic reading implies both looking down on those who "need" recourse to married life and abandoning them to a life that is not a robustly *moral* life.

Abandoning instead this stoic account of marriage, as we think we must, we are free to understand Paul's notion of **burning** in a way that opens the theological horizon of the term already set out in 3:13. Although the imagery of burning is certainly open to a psychological reading that emphasizes the sense of being consumed, which comes with progressive indulgence in *porneia* (as in porn addiction), the image of destruction through fire, including the forensic association developed in chapter 3, is also within view. By describing as "burning" the life that is the antithesis to chastity, Paul brings the phenomenology of sin as entrapment and the horizon of divine judgment into his discussion of human sexuality. To take Paul's choice of wording seriously at this point is to wrest his reference to "burning" away from its familiar association with high libido by way of a reading in which "burning" is linked to the divine judgment of the works of believers (>3:13). This theological reading casts sexual sin as having a trans-individual nature that threatens the whole congregation through the burning judgment provoked by individuals within it. If individual Christians refuse to deal with

---

14. McCarthy, *Sex and Love in the Home*, ch. 2.

this burning, they risk setting fire to the church, as it were. It is better to marry, Paul suggests in 7:2, than to expose one's self and the body of Christ to the divine judgment that the reign of *porneia* invites. This is not to deny that the way this burning actually unfolds may be discussed in terms of being "consumed by passion." But the psychological account must be understood as a second-order resonance of the primary theological meaning, in which the emphasis falls on the *destruction* burning entails.

Excursus: Sex and the Apostle

Since we have managed to draw even a notion so obviously evocative of psychosomatic interpretations as "burning" into our political reading, the reader could be forgiven for asking whether we have indeed developed an overly unifying reading that does not do justice to divergent texts—so departing from our avowed adherence to Hans Ulrich's counsel that every word of scripture demands its own hermeneutic. We can only respond by testifying that it was only as we allowed the angular passages in the chapter to force us to rethink our initial assumptions, and by insisting on doing justice to the plain sense of the text, that we have been both compelled and enabled to liberate Paul from clichéd portrayals in which he appears to be a bad pedagogue, a cynical polemicist, or a stoic bore. Liberating Paul from such conventions has freed us to hear his apostolic voice with its genuine authority while at the same time becoming more aware of the exegetical and conceptual constraints and aporias of various readings that go with the clichés.

For example, a reading that bypasses the trap of a traditional "concession" interpretation allows Paul to appear surprisingly comfortable with human sexuality in commending, if not commanding, a healthy, fit, and regular sex life to married couples. After all, the Apostle happily exhorts married believers to engage more in sex than those romantics would admit who have taught us to look down on him as erotically obtuse. But more importantly, Paul's account of nonproprietary sex frees couples from treating the bedroom as a sphere of power play by liberating them from the idea that because they own their bodies, sexual relationships can only result from contractual negotiation between "consenting adults" who will naturally deploy what "assets" they have for maximum tactical advantage. Paul's portrayal allows Christian couples to understand sex as something quite different than an arena for the war of the sexes, and marriage as something more than a sheer *agon* in which only one can triumph, while the other is made subservient.

It is vital to read Paul's approach in this whole chapter against the backdrop of alternatives it rules out. If sex is not understood as Paul describes it—namely, as a duty, that which love "owes" to the spouse—the gate swings wide open to conceive of it as a mean to other ends. To do so is to force sex uncomfortably close to prostitution in being treated as a possession that must be traded for adequate payment, as those critics perceptively noted who saw conceptions of exchange and debt as built into the Kantian definition of marriage, framed as it is by conjugal rights. We only grasp the liberating force of Paul's portrayal when we grasp that as a whole it drives toward the affirmation of 7:15b: **It is to peace that God has called you.**

Even in the context of issues that we tend to group under the heading of "sexual ethics" Paul is summoning believers to no other *telos* than the one that is given to the life of the church as a whole, that is, to live as the body of reconciliation and peace (Eph 2). Patterns of sexual intimacy among Christian couples should bear witness to and draw from the power of this reconciling community. It is precisely the practice of chastity, the nonproprietary way of owning one's body and that of the spouse, that has the capacity to transform the war of the sexes into that **peace that God has called you** to. While we tend to think of sexual ethics as "personal" ethics and of "peace" as a political concept, Paul invokes precisely the language of peace to name the dynamic that drives out strife in the sexual realm. Rather than being imposed onto Paul's text, our political reading thus accounts for the fact that again at a pivotal moment in a discussion that seems to us not to demand it, in 7:15 Paul draws on the grammar of *oikodome* to give orientation to his approach to a material discussion.

But will this approach really go so far as to absolve Paul of the charge of reinforcing patriarchalism in this chapter? Does not the slogan with which the chapter opens, "It is good not to touch a woman," present a characteristically male perspective on sexuality? Perhaps. But a reading that goes down this track can only be sustained by overlooking Paul's implicit equalization of the male viewpoint by strongly valorizing its counterassertion, "It is equally good for a woman not to touch a man." The same pattern can be detected in Paul's description of divorce in 7:11, where he challenges the Jewish pattern, in which only men could divorce, by simply asserting that women are also capable of divorce. One way to keep Paul in the patriarchal box is to read his admission of the egalitarian nature of divorce as a concession to Hellenistic Christians for whom female divorce was possible. But in line with his earlier egalitarian inversion of the male gaze in 7:4, we prefer to read this as a principled shift. To do so is to discover that the Paul who has surprised us so many times thus far can again prove himself capable of breaking our stereotypes, in this case the all too familiar characterization of Paul as "the patriarchal misogynist."

Here again, to approach Paul as he comes to us in this text not simply as an author but as an apostle is to render his discussion of sexuality an address to our time and space as direct as it was to the Corinthians. If we are to find liberation from the dead ends and confusions of our lives today, it will only be as his texts are freed from *our* misreadings, which mask the way in which his gospel is for *us*. If we, as a generation, feel a characteristic set of frustrations, confusions, and constrictions in the Christian life, it is imperative to begin looking for the symptoms of our malaise by reconfiguring our instinctive perceptions that Paul is a boring stoic or an authoritarian prig, a maudlin teacher, and so forth. Reading Paul's summons as those of an apostle means understanding that the liberating insights that will emerge as we read can only occur as we let him break free of the stereotypical readings by which we habitually distance him from the circumstances of our lives.

The Place of Chastity

> [10]To the married I give this command—not I but the Lord—that the wife should not separate from her husband [11](but if she does separate, let her remain unmarried or else be reconciled to her husband), and that the husband should not divorce his wife.
>
> [12]To the rest I say—I and not the Lord—that if any believer has a wife who is an unbeliever, and she consents to live with him, he should not divorce her. [13]And if any woman has a husband who is an unbeliever, and he consents to live with her, she should not divorce him. [14]For the unbelieving husband is made holy through his wife, and the unbelieving wife is made holy through her husband. Otherwise, your children would be unclean, but as it is, they are holy. [15]But if the unbelieving partner separates, let it be so; in such a case the brother or sister is not bound. It is to peace that God has called you. [16]Wife, for all you know, you might save your husband. Husband, for all you know, you might save your wife.
>
> [17]However that may be, let each of you lead the life that the Lord has assigned, to which God called you. This is my rule in all the churches. [18]Was anyone at the time of his call already circumcised? Let him not seek to remove the marks of circumcision. Was anyone at the time of his call uncircumcised? Let him not seek circumcision. [19]Circumcision is nothing, and uncircumcision is nothing; but obeying the

> commandments of God is everything. ²⁰Let each of you remain in the condition in which you were called.
>
> ²¹Were you a slave when called? Do not be concerned about it. Even if you can gain your freedom, make use of your present condition now more than ever. ²²For whoever was called in the Lord as a slave is a freed person belonging to the Lord, just as whoever was free when called is a slave of Christ. ²³You were bought with a price; do not become slaves of human masters. ²⁴In whatever condition you were called, brothers and sisters, there remain with God.

Verse 10 is typically read to be demarcating a new topic in chapter 7, with verses 1–9 being understood to be concerned with sex, verses 10–16 with divorce and miscellaneous cases, before a concluding return to questions of sex in verses 25–40. Having abandoned the search for any thick theological coherence of the chapter as a whole, taking this approach makes it easy to imagine that Paul's discussion in 7:1–9 then turns to preempt the following reply: "You are commending sex and marriage, but what if my spouse fails to provide me with the sex I deserve? Does this not give me license to seek it somewhere else?" Clearly this is an untenable question in the light of the reading of 7:1–9 we have offered. Our reading thus continues by taking the ensuing discussion to be Paul's denial of divorce as a legitimate response to sexual problems in marriage, which he refutes as vigorously here as he refuted the solution of consorting with prostitutes in chapter 6.

For Paul neither sexual frustration nor religious differences count as viable occasions for divorce among Christians. By explicitly summoning couples to **stay where you were called** Paul even goes so far as to suggest that the hunt by a married person for a justification for divorce is itself already an escape strategy. On our reading the *cantus firmus* of this section remains the elaboration of the theme of chastity Paul opened at the end of chapter 6 and has continued to develop to this point in chapter 7. In Paul's account of human sexuality the various forms of *porneia*—whether going to a prostitute or marital rape—are all revealed to be variations on the strategy of running away, forms of flight from the task of owning our bodies in a theologically framed and socially engaged manner.

Our constructive reading of the long and complex arc of this next part of Paul's argument begins by picking out the terms and phrases he repeats, a repetition we take to be highlighting his core concerns for his readers. By coming to terms with these core emphases we can make better sense of the apparently haphazard collection of material topics on which the discussion in the remainder of the chapter touches. Notice first the sort of authority to which Paul appeals as he explicitly turns to address the married in Corinth: **I give this command—not I but the Lord** (7:10). This opening heightens the gravity of his ensuing instruction and is reiterated and intensified in 7:19b, where he insists that **obeying the commandments of God is everything**.

Such a formulation immediately provokes an interest in the content of the command Paul is so strongly emphasizing, and it seems that his answer is fairly direct in that a specific injunction punctuates the discussion no less than five times: **Let each of you remain in the condition in which you were called** (7:20; see 17, 18a, b, 22, 24). The rhetorical structure of this presentation parallels the one we saw in 1:10 in which Paul's central point, that the Corinthians seek unity, was reiterated by using four more explicit terms to indicate precisely the content of the unity he was enjoining. Paul does the same here in order to make his central emphasis clear, telling the Corinthians to stay put by repeating and slightly varying this one point.

His first deployment of the exhortation to remain emphasizes the relation of teaching with divine authority. By saying that this teaching **is my rule in all the churches** (7:17b) Paul presents himself as the vehicle of God's commandments. The other instances explain why this command is gospel and not law. **Remaining** where one was **called** is an opportunity not a curse, 7:21b indicates, so the believer can **make use of your present condition now more than ever**. A final, richly polyvalent formulation in 7:24 brings the discussion to its theological climax: **In whatever condition you were called, brothers and sisters, there** *remain with God*. To make proper use of one's marital condition, then, is to remain with God. But what could such an exhortation entail in the concrete? Here the common directive to chastity helps considerably in perceiving a clear set of internal relationships between what seems to be an odd collection of problems Paul addresses among the Corinthian Christians: the problem of the unbelieving spouse, the problem of circumcision, and the problem of living as a Christian slave.

Paul's exhortation to **remain in whatever condition in which you were called** raises the question for the hearer of what Paul means by one's "calling." Does he mean the various stations of life (marriage, celibacy, etc.) or does he have in mind the spiritual life that is to be pursued inside or outside of those stations? The formulation of 7:17 has become the primary lens through which Paul's language of calling has been interpreted in wide swathes of the Christian tradition, in which this question is answered in terms of stations or social strata of life: **let each of you lead the life that the Lord has assigned, to which God called you**. It is important to note, however, that the majority of Paul's references to "calling" are temporally qualified references—twice in 7:18, and repeated in 20, 22, and 24: **remain in whatever condition you** *were* **called**. This suggests that this passage is working with a notion of calling as a temporal interruption that reconfigures social space. "When God's call to become a Christian came," we overhear Paul say, "God also opened your eyes to the setting that is particularly yours for developing your specified calling, that is, the call to grow in chastity." The one universal Christian vocation to love is here being specified in concrete terms, as the Apostle winds through the different permutations of the presenting theme of this chapter—human sexual life.

It would be easy but mistaken to read Paul's appeal to "stay" or "remain" as a conservative reinscription of the social divisions of his day, as if he was baptizing social conservatism. The liberating and indeed socially fertile implication of his call to stay put is better understood as specifying in concrete detail that the pursuit of chastity is only begun in earnest when Christians refuse to flee the one form of existence that God has assigned to each as the respective occasion to learn and grow in chaste love.

Such a reading presumes that Paul's explicit interest here is not in defining and defending the institution of marriage per se as a divinely ordained vocation within the social sphere. Instead, his focus is on explicating in detail the promise of marriage as one of several locations to which divine providence may assign the believer in order that they might live out the one vocation of chaste love. Such an account of vocation may well come as a liberating word to those young or not so young Christian adults who obsess about ferreting out God's hidden answer to the question of whether or not they are called to marriage. This obsession often takes the unfortunate form of suspending the work of coming to terms with the setting in which they find themselves put and, ironically, in which the habits of chastity might be developed that would prepare them for marriage, should a willing and suitable partner come their way.

Paul concludes his series of repeated exhortations to "remain where God's call found you" with the clarification παρὰ Θεῷ (*para Theō*, **with God**. The preposition *para* has a rather wide semantic field allowing a variety of readings, each of which may express important facets of what Paul is setting out as the promise of "remaining." When believers embrace their place as the location given to them by God they remain "under God" (which is to obey his command) as well as "before God" (keeping his role as judge before them), and they linger "with God" (bathed in his grace).[15]

Addressing another exegetical crux takes us further into the question of how Paul's discussion here can be understood as explicating the responsibility of Christians to learn to own their bodies wherever the call of Christ reaches them. The exegetical question turns on what we make of Paul's

---

15. BDAG, 1210.

comment to Christian slaves, that **even if you can gain your freedom, make use of your present condition now more than ever**. Very few Christians through the centuries have read this verse to be a suggestion by Paul that slaves remain in their state to make use of it even when freedom is on offer.[16] Luther offers a strong version of the traditional Christian line, proposing that the drift of 7:22 (**For whoever was called in the Lord as a slave is a freed person belonging to the Lord, just as whoever was free when called is a slave of Christ**) makes the default presumption of Christians that slaves ought to be freed. Taking our cue from this reading, we offer a third reading of the invitation to **make use of your present condition now more than ever** that broadens its applicability by taking it to encompass all the situations discussed in this chapter—the Christian with the unbelieving spouse, the Christian who is uncircumcised and struggling with pressures to remedy this condition, and the Christian who is a slave. On our reading Paul has no interest in offering a general account of the permissibility of slavery or of circumcision among Christians. Rather, he presents slavery and circumcision as particularly telling contexts in which proprietary conflicts exist over Christians' bodies and therefore as the sorts of contested settings in which the one calling to chastity (as ownership of one's body) must be pursued. Such situations are particularly pregnant opportunities for Christians to discover the practical meanings of having nonproprietary ownership over their bodies.

Luther was on the right track, then, in moving to interpret 7:21b in light of verse 22, where Paul insists that wherever one is called, one belongs to the Lord. In the final analysis this theological conclusion rests on the Apostle's reiteration of the ontological supremacy of Jesus Christ as Lord presented in 7:23: **You were bought with a price; do not become slaves of human masters**. The invocation of the crucifixion and lordship of Christ impels Paul's refusal of bondage to any other lordship, whether to the unbelieving spouse, the representatives of religious traditions (circumcision), or slave owners.

The Apostle's central concern is to demonstrate what happens when believers, assuming they can be more effective in their Christian life by escaping from their given social contexts, are met with the claim that their quest is in fact a flight, an evasion of the imperative to grow in chastity. To flee from this imperative can only be into the "law" of *porneia*, the no-place of restless self-referential movement in which true belonging and ownership can never materialize. Recalling our discussion at the end of chapter 6, we see again Paul's hypersensitivity to the self-destructive paths humans follow

---

16. Swartley, *Slavery, Sabbath, War and Women*, ch. 1.

into spaces and realms where they will find no place to settle. He tirelessly commends the command of the God who directs his creatures to the social spaces he has given them as occasions to grow in chaste love. Paul's message is not that "everybody should be waiting to learn what is their assigned vocation." Rather, with his drumbeat emphasis on remaining *where God found you*, he aims to commend the kind of ownership of one's body that demands growth in discipline in the circumstances immediately at hand. Through such discipline Christians come to have substance as they are substantively connected to the bodies they already have and the social realm in which they already exist. Peace cannot be chased, but only discovered.

The opening mistake in reading 7:2 that we have seen to break the back of the chapter on the rock of an assumed either-or between marriage and celibacy naturally culminates, we would suggest, in the fetishization of calling. This is a fetishization, ironically, that makes people "burn." People are thus forced into burning not by the force of passion but in having continually to ask themselves whether or not they have passion that vouchsafes their vocation to marriage. Such a burning will have a double edge in that their over-occupation with this one question will make them literally burn time and the resources of the soul that could have been used to fuel the pursuit of love and self-ownership in the many forms it can take. The burning judgment that falls here is, hence, one on idolatry, not one on persons, stations of life (marriage), or a particular human faculty (passion). The tragedy of the restless preoccupation with the question "*What is my calling?*" lies in the fact that it tends to make those engaged in it rather lonely, in contrast to the immanent social dynamics of the pursuit of chastity that draws people out from the place they already inhabit.

The political reading we have been developing has alerted us to the remarkable fact that Paul displaces the question "Is this my calling?" with an exhortation to look around at what happens when you embrace within your particular social matrix a life of joyful, responsible ownership of your body in chastity. To that end, in 7:14 the Apostle points out that **the unbelieving husband is made holy through his wife, and the unbelieving wife is made holy through her husband**, and that by the same power the children **are holy**. Once again there is no hint here of a mystical diffusion of holiness. Instead, Paul is making a mundane extension of this argument to this point, that when a Christian lives in loving union with a nonbelieving spouse, the claim that Christ has on the Christian and the resonance of Christ's love in her life cannot leave the other spouse unaffected. The potential of this "preaching through life" allows Paul quite unselfconsciously to raise the hopes of his readers in 7:16: **Wife, for all you know, you might save your husband. Husband, for all you know, you might save your wife**. Chastity is not only a response to God's will or command but also provokes a response from others with whom Christians are in such close social contact.

This is not to suggest that 7:16 is easy to interpret, especially if "the net result of a century of critical endeavor has been to envelop this verse in ever greater obscurity."[17] Since the Reformation, in particular, for all the emphasis it put on justification through personal faith, we instinctively shy away from any suggestion that a human being (whether spouse or any other) can be the causal agent "saving" another human being. This leads one to suspect that Paul's claim that one spouse may be "made holy" through another is not pointing to salvation strictly but more modestly to a *sanctifying* influence that one person can have on the other. Jerome Murphy-O'Connor parallels our emphasis on chastity as a lived activity of faith by arguing that holiness in scripture is not an ontological bestowal, but "for Paul is essentially a dynamic concept," which demands of believers "a continuous effort of fidelity."[18] The pagan partner or child of the believer may not personally believe in Jesus Christ, but they may well pick up "a pattern of behavior that is analogous to the conduct expected of the *hagioi*."[19] Murphy-O'Connor is nicely attuned to the patterns of influence on spouses or children as exerted by the behavior of believers that were as likely to have been occurring in the early church as today. But is it an accurate reflection of Paul's line of thinking to conclude with Murphy-O'Connor that the believer is warranted in hoping that true saving faith will come into existence if a spouse or child adopts habits of behavior from a Christian? A trend in contemporary theology has been to answer this question increasingly in the affirmative, to the extent that the role of practices in the formation of Christian virtue has been understood to be the vector for the acquisition of Christian holiness.

Listening to Paul at this point might be aided by a distinction Luther once suggested that differentiates between *selig* (saved) and *heilig* (holy).[20] Both concepts describe the dynamics of the one faith, but while justification (*selig*) is a direct effect of the faith that saves through grace, in sanctification (*heilig*) faith works not immediately, the Reformer notes, but is mediated through those worldly stations such as marriage that concern Paul in this chapter. Luther helps us understand Paul better here since his way of distinguishing between justification and sanctification highlights the decisive role of faith in both processes. As he does so he also draws attention to the mediating role of elementary forms of creaturely life in sanctification, thus

17. Murphy-O'Connor, JMO, 43.
18. Ibid., 48.
19. Ibid., 49.
20. WA 26:505.20f; LW 37:365. See also Bayer, *Freedom in Response*, 112–13.

helping explain why Paul could be so unsurprised by a "rubbing off" of faith from one spouse to the other in and through marriage.

Acknowledging the sophistication in these attempts to maneuver round Paul's expressed hope for the spouse to be "saved" (as the Greek term σῴζω actually entails) by discussing the proximity of sanctifying faith to saving faith, we need not understand Paul as overstretching the matter, if we understand the practice of chaste love as one that naturally attracts others to the fullness of that form of life to which this particular conduct organically belongs. If chaste love is an authentic expression of the Christian faith, it is at the same time, and due to its provocative nature, an invitation into this same sanctifying love *and* saving faith. The crucial point at which Luther invites us to go beyond Murphy-O'Connor is in his awareness that the Greek language of *hagioi* is not merely moral language. Although phenomenological observation may indeed spot moments of influence describable in terms of patterns of conduct, the inseparability of justification and sanctification will mean that the adoption of moral patterns that we associate with Christian faith will eventually culminate in a full adoption of what underlies that conduct, that is, faith in Jesus Christ. If the spouse's behavior does not reach this terminus, the adopted patterns will eventually be rendered hollow simulacra of holiness. But the language of sanctifying (ἡγίασται/*hēgiastai*, "will be sanctified") is used nowhere in the New Testament in such a merely moral way. It would seem inconceivable for Paul to assume that someone could be holy but unsaved, as these two concepts describe two sides of the same coin.

Our theological resistance to interpretations that allow for a separation between holiness and salvation invites a deeper phenomenological reading. We can certainly imagine people becoming more and more sympathetic to the morals of Christian faith, adopting Christian habits in wider and deeper ways, but without the willingness yet to embrace the confessional aspects of the faith that underlie that conduct (one of the dynamics that has been described with the term "Christendom"). But the question one needs to ask here is whether being attracted to Christian conduct is not in fact always more than what it appears to be. Attraction is a multilayered phenomenon. We might feel ourselves attracted to, say, the looks of a particular person, but what do looks mean? How can we be sure that we are *simply* attracted to the outer layer of someone's physiognomy? "Looks" are always "outlooks," the way that a person "looks at you." Eyes are attractive not simply because they are a lovely shade of blue but because of the way those eyes are turned upon you, which promises a whole inner cosmos "behind blue eyes" (as put definitively by The Who) to explore, which is in fact the animating source of the attraction.

This deeper layer of attraction can in the final analysis only be an attraction to *what* someone does, not *how* they do it, which is why it is easy to imagine finding a supermodel genuinely unattractive. The warm way in which a spouse may receive a loving gesture that does not pressure the other, for instance, if it is to become more than a simple biological response, can only be so through the acknowledgment that it represents a *what*: chaste love. If one is attracted to the other's behavior for no other reason than that it makes one's own life better, this immediate reaction will never be transcended by the movement to discover the nature and the source of that conduct. In this way the "rubbing off" effect will fade into a mere acted semblance of Christian chastity.

On this account Paul might simply have expressed good confidence in the eventual salvation of children of a Christian parent, given the extent of influence parents have on their children. Instead, he uses strangely factual language: **now that they *are* holy**. Our theological account thus far allows no plausible explanation for this factual characterization of the holiness of children other than to assume that Paul is speaking here of children who, because born to a believing parent through the logic of the covenant,[21] are due baptism whether or not they have in fact been baptized.[22] A theological account must refuse any simple paralleling of the "rubbing off" effect of a spouse on their mate with the parents' effect on a child.[23]

In our view Paul seems to presuppose two distinct yet inseparable ways in which the inseparability of justification and sanctification can be presumed. One is through the influence of behavior, the other way is via baptism. The distance between the two is destined to shrink in size, however, the better we understand that baptism, even of infants, was understood not as a transition from one soteriological state to another, but emphatically as an induction into a new form of existence. As the rites of baptism develop in the first Christian centuries it becomes clear that baptism was seen as bestowing not merely a forensic claim but also a whole range of patterns of

---

21. Collins, RFC, 266-67.

22. Calvin, JC, 149-50.

23. Historical critics are continually tripped up at this point by their search for an ancient precursor operating at the level of a homogenous ontology of pollution. Deming is characteristic here: "If the children were holy by virtue of being baptized, then Paul could not prove from their holiness what he wants to prove, namely, that a Christian makes his or her unbelieving partner holy; and if the conceded point in Paul's argument was that baptism secured the holiness of children, it is difficult to see why this whole matter surfaced in the first place, for the believing spouse was also baptized and therefore should be in no more danger of pollution than the children" (*Paul on Marriage and Celibacy*, 131 n. 94). That which is "difficult to see" from a historical-critical perspective proves far more visible from a theological point of view.

perceiving the world and acting in it that made ancient interpreters speak of the "baptismal character."[24] Baptism is seen as extending into a lifelong practical lesson in receiving a new lordship. In a similar vein, in Romans 14:13 and Galatians 3:27 Paul emphasizes the sanctifying implications of baptism by using the metaphor of baptism as "putting on Christ."

Eastern baptismal rites are shaped to this day by the ritual calling down of the Spirit on specific body parts, even organs. What is asked for in prayer for these body parts has a palpable moral dimension in that the petitions seek the bestowal of specific spiritual gifts that will be needed for a life of Christian holiness. So the anointing by oil of the ears of the baptized is meant to render them good listeners, of the mouth to prevent lies, of the hands as organs of good works, and of the feet to make them fit for the pilgrimage to the eternal city. Such a baptism is an emplacement in the fullest sense, a resistance to whatever spheres of influence might otherwise determine the life of the human being in all of its particulars. Baptism is a placement of a human being inside that "chastened" love that marks a life as specifically Christian.

Granting such primacy to the baptismal transformation does not deny but includes a number of educational effects, from openness to the influence of patterns of conduct to the individual's induction by the community into the life-form of confession. In short, in baptism something is *given* that must also be *pursued*. Hence we find the same inseparability of justification and sanctification that grounds our account of the effectiveness of enacted witness. Following Paul's flow of argumentation we first saw this inseparability in terms of the connection that moral behavior has, perhaps imperceptibly, to its basis in justification. With the example of baptism we see the same emphasis from the other side, as an emphasis on sanctification understood as an objective change of soteriological status that must still come to have a moral extension.

Excursus: Theology and Phenomenology

Our criticism of Murphy-O'Connor has granted his phenomenological observation despite our final assessment of his reading at this point being less than genuinely theological. Having now clarified the reasons why a theological reading such as the one we propose best unifies the chapter (advanced, as it had to be, by way of an account of the relation between justification and sanctification), it is entirely appropriate to enter a discussion of the role of

---

24. Wannenwetsch, "Die ethische Dimension der Liturgie," especially the subsection "Leben aus der Taufe als Einübung in die 'Neue Schöpfung,'" 387–89.

phenomenological observation in theology free from the secret fear that we will undermine our theological claims by so doing. Quite to the contrary, we assume that diving deep into theological truth forces believers toward a more persistent phenomenological attentiveness. Such a stance draws the theologian into the vicinity of those strands of modern philosophy that resist the epistemological foreshortenings associated with both the regnant philosophical empiricism and its major rival, philosophical idealism.[25] Though as we have seen Paul does not offer a detailed explanation of how the "rubbing off" effect that he assumes to be happening might pass over from "mere" behavioral change to become real, vibrant faith, in the end he does not need to develop such an account in order to urge the Christian practice he is enjoining.[26] A more elaborate explanation would not directly advance his presentation of the theme that we have suggested to be the core of his interest: describing the ways in which kenotic social proximity and communication might be materially carried out as Christians seek to "know nothing" but the crucified Christ.

Our assumption that the unspoken moves in Paul's thought fully cohere with his explicit discussion offers the advantage of allowing us to learn how justifying faith might be understood as drawing us into deeper attention to the many layers and currents that characterize the existence of the whole mobile and diverse created realm. One effect of taking this approach is visible, we hope, in the form this commentary has taken. Our approach is "suggestive" in the sense of presenting insights that are not fully and definitively explored, however textually grounded and substantive the initiatives they provoke might be. Our interest is in a reading alert to openings that might be glimpsed between Paul's word choices and contemporary concerns to which, we discover, Paul may have something useful to say. Such a procedure must be distinguished from reading strategies that aim to "evoke associations" or "open dialogues." The openings that we glimpse are not just pointers to further worlds of discourse on which the text might have a bearing but windows that might be opened, paths that might be gone down. It is our conviction that these windows need to be present, as we read

---

25. "Empiricism cannot see that we need to know what we are looking for, otherwise we would not be looking for it, and intellectualism [Cartesian idealism] fails to see that we need to be ignorant of what we are looking for, or equally again we should not be searching. They are in agreement that neither can grasp consciousness *in the act of learning*." Merleau-Ponty, *Phenomenology of Perception*, 33; emphasis in original. See also Heidegger, *Phenomenology of Religious Life*, especially Part Three.

26. In this subsection we offer this elaboration of his position in general sympathy with how such processes are described in phenomenology. For example, Merleau-Ponty explores something like the "rubbing off" effect in his careful investigation of how mass movements can arise in *Phenomenology of Perception*, Part III.3.

the text, because a particular light that shines in from them is necessary for us to comprehend what is being said in 1 Corinthians.

In the course of our discussion of the "rubbing off" effect, the phenomenology of attraction seemed to us something that we needed to bring in to help us make sense of Paul. It is part of the particular calling of each generation to seek the influx of light from all sorts of debates that define our comprehension of any issue, whether the terms of these discourses are inherited or more genuinely created by our contemporaries. To affirm that scripture is a "light unto my path" (Ps 119:105) should not be taken as a denial that this light may illumine our current circumstances through a variety of windows. Neither does this suggest that the more light we get the better, and so every window in sight should be opened. This is the strategy of reader-response approaches in which it is assumed that scripture is an inert and dark text that only comes to life when people with different perspectives reflect back whatever they think they can see in it. The sort of biblical exegesis that we are proposing takes place in the midst of lived experience that is not afraid to listen both to scripture and to the most detailed observers of the creaturely realm. These observers, like us, are also affected by the subtle influences, dare we say the "rubbing off" effect, of being only able to think as creatures surrounded by the good gifts of their creator.[27]

Christian Discernment in Intensified Time

> [25] Now concerning virgins, I have no command of the Lord, but I give my opinion as one who by the Lord's mercy is trustworthy. [26] I think that, in view of the impending crisis, it is well for you to remain as you are. [27] Are you bound to a wife? Do not seek to be free. Are you free from a wife? Do not seek a wife. [28] But if you marry, you do not sin, and if a virgin marries, she does not sin. Yet those who marry will experience distress in this life, and I would spare you that. [29] I mean, brothers and sisters, the appointed time has grown short; from now on, let even those who have wives be as though they had none, [30] and those who mourn as though they were not mourning, and those who rejoice as though they were not rejoicing, and those who buy as though they had no possessions, [31] and those who deal with the world as though they

---

27. "It is through my relation to 'things' that I know myself; inner perception follows afterwards, and would not be possible had I not already made contact with my doubt in its very object." Merleau-Ponty, *Phenomenology of Perception*, 445.

had no dealings with it. For the present form of this world is passing away.

³²I want you to be free from anxieties. The unmarried man is anxious about the affairs of the Lord, how to please the Lord; ³³but the married man is anxious about the affairs of the world, how to please his wife, ³⁴and his interests are divided. And the unmarried woman and the virgin are anxious about the affairs of the Lord, so that they may be holy in body and spirit; but the married woman is anxious about the affairs of the world, how to please her husband. ³⁵I say this for your own benefit, not to put any restraint upon you, but to promote good order and unhindered devotion to the Lord.

³⁶If anyone thinks that he is not behaving properly toward his fiancée, if his passions are strong, and so it has to be, let him marry as he wishes; it is no sin. Let them marry. ³⁷But if someone stands firm in his resolve, being under no necessity but having his own desire under control, and has determined in his own mind to keep her as his fiancée, he will do well. ³⁸So then, he who marries his fiancée does well; and he who refrains from marriage will do better.

³⁹A wife is bound as long as her husband lives. But if the husband dies, she is free to marry anyone she wishes, only in the Lord. ⁴⁰But in my judgment she is more blessed if she remains as she is. And I think that I too have the Spirit of God.

In the section beginning with verse 25 Paul not only addresses a different practical question, the question of how best to deal with virgins, but also explicitly positions his comments as expressing a different *type* of authority as he treats the issue: **I have no command of the Lord, but I give my opinion**. But we will best understand the flow of the remainder of the chapter if we suspend for now the discussion of what sort of authority Paul is setting out with this introductory phrase that so markedly differs from the assertion that, to this point in the chapter, he is presenting the Lord's command. The best place to begin our investigation of this section is by looking at the role the imminence of the *parousia* plays in Paul's treatment in order to discern the relation of his enjoinder to **remain as you are** to the conditional claim **in view of the impending crisis** (7:26).

It seems clear that whatever we take the expression διὰ τὴν ἐνεστῶσαν ἀνάγκην (*dia tēn enestōsan anankēn*) to mean, it plays a crucial role in Paul's assessment of the various life situations he addresses and determines the tactics he will propose for how best to live in light of this "crisis." The NRSV rendering of 7:29, **the appointed time has grown short**, provides us with both a conundrum and its key. The majority of commentators understand this phrase along the lines of the NRSV as indicating that the world is "running out of time." Thiselton extends this temporal resonance with his translation "limits have been placed on the critical time." Although this explanation seems especially inviting to readers in the postindustrial West who have been thoroughly inculcated into the rule of *chronos*—standardized, measurable, and apportioned time—such a reading blatantly overlooks that in the Greek the word used for the time grown short is not χρόνος (*chronos*) but καιρὸς (*kairos*).

Whereas *chronos* names the experience of a flow of time that is always lost, *kairos* is time that can only be given. For the Greeks *kairos* was a mode of human participation in the time of the gods, and the Christian adaptation of this concept depicts *kairos* as the vestibule of the Creator's presence. Thiselton's rendering as "critical time" is therefore apposite in indicating what is at stake here: a sharing in God's presence, a presence that is inevitably a crisis for humans in that it literally "cuts into" human indifference. Understanding oneself as having been made a participant in kairotic time is therefore synonymous with having been invited to "take off the old and put on the new," or to "put on Christ," as Galatians 3:27 puts it.

The full expression in 7:29 is ὁ καιρὸς συνεσταλμένος ἐστίν (*ho kairos synestalmenos estin*), which, taken literally, suggests a compression of *kairos* ("the time having been shortened"). It is particularly striking that though *kairos* by definition indicates an intensified form of temporality, Paul uses an expression indicating a further intensification of *kairos*. As fallen creatures who cannot evade the claims that *chronos* makes on our lives, culminating as they do in death, our experience of time makes us imagine that even *kairos* must have a duration. This makes it all the more important to be mindful of the categorical difference Paul is signaling with his emphatic use of *kairos* language here. What the Apostle has to say about the best way for virgins to handle themselves is qualified by setting the discussion within the intensified time that is one of the characteristic New Testament descriptors of the kingdom of God (Mark 1:15).

Commenting on the pregnant expression of 7:29, the post-Christian philosopher Giorgio Agamben catches the challenge to current social configurations that this account of time presses on the church of our day:

> Just as messianic time transforms chronological time from within, rather than abolishing it, the messianic vocation, thanks to the hōs mē, the "as not," revokes every vocation, at once voids and transforms every vocation and every condition so as to free them for a new usage ("make use of it"). . . . Just as messianic time

is not some other time but, instead, an integral transformation of chronological time, an ultimate experience (an experience of the last things) would entail, first and foremost, experiencing penultimate things differently. In this context eschatology is nothing other than a transformation of the experience of the penultimate.... Paul expresses the messianic relation between final and penultimate things with the verb katargein, which does not mean "destroy" but, instead, "render inoperative." The ultimate reality deactivates, suspends and transforms, the penultimate ones—and yet, it is precisely, and above all, in these penultimate realities that an ultimate reality bears witness and is put to the test.[28]

Given the backdrop of this juxtaposition of *chronos* and *kairos*, and mindful of the Apostle's pointing to the passing away of the schemas of this life, we are now in a much better position to grasp the nature of the list of activities Paul characterizes with the conjunction **as if** in 7:29–31.

A straightforwardly chronological understanding of "running out of time," taken in the sense of a temporal resource that drains away, would inevitably engender an inadequate account of Paul's famous (and enigmatic) *hōs mē*, **as if**, logic. If we read this "as if" through the presumption of time as *chronos*, we will have to take Paul to be disparaging the time that remains, effectively if not explicitly demeaning the created order. On such a reading Paul would be understood as saying, "while doing X or Y, make sure that you don't *really* do X or Y: don't invest yourself in what you do, whether emotionally, sexually, economically, or politically." In contrast to this yet again stoicized Paul, the Paul we encounter in these passages is affirming of the stability and givenness of created orders. After all, without such an affirmation, what would be the value of the effort he has spent counseling those who live in these orders, paradigmatically that of marriage? If the shortness of time conceived as a limited chronological progression was the determinative factor for Paul's pastoral efforts, it would be difficult to explain why believers should invest in long-term commitments such as marriage or educating children, since such activities could never reach fruition.

Those schooled in the theological tradition of Luther's *Ständelehre* (doctrine of the estates/institutions) will find it hard to overlook an implicit reference to the elemental orders of created life in Paul's list of examples in 7:29–31, specifically the *oeconomia* and *politia*. Not only does Paul mention the trials of marriage in this compressed time (no surprise, given the topic of this chapter) but he also notes changes in activities taking place

---

28. Agamben, *Church and the Kingdom*, 18–19.

in the economic sphere of human existence (**buying**) and in the political realm (**dealing with the world**). It would be a mistake to read these hints at enduring features of divine institutions as representations of the schema of this world that Paul characterizes as passing away in 7:31. The fact that an emphasis on the creaturely life of the affections (**mourning** and **rejoicing**) is aligned with Paul's dealings with these institutions should provide ample warning not to conflate the institutions and the schemata that are passing away. After all, rejoicing will not cease when this passing world ceases but instead will remain the central, almost summative, characteristic of life in the eternal kingdom.

Having argued, then, that the awareness of the compressed *kairos* that Paul is advocating is not a marginalization of the claims that creaturely life makes on temporal existence, we must therefore recognize the way in which the Apostle is summoning the Corinthians to genuine engagement with the world. In other words, the *hos me* is to be interpreted as calling believers to fully engaged action *within* kairotic time, not a *semblance* of action in a chronological time that is almost over (which is why the "as if" rendering of *hos me* has tended to send commentators down the wrong interpretative tracks). What this passage amounts to is a call to action as the enactment of critical discernment.

Such discernment appropriately expresses an awareness that **the present form of this world is passing away** (7:31b). It is through acquiring discernment that true human action can begin to be enacted by those caught up in the σχῆμα (*schēma*) of the old aeon. A clear hint that the Apostle is to be read in this way can be discerned in his clarification that what is passing away is not *time* but the schema of this world: τὸ σχῆμα τοῦ κόσμου τούτου (*to schēma tou kosmou toutou*). This passing is expressed in the present tense (παράγει/*paragei*), not in the future tense ("will pass away") or in the aorist tense ("has begun to pass away"). The present-tense expression compels us to understand Paul's qualification as concerned with the *nature* of the schema of the world: the *schemata* of this aeon are not solid and enduring but are characterized by their ephemerality. One can be caught up in them, but this is to be trapped in something in which one can never exist in the full sense of the word. The schemes are "forever passing" (*paragei*), always in flux and incapable of providing rest. They are fractured space and time existing only in a dissipating sense.

The opposite of the space-time of the *schemata* is the *kairos*, which offers a dwelling for humans in its very compression and thereby opposes their dissolution in the schema of the world. Whereas the *schemata* diffuse and disperse human existence, breaking us into disarticulated fragments, *kairos* time marks the sequence of our being reconfigured, brought into a shape and so made whole. Being caught up in the schemes of the world is to be buffeted by endless and fruitless quests for a dwelling where there is none to be had. Because they have an acquisitive form, these schemes trap and hold human beings by offering a false hope that obscures their true nature as passing illusions, one of which Paul has already described in detail, *porneia* (>6:12-20). Our discussion above ("Excursus: Theology and Phenomenology") explains why we feel free to assume that Paul has a background theology of creation and the institutions in place. It seems highly unlikely that he is suggesting that the "passing" of the schemes of the age will take with it the fundamental creaturely necessities of marital, economic, and political existence (7:29-31). On the contrary, creation names that which is revealed in *kairos* time as capable of actually being had or done, precisely in place of and opposition to what is only virtual or hypothetical. In sum, Paul is here summoning the faithful into a mode of existence that does not conform to the schemata of the age, just as he does in his famous caveat in Romans 12:2: μὴ συσχηματίζεσθε (*mē syschēmatizesthe*): "Do not be conformed to the schemata of this age."

Having clarified the basic framework that situates this section, we are prepared now to deal in more detail with the various activities Paul characterizes under the kairotic logic of *hos me*.[29] It seems best to begin with the one example in which the finite form of the verb sets it apart from the participle construction that precedes the other examples: **those who buy as though they had no possessions**. Thiselton's translation of μὴ καταχρώμενοι (*mē katachrōmenoi*) as "not hold possessions" is helpful in drawing attention to the difference between a taking and appropriately using, on the one hand, and a more acquisitive and proprietary interest in securing and retaining of something purchased, on the other. We take Paul's emphasis on the categorical difference between the two modes of dealing with the goods of the world (buying vs. possessing) to indicate the grammar underlying his understanding of the other examples. This rendering rests not only on the one linguistic observation just discussed, but on the fact that such a reading meshes well with our account of the way in which the *schemata* of the world are best understood as expressions of a proprietary attitude characterizing those who remain trapped in their reign.

In keeping with this grammar, we can then paraphrase what Paul says about emotional patterns (**mourning** and **rejoicing**) by taking mourning as our example: "Mourn, but only those things that creatures mourn, not as if absorbed into it, following it into despair, as if the future had been

---

29. The following sections draw on exegetical insights first developed in Wannenwetsch, *Die Freiheit der Ehe*, 240-52.

extinguished." In being alert to the compressed *kairos*, such mourning knows that the parameters of this affective expression are oriented by an awaiting of the coming of the Lord, whose presence is sought rather than feared. This type of waiting does not allow itself to slide into the despair and escalating desperation that accompany the view of human action as taking place within an ever-shortening span of available time.

As we turn to consider how Paul develops these themes in relation to the issue that has been his target of practical concern (the married life), we must first recall that the participial construction that introduces this example (as it does every other, with the exception of "buying") compels a reading that understands his central interest to be the *form* of action instead of a *state* of affairs. In so doing he takes up the prophetic assumption that the day of the Lord supervenes on the normal course of life, including even the celebration of weddings and births (Joel 2:16; see Luke 23:29; Rev 18:21–23).

Those who have wives are therefore not simply "the married ones" but the married ones insofar as they really practice a mode of *having* one another as *spouses*. This is to rule out not only an Encratite-type reading ("even though you unfortunately happen to be married, act as though you are functionally single") but also "Josephite" readings ("even though you are married, don't enact it in physical consummation"). While "having" wives should certainly be understood in the full sense of marital life, including its sexual aspects, the main clue that must be noted here is that, as in all the other examples, Paul is again giving *moral* counsel, treating what the believers are summoned to *do*. This suggests that the formulation here is a kind of shorthand expression for the more elaborate theology of chastity we detected running through the chapter as a whole, which is to say: "own each other as spouses as though you were not possessors but must repeatedly receive one another as gifts in light of the upheaval the proximity of the Lord is bringing about."

We should attend next to the three positive statements Paul uses to explain his pastoral reason for introducing the *kairos* discussion. He wishes to let the Corinthians in on what he considers a universal truth: **those who marry will experience distress in this life**, and given this view, he offers a solicitous pastoral comment, **and I would spare you that** (7:28b). In the context of his discussion of marriage, his overarching point is to express his hope that the Corinthians might be **free from anxieties** (32a), a comment he offers **for your own benefit, not to put any restraint upon you, but to promote good order and unhindered devotion to the Lord** (35).

The phrase in 7:34, **and his interests are divided**, presents us with a text-critical problem. Two textual witnesses exist, including one that proposes a quite different interpretive trajectory by suggesting that marriage *compromises* the loyalty of the spouses to the one Lord. The other tradition allows a much stronger positive reading of marriage as a *way in which* to love the Lord. This textual witness must be the preferred one, as it is in harmony with Paul's overarching interest in promoting **good order and unhindered devotion to the Lord,** which he considers both the married and the celibate to be in the position to pursue. If Paul were now to suggest that marriage is inferior to the single life in diluting one's devotion to the Lord, he would, in effect, be undermining his earlier discussion.

How we characterize Paul's claim that the **married one is anxious … to please** will also be critical in shaping our reading of his moral advice in this section. The Greek term ἀρέσκειν (*areskein*, "to please") has a juridical overtone in classical Greek and implies an obligation on the part of spouses to uphold certain responsibilities associated with the married state of life. This overtone should help caution us against a surface understanding of "pleasing" such as the one Aquinas assumes in interpreting the passage:

> A woman's apparel may incite men to lust, according to Prov. 7:10, "Behold a woman meeteth him in harlot's attire, prepared to deceive souls." Nevertheless a woman may use means to please her husband, lest through despising her he fall into adultery. Hence it is written (1 Cor 7:34) that the woman "that is married thinketh on the things of the world …"[30]

It is safe to assume that Aquinas's judgment here is colored by his adherence to the Augustinian account of sexual desire, in which the notion of *concession* is key, and also to the distinction, adopted from Greek philosophy, between the life of contemplation (*vita contemplativa*) and the active life (*vita activa*). Within this distinction as it had come to be imported into the *corpus Christianum*, the contemplative life of the religious was understood as the higher calling, whereas the active life to which marriage (which included the whole sphere of the *oikos*) belonged was seen as a lower, "common" vocation, as it represented the sphere of following the "commandments" merely as opposed to the (higher) "counsels."

As we have noted before, this tradition of thought sits, as a whole, uneasily with the grain of Paul's theology as a whole. The Apostle is certainly aware of different legitimate ways to live the Christian life, as displayed in the difference between married and unmarried states of life, but the account he develops of these differences develops at a practical rather than an ontological level. In ontological terms the Apostle has presented all legitimate

---

30. Aquinas, ST II–II.169.2.

stations of Christian life as being of equal value, and Christians are therefore free to prefer one vocation over the other, precisely for practical reasons that depend on individual discernment.

If, on the other hand, we prefer to read the passage by following the lead of the (in our view inferior) textual version of the "divided" passage (7:34), and assume a bifurcation between the active and contemplative life as of a lower to a higher calling, then marriage must be defined as a life of divided loyalty almost inevitably inferior to the wholeness and completeness only the contemplative life can afford. On this reading a concessionary ethic will follow that seeks to be continually reconfirmed by readings like that which Aquinas offers, first finding a concession to marriage because of lust, and then extending it with the concession of allowing a husband's demand that his wife "tart up."

Were we to succumb to the temptation held out to us from the first verse of this chapter to understand marriage as an intrinsically compromised state, we would be forced continually to explain why a spouse's sexual delight must be understood as some variant of vain self-indulgence. For Aquinas any attention by a spouse to the sexual aspects of the marital partner must be a sin. It therefore cannot be affirmed, but only allowed as a venial sin. That Paul can imagine a very different way in which "to please" comes out in Romans 15:2, where he uses the language of pleasing in the context of *oikodome*: "Each of us must please our neighbor for the good purpose of building up." With the grain of Paul's overall account of chaste love, as we have seen him develop in the last two chapters, it is altogether plausible to understand the vocation of married lives of believers as a distinct part of that building up of the body of Christ, which presupposes a far wider account of "pleasing that special neighbor" that is your spouse than a narrow discussion of "attire" could bring into view.

Grasping the pastoral nature and purpose of Paul's discussion in 7:25–40 will be decisive if we do not wish to misconceive the degree of authority Paul expects this passage to exert. It is all too easy to begin by observing that the whole long passage, right through to the end of the chapter, is framed by Paul's explicit announcement of a more modest claim than we typically associate with an apostolic injunction. This might tempt us to ignore the reality that not everything he presents in this passage is mere opinion or tentative suggestion. On the contrary, Paul speaks here from firm convictions, and because he does he can be correspondingly certain no authoritative pronouncement is necessary for important questions of individual vocation. He is as clear about the necessity that Christians live into the *kairos* as he is about the need for Christians to be weaned off the ephemeral schemes of the world. Having previously demonstrated the principled equality of the various vocations in which chaste love is to be lived out, Paul can now, on the basis of these certainties, allow scope for individual and local church communities to deliberate about the best possible tactics for Christians responding to these certainties in light of the specific contexts in which they live. Paul's central interest is in setting out what is nonnegotiable for Christians and in showing how these nonnegotiables situate their true freedom of judgment and discernment.

Having seen Paul unambiguously stating his beliefs about the ontological reality of the times and conveying them through pastoral solicitude for his readers, we are now prepared to see why he intentionally takes a step back from his pastoral authority in the opening and closing verses of this section: **Now concerning virgins, I have no command of the Lord, but I give my opinion as one who by the Lord's mercy is trustworthy** (25); and **in my judgment she is more blessed if she remains as she is. And I think that I too have the Spirit of God** (40).

These opening and closing statements are easily read in either a weaker or stronger sense than Paul gives them. We might read them as gentle self-deprecating indications that Paul does not have the capacity or necessary information to make recommendations to specific Corinthian believers on how they should approach particular decisions about marital status. On the other hand, we might take them to be covert commands that are in reality an iron fist in a velvet verbal glove. Our reading takes neither of these routes. We argue, rather, that Paul's affirmation that his apostolic authority simply does not extend as far as the responsibility to dictate life decisions of individual believers flows directly out of the clarity of his theological insight into the state of the times.

It is precisely because Paul's apostolic speech offers the Corinthian community a clear theological vision of the ultimate context of their action that he can make way for their own deliberation and discernment. He thus proffers general opinions ("better to remain") alongside reminders that these questions are ones that individuals and couples must discern within the particular limits and opportunities in the community. While not utterly "indifferent," these matters are only of ultimate significance insofar as they require distinctive appraisals through the discernment of faith. Paul wishes all Christians to grasp that all legitimate states of life remain nothing more than settings within which the one calling to chastity must be continually embraced. With that vocation clearly discerned, **Let him marry as he wishes; it is no sin ... she is free to marry anyone she wishes, only in the Lord** (7:36b, 39b).

In contrast to readings that presume *chronos* as the basic frame of reference and that lead into dismissals of the contemporary authority of this passage on the basis of the historical judgment that Paul was wrong in his expectation of the imminent *parousia*,[31] a reading that presumes the ongoing theological importance of *kairos* in this passage will also expect the attitude to which Paul summons the Corinthians to be one that is valid for every new generation of Christians. We resist Thiselton's translation "limits have been placed on the critical time" (7:29),[32] because every generation of Christians must be seen to inhabit the critical time. An appropriate alertness to *kairos* that is necessary for all Christians is evaded when we overlook the structural point that, according to Paul, it is the *schemata of the world* that are fading away, not time as understood on a dwindling chronological scale. The critical force Paul sees the *kairos* to continually exert has the effect of foregrounding the perennial importance of Christian discernment. Christians cannot evade the continual need to discern between those places where creatures can find a genuinely hospitable place to dwell and those socio-spatial configurations of their existence, whether in stoic or libertarian guise, that will only ever be conducive to an endless state of flight.

We conclude by returning to the point from which we began. Our initial discussion of the *porneia*-chastity polarity can now be understood as clarifying the schemata-institutions polarity. To invest oneself in the pursuit of *porneia* is to be claimed for the passing schemes of the age. Conversely, to pursue chastity is to own one's creaturely constitution and so to belong in a divinely delimited context in which human life and relationship can truly flourish. Discernment in the realm of human sexuality—whether of the difference between *porneia* and chastity or of what is concretely entailed in the flight from *porneia* to chastity—provides a model of the larger movement from the schemata of this age into habitable creaturely life as revealed by the integrative force of *kairos* time. In any sphere of human existence, owning without possession can only genuinely occur through dwelling "in" the *kairos* as it interrupts the entrapment in acquisitive proprietorship that a merely chronological existence prescribes.

---

31. As Hays surprisingly does (RBH, 133).
32. Thiselton, ACT, 114.

1 Corinthians 8

Conscience: Self-Knowledge as Loving Social Knowledge

> ¹Now concerning food sacrificed to idols: we know that "all of us possess knowledge." Knowledge puffs up, but love builds up. ²Anyone who claims to know something does not yet have the necessary knowledge; ³but anyone who loves God is known by him.

It is commonly assumed that Paul turns to address another distinct ethical case in chapter 8—the problem of food offered to idols. While there must have been a previous letter in which the Corinthians pressed him to respond to a question they experienced as highly controversial and that once again threatened to open a rift in their community, a close reading of Paul's argument will reveal that his key concern is not to settle the question of whether "to eat or not to eat."

We will enter the flow of his argument in this chapter by taking up the term Paul highlights in the pointed conclusion of the chapter, **conscience: when you thus sin against members of your family, and wound their *conscience* when it is weak, you sin against Christ** (8:12). If there are hence good reasons to understand the chapter as a whole as organized around this concept of conscience (which also appears in verses 7 and 10), we should be wary of smoothly reading into Paul our modern conception of conscience, conceived, as it is, as the human faculty responsible for generating moral judgments.

A more fruitful approach begins by attending to the linguistic components present in the Greek term most often translated "conscience": συνείδησις (*syneidēsis*). Both this Greek concept and its Latin translation, *conscientia* (the root of the English term "conscience"), describe a form of knowledge in which the one who has that knowledge holds it "together with" (Gk. συν-, Lat. *con*-) something else. As we read Paul, then, we need to operate within a root account of conscience denoting a *form of knowledge* as opposed to a *faculty* of the human mind. The decisive question to which we will hope to find an answer in this chapter concerns what it is that accompanies this form of knowledge. In other words, how is the *syn-* or *con-* element in that knowledge to be understood? What *sort* of knowledge is it that Paul assumes is needed among the Corinthians if they are to resolve their rift over the appropriate Christian behavior as regards eating food offered to idols?

A viable working definition would understand conscience as a concomitant form of knowing who we are and therefore what is due for us when we act as human beings. Here we use the somewhat awkward language of "due" in a manner that will take on a semi-technical meaning in the following discussion, and denotes that which is genuinely fitting for humans. That which is fitting is owed in responsibility not only to others, but to one's self. Within the orbit of such a definition, conscience is then describable as a form of self-knowledge located within the teleology of human agency, its being directed towards "ends" that need to be grasped in human agency in order for it to be sound. It is within this tradition of understanding conscience as a form of located self-knowledge that the modern account of conscience as levying moral judgments emerged and became dominant. This later account pictures conscience as a sort of judge in our head that accompanies actions by either remaining silent or announcing condemnations. Reading Paul's deployment of the concept in this chapter without this particular bias, however, suggests that this way of tying the *syn-* or *con-* element to the self significantly narrows the scope of meaning available in this usage. The flow of Paul's treatment in this chapter makes it difficult, if not impossible, to ignore his more social understanding of conscience as a mode of knowing one's self *together with* others, rather than in isolated moral interiority.

Returning to the first verse of the chapter, it is apparent that Paul understands the Corinthian dispute about eating food offered to idols as resting on an underlying clash between two rival forms of knowledge: one type of knowledge that **puffs up**, and another that **builds up**. Paul does not explicitly deploy the language of conscience to characterize the knowledge that builds up. But he does develop a sequence of characterizations of its negative counterpart, the weak conscience, and in a manner that invites us to pay special attention to the asymmetry in his treatment. Given contemporary understandings of conscience, it is remarkable that Paul never even hints at a concern with the "healthy conscience." Instead, he directs the attention of his readers away from the respective *state of conscience* (good, healthy, bad, unhealthy) to what the action it shapes *effects in others*. What is missing in the (self-)knowledge that puffs up is precisely the awareness of what this type of knowledge does to other "con-sciences." Hence our suggestion that this chapter is best read as a discussion of two rival forms of self-knowledge: one that does know all things through the focal point of knowing the self, and another that might truly be termed "*con-scientia*," as it describes a way of knowing the self "together with others," and vice versa.[1]

Paul clarifies the differences between the two types of knowledge by making a number of fresh starts in this section, some of which are more obvious than others (such as the puffing up/building up polarity). Verse 2 draws attention to claims **to know something** (ἐγνωκέναι τι/*egnōkenai ti*), claims that Paul sets in contrast to **the necessary knowledge** (δεῖ γνῶναι/ *dei gnōnai*). Philological details allow us to describe this second contrast in structural terms. The perfect tense form in which the Greek renders the participial form "knowing" indicates an achieved, acquired, or possessed type of knowing that relates the knower to its respective objects as to a "something" (Gk. τι). Such knowing could be said to draw in bits of information in an isolated and objectifying fashion, because it is disengaged from any attempt to know one's self or interact with other people in the world.[2]

Having been alerted to the subtle way in which Paul characterizes this isolated and isolating form of knowing prepares us also to grasp an important nuance in his rendering of the rival to this knowledge as **the necessary knowledge**. The structural significance of the contrast indicated here is underplayed if we assume a simple part-to-whole relationship between the two terms. The Greek *dei* does not so much denote necessity but what is specifically required in relation to each agent. This would suggest the translation "does not have the knowledge due to him or her." Within the Greek logic *of dei*, which can also refer to standards of decency, the knowledge that individuals "ought" to have cannot be abstracted from the specific characteristics of a person and his or her respective role in society. Augustine famously deployed this sort of rationale in the course of a discussion on Christian participation in warfare. Even though everyone knows what war is in general, the knowledge due a soldier of what is entailed in a given war with respect to, say, its legitimacy differs substantially from the knowledge due his general. The difference in associated forms of knowledge has the moral consequence that the soldier and the general have varying degrees of responsibility in its prosecution.[3]

What type of knowledge, then, is due the Christians Paul is addressing? We are provided with a clear answer to this question in verse 3, but not

---

1. We will use the artificial spelling "con-science" throughout this chapter as a reminder that we are speaking of Paul's usage of conscience as an active knowing-with rather than the modern conception of knowledge as an anthropological faculty.

2. Barrett well captures both the acquisitive and isolating aspects of this knowledge with his translation "some piece of knowledge" (CKB, 190).

3. Augustine, *Reply to Faustus the Manichaean (Contra Faustum [Manichaeum])*, XXII.75.

without raising an associated set of new questions. This short verse has two widely attested textual variants, either of which answers our question in a theologically plausible fashion, and both of which are mutually illuminating. The one and possibly earlier variant is "if anyone loves, he or she has experienced true knowing" (Thiselton's translation), the other being **anyone who loves God is known by him**.

In the first variant we hear Paul saying *in nuce* what he has elaborated in more detail in Philippians 1:9: "that your love may overflow more and more with knowledge and full insight to help you to determine what is best." In both formulations love is seen as the matrix of knowledge, the grammatical subject that overflows in knowledge. This entails that love itself is characterized as a way of knowing that can and should be abundant. Love is in no way blind, as the cliché avers, but awakens agents to recognize and embrace reality as it actually exists.

The second variant, echoing another famous Pauline passage, "then I will know fully, even as I have been known" (1 Cor 13:12b), by no means supplants the first variant's connection of love and knowledge but goes some way in clarifying the theological basis on which the first variant implicitly operates. The "required knowledge" that love is capable of generating is knowledge that comes from first being known. It is a "capacity" that is itself received in relation rather than being self-generated. This leads to the question of what we humans apprehend in the state of being "known by God." Beyond mutual acquaintanceship, when God "knows" someone, that person is pulled into a salvific relationship. With this formulation we understand Paul, like other writers in the New Testament, to be working within the Old Testament concept of זכר (*zkr*), which denotes God's "remembering," specifically of his covenant (Ps 105:8; Luke 1:72). Such divine remembering is as effective as God's word, which does what it says. When God, for instance, is said to "remember" Noah, what is denoted is a concrete rescue from the flood for him and his family and the animals with them (Gen 8:1).

The efficient power of divine knowing or remembering (to rescue or save creatures by God turning his countenance to them) is crucial to keep in mind even as it raises the question of how we are to understand "being known" by God as those who are necessarily *inside* the experience of being a human recipient of this knowing. If raising this question is taken as tantamount to a demand for a psychological explanation, a variety of such explanations may well be suitable as long as it remains clear that such inquiries are driven by a theological interest in investigating how God's ways with his people fully incorporate the materiality of the human condition.

To be known by God means to be liberated from that fear which drives people into the vain enterprise of trying to make themselves known to God.

To know that we are known by God, given a name by which God calls us, rules out all desperate attempts to create a name for ourselves by seeking existential experiences or forms of self-display that would elevate us over our fellow creatures. This Augustinian twist suggests a reading of the longer textual variant as at least implicitly addressing what might stand in the way of, or might even be perverted into, a form of acquisitiveness toward that "loving knowing" which the shorter variant calls forth. After all, to *know something lovingly* is different than *loving to know something or someone*.

Knowing Nonexistent Gods?

> ⁴Hence, as to the eating of food offered to idols, we know that "no idol in the world really exists," and that "there is no God but one." ⁵Indeed, even though there may be so-called gods in heaven or on earth—as in fact there are many gods and many lords— ⁶yet for us there is one God, the Father, from whom are all things and for whom we exist, and one Lord, Jesus Christ, through whom are all things and through whom we exist.
> ⁷It is not everyone, however, who has this knowledge. Since some have become so accustomed to idols until now, they still think of the food they eat as food offered to an idol; and their conscience, being weak, is defiled.

Having laid out the contrast between two forms of knowing, Paul is now in the position to deploy it to unravel the knot the Corinthians have put before him: the problem of food offered to idols. He introduces this discussion by paraphrasing the statement of 8:1, **Now concerning food sacrificed to idols: we know that "all of us possess knowledge."** He further specifies the content of this puffed-up knowledge in relation to what Paul himself also affirms: **"no idol in the world really exists,"** and **"there is no God but one"** (8:4). Although the content of this knowledge seems to be straightforward and indisputably Christian, Paul is soon to unsettle the Corinthians' certainties on this score. He does so by pursuing a sequential train of thought from verse 4 to verse 6 that requires a particularly sensitive reading if we are not to end up understanding the Apostle to contradict himself from one sentence to the next. The potentially troubling aspect of this discussion lies in the rather different ways in which the question of the "existence" of idols is handled.

What has been flatly denied in 8:4 (**no idol in the world really exists**) seems to be contrastively affirmed in the subsequent verse, **in fact there**

are many gods and many lords. The way in which the two sentences are connected by the Greek conjunctive particles *kai gar* (as rendered "indeed" or "for indeed" in most English translations) rules out any attempt to understand 8:5 as Paul's refutation of the earlier slogans. We must hence find a way to read 8:5 as an interpretative qualification of what is affirmed in agreement with the Corinthians in 8:4, and which is then further theologically clarified in the subsequent verse.

On the question of the existence of idols, it is worth initially observing that in the "profane" Greek, εἴδωλον (*eidōlon*) refers to "shadow images of the dead."[4] This definition points to a lack of reality behind the appearance of the idol that helps explain the appearance of a common Judeo-Christian polemic in 8:4—because there is no God but one, no other god in the world really exists. The second slogan must therefore be understood as the foundation of the first. The notorious tendency of the Greek language to have sentences without verbs, in a manner that many other languages cannot, bequeaths us, once again, a dilemma that is more than a mere problem of translation. A literal rendering of the Greek expression in 8:4 would be "we know that no idol in the world" and that "no God except the one." A translator's natural instinct will be to fill out the space for both missing verbs with the one concept of *existence*. But by doing so, an interpretative pathway is opened that will easily undermine our capacity to understand the consistency in Paul's argument. Rather than filling the grammatical gaps in either case with a univocal concept of "existence," we are better served by attending to a crucial difference in the way in which this concept can be applied to God, on the one hand, who is "being" rather than an instance falling under this rubric, and the "gods," on the other hand, whose "shadowy" existence is of an eternally different kind.

It is only with the force of this comparison in mind between the forms of "existence" of God and of idols that we can understand Paul not to be contradicting himself in 8:5 when he speaks as though idols, who have been just said to not exist, do have a real existence. Here Paul uses a verb that lays a particular emphasis on their specific mode of existence as **so-called gods**. Quite obviously, Paul does understand these gods and lords to be real efficient causes in the world: these so-called gods are more than mere projections of the subjective consciousness of humans. This is why we cannot commend the tendency to smoothly harmonize 8:5 with verse 4 by way of translations such as Thiselton's: "For even if there really exist, for the sake of argument, so-called gods . . ." The error here is to conflate the qualification that idols exist *for those* who worship them, or are at least tempted to

---

4. Rienecker, *Sprachlicher Schlüssel zum Griechischen Neuen Testament*, 369.

worship them, with a relativization of their existence in the world. While it is true that their reality is not of the same *type* as the reality of the triune Creator of all things, this is not the same as saying they are simply nonexistent. All creation has a genuine existence of its own, which differs in kind from the existence of the One who created all things.[5]

The particular dialectics that allows us to say that idols do not exist, and yet exist, was captured in a particularly illuminating fashion by Luther. His observation (frequently attributed to but in fact adopted by Calvin) that the human heart is an idol factory takes into account Paul's characterization of those gods that exist as "so-called" gods. But it further explicates Paul's point by indicating that these gods are really called into being by those who call upon them by putting their hope and trust in them. "That now, I say, upon which you set your heart and put your trust is properly your God."[6] Luther's account is quite obviously informed by Old Testament depictions of the idols, such as the ridiculing of foreign deities as mute and deaf clay figures in Psalms 115:5 and 135:15–18, as "those who have mouths but do not speak, have eyes but do not see, and have ears but do not hear." The interesting twist observable in these passages is that the potential arrogance of the monotheist over the pagan or Gentile idol worshipper is characteristically undermined by the admission of a type of formative power they attribute to those mute beings. Idols are said to be effective in conforming their worshippers to their own image, making those who worship them, too, end up as "ones who have ears but cannot hear": "those who make them will be like them" (>13:1).

Augustine conceptually articulated this idol-generating capacity in terms of the conflation of *uti* (use) and *frui* (enjoyment) characteristic of fallen humanity. Those who have slipped from merely using the things of the world into making created things direct objects of their love end up

---

5. And, we must not forget, this "existence inversion" was already set out in 1:29. "God chose the ignoble things of the world [*agenē*, *ignobilia*, says the Vulgate] and the contemptible things, and also the non-beings, in order to annul the beings (*kai ta mē onta, hina ta omta katargēsē*)—in order that no flesh should glorify itself before God." Marion, *God Without Being*, 89.

6. "What is it to have a god? What is God? Answer: A god is that to which we look for all good and in which we find refuge in every time of need. To have a god is nothing else than to trust and believe him with our whole heart. As I have often said, the trust and faith of the heart alone make both God and an idol. If your faith and trust are right, then your God is the true God. On the other hand, if your trust is false and wrong, then you have not the true God. For these two belong together, faith and God. That to which your heart clings and entrusts itself is, I say, really your God." Luther, *Large Catechism*, 365.

conforming to these objects in a manner best described as a form of servitude.[7] In this chapter Paul's central concern is to respond to those believers who are frustrated by the servitude of other believers who still reside in the sphere of influence that exists for those habituated to idol worship: **Since some have become so accustomed to idols until now, they still think of the food they eat as food offered to an idol.** Paul needs to explain how this servitude is carried or maintained, especially in the case of those whose confession of Christ entails confessing liberation from the power of the gods over human life. The core problem of the chapter, then, is once again not the presenting problem of eating food offered to idols, but the root dilemma that drives it, one that remains live in the church today: how are Christians to negotiate life with other Christians when some do not feel and live out that which they confess, while others look down on them, presuming themselves to be more "advanced" in faith?

When Paul speaks of those whose habituation **until now** (or "up to the present") has been to idol worship, it may seem he is using rather sloppy language. He is not, after all, speaking to those outside the Christian body but to believers who have turned to Christ and adopted corresponding new patterns of life. But it is precisely because Paul is addressing *Christians* that the problem of habituation and the associated questions of conscience it raises become acute. There are those who have indeed received Christ and come to adopt the correct dogma ("one God") but who are still lacking knowledge of the type that we described earlier as *con-scientia*. In other words, their "knowing" of the Christian *doctrina* has not fully permeated every aspect of their lives, including the emotional and aesthetic affinities, due to their longstanding habituation in the old life.[8] The new life and the new knowledge that represents it has not yet become the daily "companion" (συν-είδησις/*syn-eidēsis*) that is characteristic of the knowledge that Paul says is due (δεῖ/*dei*).

There is a risk here that we will slip into another typology of graded knowledge, as happened in the Christian accounts of *gnosis* in the third and fourth centuries that embraced the idea (classically defended by Origen) of there being different classes of Christian knowledge and maturity. Paul, too, is employing notions of gradual growth in knowledge and clearly presumes

---

7. Augustine, *On Christian Teaching*, I.3–40.

8. This problematic was a core concern of the Reformation: "This distinction [between faith in God and in our own works] is easy to speak of; but in experience and practice it is the most difficult of all, even if you exercise and practice it diligently. For in the hour of death or in other conflicts of conscience these two kinds of righteousness come together more closely than you would wish or ask." Luther, *Lectures on Galatians Chapters 1–4* (1535), in LW 26:10.

there to be those who deploy their knowledge in the role of spiritual parents, but the thrust of this whole chapter is again directed against the reification of these observations into types or classes among Christians. Paul never refers to those who cause the weak to fall as "the strong ones," which we read as a refusal to ontologize different states of knowledge. It is precisely the Corinthian aspiration to such a classifying schema that Paul is refusing.

With the caveat **It is not everyone, however, who has this knowledge**, Paul cannot, therefore, be referring to a class of have-nots who could be contrasted with another class possessing the required knowledge. This point is reinforced if we pay attention to the Greek expression that circumvents the language of possession refused in 8:2, instead turning the subject of the sentence around literally to read "this knowledge is not in everyone." Given the force of this wording we must conclude that the majority of translations that employ the language of having or possessing (NRSV, Thiselton, Barrett) are obscuring the decisive structural distinction here. Even the sort of knowledge that might be claimed as a possession (the one that "puffs up") is not really one that one can genuinely "have," as Paul reveals that those who claim to possess such knowledge are in fact the ones who are being possessed—caught up in a nexus of pretentious claims that rob them of their true agency. The delusionary character of such knowledge will become more obvious as the chapter progresses, but to call such knowledge presumptuous is to insist that any knowledge that really matters inevitably lays claims on those who claim to possess it. Thiselton seems to grasp this aspect well, at least in relation to one type of knowledge, when he renders 8:7b as "Some are still gripped by the idol." In the light of our discussion to this point it strikes us as not implausible to render the first two phrases of 8:7 symmetrically, thus yielding: "not everyone is possessed by this new knowledge that is due, for some are still possessed by the knowledge that is of the idol."

In 8:6 Paul introduces what biblical scholarship has identified as an older liturgical formula, most likely related to baptism. He links this verse with the previous verses through the contrastive conjunction ἀλλα (*alla*, "but"). Noticing the parallelism of members employed here as typical of poetic language might suggest that Paul's addition to the traditional material is ἀλλ' ἡμῖν (*all' hēmin*, "**yet for us**"). If this "for us" is introducing a contrast, it invites us to read the preceding verse as a general statement about the religious proclivities of human beings. This is to read 8:4–6 as an argumentative sequence that begins with the common doctrinal formula **there is no God but one** (8:4) and moves into an elaboration of how this affirmation is worked out in light of the confusing and overlapping claims of the many lords of the world. It is the confession that first reveals what the oneness of God means for all human beings (8:5) and then what it means for those who are liberated from the cacophonic liturgies of the world (8:6) to which the *homo religiosus* is otherwise inescapably subjected.

Paul seems to make reference to the traditional acclamation because it offers him a way of describing the reality of the Christian life as an ongoing process of liberation **through him**. With this move he insists that the process of liberation from the grip of the idols cannot be accomplished through any ready-made formula, including quoting the right doctrinal formula. None of these will produce the knowledge that is due. It is the agency of the **one Lord, Jesus Christ, through whom are all things and through whom we exist** that propels the process of bringing believers into conformity to the image of the New Adam by wresting them away from trust and reliance on the rival images offered by the idols of this world.

What is striking about the Apostle's deployment of this liturgical acclamation is how he uses it to shift attention away from the dilemma assumed in the Corinthians' debates about eating idol food—the question of the *existence* of God and the *existence* of idols. The new emphasis, resting on his account of the difference between the two types of knowledge, focuses on the problem of *our* existence, framed by the traditional formula's direction of attention to the figure *through whom* **we exist**. The trinity of prepositions in 8:6—**from whom, for whom,** and **through whom**—turns out to be more than a formulaic trinity, since raising the theme of our existence through Christ points beyond the role of the second person of the Trinity as mediator of creation toward the inclusion of the Spirit's work in mediating the new existence of the believer in Christ.

This Trinitarian expansion of the earlier discussion about the knowledge appropriate to the Christian invites comprehension of why Paul's use of the liturgical formula has to be termed "existential," in the fullest sense of the expression. As genuinely human beings, as creatures of **the Father, from whom are all things and for whom we exist**, we can know the things of the world truly only through the confession that we are claimed by their existence as creatures of the same Father. Everything we know is existential because we cannot distance ourselves from the objects of our knowledge as unrelated items "out there" in the world. In short, the claim **to know something** (8:2)—isolated or objectified bits of data—is an impossible one to make in the Christian faith.

The upshot of this recognition is aptly expressed in the climactic ending of the acclamation that our knowledge of everything is to be rooted in a form of knowing ourselves precisely as those who exist of him and for him. With this affirmation the acclamation can emerge in its genuine Trinitarian roundedness: the knowledge due the Christian is to know oneself only and precisely as "emplaced," redeemed, and conformed: as placed in the creation of the Father, as redeemed through the Son, and as being conformed to him in our lived existence by the reconciling activity of the Spirit. By contrast, the claim to know "something" is tantamount to confessing that we know something we do not love and cannot situate in the existing economies of relationship among persons human and divine.

Those who worry about the tendency in modern Christian theology to reduce claims about God to claims about human religion may well be concerned about the emphasis we have found in Paul on the existential character of knowledge. We share the concern that various modern theologies have converted Luther's existential theology of the Word into a Schleiermacherian existential theology of faith or even a philosophical existentialism that does without reference to God altogether. But Paul's formulation suggests that we take this worry one step too far when we try to meet this problem by denying any role for human self-knowledge in Christian theology and faith. The critical question is rather what form such knowing of the self might appropriately take, what status we ascribe it, and for what purpose we claim it. Any answer to these questions that Christian theology might undertake must not fail to take a close listening to what Paul has to say on the importance and vulnerability of human con-science in his attempt to help the Corinthians cut through the Gordian knot of the idol food problem.

As Paul has indicated in 8:7b that the problem of the weak conscience is a matter of the continuing force of habit and the dissonant feelings when confronted with certain practices, the passive construction of the expression **and their conscience, being weak, is defiled** throws open the question of agency: who is actually responsible for defiling such consciences? What Paul has already said is that there are two agents involved in this process of defilement—the one who eats in bad conscience, and the idol with its power to draw the worshipper into its own image. Now the Apostle is gently opening up his final theme by hinting that there may be a third agent involved in such defilement—the fellow Christian. To alert this third party that they might be involved in defiling the consciences of their fellow brothers and sisters, he engages the slogans by which they are defining their relation to the weaker consciences in question.

Appetite for Destruction

> [8]"Food will not bring us close to God." We are no worse off if we do not eat, and no better off if we do. [9]But take care that this liberty of yours does not somehow become a stumbling

block to the weak. ¹⁰For if others see you, who possess knowledge, eating in the temple of an idol, might they not, since their conscience is weak, be encouraged to the point of eating food sacrificed to idols? ¹¹So by your knowledge those weak believers for whom Christ died are destroyed. ¹²But when you thus sin against members of your family, and wound their conscience when it is weak, you sin against Christ. ¹³Therefore, if food is a cause of their falling, I will never eat meat, so that I may not cause one of them to fall.

"Food will not bring us close to God." We are no worse off if we do not eat, and no better off if we do. Scholars debate whether the second phrase is Paul's *response* to the first indisputable slogan, or if it is *part of* a longer slogan Paul is quoting. The Apostle appears to be in agreement with both slogans, as long as we keep the focus entirely on the physicality of the meat. Nothing about its materiality poses an immediate threat and in that sense Paul certainly agrees that food is not soteriologically relevant, as it might be imagined to be in so-called primitive religious ideas about the ingestion of hidden particles that, like maggots, eat people from within. Having already confessed the goodness of creation in 8:6 it would be absurd for him to agree that meat itself could be the source of the problem associated with idol food. The problem, somehow, is *eating*. This line of reasoning leads us to side with the minority of interpreters who, against the translators of the NRSV, read this whole verse and not just the first sentence as a Corinthian slogan.⁹

Eating is inevitably a communicative act that, at least in principle, concerns a human-object relation to the food being ingested but in practice always entails a relation to other people, from cooking for or serving others up to full table fellowship. Foreshadowing his approach to this topic in chapter 10, where the Apostle emphasizes the *koinonia* that table fellowship sets up either with demons or with the Lord, in the present context Paul refutes the Corinthian slogan by reference to the social aspect of human eating. It is the *individualistic* framing of both sentences in 8:8 that hints that Paul would understand both slogans to contradict his central emphasis: what is relevant in this situation is not the individual's relation to God or to items of food in isolation, but primarily the Christian's relation to other believers. The Apostle's response, then, must begin not in 8:8b, but in verse 9: **But take care that this liberty of yours does not somehow become a stumbling block to the weak.**

---

9. Murphy-O'Connor, JMO, ch. 7, "Food and Spiritual Gifts in 1 Corinthians 8:8."

With this response Paul is not simply refuting the Corinthians' slogans but showing them why it is impossible to carry these slogans out in lived human existence. Their own eating idol food is not unselfconscious, but is in fact a statement about their liberty that in their minds elevates them over those who cannot eat with the same sense of detachment. Any one of them might well have overcome any thought of the idolatrous associations of the food for themselves, but as they have been liberated from that idol, their liberated eating has in fact but replaced it by assuming their progress in the Christian life to be a statement of superior freedom. And by making such a statement they in fact quite directly confront their fellow believers. It is this social signification that is Paul's prime concern: **But take care that this liberty of yours does not somehow become a stumbling block to the weak** (8:9). The NRSV renders as "liberty" the Greek ἐξουσία (*exousia*), which is more appropriately translated as "power," "might," or, as Barrett sensibly suggests, "authority." The same word is used, for example, to characterize the peculiar force of Jesus's own proclamation (Matt 7:29). The term "authority" always indicates a relational form of power, not a power simply to make something happen but the power to make something happen that affects someone else, typically through moving him or her in the direction of what the bearer of authority intends. This is the authority the self-proclaimed strong ones exercise as they eat, whether they acknowledge it or not. It is because this exercise of power is already at work that Paul can speak of their power to somehow **become a stumbling block to the weak**. The attempt made by the "strong ones" to deny the full scope of their *exousia* therefore amounts to a strategy to deny the responsibility toward others associated with all human action, and in particular within the community of believers (>6:13–17).

What is remarkable about this opening rebuttal is the gentleness with which Paul is inviting his interlocutors into his argument: "You have authority (*exousia*), and you exercise it before those you think of as weak—let us assume this is correct and proceed." His approach is to grant their ideas about maturity and liberty rather than sweeping them away because, once again, he will use their own ideas to make his constructive case once he inverts them. "Granting your terms," we might paraphrase, "reconsider those you think of as weak. Does your behavior, your authority to display your freedom from food rules, not invite others to emulate you even though they have some habituated discomfort about doing what you are doing?" Progressively, the Apostle's rhetoric grows more dramatic: **by your knowledge those weak believers for whom Christ died are destroyed** (8:11), and even more sharply: **when you thus sin against members of your family, and wound their conscience when it is weak, you sin against Christ** (8:12).

Thus Paul moves on to expose the true nature of their moral stance as an unwitting denial of their actual authority and moral agency.

In 8:10 Paul presents his readers with a concrete scenario (either drawing on actual reports of happenings in Corinth or setting out an exemplary situation) in order to demonstrate how the liberty/authority of the self-proclaimed strong ones actually works to cause those with weaker consciences to stumble. Paul's formulation is not intended to resolve the question of eating or not eating but to expose the forces of rivalry, display, and superiority at work in this situation—the Corinthians' anti-*oikodomic* enactment of beliefs that are on the surface completely unobjectionable.

Taking up their question about whether to eat idol food or not, Paul uses their question as an occasion to show them how their lack of love turns true statements about the one God and the ephemerality of idols into falsehoods through performatively situating them within the contradictory statement that their practice of eating loudly proclaims. In order to render the effects on other members of the body most visible, the Apostle chooses as his example a rather acute scenario that might arise in this contested realm. **For if others see you, who possess knowledge, eating in the temple of an idol, might they not, since their conscience is weak, be encouraged to the point of eating food sacrificed to idols?**

Statements made by authority *provoke* certain types of responses. For this reason the NRSV's translation **be encouraged** is too mild. The stronger affective and negative tenor of Luther's *verleitet*, "tempt," better grasps the effect of the so-called strong on weaker consciences. Tellingly, the Greek expression οἰκοδομηθήσεται (*oikodomēthēsetai*) is derived from the same root as Paul's key concept of upbuilding. Thiselton's suggested translation therefore seems most perceptive in characterizing the effect of the exercise of authority by the self-proclaimed strong as a perverted form of *oikodome*: "Suppose someone sees you . . . will the insecure person's self-awareness not be 'built' into eating meat sacrificed to the actual idol?"[10]

Because eating in a public place is one such provocation, we are entitled to imagine two likely responses from those characterized as having a weaker conscience. One type of response of the weak to the provocation of the so-called strong is to accuse them of solidifying false teaching to build a misshapen and hollow shell of a church. Such a church only apparently stands firm but is fatally flawed in its construction (>3:10–15). Somehow the strong are seducing those with weak consciences to move toward a form of flawed and unstable knowledge rather than the aforementioned "due knowledge." A different type of response that might be provoked when the

---

10. Thiselton, ACT, 132–33.

strong ones flaunt their freedom might be their angry denunciation by the weaker reactionaries: "*Real* Christians would never do such things. We don't do idol food, smoke, drink, or go with girls that do."

Paul does not discuss this latter possible response here but concentrates on the emulative scenario in which the self-proclaimed strong ones shape the behavior of those with weak consciences by drawing them into their practice of eating idol meat. In theory one might wish to understand such sharing as a mark of growth in those of formerly weak of conscience. They would, one could imagine, happily embrace the behavior and convictions of those who are mature and with theological accuracy now also confess that since there are no idols in the world, they have no problem of eating meat offered on the altars of idols. Yet such a pedagogical reading is barred by the sharp verdict of 8:11: **by your knowledge those weak believers ... are destroyed**. It is therefore obvious that Paul thinks of the invitation that the performative statement of the self-proclaimed strong issues as a temptation rather than an occasion for fostering genuine maturity in the weak.

How then are we to understand the dramatic nature of Paul's verdict as expressed in the stark language of destruction? We might imagine a kind of double effect at work here. On one hand, the authoritative display of liberty by the self-proclaimed strong ones shames the weak by exposing them in their weakness. This "shaming of the weak" would sharply contrast with the emphasis Paul has laid in his proclamation on the "shaming of the strong" (1:27). On the other hand, attention has been drawn to the danger that those with a weaker conscience might be seduced by a mere semblance of maturity, instilling in them a desire to emulate those with apparently superior knowledge.[11] But such emulation of behavior and speech without the necessary development of the affective and sensitive powers cannot be an enactment of the truth of their doctrinal confession. The weak are thus pushed into a schizophrenic situation, a mere simulacrum of the deeper and more integrated Christian life and confession Paul so deeply desires for them.

Paul's treatment suggests that a more appropriate response to those who cannot yet live in what they confess begins by appreciating them for who they are. This is not to celebrate weakness and so deny the need for further maturation but to patiently respect the unique state of growth of each fellow believer. Paul is drawing attention to the strong ones' denial of this pastoral sense of timing. He warns not only against making the weak pretend they are strong but also against any consignment of the weak and strong to unalterable classes by which some who have made some genuine

---

11. Girard, *Scapegoat*, ch. 3.

progress will be tempted to a pride that can effect the destruction of the whole.

The language of "conviction" usefully captures these considerations. A conviction is a confessed belief that has permeated our skin and bones—less like a coat we can change at will but something that has become an integral part of us. The "destruction" that Paul has in view becomes more intelligible if described in terms of the self-confessed strong ones tempting the weak of conscience to act on adopted opinion rather than from embodied conviction, thus mutilating their own integrity. This explains why Paul resorts to the strongest possible language when describing the effect that the strong ones' forceful "pedagogy" has on the weak. The Greek ἀπόλλυται *(apollytai)* is more appropriately translated as "perishing." From its other uses in the New Testament, we know that the term can well assume soteriological overtones. It strikes us as legitimate therefore to infer that Paul's concern is not only with the psychological harm that might occur when people are made to act against their conscience; his concern is also with the ways their misguided mimetic desire will eventually push them into a nonintegrated Christian life lived as an empty ideology, a nexus of ideas that only need be adopted rather than enacted as expressions of genuine conviction. These considerations explain why we understand the real threat being warned against in this chapter to be the fostering of any Christianity that bypasses the patience required to facilitate Spirit-led conformation to Christ over time. What is so destructive in what the "strong ones" hold out for emulation is the invitation to jump the queue of this Christo-formation of the whole life of faith, neglecting its affective and habitual facets.

Our understanding of the dynamics of conviction draws on work by contemporary authors McClendon and Smith.[12] But an analogous point could be made by drawing on the famous triplet in which the Reformers distinguished between *notitia* (cognitive knowledge), *assensus* (assent), and *fiducia* (existential trust) in order to indicate the essential aspects of the Christian faith. This triad is not only intended to describe the unity of faith. The existential trust by which the heart clings to God typically involves and expresses a degree of knowledge of doctrinal truths as well as cognitive and emotional assent to them. Even though this doctrinal distinction seems not to be directly applicable to Paul's concerns, we might still find it a helpful hermeneutic tool in understanding the full thrust of the Apostle's argument, especially its insistence that a genuine Christian life cannot be reduced to an expression of anything less than all three aspects of faith.

---

12. McClendon and Smith, *Convictions: Defusing Religious Relativism.*

As Paul has made it clear to the Corinthians in this chapter, it is not enough for faith to express a merely cognitive knowledge and assent to central aspects of the doctrinal tradition, a lesson he applies to both parties: the strong ones are summoned to abstain from any behavior that could invite the weaker ones to adopt a less than fully integrated pattern of faith. This would apply if they were taking up a practice of eating idol food that might be in line with what they understand is true (*notitia*) and with what they therefore might wish to comply (*assensus*), but which they cannot yet bring into line with their economy of trust (*fiducia*), shaped as it still is by their memories of past participation in the cult of idols which they associate with the meat. For the strong ones, on the other hand, their firm standing in the sphere of *notitia* (correct understanding of the goodness of all created things) leads them to an overconfident demonstration of *assensus*, underplaying the horizontal dimension that *fiducia* entails, thereby revealing the inaccuracy even of their self-styled *notitia*. Put more simply, the strong ones are effectively enacting a correct claim about creation, but in a manner that reveals their unawareness of its intrinsic linkage to the doctrine of reconciliation—for the God who creates all things good cannot be rightly served by thwarting the work of that same God to bring humanity into the reconciled peace that is the church.

Now that Paul has made his own views clear, there cannot be any doubt left that his quotation of the Corinthians' slogans is a subtle rebuke. These slogans, if followed, would fend off Paul's exhortations to *con-science* by keeping the discussion at a supposedly higher level of discourse and refusing to engage the plane of human interaction within which theologically crucial activity is happening—a syndrome we have seen before: "How can physical matters ever effect the spiritual?" (>6:13–17). Paul's retort refuses to heed the Corinthians' desire to keep the discussion on the plane of a higher-level general question, insisting that the primary issue is to **not somehow become a stumbling block to the weak.**

Notice that Paul does not grant the so-called strong any real strength in relation to the standard of the gospel. The Apostle demonstrates that the strength that they are demonstrating has no real congruence with the strength of the Spirit. The Corinthians thus fall not just a little short of the power that they legitimately possess, but are expressing the wrong type of power entirely, a power opposed to that of the cross, which is displayed in weakness (1:23—2:16). The Corinthians who think of themselves as strong on the basis of the maturity of their beliefs are therefore far from being genuinely mature Christians. Genuinely mature believers should be presumed to exercise a type of authority in the church that truly builds up rather than "building" others into a pseudo-Christian ideology of detached individual strength.

In 8:11 Paul not only explicitly states his verdict about the catastrophic nature of the affliction being visited on the weak but eventually also clarifies the question of agency that he opened up in 8:7. The Apostle has not really been interested in resolving the "eat or not eat" question here, because his main concern is to make as clear as possible that it is not merely the *behavior* of the self-proclaimed strong that tempts the weak into disintegration, but is more specifically the *knowledge* they are exhibiting that works destruction. Once again the Greek construction provides the crucial clue. Literally translated, the verse begins by stating that "it perishes the weak," a passive/neutral construction echoing the formulation in 8:7 that opened up the question about who should be understood as the agent of destruction. It is almost as if Paul invites the reader to pause and ponder the question that he then answers in the completion of the phrase ἐν τῇ σῇ γνώσει (*en tē sē gnōsei*, **in your knowledge**). Paul is now quite direct in stating that it is the self-proclaimed strong ones who, through the very knowledge in which they take pride, are the ones who affect the weak of conscience in the most exploitative way.

Another point Paul is communicating with this message is that the *mode* of knowledge possessed by those he is addressing (ἔχοντα γνῶσιν/ *echonta gnōsin*, **you who possess knowledge**) is inevitably affecting others. Even the correct doctrinal propositions, such as "there is no God but one," are never simply true but are only true in fact when verified in a specific type of *con-science*. They can thus be falsified by being presented in the isolated form of mere ideology. Because knowledge always mobilizes its holder, as indicated by the alternative of building up or puffing up, the different forms of knowledge will be either building up the Christian *koinonia* or puffing up individual members, amounting to a sort of anti-*oikodome*.

The menace of the wrong mode of knowledge is indicated by Paul's rather unexpected use of prepositions. The weak brothers and sisters are afflicted not as we might expect, *through* (διά/*dia*) the display of isolated knowledge, but literally *in* (ἐν/*en*) such knowledge. In other words, this mode of knowledge is not only instrumental, a mere means for destruction, but destroys by drawing others into its very sphere. To be affected in this way by a particular knowledge is to be drawn into a sphere of all the things that this knowledge does with you and to you, an effect reaching far beyond the simple conveyance of opinions or ideas from one person to another.[13]

13. See Paul's discussion in Romans 12:1–2 of the schematizing power of the eon that is challenged only by a transformation of the νοῦς (*nous*), the organizing center of both cognitive and affective human perception.

The self-designated strong are therefore not offering a genuine alternative to worshipping the idols; their isolated and isolating knowledge destroys the weak because its appeal is structurally identical to the pull of the idols as one that forcefully draws in and makes dumb at the same time.

Paul's diagnosis and warning has now emerged in its full severity, yet without quenching hope. By demonstrating to the Corinthians the destructive nature of their *gnosis*—its effects on the weak—Paul reveals something to them that the strong could not have understood otherwise. Only as their imagination has been drawn into the workings of someone else's weakness could those who think themselves strong be helped to discover their own potently destructive weakness so dangerously hidden from themselves. Reading Paul in this way suggests that 8:12 is a reminder of the empathetic connection that is Christ's body, a connectedness that the Corinthians' "pedagogy" of enticing the weak to emulate the strong in their pride came close to denying. This is why the Apostle has to expressly point out the intertwined fates of those who think of themselves in terms of weakness and strength. The expression **when you thus sin against members of your family . . . you sin against Christ** not only reminds them of the fact that the reality of Christ's body implies offending the head whenever one member is offended; it also points, on behalf of the body, to the fact that the things they do to one member of the body put their own membership in the body simultaneously at stake.

Finally, and most strikingly, Paul ends this discussion by calling attention to his personal willingness to repudiate the premises that drive the whole debate. In so doing he sets the self-confessed strong before a stark alternative, saying, **if food is a cause of their falling, I will never eat meat** (8:13). Paul is not claiming that "since some have fallen by seeing others eat meat I will give it up" but is setting out a point-for-point negation of the display of freedom practiced by the self-confessed strong. Whereas the strong pride themselves on a knowledge of God that makes no structural reference to the church, Paul reiterates his opening emphasis on the building up of knowledge in love (8:1) by here highlighting the contrast between his commitment to giving up his own "rights" for the community's sake with the so-called strength that can only be had in the display of freedom at the community's cost. Paul's knowledge of what is "due" on his part to the body of Christ (8:2) is thus constituted in his attachment to its members. His way of knowing his own self is through his having been bound by Christ to the wellbeing of others.

This last point echoes the temptations of modern readers, who, like the Corinthians, are often prone to judge the worth of their leaders' works according to the form of their labor, and not according to its actual value as a work built on the one foundation (>3:10–11). In this sense, food could be seen as a placeholder for any activity. Paul's interest is not in making a general rule to "stay away from anything that someone has a taboo about." He is here teaching Christians to become aware of the sort of knowledge of Jesus Christ that Christian behavior proffers to others.[14] **When you thus sin against members of your family, and wound their conscience when it is weak, you sin against Christ** (8:12). Paul makes it clear that the behavior of the strong faction is not an expression of their true authority but a display of counterfit freedom, a statement that they are compelled to make by the ideology that possesses them rather than a free act. True freedom would be prepared to refrain from not only the doing of something, but also from any need to display the licitness of doing it.

A memorable moment in the 2000 American presidential campaign provides an example of actions by well-known figures that display the mechanics of what Paul has called the wounding of weak consciences. In the Saddleback Church presidential debate, moderated by the pastor Rick Warren, John McCain sat before a supposedly Christian audience and unambiguously stated that he would be pro-life in all circumstances, to rapturous applause. But what was he actually affirming? Was he suggesting that he would support the criminalization of abortion? Was he suggesting the revocation of all federal funding of embryo research? Or what?

By suggesting these questions need not be asked and therefore only paying lip service to the claim that Christians are pro-life, McCain pushed others who also confess themselves to be pro-life into a position of not understanding what is being confessed. Those whose understanding of a pro-life position is tied to fear of the consequences of legalized abortion are encouraged to dismiss as beyond the pale all those who might be prepared to discuss whether it might be morally or legally permissible in certain circumstances. McCain thus encouraged a regression among believers into holding a pro-life confession not as a fully rounded and embodied theological belief, but as a *taboo*. An alternate response to such a statement would be to join in the denunciations of abortion advocates but without the true freedom that understands what is being rejected in the pro-life confession. This would be the regression of false and empty *assurance*. Both ways of holding a pro-life position remain solid and closed to discussion because they refuse to ask serious questions about what it means in real terms to confess Jesus's love for every mother, every new born, every orphan and widow.

---

14. Our treatment has also been influenced by the highly influential recovery of this insight by George Lindbeck, who illustrated it by analyzing what is being said when the crusader cries "Jesus as Lord!" as he cleaves the head of the infidel. Lindbeck, *Nature of Doctrine*, 64.

By inviting Christians to live their faith as an empty conceptual confession that abandons the quest for intellectual knowledge and existential engagement, McCain (inadvertently perhaps) illustrated why Paul's concerns remain important today. Christians must not resolve the moral and religious dissonances other believers experience by avoiding the middle stages of understanding in which their confession of Jesus Christ must come to have substance in lived existence. To do so is to display a disdain for building any genuine unity of purpose among the body of believers, a disdain that is in effect a repudiation of any such unity.

What are we to make in the final analysis of the fact that Paul not only refuses to validate the self-styled strong as actually strong, but also forgoes proposing any counter-habituation to "strengthen out" the weak consciences by freeing them from those fearful bonds that keep them tied to practices linked to idolatry? No picture is offered by the Apostle of a genuinely strong or healthy conscience, but only of consciences weak or wounded by their habituation in idol worship. Why does he not demand that they develop practices that foster a healthy and strong conscience?

This question is especially pressing given the recent renaissance of Christian virtue ethics, with the prominent role it gives to habituation in the Christian life. Would Paul admit the idea that one could be habituated in the knowledge due to Christians in the way in which one can be habituated into idol worship? Given the flow of this chapter's discussion, it would seem attractive to speak of *con-science* as the Christian alternative to *gnosis*. *Con-science* would then demarcate that socially alert self-awareness that is Paul's antidote to the isolated and objectifying nature of a knowledge in which others are "destroyed."

Paul's peculiar construction of knowing as being known by God (8:2–3) insinuates that there is a structural difference between the two modes of arrival at the respective types of knowledge. The observations that arise in the course of his discussion are intellectually liberating. On the one hand, we see the Apostle being well aware of the power of *habit* to "in-form" the conscience; on the other hand, his account of habit is more circumscribed than is typically presumed in current versions of virtue ethics. Yes, habituation matters, we hear the Apostle say; but the processes of Christian maturation are not reducible to a matter of formation by habits (as an outside-in movement). In a manner that is both disturbing and liberating these processes rely on a fine-tuned *culture* of "con-science" in which the inside-out trajectory is accorded a critical role: the practice of knowing oneself *with* the other, a bold locating of the integrity of one's life in the outside of the other's conscience as the form of living that is due in kairotic time.

1 Corinthians 9

Paul the "Light Traveler"?

Chapter 9 seems to invite a particularly straightforward reading and few obvious interpretative difficulties. Paul is defending his apostolate by pointing to the many sacrifices he has willingly made in its course and invites his readers to adopt a similar attitude of spiritual discipline in order to achieve the eternal prize that God will bestow on the faithful.

If we have learned one lesson in the process of reading Paul it is that when readings impress themselves on us as "straightforward," it is best to pause to ask why. For example, how much of our instinctive reading of this particular chapter has been shaped by the conflation of two major interpretative traditions, Puritan and Calvinist, which, taken together, have tended to encourage reading the Paul we find here as a heroic and sacrificially hard worker? His evident emphases on freedom, right, and reward combined with imagery of faith as an athletic competition easily sound like an ancient echoing of the familiar habits of an individualized capitalist society in which the restraint of desire is seen as a means for succeeding in a competitive striving for goods. On this reading capitalism seems not so different from Christianity; both are ways of organizing social life by codifying rewards for disciplined striving after goods: capitalism after material goods, and Christianity after the greatest of all immaterial goods—eternal life.

Isaak Dorner, a nineteenth-century Reformed German idealist, represents the ethical presumptions we tend to bring to this chapter in a particularly clear fashion.

> In the case of Christians ... [every ascetic practice] must proceed from faith, from the pleasure that is taken in the growth of the new man (for whose sake hindrances are taken out of the way), from the desire for spiritual increase (Matt 6:16f.), and from the dissatisfaction that the Christian feels with the humiliating want of freedom which he still experiences.... For while it is the aim of the Christian to overcome those habits and tendencies in his natural energies which are opposed to his spiritual

life, he seeks all the while to take these energies themselves and preserve them by making them the organs of his Christian freedom.... In self-examination (1 Cor 11:28), calm introspection, in the light of God's word and in solitude, holds the most important place; while penitential discipline consists chiefly in fighting against the predominant influence of the carnal nature, and in humbling ourselves before God, also before our neighbor should circumstances require.[1]

It will soon become clear that while Paul does use the main terms arrayed in Dorner's treatment, the Apostle offers a radically different way of fitting them together to yield an altogether different account of freedom, discipline, and the rewards that accrue from it.

In addition to inviting us to reconsider Dorner's picture of Christian piety, a close reading of Paul also directs attention away from another dominant cultural icon, the fetishization of "fitness." He will do so by fostering a new appreciation of the quest for a divinely given purpose that is extrinsic to the "projects" of our lives. Such a reading will need to trace Paul's theologically sensitive account of the "reward" for which Christians rightly hope and strive that is again different in type from any spiritual rewards that might be associated with present fitness or eternal bliss. As we have seen in previous chapters, Paul is not primarily interested in rating or denying the Corinthians' expectations of spiritual progress and aspirations to spiritual reward. Nevertheless, as he handles a sequence of wide-ranging issues, he attempts in each case to guide a transformation of their understanding of both ideas. We might characterize what he is doing as guiding their journey out of a freedom-to-choose into another freedom that the Corinthians cannot yet perceive. His account of this new freedom that the gospel offers redirects their understanding of the Christian faith by means of a re-narration of the options available within each of the ethical and missional situations under discussion in this chapter.

The emphasis on "reward" in this chapter marks it as a high point in a string of discussions that cover several axes of Paul's rounded vision of the freedom of a Christian. From the emphasis on "freedom from anxiety (about one's vocation)" that he wishes for unmarried (and married) Christians in chapter 7, Paul has moved to highlight in chapter 8 how the liberty of the Christian in all things must extend to freedom from self-indulgence and self-promotion at the expense of other believers, especially the weak. In chapter 9 the Apostle now adds as a key motif of this theology of freedom the notion that the gospel is essentially "free of charge." He identifies

---

1. Dorner, *System of Christian Ethics*, 408-10.

this cost-free attribute of the gospel as the inner purpose of his kenotic approach to the proclamation of the gospel. Because the Corinthians find his approach to Christian ministry so puzzling, Paul now sets out to offer a fully-fledged "apostolic defense" of his behavior as an embodiment of the kenotic character of the gospel. Of paramount importance for practitioners of such a stance is the refusal to set any obstacles in the path of witnessing to the gospel, to ensure that it remains "free of charge."

Ultimately, the Apostle's interest in chapter 9 is to offer a winning depiction of an appropriate Christian zeal to win people for the gospel. It is in pursuit of this end that Paul enacts his kenotic apostolate with its willingness to become "all things to all people," a becoming that requires discipline and bodily renunciation. What follows, then, is a careful and passionate examination of the phenomenon of gospel preaching and the discipline it demands of the believer. When read as another installment adding depth to his account of freedom, the interposition of the discussions of this chapter between chapters 8 and 10, both of which treat the issue of idol food, makes perfect sense. What might seem to be a possible interpolation or detour disturbing Paul's treatment of that topic becomes comprehensible as a step backward by Paul in order to offer a more fundamental account of the theological premises that organize his emphasis on freedom.[2] A transition in genre or mode of thought is already indicated in the shift in Paul's use of pronouns, moving as he does from third to first person in the last verse of chapter 8: "I will never eat meat, so that I may not cause one of them to fall." The first verse of chapter 9 follows smoothly in this train, remaining in the first person singular but turning directly to the Corinthians with a string of stinging questions.

> [1] Am I not free? Am I not an apostle? Have I not seen Jesus our Lord? Are you not my work in the Lord? [2] If I am not an apostle to others, at least I am to you; for you are the seal of my apostleship in the Lord.
> [3] This is my defense to those who would examine me.

These paragraphs have often been labeled Paul's "apology," because in them he defends himself against **those who would examine me**. What are the concrete charges he thinks it necessary to ward off?[3] More penetrating

---

2. "There is now general agreement that ch. 9 is not an intrusive element from another letter, but a classical *digression* in a typically Pauline A-B-A pattern." Murphy-O'Connor, JMO, 120.

3. "Examine" is a weak translation of the Greek ἀνακρίνουσίν (*anakrinousin*) (as in 4:3), which is a present participle that suggests that Paul may well be referring to concrete charges in a letter he had received. See Hays, RBH, 149.

patristic commentators speculated that Paul was facing a challenge to the consistency of his ways, with the Corinthians suspecting Paul's practice was not up to the standard of his theory. "Paul . . . you practice discipline in word only," as Chrysostom paraphrases the challenge.[4] In agreement with this construal, we see the Corinthians indeed pressing such a challenge, to which Paul responds by defending the internal theological consistency of his practice in order to explain why his behavior ought not to be understood as the Corinthians presume. Their suspicions have arisen on the basis of mistaken assumptions about the appropriate behavior of apostolic authorities, which the Apostle Paul now exposes as theologically misguided.

Based on his previous characterizations of the spirit that prevailed in the Corinthian church, Paul has chosen to mount his defense by taking up the two major terms being invoked by his objectors: "freedom" and "authority." It again displays Paul's own inner freedom that he does not shy away from responding to the Corinthians' implicit challenge to narrate Christian freedom by way of discussing the peculiar ἐξουσία (*exousia*) that characterizes new life in Christ. Given the terms around which this scuffle will unfold, the widespread tendency in contemporary translations to render *exousia* as "right" unfortunately obscures crucial aspects of Paul's theological response to the misguided Corinthian account of freedom.

Given Paul's understanding of proclamation as always addressed to a particular audience, it is again important to recognize the difference between modern rights language and his language of *exousia*. The modern account of freedom as the noninfringement of individual rights almost forces on us a reading of Paul's defense of his freedom as a tale of heroic sacrifice. Such readings uncannily reproduce the high medieval approach in which Paul's tent-making activity was presented as the paradigmatic supererogatory action: action beyond what was formally required by his vocation to preach the gospel, undertaken by choice and therefore of special merit (>6:7–8). In this way the label "supererogatory selflessness" can be said to indicate the core value being protected in both modern and ancient schemes.

As its usage throughout the New Testament testifies, however, *exousia* ("power") is by definition always power enacted, the *particular* might revealed in a given "mighty act." *Exousia* never describes a sheer potency whose holder has an option or choice whether to exercise it or not. This is why for Paul the *exousia* of God is intimately connected with discernments about the appropriate mode of its discharge in any concrete circumstance. The way he portrays the freedom of apostolic *exousia* in this chapter is therefore deeply at odds with a common contemporary reading in which

---

4. Chrysostom, *Homily* 21, PG 61:169–71, quoted in JK, 145.

freedom is conceived as choosing from the wide range of licit actions and maintaining that this freedom is not compromised even when some such licit possible courses of action are not taken out of deference to the limitations of others. We will see that this common reading of the "sacrificing" or "limiting" of one's true freedom out of deference to others is precisely the point at which manipulative interpersonal dynamics emerge that in effect levy a "charge" for the gospel being offered.

The problematic implications of freedom defined as the heroic sacrifice of forgoing legitimate rights is starkly displayed by predicaments in which modern missionaries have occasionally found themselves. Pursuing a call to the "ends of the earth," well-meaning Western Christians have felt that "compulsion presses upon me" (Thiselton's translation of 9:16) to travel to "remote" places to evangelize people in what could only be experienced as culturally "primitive" settings. The temptation felt by some, expressed by a few, but displayed by many in their obvious yearning to be "back home" was that the greatness of the reward they could expect for such sacrifices might be inversely related to the deprivations in the dark places of the mission field.

The novelist Barbara Kingsolver has creatively expressed the humor and the horror of this dilemma in her depiction of the Price family's missionary journey into the Belgian Congo. Able only to take one suitcase on the small plane that will deliver them to their mission field, mother and daughters decide to wear multiple layers of clothing with some of their most precious items stuffed underneath. One of the daughters narrates a crucial moment of the journey:

> We came from Bethlehem, Georgia, bearing Betty Crocker cake mixes into the jungle. My sisters and I were all counting on having one birthday apiece during our twelve-month mission. "And heaven knows," our mother predicted, "they won't have Betty Crocker in the Congo."
>
> "Where we are headed, there will be no buyers and sellers at all," my father corrected. His tone implied that Mother failed to grasp our mission, and that her concern with Betty Crocker confederated her with the coin-jingling sinners who vexed Jesus till he pitched a fit and threw them out of the church.[5]

As their small plane spit the Prices out in their new jungle home, they were surprised and horrified by the sweltering heat and torrential rain that immediately turned their carefully stowed cardboard boxes of cake mix to mush. The zealous father takes such losses to be inconsequential, being a "light

---

5. Kingsolver, *Poisonwood Bible*, 15.

traveler" no doubt attracted to the Paul who seems to appear on the surface of 1 Corinthians 9. That Paul, siding with the Jesus who tells his disciples to take nothing with them on their missionary journeys, neither money nor extra clothing (Matt 10:9–10), exemplifies for Nathan Price that the proper missionary servant of the gospel needs nothing but a machete and a Bible. In whatever cultural guise it may appear, the ideology of supererogatory sacrifice begins simply: by puffing up one's legitimate rights so that forgoing them appears amply heroic. The missionary father in Kingsolver's novel can only sustain his own image of the perfect sacrifice by relying on the practical support provided by those family members who not only carry twelve layers of clothing through the jungle, but in so doing incur the mark of spiritual weakness and compromise. And perhaps more dangerously, the establishment of moral high ground in this way easily becomes a destructive resource for psychological blackmail. This sort of pressure seeks the compliance of the intended addressees of one's own heroic efforts by making them aware of what sacrifices have been made "on their behalf."

As familiar and compelling as the prevailing nexus between a particular account of freedom, rights, and sacrifice appears to us, do we really find it in Paul's discussion here? It is true that the Apostle indicates to the Corinthians that he has forgone legitimate claims, and we do find in this chapter the language of reward attached to such asceticism. But if we attend closely to what Paul delineates as his reward, the whole equation begins to change. The reward, which he considers his prize, is not that which is due as repayment for giving up legitimate rights or the ensuing magnitude of his sacrifice, but is instead the reward that comes with seeing the gospel find its mark in the hearts of others won for the gospel.

The Fruits of Spiritual Labor

> [4] Do we not have the right to our food and drink? [5] Do we not have the right to be accompanied by a believing wife, as do the other apostles and the brothers of the Lord and Cephas? [6] Or is it only Barnabas and I who have no right to refrain from working for a living? [7] Who at any time pays the expenses for doing military service? Who plants a vineyard and does not eat any of its fruit? Or who tends a flock and does not get any of its milk?
>
> [8] Do I say this on human authority? Does not the law also say the same? [9] For it is written in the law of Moses, "You shall not muzzle an ox while it is treading out the grain." Is it for oxen that God is concerned? [10] Or does he not speak entirely

> for our sake? It was indeed written for our sake, for whoever plows should plow in hope and whoever threshes should thresh in hope of a share in the crop. ¹¹If we have sown spiritual good among you, is it too much if we reap your material benefits? ¹²If others share this rightful claim on you, do not we still more?
>
> Nevertheless, we have not made use of this right, but we endure anything rather than put an obstacle in the way of the gospel of Christ. ¹³Do you not know that those who are employed in the temple service get their food from the temple, and those who serve at the altar share in what is sacrificed on the altar? ¹⁴In the same way, the Lord commanded that those who proclaim the gospel should get their living by the gospel.

That the Corinthians perceived Paul's behavior as odd is indicated by his comment in verses 5 and 6, in which Paul marks the contrast with **other apostles and the brothers of the Lord and Cephas,** who obviously traveled with an entourage and were happy to be hosted by the respective churches they visited. Paul therefore must not only explain the particularities of his behavior but at the same time indicate why he goes about his ministry in such a different manner than his fellow apostles. The perceived oddity of Paul's kenotic, self-emptying form of life (>2:1–5) may even have encouraged some to go so far as to question his apostolic credentials altogether.

Paul's response to these challenges begins with a reminder of the particular bond he shares with the Corinthian church in having fathered it. He draws attention to this special relationship by calling them **the seal of my apostleship**. While Paul's mission has its origin on the road to Damascus in Christ's own calling (**Have I not seen Jesus our Lord?**), his apostolate only comes into its own when the Word sown comes to flourish in the faithfulness of the church communities he is serving. Indeed, the *exousia* of the Apostle is by definition something that proves itself only in its actual discharge rather than being proven by his former act of foundation (>1:2–3). Thus it is part of maintaining and proving his authority that he remains engaged and responsive to the ongoing challenges of his churches. He is thus re-establishing his apostolic authority precisely by explaining how his behavior must retain its character as an exemplary existence that stands over and above the community's expectations about appropriate behavior.

Our first interpretative clue to Paul's response to his challengers comes when we consider closely the three "rights" he discusses here, namely, **to our food and drink, to be accompanied by a believing wife,** and **to refrain from working for a living**. Because these examples all seem to be related to the question of Paul's particular way of discharging his apostolic authority, we do not think they are randomly chosen. Insight is gained into the nature of the Corinthians' complaint when we ask what the three examples of rights have in common that Paul says he is forgoing. Since the right to **food and drink** is addressed extensively in the chapters preceding and following the present chapter, we can focus on the nature of his reservation by investigating the two other contested issues: traveling with an entourage and refraining from working for a living.

Both such "rights" could easily be understood as symbolically representing the status the Corinthians associated with apostolic authority. Hays helpfully draws out in some detail how Paul's insistence on paying his own expenses by journeyman tent-making unsettled the Corinthians by placing him outside of the usual cultural trappings associated with spiritual teachers, who were recognized and honored in ancient society through patronage. In working for his living Paul refuses both itinerancy and patronage—the main markers of spiritual authorities of the day.[6] A contemporary example of this convention can be found in churches that find it a source of pride that their minister is well remunerated and drives a luxury car—a tendency put in sharp relief by the understandable practice of some socially and financially deprived African American churches that see the pastor as the icon of the community's hope for the financial and social respectability that it has been so cruelly denied. Within such cultural frames, refusing these marks of spiritual authority would inevitably give rise to suspicions that ministers without such signifiers of prestige must lack them because they lack spiritual power.

It was these sorts of suspicions about genuine power and authority that were raised in the first Christian centuries by traveling without an entourage. True spiritual authorities would be expected to have attendants who looked after their more mundane needs while they were concerned with loftier matters. By showing up with his tent-making toolbox and setting up his stall in the marketplace, Paul must have frustrated the expectations the Corinthians associated with a leadership figure of the universal church. Because the church fathers were largely persuaded by the reading of chapter 7 that made celibacy the higher state of Christian life, they were here prone to debates about whether γυναῖκα (*gynaika*) means "wife" or "woman"

---

6. Hays, RBH, 146–48. The emphasis Hays puts on Paul's approach to receiving pay as an intervention designed to reshape the way all parties in the Corinthian church understood themselves as members of a political community *sui generis* is far preferable to accounts that read his forgoing pay as merely a ministry strategy designed to win converts. John Goodrich, for example, without having an explanation for the historical matrix that might make this a winning evangelistic formula, nevertheless concludes that "the weak believers therefore were those to whom Paul wished to accommodate by refusing material support" (*Paul as an Administrator*, 170).

(perhaps "virgin") (>7:1–6), a preoccupation related to their tendency to project back into Paul's day their image of the bishop's traveling entourage.[7] But even as they did so they appear to have grasped the core charge Paul is resisting, namely, that he displays an appalling lack of the external signifiers that would naturally be expected to accompany his apostolic authority. Even the most minimal version of "entourage," the right to bring the single figure of a wife on the apostolic travels, is still raising the question of appropriate markers of apostolic status—not unlike the status marker sought by contemporary academics whose invitations to come to another city are hoped or expected to include the polite addendum "we would be delighted if your spouse could join us and will be happy to reimburse your joint expenses."

It is common to read this discussion as an affirmation by Paul that any sort of legitimate work generates an entitlement to payment. Here the modern presumption is that, if one has a right, one no longer needs to beg or even give thanks but can expect to receive what is due without further discussion.[8] This reading would understand Paul to be emphasizing ever more emphatically the magnitude of the claims he has forgone, making him appear as one deserving of the greatest reward in having given up the most extensive set of rights—those due an apostle. If, however, we take a more serious look at the details of Paul's apology, such a reading starts to fall apart rather quickly.

In the first instance, if Paul was trying to defend a sacrifice on his part, why should he make the same point that material work deserves material reward three times in 9:7? In theory this could be a mere rhetorical gesture drawing attention to his point by employing a variety of illustrative images, but we shall soon discover a deeper theological purpose behind this emphasis. Paul draws first on what appears to be a natural justice argument, followed by a scriptural proof. The rhetorical questions that frame each of his examples within the natural justice argument (**Who at any time . . .**) seems to suggest the plausibility of a principle that work always deserves material reward, a plausibility then reinforced by references to the biblical traditions of the Old (**Does not the law also say the same?**) and New Testament (**In the same way, the Lord commanded that those who proclaim the gospel should get their living by the gospel**).

The variety of the three examples he then cites, however, may well offer us the key to a different interpretative take on the whole chapter. Could it be of significance that the sheepherder would not expect a return from

---

7. Augustine, *Work of Monks* 5–6, CSEL 41:538–40, quoted in JK, 147

8. Jeffrey Stout positively assesses this modern account of rights in *Democracy and Tradition*, 205–7, to which Hauerwas insightfully responds with a Christian defense of begging in *Performing the Faith*, 241.

his work in the form of fruits, nor the soldier in the form of milk, but that each of these professions is entitled to a form of return that corresponds to its respective type of work? Raising such a question opens up a reading according to which the plurality of examples is not aimed at providing an illustration of the simple principle that any type of work should be rewarded with pay; what the variety of examples rather point toward is a quite different principle of correspondence: that *different types of work garner rewards concomitant of the type of labor being undertaken.*

This insight puts us in a position to understand what Paul is doing when he then shifts attention from the series of examples of material work to the spiritual work of proclaiming the gospel in verse 11: **If we have sown spiritual good among you, is it too much if we reap your material benefits?** In light of the principle of concomitant reward, the answer that we hear Paul give to his own question would be "no, of course not, spiritual work might well be rewarded with material benefits." Nevertheless, we understand his main purpose in this discussion to be the redirection of the Corinthians' attention toward the genuine correspondence of spiritual work with spiritual reward.

Paul will open his constructive case by asking the obvious and crucial question later, in 9:18: **What then is my reward?** His answer will explicate the spiritual return that he finds in witnessing the unobstructed power of the gospel to win new members for the body. Without preempting that discussion, we only note here that even though Paul contrasts the spiritual reward he expects with material compensation (**What then is my reward? Just this: that in my proclamation I may make the gospel free of charge**), at the same time he seems to assume that for this reward to be spiritual does not imply that it is immaterial. After all, the unobstructed *exousia* of the gospel is adding ensouled *bodies* to the church roll, bodies that gather around the Lord's Table to eat and drink together and thus to share in Christ's body.

Without setting up a simple juxtaposition of spiritual and material, it seems to us that the key distinction is between a reading of 9:4–14 that simply emphasizes the principle "pay for work" and one that draws attention to the principle of concomitant reward in which rewards come in different kinds according to the type of work being undertaken. Such an account is necessary to keep the apostolic mission oriented by a desire to keep the gospel "spiritual," which is to say, free of charge. Though not dismissing the first principle out of hand, it is now firmly subordinated to the priority of a free gospel. To frame the matter in these terms is to set up a hierarchy that makes discernment possible about whether and when the core reward Paul receives from the free gospel is being encouraged or discouraged in any given case by taking advantage of the principle of natural justice that work deserves pay.

The fascinating thing about where Paul is leading us begins to become clear in his quotation in 9:14 of the words of Jesus, drawn from Matthew 10:9–10: **In the same way, the Lord commanded that those who proclaim the gospel should get their living by the gospel.** In the Gospel, Jesus is explicitly demanding that the apostles "travel light" on their missionary journeys, taking neither money nor extra clothing. Paul, however, draws on this teaching to *invert* its clear conclusion that "the worker is worth his pay,"[9] citing Jesus's saying precisely in defense of his desire to *not* rely on the churches for his reward, as embodied in his practice of paying his own way through tent-making.[10]

On our reading this striking inversion is not a contradiction of Jesus's command but an exploration of its full scope. Not trying to tie Christian ministry and life to one set of formal assumptions about payment-for-work, Paul instead loosens this linkage in the service of the freedom of the gospel. It is in order that the *gospel* travel without "money or cloak" that Paul can sometimes embrace and sometimes refuse the natural principle of the right to pay-for-work. Service to a gospel that travels light sometimes demands itinerancy (as various Christian mendicant movements have stressed[11]), is sometimes thankful for and comfortable with the patronage of the rich (which Paul is seen gratefully accepting in Philippians 4:10–18), and sometimes entails self-supporting labor from its ministers. The key here is to resist the urge to hear definite answers about which image those who proclaim the gospel should *always* project, whether it be that of the itinerant self-sustainer, the rugged "purseless" itinerant, or the sophisticated recipient of the patronage of a wealthy Christian. What Paul is calling for instead is the agile, pragmatic discernment that emerges out of the radical hierarchy of the two priorities at stake.

This refusal to freeze Paul's comments about pay-for-work into a fixed frame here suggests two ways of moralizing this discussion about work and reward that need to be avoided. One is the tradition of interpretation that finds in this passage a single takeaway message: that churches pay their ministers properly. An inverted version of this moralized reading remains focused on the issue of payment but makes Paul's *refusal* to be paid by the

---

9. Murphy-O'Connor expresses surprise at how often this has been overlooked in modern commentaries. He does, however, go further than we will in suggesting that Paul "refused to give [Jesus's] commands the force of law" (JMO, 120–23).

10. This leads Gordon Fee to call it "one of the strangest arguments on record" (*God's Empowering Presence*, 140).

11. Johnson, *Fear of Beggars*, chs. 1–2.

Corinthians the principled model. This latter approach tends to rest on a sociological insight that equates patronage with a "patronizing" and often manipulative relationship, something to be avoided at all costs. Hays, for instance, concludes his treatment of this passage with the exhortation that "anyone whose vocation is to proclaim the gospel should stop and ask from time to time, 'Who is footing the bill for me to do this, and what implications does that have for the content and integrity of my ministry?'"[12] While this is certainly a good question to ask, the conclusion that it is in this question that we find the core message of this discussion rests on a conflation of Paul's actual lodestar, **nothing in the way of the gospel**, with the simple equation by which the "gospel free of charge" is taken to mean that the preacher must, in principle, be paid only in such a way that he will be able in his proclamation and leadership to rise above the agendas of those who fund ministry.

The demand to rise completely above the influence of money reveals a hermeneutic of suspicion that can easily miss the force of Paul's own prioritization of seeking the gospel's freedom. This priority even seems at times to demand that the Apostle willingly embrace being hosted and sustained by a wealthy church, with all the inevitable influences this entails. As his letter to the Philippians demonstrates, there were times and circumstances in which Paul was willing to be hosted by a church without feeling the need to voice concern over being manipulated by such patronage. In Corinth, however, given all we know about the particularities of this very different place, the fear of being trapped by a patronage relationship was far from unfounded. This is most evident in Paul's critique in chapter 11 of some characteristic habits that had developed in the Corinthians' eucharistic celebrations. Leaving our more detailed commentary for later, it will suffice here simply to note that Paul laments that the Corinthians are spoiling the holy meal by celebrating in a manner conforming to the standards of patronage. He insists that the setting of the sacrament in the house of a rich patron must not be taken as a license to configure the way this particular meal is taken in: it must not, he will insist, recapitulate the meals of the rich of the day in which guests were treated differently according to their social standing (>11:20-22).

Our reading raises uncomfortable questions about the historically predominant interpretation of this section as expressing Paul's concern that churches be conscientious about paying their ministers. We have discovered quite the opposite: that churches ought not to make an inviolable principle out of any one financial arrangement, Paul himself setting the example of a

---

12. Hays, RBH, 157.

minister whose account of reward for spiritual labor is maximally adaptable to circumstances so that a gospel beyond price can actually come without a price tag.

The most delightful comments on this chapter in the tradition of interpretation direct attention to how Christians are to understand their lives as they muse on Paul's quotation of the Old Testament law: **"You shall not muzzle an ox while it is treading out the grain"** (Deut 25:4).[13] It will by now be clear why we read this reference to point forward to 9:10: **whoever plows should plow in hope and whoever threshes should thresh in hope of a share in the crop**, as further elaborating Paul's encouragement for Christians to hope for the appropriate "crop" from their spiritual work. Here the agricultural examples suggest a distinction explicitly set out elsewhere between καρπὸν (*karpon*, "fruit") and δόμα (*doma*, "donation" [see Phil 4:17]). What the spiritual laborer is to hope for as the reward of their labor is its own particular fruit, while donations that are different *in kind* may well be offered, and may be gladly accepted. With this distinction firmly in mind, a spiritual reading of the three examples in 9:7 becomes increasingly plausible, based on the observation that the images of the soldier, vinedresser, and shepherd are all biblically pregnant images of gospel ministry.

If we now propose that the three images of work Paul offers may also be allegorically related to preaching the gospel, it is an interpretative move that is only viable once we have followed the argument closely as a literal reading and now sense it opening into further implications. That literal reading of the passage as a whole has set up a spiritual resonance in the three examples Paul chooses in 9:7. Immediately jumping onto the bandwagon of an analogical reading would not only deny the dignity of our fellow creatures (rendering the oxen no more than a cipher for what is actually an injunction for humans, as suggested by the line **Or does he not speak entirely for our sake?**) but would also short-circuit our hearing the more basic points Paul is trying to make. The term πάντως (*pantōs*), if translated as "entirely" to yield the implication that "this is written *exclusively* on our behalf," could be seen as an invitation to immediately jump to the spiritual level. Verse 9:10b, however, forestalls this reading in stating, **It was *indeed* written for our sake**. No reading is therefore appropriate that would highlight God's providential concern for the human species by belittling divine concern for other animals. To assume that God cares only for humans will thus produce a hermeneutical short circuit by moving the interpretation directly to the analogical level and so missing crucial shifts of attention that

---

13. Dolbeau, "Sermon inédit," 286, and Chrysostom, *Homily* 21, PG 61:173–74, both quoted in JK, 149–50; Calvin, JC, 188; Thiselton, ACT, 139.

Paul's discussion seeks to induce. An overly hasty movement to the level of spiritual or allegorical reading thus deprives the reader of access to the real spirit of the letter in not taking the time to travel the whole route Paul has laid out for his readers.

We are approaching a turning point in the chapter as marked by the strong negating conjunction **nevertheless** in 12b. This is paralleled in 9:15 by the introductory formula, **But I have made no use of any of these rights**. Verse 12b could be understood as a compact summative account of the whole of Paul's *apologia*: **Nevertheless, we have not made use of this right, but we endure anything rather than put an obstacle in the way of the gospel of Christ**. Here the Apostle does not remain content to mark the contrast between himself and others with regard to **this rightful claim on you** but hastens to add that his forgoing of all potentially valid claims is an enduring with a purpose—a purpose highlighting the core characteristic of Paul's apostolate: to not obstruct the gospel. It will be pivotal for our understanding of Paul's overall argument to get a clearer view of what it might entail to **put an obstacle in the way of the gospel of Christ**, and how he understands the material and spiritual grounds by which the gospel could be kept free of charge.

Boasting of the Gospel's Freedom

> [15] But I have made no use of any of these rights, nor am I writing this so that they may be applied in my case. Indeed, I would rather die than that—no one will deprive me of my ground for boasting! [16] If I proclaim the gospel, this gives me no ground for boasting, for an obligation is laid on me, and woe to me if I do not proclaim the gospel! [17] For if I do this of my own will, I have a reward; but if not of my own will, I am entrusted with a commission.

In 9:15 Paul wards off a possible misunderstanding that he might have invited with his enumeration of the "rights" appropriately claimed by an apostle: **nor am I writing this so that they may be applied in my case**. It is almost as though Paul begins to detect the growing gravitational pull of what we labeled the "heroism of sacrifice," the ideological nexus in which rights are writ large, waiving those rights written larger, and the resulting claim to moral "high ground" garishly displayed in huge neon letters. These neon letters could hardly be overlooked as an invitation to the Corinthians to compensate Paul for the sacrificial attitude he has displayed. Paul wastes no rhetorical effort rejecting any such interpretation, and directly repudiates it in the strongest possible terms: **I would rather die than that**. Given the cultural expectations in his context, we can safely assume that Paul's central aim as he negotiates the issue of pay turns on the questions of how activity in this sphere might set obstacles in the path of the freedom of the gospel. Just as he has "lowered" himself out of care for the "weak" brethren to forgo eating meat offered to idols (>8:13), in the same manner he has "lowered himself to the social status of the weak by refusing the patronage of the rich and becoming a manual laborer," Hays concludes.[14]

Although in other parts of his letter Paul is not shy to engage in a kind of boasting (>5:11–13), there is in fact no boasting going on in this passage. The Greek term καύχημά (*kauchēma*) is a noun that is appropriately translated as the **ground** on which any boasting by Paul, were he to engage in it, would rest. But stating a wish not to be deprived of such a ground is to be distinguished from actual boasting. This Paul makes unambiguously clear in his argument from 9:16 onwards, in which his proclamation of the gospel is in view, an activity that he insists offers no grounds for boasting whatsoever.

His explication of the two potential grounds for boasting begins with the Apostle's renunciation of legitimate claims that might have sparked boasting from him, had he believed in something like supererogatory works. But precisely because his mission to proclaim the gospel freely determines everything for the Apostle, boasting of any kind is rendered a practical impossibility: not only boasting about being a proclaimer of the gospel but also boasting about sacrificing for its sake. In theory, because the worker is worth pay, waiving what one is due gives ample grounds for boasting. But within the framework of Christian mission, which is inescapably practical, even this seemingly legitimate boasting becomes impossible; the theoretical possibility that one might boast is reduced to nothing because it would "put a charge onto the gospel," so obstructing its freedom. The core insight Paul again reiterates here is that the nature of the gospel is such that it must exist in freedom, and demands of its proclaimer the relinquishment of anything that might fetter this freedom, be it material or spiritual. The gospel must not be fettered, whether by taking money for its proclamation or boasting of not taking any.

Paul's insight into the inescapably free nature of the gospel, which exists solely to "win" people and ceases to exist once harnessed for private gain or forced onto others, is associated with the notion of ἀνάγκη (*anankē*)—**an obligation . . . laid on me**. The gospel is free and kept as such precisely if and when its proclaimer appropriately grasps the compulsion (*ananke* is

---

14. Hays, RBH, 154.

an even stronger term than "obligation") that drives him or her into proclaiming it, which in turn makes even the idea of boasting totally alien. This emphasis is developed in 9:17 with the help of two new concepts: **For if I do this of my own will, I have a *reward*; but if not of my own will, I am entrusted with a *commission*.** To boast is to tout one's own contribution to proclamation and so to manufacture one's own reward, but Paul insists that the free proclamation of the gospel not be construed as a project arising in any way from human volition. The Reformers elaborated this insight from Paul's theology with their conception of the "alien word of God," the *verbum alienum Dei*. For a proclaimer of the gospel, which *claims me*, there is nothing to claim *for me*.

Excursus: Supererogation

Paul's introduction of the concept of a **reward** (μισθός/*misthos*) accruing for a praiseworthy voluntary act was to be taken up in the later doctrinal development of the concept of "supererogatory works," backed by an Aristotelian philosophy of action. Here any action that goes further than what is required of ordinary Christians is considered worthy of extra praise, as when a higher course of action is chosen over another available and permissible option. What this teaching exalts is not primarily a certain type of action, such as the enactment of a generically recognizable good act with particular qualities or one that is exceedingly good on a gradual scale, but a specific type of investment of the will that is meritorious in its striving for perfection by "sacrificing," as it were, the permitted, the good, and the better for the very best, a course of action that can therefore be said to be the highest form of actualizing the peculiar freedom with which the human species has been endowed. Origen's comment on 9:16-17 offers a nascent account of supererogation: "For example, while a person who does not commit adultery or murder has no ground for boasting, one who lives a life of virginity does."[15] By explicitly referring to these verses as "a general teaching," Origen helps us see how a general doctrine of supererogatory works can emerge only by abstracting Paul's comments on boasting and reward from their context in 1 Corinthians with its emphasis on the freedom of proclamation.

The English term *supererogation* was coined for theological usage and derived from the Latin *erogare*, meaning to pay or expend, which appears prominently in the Latin Vulgate version of Jesus's parable of the Good Samaritan. Having rescued the injured neighbor, the Samaritan cares for him and takes him to an inn where he tells the proprietor to further care for him,

---

15. Origen, *Homilies on 1 Corinthians*, 512, quoted in JK, 153.

promising to reimburse his expenses, recounted in Luke 10:35 as "whatever you spend besides" (*quodcumque supererogaverus*). In addition to this act by the Good Samaritan, Zacchaeus's superabundant restitution (Luke 19:8–9) and Paul's supporting himself as he ministered (Acts 20:34; 1 Thess 2:8–9) had become by the medieval period the three paradigmatic examples of Christian supererogation. The moral rule set by these examples was formalized in Thomas Aquinas's highly developed distinction between commands that all must obey and counsels that some might observe if they wanted to live a "higher" Christianity.[16] The Reformers rejected the presuppositions of this line of argumentation, believing that human beings could in truth obey neither Christ's counsels nor his commands. Christians, Luther taught, must be constantly thrown back into grace and toward love of the neighbor without hesitation, or reckoning—completely without reserve.[17]

Luther thus repudiated the medieval bifurcation between following Christ's commands (charity, understood through the cardinal virtues) and his more strenuous counsels (poverty, chastity, and obedience). This distinction had come to define the boundary between laypeople and those in religious orders, with the nomenclature of "vocation" exclusively linked to the "higher way."[18] Calvin expresses the protest of the magisterial Reformation against this two-tier Christian morality thus: "Since we are unduly inclined to hypocrisy, this palliative ought by no means be added to soothe our sluggish consciences."[19] Such disavowals were to have a long history in Protestant theology, as marked by their anathematization in the Anglican Thirty-Nine Articles.[20] It is hardly going too far to say that the spark that lit off the Reformation was a theological resistance to this notion of a "higher way" and the bifurcation in the *corpus Christianum* that it fostered. Such

---

16. Aquinas, ST I.II.108.2–4.

17. Luther, *The Freedom of a Christian* (1520), in LW 31:348; *Treatise on Good Works* (1520), in LW 44:33.

18. See Aquinas, ST II.II.185.6.

19. Calvin, *Institutes*, 2.8.58. Calvin repeats this criticism at greater length in his commentary on 1 Corinthians 9:18: "The Papists try to find support in this verse for works of supererogation.... Paul did indeed go beyond what was normally required of pastors in their calling, seeing that he did not take the pay, which the Lord allows pastors to take. But it was part of his duty to take steps against every possible cause of offence, which he saw would arise. Now, he was aware that there would be no further progress for the Gospel, if he were to take advantage of his right; but even if that was something unusual, I maintain, however, that he offered to God no more than he was bound to give ... let there be an end to the use of the term [supererogation] itself, for it is bursting with devilish pride" (JC, 193–94).

20. "Workes of supererogation, can not be taught without arrogancie and impietie." Art. 14, cited in O'Donovan, *On the Thirty-Nine Articles*, 141.

moral clauses of exception appeared to cut the vital cord of transformative faith to yield a culturally conservative and conformist Christianity for the masses who were held only to minimum standards of Christian morality.[21]

That Paul's tent-making should have played, alongside Matthew 19, a starring role in the development of this doctrine of supererogation strikes us as rather odd, given the fact that he so bluntly juxtaposes the nexus of voluntary action and reward with his characterization of the gospel's very different mode of operation: **For if I do this of my own will, I have a reward; but if not of my own will, I am entrusted with a commission.** It is crucial for understanding Paul's account of his mission (and reward) that we take seriously his insistence that his mission was a divine commission and not a matter of his own willed choice.

The Greek term that is translated as **commission** in the NRSV is οἰκονομία (*oikonomia*, "house holding"), which might even be understood in terms of "holding an office." Office holding certainly creates a sense of obligation not unlike the sense of compulsion Paul has noted as a feature of his vocation, but it also opens up once again the reward discussion with a complicating statement. Having just stated that the task into which one is externally *compelled* cannot yield a reward, how can Paul now ask, since I have been *commissioned*, what then is my reward? Even though the argument to this point has been rather winding, first ruling out the notion of reward altogether, only to allow it under certain conditions later on, what has become certainly clear is that the reward to which the Apostle refers from 9:18 onward has to be of a fairly counterintuitive kind. Paul seems to be closing his discussion of the question "what is my due?" as a lead-in to a related but significantly different account of reward that orbits around the question "what is the goal or *telos* that Christian proclamation seeks?"

The Rewards of Watching the Gospel at Work

> [18] **What then is my reward? Just this: that in my proclamation I may make the gospel free of charge, so as not to make full use of my rights in the gospel.**

This verse marks a shift of focus from the question regarding the freedom of human agents (whether or not to act out their legitimate rights) to a new theme: the freedom of the gospel as the main protagonist in the divine economy. It is a change in tack that will allow Paul to turn the tables on common-sense definitions of reward that run afoul of theological sense. The

---

21. Luther, *Martin Luther's Ninety-Five Theses*, theses 44–45.

reward for proclaiming the gospel as Paul describes it here is itself a proper aspect of that gospel rather than garnering an "alien" quantifiable return for its proclaimer. It is not subsequent to the proclamation of the gospel, nor is it different in kind, like the monetary remuneration for physical labor in which the currency of the payment has no material correspondence to the type of work done. Since the true reward for the proclamation of the gospel is tied up with its own proper fullness, it is *only* rewarding when it is truly **free of charge**.

What we need to uncover is what Paul experiences as the reward intrinsic to the gospel's own proper and life-giving operation. One interpretative possibility is to run this passage through the Aristotelian notion of praxis as the emphasis on "practices" in moral philosophy and theology over the last thirty years would suggest. This reading understands "rewarding" experience as associated with a fitting execution of a particular type of action. "The act and its 'reward,'" writes Thiselton, "are linked by 'internal grammar' like the delight of giving a gift to a loved one, not by external cause and effect. . . . To learn to play a Bach organ fugue or a Beethoven piano sonata 'brings' a reward in the very joy of playing it."[22] Here the preaching of the gospel is conceived as rewarding precisely in being a humanly (self-)satisfying performance.

Such a reading, precisely because it must be so keenly self-aware, inevitably links a demand to the gospel message: that delivering it be a pleasurable and satisfying activity for the *preacher*. In contrast, Paul's approach to reward shows him rather excited to be granted the experience of being a first-person witness to the operation of the gospel's power *in others*. What engages him is to remove all the stage props that might manipulate people's reactions in ways that obscure the agency of the gospel. On our reading Paul's reward can therefore by definition not be attached to his or the church's performance, but must be linked to the display of the gospel's own power. The "reward" that Paul is discussing here is therefore *extrinsic* to Paul's activity on the grounds that, theologically speaking, only God can bestow a reward that is so different in kind from the reward that comes with any skillful human activity.

This is to suggest that Paul is *resisting* that very type of preaching that seeks delight in the aesthetically well-turned phrase. It is this attunement to the human pleasure of such a performance that we have been suggesting places a "charge" on the gospel, effectively muffling its own action. Paul is keenly aware of this problem and refuses to place any such charge on his message by implicitly or explicitly asking for a payment different in kind,

22. Thiselton, ACT, 142–43.

whether money, respect, or the pleasure of delivery. This observation is reinforced by the textual clues in 1 Corinthians 1:16-17 indicating that Paul is relatively unconcerned in this letter with achieving a flawless text. His is not the enactment of a performance so perfect or aesthetically pleasing that the very communicative act is itself the only reward that can be expected. In the reward Paul is hoping for, it is the well-functioning of the gospel that counts, its winning over those who are now far away. As such, the activity of proclamation in which he invests himself is not properly narrated through an Aristotelian idea of praxis in which it is assumed that the pleasure that arises in a human activity is in achieving the *telos* whose origin is within the human agent.[23] Preaching is only the preaching *of the gospel* if it is a means to an end extrinsic to the activity itself.

Paul's characterization of his reward as tied to the preservation of the freedom of the gospel is so insistent that it almost appears that its success is completely extraneous to the success or failure of his own performance in the act of proclamation. While the Apostle seems open to this being the case, and gives us no hint that he feels himself to be owed a "successful" or "happy" life for serving the Lord, he nevertheless speaks of **my reward** (9:18). He thus calls us to acknowledge that there must be a way to understand the person of the Apostle as genuinely partaking in the reward that he insists on defining in terms of the wellbeing of a separate agent, the gospel. His own way of putting it suggests that his efforts are moving him into the vicinity in which this free gospel is at work, for which he would endure everything if necessary (9:12b). As he says in 9:23, **I do it all for the sake of the gospel, so that I may share in its blessings**. He finds himself rewarded by basking in the reflected light of the active and living gospel as it claims human lives and liberates them from their bondage.

While it is obvious that Paul therefore expects his **share** within the workings of the gospel, the NRSV translation obscures another significant feature of his argument. A literal translation of the consecutive construction (**so that . . .**) in the second half of 9:23 would be, "so that I may become a co-partaker with it [the gospel]." The first syllable of συγκοινωνὸς (*synkoinōnos*), *syn-* ("together with"), indicates that the reward to which Paul understands himself entitled as a proclaimer of the gospel is not properly understood as an individual eternal reward.[24] Nor is this notion of reward to be subsumed under an economic model of stewardship in which Christians are assumed to have been given a "deposit" that they must invest

---

23. Aristotle, *Nicomachean Ethics*, 1099a8-21.
24. Hauck, "koinos," in Kittel, *Theological Dictionary of the New Testament*, 3:804.

well if they are to be "paid off" in the afterlife (a notion those of us living in capitalistic societies are susceptible to).[25]

The proclaimer's share in the gospel is instead envisioned as springing from a sharing in the lives of those "won" by the gospel—now in the church and then in the eschatological city. This is why the object of Paul's hope is to have a share in *the gospel*, not "its blessings." The NRSV mistranslation of the "together with" that is the heart of this passage springs from an individualist presupposition: that the rewards of gospel proclamation accrue to *individuals* in order to be received sometime *in the future*. This rendering obscures Paul's point that what he hopes to share in is the *present* gathering of the community by a powerful gospel. The community the gospel gathers is of course an eternal one, but his hope is to enjoy it in his present time and place.

It should come as no surprise that the eschatological presuppositions we bring to the text easily tint our respective readings at this sensitive point. Our eschatological imagination provides the horizons, in the Husserlian sense, within which the various understandings of reward must be situated. It is in fact not only a difference in eschatological expectation (individualist vs. social, present vs. realized vs. future) that is at stake here; two wider rationalities are in play that Paul directly contrasts with each other. Thiselton's rendering of Paul's expression in 9:17, **I have a reward,** as "I am in the realm of reward"[26] is an interpretative translation that nicely encapsulates the reading we have proposed. But an important rival language game both grounds and reflects a rival form of life. Our interpretation has seen Paul resisting that form of life that moves from a concern to serve one's own rights and freedom of choice (>9:1–15) to an interest in securing individual rewards by way of making sacrifices. It is thus an approach that Paul has already rejected that prompts readers to read the whole chapter within a horizon of individualized eschatology.

---

25. This capitalist reading is vigorously defended by John Goodrich. He frames Paul's entire apostolate within an economic framework by taking Paul's language of being in servitude to God's will as an indicator that Paul is presenting himself as an ancient private (slave) administrator. He thus concludes from the passage under discussion that "as God's commercial administrator the chief objective of [Paul's] apostolic administration is to generate a 'profit' for his divine principal" (*Paul as an Administrator*, 193). "Paul refuses to accept a wage from the Corinthians because such an act of self-sacrifice enables the gospel to advance further in Corinth, a noteworthy accomplishment which Paul can confidently identify, or boast in—as a demonstration of faithfulness to his commission (4:2). Thus, Paul forgoes his rights to an immediate financial payoff in order to ensure that he will receive his incorruptible prize (9:24–5), an eschatological wage (3:8, 14) to be issued along with his master's praise (*epainos*, 4:5) at his return" (ibid., 195).

26. This translation of 9:17 is discussed in Thiselton, ACT2, 696–97.

Our negative verdict on any suggestion that the Christian should orient their life according to the hope for the reward of personal heavenly commendation rests on the fact that if we read this chapter in this way we will eventually be drawn into the constricting embrace of the "rights-choice-sacrifice" language that is clearly Paul's target in this chapter. We would also severely compromise our reading of his reasons for resisting the idea of spiritual gifts as personal possessions (>1:11–12; 12:12–13). We recall this point now because these are mutually exclusive hermeneutical stances: inhabiting one or the other will strongly shape our reading of the last sentences of this chapter, when Paul combines the summons to exercise self-control with the hope to receive an imperishable wreath (9:25). This passage would seem almost impossible to extract from the horizon of individualized eschatology if taken on its own instead of being read, as we are proposing, through the lens of Paul's subversion of individualized reward language in 9:17–18.

Excursus: Paul's Formation of the Self

Paul not only observes the gospel at work; he tells us in 9:22 that it is changing him: **I have *become* all things to all people, that I might by all means save some.** On our reading, since Paul's understanding of the "becoming" being indicated here (γέγονα/*gegona*) is an open-ended eschatological one, he must understand it in terms of a process of discovery and exploration,[27] of coming to terms with what the gospel will reveal about him and those to whom he preaches as it binds them to each other. What seems obvious to Paul is that in order to become "all things to all people" there must be renunciations, concrete abdications of his legitimate claims. Only in the midst of the complexities of his mission will he learn exactly which renunciations will best serve the freedom of the gospel.

A brief philosophical excursus on the type of formation being envisioned here will clarify what sort of exercises or disciplines might accompany this account of becoming and formation. We have already noted the Aristotelian performance account of this process: becoming a more skilled or virtuous practitioner is rewarding on its own terms. The ascetic and still dominant reading of Paul's "becoming all things to all people," in contrast, emphasizes the chiseling away of the current self by ascetic habits that remove the accidental and culturally dispensable aspects of the self to reveal its eternal and enduring eschatological core.[28] Here the reward of the discipline involved in being made new by the gospel is tied up with the glimpse

---

27. Lindemann, *Der Erste Korintherbrief*, 213.
28. Deluz, *Companion to 1 Corinthians*, 119–20.

it affords of our perfected state, the "I" purged of all sin and mutability, the God-like eternal image of God within us.

Our reading finds Paul to be closer to a counter-Enlightenment philosophical tradition in which the disciplines associated with becoming are oriented not by a known teleological outcome nor the pleasure of performance but by fidelity to a new reality that has to dawn on us and that questions our certainties about ourselves and our future. Highly attuned to the human tendency to plan and project designs onto others, and recovering the centrality of wonder in ancient philosophy,[29] Nietzsche insisted that philosophy only begins when we allow ourselves to admit that we know precious little about ourselves and others.[30] Later interpreters have criticized the solipsistic obsession with the subject's self-overcoming implicit in this way of beginning. Heidegger, for instance, refocused Nietzsche's account of philosophy by emphasizing that human beings come into truth only as their false *schemata* of perception are punctured by the instances in which external reality refuses to conform to their expectations (>Excursus: Theology and Phenomenology). He insisted that our only hope of becoming truthful beings capable of escaping the undertow of our will to dominate and our projections about how we would like the world to be is to devote ourselves to being faithful to an otherness that breaks in on us, forcing us to more closely attend, become responsive, and conform to what has been revealed.[31] In this tradition discipline names the effort we invest in incorporating an externally appearing truth into our current habits of life. In the process of human transformation understood in these terms, the intellectual and volitional task is to learn to link what I think I currently know and live with that not-previously-known which has come to command my attention.[32] The antitheses of discipline, then, are inattentiveness and forgetfulness.

The eschatological openness of the Apostle's account of discipline is positioned to resist both the ancient/Enlightenment moral axiom that the task of ethics is to "know thyself," and its post-Nietzschean reformulation as "take care of yourself," later and most famously elaborated in the work of Michel Foucault.[33] What Paul is resisting with his account of Christian mis-

---

29. Chappell, *Knowing What to Do*, ch. 12.

30. Nietzsche, "On Truth and Lying in a Non-moral Sense," in *Birth of Tragedy*, 139–53.

31. Heidegger, *Nietzsche*, vol. 1, *The Will to Power as Art*, I.16.

32. "There is always only one question in the ethic of truths: how will I, as someone, *continue* to exceed my own being? How will I link the things I know, in a consistent fashion, via the effects of being seized by the not-known?" Badiou, *Ethics*, 50.

33. Foucault, "Technologies of the Self," in *Ethics*, 223–51.

sion and ministry is the emphasis of both formulations on the cultivation of a "self." In the perspective the Apostle offers, my "self" is an eschatological entity that is not entirely known to me and can only be discovered in caring for everyone and everything loved by Jesus Christ. This is to understand that Paul's eschatological perspective is determining his ethical perception, both being understood as the primary entailments of faithfulness to the Christ who has appeared to him.[34] This Christ has revealed to him a church and a mission that have claimed his whole being,[35] stripping him of any ideal pictures he might have had of himself in some form of pristine isolation, an imaginary form toward which he might strive in exercises of body or soul.

Thus for the second time in this chapter we see a nested framework of priorities, this time in Paul's understanding of self-discipline. His first and most basic priority is embodied in his resolve to **endure anything** (9:12) in service to the gospel's agency. In order actually to accomplish this endurance, however, Paul embraces an active punishment and enslaving of his body (9:27), which does not *define* fitness but *serves* whatever fitness will be gained as he follows the turbulent path of the gospel. We have become sensitive in a postcolonial era to the violence that is associated with the demand that some people understand themselves as deviants and conform to what is defined as normal by the ruling majority. This is what Foucault called "subjectification."[36] We take Paul to be offering a rival account of this process in that he believes that human beings are only *made* subjects by being claimed by others. Paul not only embraces this strikingly countercultural claim, but actually presents his being claimed by others as the mediatory activity through which he is being conformed to the living Jesus Christ.

Given this christological structure of Paul's account of Christian discipline, the dominant patristic reading of **only one receives the prize** (9:24b) seems apposite, here explained by Origen:

> Paul says that one receives the prize, although many compete. All those who are being saved are one and one body (Gal 3:28; 1 Cor 12:12). For we are all one bread and we partake of the same bread (1 Cor 10:17). And you are all the body of Christ (1 Cor 12:27). All, then, applies to those who are being saved, but there is one who receives the prize.[37]

34. Ulrich, *Eschatologie und Ethik*, Part I.
35. Barth, CD IV.3.1, 198–211.
36. Heller, "Power, Subjectification and Resistance," 78–110.
37. Origen, *Homilies on 1 Corinthians*, 514, quoted in JK, 157. When not evading this question entirely, modern commentators are usually content to assert that Paul's point is not about winning prizes at all but is exclusively about self-control. See Fee, *First Epistle to the Corinthians*, 435; Collins, RFC, 361; Witherington, *Conflict and Community*, 214.

As he speaks about Christian self-discipline, then, the Apostle can thus hardly mean: "Each of you must run for your own prize." He is instead insistent that Christ's victory is the one victory over the powers and principalities of the world, within which the individual believer's striving is comprehended. This would make the aim of Christian self-discipline to be conformed to "Christ, and him crucified" (1 Cor 2:2).

An important effect of this construal is its de-emphasizing of the role played by "winning" in Paul's account of discipline, which aims to increase his hearers' understanding of the danger of running the *wrong* race.[38] The challenge of the Christian life is to become aware of and engaged in competing in the right race; not any race will do—only the race that has been set before each believer counts if he or she does not wish to **run aimlessly** (9:26a). If only *one* truly wins, the believer's discipline is only spiritually viable insofar as it serves and facilitates Christ's victory. Because it is *Christ's* race, it is first and definitively a race to win *others*. This is the one race that must be *set* before sinful beings, and to run it human beings must repent of their infatuation with other competitive goals in order to willingly embrace the one race. This suggests the following gloss of 9:24: "Run in such a way that you may win *by participating in Christ's victories*."

Paul's discipline thus goes beyond asceticism in his pursuit of a thoroughgoing emptying of his own designs. This discipline consists in an active process of fighting those self-images and cultural habits, however ingrained and unconscious, that bar him from remaining faithful to the Christ who has appeared to him and bound him to other human beings. To those who misdirect their disciplinary efforts by competing for spiritual gifts or, as today, obsess about their attempts to achieve the "perfect" body (whether muscular or emaciated), Paul's response is not to urge any *relaxation* of Christian self-discipline, but rather its *redirection*.

Becoming and Being Made All Things

> [19]For though I am free with respect to all, I have made myself a slave to all, so that I might win more of them. [20]To the Jews I became as a Jew, in order to win Jews. To those under the law I became as one under the law (though I myself am not under the law) so that I might win those under the law. [21]To those outside the law I became as one outside the law (though I am

---

38. "Although people may claim to perform good works before faith, works that seem praiseworthy to onlookers, such works are vacuous. They look to me like someone running with great power and at high speed, but off course." Augustine, Exposition 2.1 of Ps 31, in *Expositions of the Psalms*, 1:365.

> not free from God's law but am under Christ's law) so that I might win those outside the law. ²²To the weak I became weak, so that I might win the weak. I have become all things to all people, that I might by all means save some. ²³I do it all for the sake of the gospel, so that I may share in its blessings.

Up to this point Paul has developed his apology for the kenotic apostolate he embodies by explaining why his renunciation of rights is necessary to preserve the freedom of the gospel in the course of his proclamation. In the famous passage now before us he describes with some precision how the kenotic character of his mission positions him within varying cultural and religious contexts. It is striking that he begins this new train of thought with the same terminology just deployed to characterize the *telos* of his mission as devoted to keeping the gospel "free of charge." Ἐλεύθερος γὰρ (*Eleutheros gar*, "for, as one liberated . . .") begins this passage, echoing the chapter's opening question, **Am I not free?** At this point in Paul's argument it is apparent that the specific type of freedom he is now positively claiming has come into being as a direct result of his commitment to "enduring anything." The merely theoretical and negative freedom of choice expressed in the opening line of questioning has thus been completely displaced by the new and positive freedom that draws him into many different cultural spaces.

The translation of the NRSV is particularly infelicitous at this point, however, in the insertion of **though**, not present in the Greek. More importantly, it sends readers in the wrong direction, the concessive participle **though** now suggesting a reading in tune with a classically liberal account of freedom: "even *though* I am free from any *a priori* commitment to anyone, and therefore free to do what I want, I have *still* (laudably) resolved to make myself serviceable to everyone." To put the contrast in such terms also suggests a personal understanding of **all** (πάντων/*pantōn*), a reading Thiselton's translation explicitly espouses: "no slave to any human person." Though not implausible to imagine that potentially compromising alliances to human patrons, for instance, are in view here, reading *pantōn* broadly seems the best option. This would mean to understand this **all** as being inclusive of anything that might put an obstacle in the way of the gospel, including conceptual schemas like the rights-sacrifice-boasting-reward nexus from which we have seen Paul distancing himself.

Our more expansive reading of Paul's freedom from "all things" has the advantage of avoiding the trap of a traditional approach represented by Origen. The great Alexandrine understood the Apostle to be claiming to be free from all sin, and so "the perfected apostle."[39] We think it preferable to retain the unspecified character of this expression, because while Paul knew that in order to be able to become **all things to all people** there must be renunciation, he also realized that what must be renounced in a particular missionary situation cannot be foreseen and hence be solidified in a fixed list. Preserving the openness of the "all" here follows from our suggestion that it will be only in the midst of the complexities that come with his mission, as he rubs shoulders with people on the other side of various cultural divides, that he will learn precisely what renunciations will best serve to preserve the freedom of the gospel in any given circumstance.

Finally, reading Paul's freedom from "all" as a narrowly personal reference short-circuits the logic assumed in the formulation of 9:20a: **To the Jews I became as a Jew, in order to win Jews**. Note that Paul first uses the definite article "*the* Jews" at the beginning of the statement, but then omits the article for the final noun. Paul's insistence that he did not come to win *the* Jews, but individual *Jews* makes perfect sense in light of the "free," that is, noncoercive character of gospel proclamation he has outlined, which can always only hope to win individual human beings, not groups as a block. A pneumatological point underlies this clarity: the Holy Spirit's work is not to collectivize but to individuate, to give and guide each person in the particular way that will honor and so bring to fruition their irreducible Christlikeness while situating each person in their assigned place within the body of Christ. The discipline associated with Paul's sharing of the gospel with others thus makes him *more* the person he was created to be, allowing him a more "fitting" pursuit of his ecclesial vocation as an apostle.

When discussing his devotion to the gospel, Paul is happy to use the active language of enslaving *himself* in order to emphasize his determination to conform his patterns of living to the demands of the gospel. But when he speaks about the *addressees* of his proclamation, such as Jews and Gentiles, he switches into the language of becoming. He does not "enslave" others as he does himself, but "becomes like" them. On one hand this is another example of the pneumatological sensitivity displayed in his refusal to address "the Jews" as a single or homogenous mass. It is crucial here to note that the Greek verb ἐγενόμην (*egenomēn*, to "become like") is in the middle voice, which is impossible to render in English, being situated between the active and passive voices. By using the middle voice here the Apostle is suggesting that "to become" is to be *engaged* in a process (so being "active") but in the mode of *responding* to larger forces driving the process as a whole (and so "passive"). The will of the individual thus does not *define* a range of options

---

39. Origen, *Homilies on 1 Corinthians*, 512, quoted in JK, 154.

to be *chosen* but *embraces* or *rejects* that which must first be *discerned*. The implication of this language shift is that Christians must not think that they can "make themselves," whether in the sense of driving their own biographical project or even in the sense of making themselves "as" others. Rather, Christians understand the making of their lives to be a divine prerogative that they experience only under and within the operation of the gospel.

Deference to the prerogative of the divine *poiesis* ("making") is not the only aspect in Paul's discussion that should keep Christians from speaking as if they could "make themselves as" someone else. His shifting to the language of "becoming" points to the fact that missional empathy can never be conceived as a unilateral supply-side activity driven by the evangelist. The language of *making* is always tied up with the application of force to change something or someone's current form.[40] In contrast, the language of *becoming* helps us understand Paul's theological stake in positioning the aim of his action as "winning" others (9:20). It is one of the crucial lessons of missionary work to the present day that this "divine making" and "human becoming" must never be confused.[41] There are all too many ways to short-circuit the patient process of "becoming as" others by utilizing manipulative means to make quick entries into the territory and then presumably "into the hearts" of those one wishes to evangelize. A related short-circuiting of the gospel's freedom is to undertake mission as a sort of headhunting expedition. Here the rights-sacrifice-reward complex suggests imagining the gospel as the offer of a prepackaged product by those pictured as standing above and unaffected by the "recipients" it might attract.

In the famous outreach effort to the Waodani tribe in the Amazon jungle, recounted in countless hagiographic books and the movie *End of the Spear*, the first wave of active preaching by Jim Elliot's group of missionaries was largely unsuccessful because the band of exclusively male preachers did not begin by learning the language of the group to whom they were reaching out. Instead, they literally descended upon them in the alien contraption of an airplane. Linguistic incomprehension and cultural misunderstanding quickly spiraled into a bloody end to the first act of this mission outreach, as the culture to which the missionaries had insufficiently accommodated themselves reciprocated with their own "forced entry"—the sharp end of a

---

40. Commenting on the violence inherent in Plato's account of *poiesis*, Hannah Arendt draws attention to how Plato conceives the work of the craftsman. For him to make is to imprint an idea, such as an imagined chair, onto a substrate such as wood in order to fabricate an envisioned artifact. "This element of violation and violence is present in all fabrication, and *homo faber*, the creator of human artifice, has always been a destroyer of nature" (*Human Condition*, 97).

41. Jennings, *Christian Imagination*, 102–12.

spear! Only by refusing to defend themselves in the last moments of their lives did the missionaries open a window to genuine communication with the Waodani. The much more eloquent offer of the gospel came in this story's second act, and was performed by the dead men's widows. The widows invited trust by again going to the tribe, this time in complete vulnerability. Unarmed, on foot and with their young children, they exposed themselves to the very people they knew to be the killers of their husbands. Without airplanes and gifts of trinkets, it was these widows who embodied a gospel that "travels light" by exposing their vulnerable and unarmed bodies and even those of their children to the mercy of those others they wished to win for the gospel.

Such a willingness to enter foreign cultural space, with all the embarrassment and powerlessness it will entail, is a prime example of the evangelistic *kenosis* Paul is commending. We must be prepared to become vulnerable by attempting to be "as" others in order to be "with" them. The understanding of "traveling light" presumed by the missionary father in *The Poisonwood Bible* with which we opened our discussion of this chapter thus emerges as the antithesis of this vulnerable exposure, characterized as it was by a pride in "forgoing anything" (>8:8–13) and a refusal to "become like" those to whom a correspondingly misshapen gospel is preached. It was the missionary widows, not the zealous missionary father, who practiced submission to the law of the prize in their willingness to embrace the cultural accommodations entailed in meeting those to whom they had been entrusted and commissioned.

If the enculturation of the gospel is to be genuine, those who preach it will have to be transformed as they engage with the cultural forms and perspectives of those to whom the gospel is being freely offered. Paul does not understand this enculturation to begin with some act of cultural erasure that precedes taking up the habits and patterns of another culture. Neither does his kenotic empathy license complete and indiscriminate accommodation to the culture of those he wishes to win for the gospel. He makes this crystal clear in 9:21, **though I am not free from God's law but am under Christ's law**, a kenotic account of Christ's law that recurs in Paul's writings: "Bear one another's burdens, and in this way you will fulfill the law of Christ" (Gal 6:2). Empathetic evangelism does have its proper limits— Paul would not join the Corinthians' excursions to brothels or law courts, which he censures in chapter 6, to take two obvious examples.[42] Building a catalogue of the immoral activities he felt Christians needed to avoid is no doubt possible, but for our purposes it is coming to terms with the way Paul

---

42. See Gooch, *Partial Knowledge*, 131–39.

understands the positive discipline demanded by his pursuit of the gospel that is most important.

What is obvious is that as he follows the liberating gospel Paul feels blissfully free from concerns so prominent today about preserving some stable cultural configuration of his identity. The Apostle is free from the compulsion to engage in identity politics not out of some facile claim that he is "beyond culture," but because his true identity is solely grounded in Christ, the same Christ whom he knows he will discover if he attends to the others he encounters within the working space of the gospel. Trusting that the eschatological future of humanity is never absent in any face he meets, Paul has been liberated in the missionary endeavor from the temptation to try to "make" Christians through powerful techniques of persuasion. Instead, for Paul evangelism amounts to seeking to discover the presence of Christ in those who do not yet know this presence. Only on this basis can the business of "becoming as" those others be freed from the fear that breeds coercion—the fear of losing one's own identity.

The significance of Paul's employment of "becoming" language is confirmed by another linguistic detail. While he does not claim to be simply or completely enculturated as a Jew or a Gentile, inserting a relativizing "as" (ὡς/*hōs*)—**I became *as* a Jew . . . *as* one under the law . . . *as* one outside the law**—there is no such distancing participle when Paul claims to have become weak to the weak: **To the weak I became weak, so that I might win the weak**. Why the need to use indirect constructions with regard to cultural-religious groups that are unnecessary in relation to the weak? Though the Apostle is free to be unconcerned about the cultural stability of his own identity, this freedom in the gospel does not imply a license to override the dignity of his host culture, which any claim to have completely taken it on would entail. It is therefore to be understood as a mark of respect that he becomes "as" Jewish as necessary, and does not claim to "be" Jewish when reaching out to Jews. The fact that Paul could well make (and make credible) the claim to actually *be* a Jew, as warranted by his being the son of a Jewish mother, only heightens the significance of this unpretentious, noninvasive approach over against any possible host culture. In order to bring the gospel free of charge to the Jews, it is not enough for Paul to be *(of) Jewish (origin)*; rather, he must become *as* **a Jew** to them in no less a way than the one in which he needs to become *as* a Gentile to the Gentiles. The distance to the respective culture that is to be overcome in this kenotic approach is not measured by any common scale of measuring the distance between cultures but is measured by the distance from the identity that defines Paul's life and mission: in Christ.

The weak, on the other hand, to whom Paul becomes weak without the distancing particle *hos,* cannot be described in terms of membership in any sociocultural group—units that always threaten individuals with the specter of accommodation and absorption. The weak whom Paul wishes to join are those whose existence is a living invitation for Christ to enter and indwell them. Such weakness encapsulates the core of Christian existence as a life of dependence on grace. What the weak still need, and what Paul correspondingly needs to bring them by becoming weak himself, is no more or less than to help them understand the pneumatologically privileged character of their lives as an open invitation for grace (>12:21–26).

Linguistic differences also indicate that Paul has a differentiated understanding of groups in their respective relationships to the law. There are those **under** (ὑπό/*hypo*) the law, the Jews; there are those **without** or **outside** of it (ἀνόμοις/*anomois*), the Gentiles; and there are those **under Christ's law**. In the original Greek the latter expression, ἔννομος Χριστοῦ (*ennomos Christou*), is a highly interesting combination of a spatial preposition, ἐν (*en*), and a noun, νόμος (*nomos*), that would be literally rendered "en-lawed." This compact expression invites us further to consider what precisely is at stake in the question of the enculturation of the gospel. While the laws of cultural etiquette are in themselves no longer binding for Christians, it does remain possible to move into the realm these laws hold open, to enter into and move freely within or outside their various spheres of influence. In contrast, the law of Christ cannot so easily be conceptualized in a framework of spatial negotiation. The gospel, in other words, is not like the Aristotelian category of "relation," that is, determined by the varying distance of the two entities that are literally kept within sight of each other.

Unlike the laws of culture, the law of Christ is not so much a sphere of influence but infuses Christians in a manner that empowers them to follow the progression of the gospel into all human sociocultural spheres, penetrating and transforming the patterns and game-rules by which they function—their "laws." As the spear of the Indian passes fatally into the flesh of the missionary, his refusal to retaliate allows the law of Christ to be tangibly present in a manner that penetrates and eventually transforms the cultural laws that sustain a culture of war.

How do we actually see Paul enacting this "becoming like" in the broader context of this letter? Is there any material evidence that he has given up anything to be with and "as" the Corinthians? Origen is the one church father who discusses this question in some detail, mentioning Paul's famous sermon to the Athenians as an example of the Apostle's accommodation to others' beliefs. He cites as examples of Paul's becoming "weak to the weak" his willingness to allow those "burning with desire" to marry, and showing sympathy for those who have lost their husbands. Although we find some of the examples Origen gives less than convincing, the question remains an insightful one. Though also rejecting his interpretation of Paul's "all things to all men" as being the highest level achievable in a schema of five categories of spiritual existence,[43] we would nevertheless like to enter the inquiry Origen opens into the linkage between Paul's weakness and his sympathy toward the real-life problems of the Corinthians.

Many of the instances of sociocultural accommodation Paul might have made on behalf of the Corinthians are lost in the mists of history, but a few have left obvious enough traces. We know that Paul was willing to eat with Gentiles, and the discussions reported among church leaders in Acts 15 and Galatians 2 reveal that one of the driving impulses of his mission to the Gentiles was to overcome the towering barriers various cultural conventions presented to eucharistic table fellowship (>ch. 14). But the most remarkable and least noticed piece of evidence we have for Paul's extensive accommodation to the Corinthians is his deep and patient investment in responding to their many questions and concerns. We understand this letter as one extensive proof that Paul's becoming "as" Corinthians entails entering the conversation they wish to have, working from the site of their expressed questions and concerns rather than dictating to them what he wants them to learn. In the face of their apparent lack of docility the Apostle sits down and patiently responds to their letters, at great length and with evident care, displaying why attentiveness and accommodation must be understood as integral to his gospel—and are, in fact, the heart of his apostolate. Such teaching, like all genuine teaching, is an intrinsically kenotic activity.[44]

Fitness for the Gospel

> [24] Do you not know that in a race the runners all compete, but only one receives the prize? Run in such a way that you may win it. [25] Athletes exercise self-control in all things; they do it to receive a perishable wreath, but we an imperishable one. [26] So I do not run aimlessly, nor do I box as though beating the air; [27] but I punish my body and enslave it, so that after proclaiming to others I myself should not be disqualified.

The foregoing discussion makes it impossible to see 9:24-27 as opening a new train of thought in which Paul, having completed the case for his

---

43. Origen, *Homilies on 1 Corinthians*, 512-14, quoted in JK, 155.
44. Bayer, *Contemporary in Dissent*, ch. 5.

kenotic apostolate, now concludes by stressing the individual Christian's training in spiritual exercises as a means to receiving his or her crown of eternal glory.[45] It is true that Paul draws the argument to its pinnacle by setting before his readers the vision of the ultimate goal of the Christian life, the imperishable wreath, contrasting it with all this-worldly gains and aims. We should be wary, however, of separating this concluding exhortation from the vision Paul has developed in the previous verses with its focus on the proclamation of the gospel and the specific relinquishments necessary to keep it free. As we have seen, this account of apostolic *exousia* was configured by the extrinsic character of the gospel and its reconfiguring power in the community, and thus in the Apostle's life. As he now carefully sets his understanding of the freedom of the gospel before the Corinthians, Paul simultaneously "exhibits the superlative discipline of his own life,"[46] which is oriented by a hope for present reward.

Far from prescribing a recipe for individual spiritual fitness, as contemporary ideas of "fitness training" immediately suggest, Paul actually uses a telling term in 9:27, ἀδόκιμος (*adokimos*), that can be translated to reveal a very different constellation of meaning. Its context, **but I punish my body and enslave it, so that after proclaiming to others I myself should not be disqualified** (*adokimos*), is as difficult to understand as it is key to the coherence of this concluding section. The NRSV translation gets going in the wrong direction in two ways. First, by rendering the aorist participle κηρύξας (*kēryxas*) as indicating a temporal sequence ("after"), it suggests that preaching is a stand-alone act that will only be subsequently assessed. Such temporal logic engenders the need to conceive of the "disqualification" as occurring by means of a forensic judgment. This interpretative train is even stronger in other translations, such as that of Luther or the German *Einheitsübersetzung* that render *adokimos* as *verwerflich* ("condemnable") or *verworfen* ("condemned"). The widespread tendency to read Paul as drawing this chapter together with a concluding treatise on the conditions for passing the bar at the final judgment sits, however, very uneasily with the train of thought he has developed so far in the chapter. What sort of climax do we have here if the Apostle, who opened by explaining the almost shocking scope of his willingness to renounce what should be coming to him as the result of his concern for others (and their eschatological fate), now ends

---

45. We are aware that this reading is a departure from the consensus readings, both modern and ancient. See Thiselton, ACT2, 716; Augustine, *On the Usefulness of Fasting* 5, PL 40:710–11, quoted in JK, 157–58; Calvin, JC 197. Our reading comes closest to that of Richard Hays, who notes the communal horizon of this passage but does not discuss how this reshapes readings of the "immortal prize" as post-temporal (RBH, 156).

46. Severian of Gabala, *Commentary on 1 Corinthians*, quoted in JK, 147.

by commending a renunciation aimed at securing his own individual place in the heavenly pantheon?

It seems far more plausible to read this last paragraph as a further point in elaborating Paul's extended defense of his kenotic apostolate, which would be disqualified were he to refuse to discipline himself to conform to the task given by the gospel. The Greek term *adokimos* does indeed denote a lack of fitness, not in the abstract sense of an overall characterization so much as in direct relation to a task that requires a specific set of skills to complete. A "flabby" person may be just the right person to be one's defense lawyer, for example. It is in keeping with Paul's understanding of gospel proclamation, entailing as it does the witness of the proclaimer's entire existence, that he concludes his *apologia* by reemphasizing the purposefulness of the Christian mission as the opposite of a boxer **beating the air**. Paul would be disqualified *as an apostle* if he abandoned the church to which Christ had bound him. This present tense reading of Paul's warnings against disqualification is strongly bolstered by the term's repetition in three successive verses in 2 Corinthians in reference to a this-worldly disqualification, or failure to qualify (2 Cor 13:5–7).[47]

The point of employing this language of disqualification becomes especially evident when 9:18, **that in my proclamation I may make the gospel free of charge**, is rendered literally "that in my evangelizing I will set out the gospel free of charge." The purpose of Christian witness does express a hope to receive an imperishable wreath, but as we have seen, this reward is not construed as an individual prize merited on the basis of individual spiritual fitness, but rather as an inheriting of the communal place that comes to all who have been made fit to be a **co-partaker of the gospel**. The reward that Paul seeks that "will never fade away" (as Thiselton translates it[48]) is not to be awaited in the distant future but must continually be sought and conformed to in each present moment: the coming into being, before his very eyes, of that community which is everlasting and in which he has a rightful place by the power of the gospel. This is also to understand the reference to imperishability here as a preparatory foreshadowing of the grand chapter on resurrection to come (chapter 15), with its emphasis on the rising of *all* the saints and their union with the *one* who wears the crown (>15:22–24).

We conclude by noting one further implication of our theological observations. First a comment on the burdens a misreading of this chapter has laid on Christians: the understanding of Christianity as a training regimen focused on achieving an eternal prize has fuelled and fostered a

---

47. Collins, RFC, 362–63.
48. Thiselton, ACT2, 714.

culture of introspection that places the insufferable burden on individuals of keeping watch over whether they have done enough to deserve a reward. It has further deformed Christian mission by setting up a *culture of competitive preaching*, in which evangelists mark their success by counting how many souls they have won.[49] This is paralleled by a *culture of prophylactic evaluation*, another missiological deformation tied up with an impulse to "make" effective converts through education and discipline that are taken to be necessary precursors to fellowship and discipleship.[50] These theological deformations have in the Western world exacerbated trends inside and outside of the church of valorizing rather than questioning competitive and pedagogical accounts of society as a whole. Despite the many criticisms leveled at Max Weber's *Protestant Ethic and the Spirit of Capitalism*, his insight remains valid that versions of Christianity that have emphasized the problem of the assurance of salvation and combined it with abstemious labor as a means of achieving such assurance have entrenched a spirit of enlightened self-interest that is the matrix of the *culture of individualized economic competition*.

Some have found Paul's use of athletic metaphors to suggest, if not exactly warrant, a theology of competition, but we have seen that such a reading runs in a diametrically opposite direction to his stated intention. By stressing that one (Christ) wins, Paul here (and in the rest of the Corinthian correspondence) renders himself unusable for substantiating the claim that competitive social organization is to be seen as the most productive way to draw the best out of individual human beings or communities. Paul's whole thrust in this chapter is to stress that *any* aspiration to perform in a way that "wins" *against* others is not only intrinsically prideful; it destroys the gospel. We might even go so far as to say that in the Corinthian correspondence, competition appears only as a rival to the community of gifts in which no agonism is necessary to bring each person to their fullest flourishing (>12:14–19). In Paul's writings the *agon* motif is sharply focused on drawing attention to the importance of Christian discipline, especially bodily self-discipline, not competition itself,[51] as the vast majority of the Christian tradition clearly grasped.[52]

---

49. In his *Homilies*, Origen explicitly relates the athletic metaphor to a competition between doctrines, religions, and philosophies in which the church is involved (*Homilies on 1 Corinthians*, 514, quoted in JK, 157).

50. Jennings, *Christian Imagination*, 108–15.

51. Collins, RFC, 358–63; Pfitzner, *Paul and the Agon Motif*.

52. Pfitzner, "We Are the Champions!," in Preece and Hess, *Sport and Spirituality*, 49–69.

We must ask ourselves, not only in the realm of sport but in wider spheres of human endeavor: why does it seem to us that collaborative social forms are less productive of human flourishing than competitive ones? The last decades have certainly seen increasing sympathy among politicians in the developed West for the idea that better teaching and health care provision (to take two of many examples) will result if practitioners are pitted against one another. In opposition to this trend, the recent rise of community organizing represents one of many possible countermovements seeking institutional forms in which people's abilities to speak for and from the community can be fostered and grown. Such social structures are built on the presumption that if one member of the group "wins," it is a win for the whole community. The implications of this point for theologically understanding political structures are far-reaching. Competition is clearly one way groups can be organized with the aim of enhancing the performances of all participants, but this institutional form stands at some considerable distance from the politics of the *ecclesia* in having no internal mechanisms and no imagination for how the winners' enhanced performance might be of direct benefit to the losers.

Bibliography

Agamben, Giorgio. *The Church and the Kingdom*. Translated by Leland de la Durantaye. London: Seagull, 2012.

Aquinas, Thomas. *Commentary on the First Epistle to the Corinthians*. Translated by Fabian Larcher and Daniel Keating. http://dhspriory.org/thomas/SS1Cor.htm.

———. *Summa Theologica*. Translated by Fathers of the English Dominican Province. 2nd rev. ed. 20 vols. London: Burns, Oates & Washbourne, 1912–42.

Arendt, Hannah. *The Human Condition*. 2nd ed. Chicago: University of Chicago Press, 1998.

Aristotle. *Nichomachean Ethics*. Translated, with Introduction, Notes, and Glossary, by Terence Irwin. 2nd ed. Indianapolis: Hackett Publishing, 1999.

Atkinson, Tyler. *Singing at the Winepress: Ecclesiastes and the Ethics of Work*. London: Bloomsbury T. & T. Clark, 2015.

Augustine, St. *Expositions of the Psalms*. Translated by Maria Boulding. Edited by John E. Rotelle. 6 vols. The Works of Saint Augustine, pt. 3, vols. 15–20. Hyde Park, NY: New City, 2000–2004.

———. *Answer to Faustus, A Manichean*. Translated by Roland Teske. Edited by Boniface Ramsey. The Works of St. Augustine, pt. 1, vol. 20. Hyde Park, NY: New City Press, 2007.

———. *On Christian Teaching* [*De doctrina Christiana*]. Translated with an introduction by R. P. H. Green. Oxford: Oxford University Press, 1997.

———. *On Genesis: A Refutation of the Manichees; Unfinished Literal Commentary on Genesis; The Literal Meaning of Genesis*. Translated by Edmund Hill. Edited by John E. Rotelle. The Works of Saint Augustine, pt. 1, vol. 13. Hyde Park, NY: New City, 2002.

Badiou, Alain. *Ethics: An Essay on the Understanding of Evil*. Translated by Peter Hallward. London: Verso, 2001.

———. *Saint Paul: The Foundation of Universalism*. Translated by Ray Brassier. Stanford: Stanford University Press, 2003.

Banner, Michael. "What We Lost When (or If) We Lost the Saints." In *The Freedom of a Christian Ethicist: The Future of a Reformation Legacy*, edited by Brian Brock and Michael Mawson, 175–90. London: Bloomsbury T. & T. Clark, 2016.

Barrett, C. K. *A Commentary on the First Epistle to the Corinthians*. 2nd ed. London: Adam and Charles Black, 1971.

Barth, Karl. *Church Dogmatics*. 3/1: *The Doctrine of Creation*. Translated by J. W. Edwards, O. Bussey, and H. Knight. Edited by G. W. Bromiley and T. F. Torrance. Edinburgh: T. & T. Clark, 1958.

———. *The Resurrection of the Dead*. Translated by H. J. Stenning. London: Hodder and Stoughton, 1933.

Barton, Stephen C. "1 Corinthians." In *Eerdmans Commentary on the Bible*, edited by James D. G. Dunn and John W. Rogerson, 1314-52. Grand Rapids: Eerdmans, 2003.

Bayer, Oswald. *A Contemporary in Dissent: Johann Georg Hamann as a Radical Enlightener.* Translated by R. A. Harrisville and M. C. Mattes. Grand Rapids: Eerdmans, 2012.

———. *Freedom in Response: Lutheran Ethics; Sources and Controversies.* Translated by Jeffrey F. Cayzer. Oxford: Oxford University Press, 2007.

Bennett, Jana. *Aquinas on the Web? Doing Theology in an Internet Age.* London: T. & T. Clark, 2011.

Bonhoeffer, Dietrich. *Berlin, 1932-1933.* Edited by Larry L. Rasmussen. Translated by Isabel Best and David Higgins. DBWE 12. Minneapolis: Fortress, 2009.

———. *Conspiracy and Imprisonment, 1940-1945.* Edited by Mark S. Brocker. Translated by Lisa E. Dahill. DBWE 16. Minneapolis: Fortress, 2006.

———. *Ethics.* Edited by Clifford J. Green. Translated by Reinhard Krauss, Charles C. West, and Douglas W. Stott. DBWE 6. Minneapolis: Fortress, 2005.

———. *Letters and Papers from Prison.* Edited by John W. de Gruchy. Translated by Isabel Best et al. DBWE 8. Minneapolis: Fortress, 2010.

———. *Life Together; Prayerbook of the Bible.* Edited by Geffrey B. Kelly. Translated by Daniel W. Bloesch and James H. Burtness. DBWE 5. Minneapolis: Fortress, 1996.

———. *Theological Education Underground, 1937-1940.* Edited by Victoria J. Barnett. Translated by Victoria J. Barnett et al. DBWE 15. Minneapolis: Fortress, 2012.

Bray, Gerald, ed. *1-2 Corinthians.* Ancient Christian Commentary on Scripture 7. Downers Grove, IL: InterVarsity, 1999.

Brock, Brian. "Augustine's Incitement to Lament, from the *Enarrationes in Psalmos*." In *Evoking Lament: A Systematic Theological Enquiry*, edited by Eva Harasta and Brian Brock, 183-202. London: T. & T. Clark, 2009.

———. *Singing the Ethos of God.* Grand Rapids: Eerdmans, 2007.

———. "Supererogation and the Riskyness of Human Vulnerability." In *The Paradox of Disability: Responses to Jean Vanier and L'Arche Communities from Theology and the Sciences*, edited by Hans Reinders, 127-39. Grand Rapids: Eerdmans, 2010.

Bultmann, Rudolph. *Theology of the New Testament.* Translated by Kendrick Grobel. 2 vols. Waco: Baylor University Press, 2007.

Calvin, John. *The First Epistle of Paul the Apostle to the Corinthians.* Translated by John W. Fraser. Edited by David W. Torrance and Tomas F. Torrance. Grand Rapids: Eerdmans, 1960.

———. *Institutes of the Christian Religion: 1541 French Edition.* Translated by Elsie Anne McKee. Grand Rapids: Eerdmans, 2009.

Cervantes, Miguel. *Don Quijote.* Translated by Burton Raffel, with Introduction by Diana de Armas Wilson. W. W. Norton & Company: New York, 1999.

Chappell, Timothy. *Knowing What to Do: Imagination, Virtue, and Platonism in Ethics.* Oxford: Oxford University Press, 2014.

Collins, Raymond F. *First Corinthians.* Sacra Pagina 7. Collegeville, MN: Liturgical, 1999.

Conzelmann, Hans. *1 Corinthians: A Commentary on the First Epistle to the Corinthians.* Translated by James Leitch. Edited by George W. MacRae. Hermeneia. Philadelphia: Fortress, 1975.

BIBLIOGRAPHY

Dahl, Nils A. "The Particularity of the Pauline Epistles as a Problem in the Ancient Church." In *Neotestamentica et Patristica*, edited by W. C. van Unnik, 261–71. Novum Testamentum Supplement 6. Leiden: Brill, 1962.

Danker, Frederick William, ed. *A Greek-English Lexicon of the New Testament and Other Early Christian Literature*. 3rd ed. Chicago: University of Chicago Press, 2000.

Deluz, Gaston. *A Companion to 1 Corinthians*. Edited and translated by Grace E. Watt. London: Darton, Longman & Todd, 1963.

Deming, Will. *Paul on Marriage and Celibacy: The Hellenistic Background of 1 Corinthians 7*. 2nd ed. Grand Rapids: Eerdmans, 2004.

Dix, Gregory. *The Shape of the Liturgy*. London: A. & C. Black, 1945.

Dolbeau, François. "Sermon inédit de saint Augustin sur la providence divine." *Revue des Études Augustiniennes* 41 (1995) 267–89.

Dorner, I. A. *System of Christian Ethics*. Translated by C. M. Mead and R. T. Cunningham. Edinburgh: T. & T. Clark, 1898.

Du Boulay, Juliet. *Cosmos, Life, and Liturgy in a Greek Orthodox Village*. Limni, Greece: Denise Harvey, 2009.

Dysinger, Luke. *Psalmody and Prayer in the Writings of Evagrius Ponticus*. Oxford: Oxford University Press, 2005.

Elliot, Carl. *Better than Well: American Medicine Meets the American Dream*. New York: Norton, 2003.

Engberg-Pedersen, Troels. "Paul, Virtues, and Vices." In *Paul in the Greco-Roman World: A Handbook*, edited by J. Paul Sampley, 608–33. Harrisburg, PA: Trinity Press International, 2003.

Fee, Gordon D. *The First Epistle to the Corinthians*. Grand Rapids: Eerdmans, 1987.

———. *God's Empowering Presence: The Holy Spirit in the Letters of Paul*. Peabody, MA: Hendrickson, 1994.

Fitzmyer, Joseph A. *First Corinthians: A New Translation with Introduction and Commentary*. New Haven: Yale University Press, 2008.

Foucault, Michel. *Ethics: Subjectivity and Truth*. Edited by Paul Rabinow. Translated by Robert Hurley et al. Essential Works of Michel Foucault 1. London: Penguin, 1997.

Fowl, Stephen E., and L. Gregory Jones. *Reading in Communion: Scripture and Ethic in the Christian Life*. Grand Rapids: Eerdmans, 1991.

Fromm, Erich. *To Have or to Be?* London: Continuum, 2005.

Furnish, Victor Paul. *The Theology of the First Letter to the Corinthians*. Cambridge: Cambridge University Press, 1999.

Garland, David E. *1 Corinthians*. Baker Exegetical Commentary on the New Testament. Grand Rapids: Baker, 2003.

Garver, Eugene. *Aristotle's "Rhetoric": An Art of Character*. Chicago: University of Chicago Press, 1994.

Girard, René. *The Scapegoat*. Translated by Yvonne Freccero. Baltimore: Johns Hopkins University Press, 1986.

Givens, Tommy. *We the People: Israel and the Catholicity of Jesus*. Minneapolis: Fortress, 2014.

Gooch, Paul W. *Partial Knowledge: Philosophical Studies in Paul*. Notre Dame: University of Notre Dame Press, 1987.

Goodrich, John. *Paul as an Administrator of God*. Cambridge: Cambridge University Press, 2012.

Goossen, Rachel Waltner. "'Defanging the Beast': Mennonite Responses to John Howard Yoder's Sexual Abuse." *The Mennonite Quarterly Review* 89 (2015) 7–80.

Hadot, Pierre *Philosophy as a Way of Life: Spiritual Exercises from Socrates to Foucault*. Edited by Arnold Davidson. Translated by Michael Chase. Oxford: Blackwell, 1995.

Hamann, Johann G. *Johann Georg Hamann: Writings on Philosophy and Language*. Translated and edited by Kenneth Haynes. Cambridge: Cambridge University Press, 2007.

Handelman, Susan A. *Fragments of Redemption: Jewish Thought and Literary Theory in Benjamin, Scholem, and Levinas*. Bloomington: Indiana University Press, 1991.

Hauerwas, Stanley. *Matthew*. Brazos Commentary on the Bible. Grand Rapids: Brazos, 2006.

———. *Performing the Faith: Bonhoeffer and the Practice of Nonviolence*. Grand Rapids: Brazos, 2004.

Hays, Richard. *First Corinthians*. Interpretation: A Bible Commentary for Teaching and Preaching. Louisville: John Knox, 1997.

Heidegger, Martin. *Nietzsche*. Vol. 1, *The Will to Power as Art*. Translated by David Farrell Krell. San Francisco: Harper and Row, 1991.

———. *The Phenomenology of Religious Life*. Translated by Matthias Fritsch and Jennifer Anna Gosetti-Ferencei. Bloomington: Indiana University Press, 2004.

Heil, John Paul. *The Letters of Paul as Rituals of Worship*. Eugene, OR: Cascade, 2011.

Heller, Kevin Jon. "Power, Subjectification and Resistance in Foucault." *SubStance* 25 (1996) 78–110.

Hempel, C., A. Lange, and H. Lichtenberger, eds. *The Wisdom Texts from Qumran and the Development of Sapiential Thought*. Louvain: Louvain University Press, 2002.

Hodge, Charles. *Commentary on 1 & 2 Corinthians*. Edinburgh: Banner of Truth, 1974.

Horbury, William. "Extirpation and Excommunication." *Vetus Testamentum* 35 (1985) 13–38.

Horrell, David. *Solidarity and Difference: A Contemporary Reading of Paul's Ethics*. London: T. & T. Clark, 2005.

James, William. *The Varieties of Religious Experience: A Study in Human Nature*. London: Longmans, Green, 1928.

Jennings, Willie James. *The Christian Imagination: Theology and the Origins of Race*. New Haven: Yale University Press, 2010.

Johnson, Kelly. *The Fear of Beggars: Stewardship and Poverty in Christian Ethics*. Grand Rapids: Eerdmans, 2007.

Kant, Immanuel. *The Metaphysics of Morals*. Translated and edited by Mary Gregor. Cambridge: Cambridge University Press, 1996.

Kierkegaard, Søren. *Works of Love*. Edited and translated by Howard Hong and Edna Hong. Princeton: Princeton University Press, 1995.

Kim, Yung Suk. *Christ's Body in Corinth: The Politics of a Metaphor*. Minneapolis: Fortress, 2008.

Kingsolver, Barbara. *The Poisonwood Bible*. London: Faber and Faber, 1999.

Kittel, Gerhard, ed. *Theological Dictionary of the New Testament*. Translated and edited by Geoffrey W. Bromiley. Vol. 3. Grand Rapids: Eerdmans, 1965.

Kovacs, Judith L., ed. and trans. *1 Corinthians: Interpreted by Early Christian Commentators*. The Church's Bible. Grand Rapids: Eerdmans, 2005.

Lebron, Tim. *Wittgenstein's Religious Point of View*. London: Continuum, 2008.

BIBLIOGRAPHY

Lindbeck, George A. *The Nature of Doctrine: Religion and Theology in a Postliberal Age.* Philadelphia: Westminster, 1984.

Lindemann, Andreas. *Der Erste Korintherbrief.* Tübingen: Mohr Siebeck, 2000.

Locke, John. *Two Treatises on Government.* Edited by Peter Laslett. Cambridge: Cambridge University Press, 1988.

Longenecker, Richard. "Ancient Amanuenses and the Pauline Epistles." In *New Dimensions in New Testament Study,* edited by Richard Longenecker and Merrill Tenney, 281-97. Grand Rapids: Zondervan, 1974.

Luther, Martin. *The Large Catechism (1529).* In *The Book of Concord: The Confessions of the Evangelical Lutheran Church.* Translated and edited by Theodore G. Tappert. Philadelphia: Fortress, 1959.

———. *Martin Luthers Epistel-Auslegung.* Vol. 2, *Die Korintherbriefe.* Edited by Eduard Ellwein. Göttingen: Vandenhoeck & Ruprecht, 1968.

———. *Martin Luther's Ninety-five Theses: With Introduction, Commentary, and Study guide.* Edited by Timothy J. Wengert. Minneapolis: Fortress, 2015.

———. *Luther's Works.* Edited by Jaroslav Pelikan and Helmut T. Lehmann. American ed. 55 vols. St. Louis: Concordia; Philadelphia: Fortress, 1955-86.

Malesic, Jonathan. *Secret Faith in the Public Square: An Argument for the Concealment of Christian Identity.* Grand Rapids: Brazos, 2009.

Marion, Jean-Luc. *God Without Being: Hors-Texte.* Translated by Thomas Carlson. Chicago: University of Chicago Press, 1991.

Martinez, Florentino Garcia, ed. *Wisdom and Apocalypticism in the Dead Sea Scrolls and in the Biblical Tradition.* Louvain: Louvain University Press, 2003.

Martyn, J. Louis. "De-apocalypticizing Paul: An Essay Focused on *Paul and the Stoics,* by Troels Engberg-Pedersen." *Journal for the Study of the New Testament* 24 (2002) 61-102.

McCarthy, David Matzko. *Sex and Love in the Home: A Theology of the Household.* London: SCM, 2001.

McClendon, James Wm., Jr., and James Smith. *Convictions: Defusing Religious Relativism.* Rev. ed. Valley Forge, PA: Trinity Press International, 1994.

Merleau-Ponty, Maurice. *Phenomenology of Perception.* Translated by Colin Smith. London: Routledge, 2002.

Miller, Colin D. *The Practice of the Body of Christ: Human Agency in Pauline Theology after MacIntyre.* Eugene, OR: Pickwick, 2014.

Murphy-O'Connor, Jerome. *Keys to First Corinthians: Revisiting the Major Issues.* Oxford: Oxford University Press, 2009.

Nietzsche, Friedrich. *The Birth of Tragedy and Other Writings.* Edited by Raymond Guess and Ronald Speirs. Translated by Ronald Speirs. Cambridge: Cambridge University Press, 1999.

———. *Aus dem Nachlaß der Achtziger Jahre;* in *Werke in drei Bänden.* Edited by Karl Schlechta. Vol. 3. Darmstadt: Wissenschaftliche Buchgesellschaft, 1994.

O'Donovan, Oliver. *On the Thirty-Nine Articles: A Conversation with Tudor Christianity.* Exeter: Paternoster, 1986.

Origen. *Homilies on 1 Corinthians*: "Documents: Origen on I Corinthians" [fragments from catenae]. Edited by Claude Jenkins. *Journal of Theological Studies* 9 (1908) 232-47, 353-72, 500-514; 10 (1909) 29-51.

Pfitzner, Victor C. *Paul and the Agon Motif: Traditional Athletic Imagery in the Pauline Literature.* Leiden: Brill, 1967.

Preece, Gordon, and Rob Hess, eds. *Sport and Spirituality: An Exercise in Everyday Theology*. Adelaide: ATF, 2009.

Rees, Geoffrey. *The Romance of Innocent Sexuality*. Eugene, OR: Cascade, 2011.

Rhees, Rush. *Rush Rhees on Religion and Philosophy*. Edited by D. Z. Phillips and Mario Von der Ruhr. Cambridge: Cambridge University Press, 1997.

Richards, Ernest Randolph. *The Secretary in the Letters of Paul*. Tübingen: Mohr, 1991.

Rienecker, Fritz, ed. *Sprachlicher Schlüssel zum Griechischen Neuen Testament*. Giessen: Brunnen, 1977.

Rosenzweig, Franz. *Der Mensch und sein Werk: Gesammelte Schriften*. Edited by Reinhold Mayer and Annemarie Mayer. 4 vols. Dordrecht: Martinus Nijhoff, 1984.

———. *The Star of Redemption*. Translated by Barbara E. Galli. Madison: University of Wisconsin Press, 2005.

Santner, Eric L. *On the Psychotheology of Everyday Life: Reflections on Freud and Rosenzweig*. Chicago: University of Chicago Press, 2001.

Schleiermacher, Friedrich. *On Religion: Speeches to Its Cultured Despisers*. Translated by John Oman. Introduction by Rudolph Otto. New York: Harper & Row, 1958.

Serres, Michael. *The Five Senses: A Philosophy of Mingled Bodies*. Translated by Margaret Sankey and Peter Cowley. London: Continuum, 2008.

Shuman, Joel James, and Keith Meador. *Heal Thyself: Spirituality, Medicine, and the Distortion of Christianity*. Oxford: Oxford University Press, 2003.

Spaemann, Robert. *Persons: The Difference between "Someone" and "Something"*. Translated by Oliver O'Donovan. Oxford: Oxford University Press, 2007.

Staab, K., ed. *Pauluskommentar aus der griechischen Kirche aus Katenhandschriften gesammelt*. Münster: Aschendorff, 1933.

Stout, Jeffrey. *Democracy and Tradition*. Princeton: Princeton University Press, 2004.

Stuhlmacher, Peter. "The Hermeneutical Significance of 1 Cor 2:6–16." Translated by Colin Brown. In *Tradition and Interpretation in the New Testament: Essays in Honor of E. Earl Ellis for His 60th Birthday*, edited by Gerland F. Hawthorne and Otto Betz, 328–47. Grand Rapids: Eerdmans, 1987.

Swartley, Willard. *Slavery, Sabbath, War and Women: Case Issues in Biblical Studies*. Scottdale, PA: Herald, 1983.

Taylor, N. H. "Conflict as Context for Defining Identity: A Study of Apostleship in the Galatian and Corinthian Letters." *HTS Teologiese Studies/Theological Studies* 59 (2003) 915–45.

Thiselton, Anthony C. *First Corinthians: A Shorter Exegetical and Pastoral Commentary*. Grand Rapids: Eerdmans, 2006.

———. *The First Epistle to the Corinthians: A Commentary on the Greek Text*. Grand Rapids: Eerdmans, 2000.

Ulrich, Hans G. *Eschatologie und Ethik: Die theologische Theorie der Ethik in ihrer Beziehung auf die Rede von Gott seit Friedrich Schleiermacher*. Munich: Chr. Kaiser, 1988.

Verhoef, Eduard. "The Senders of the Letters to the Corinthians and the Use of 'I' and 'We.'" In *The Corinthian Correspondence*, edited by R. Bieringer, 417–25. BETL 125. Leuven: Leuven University Press/Peeters, 1996.

Wannenwetsch, Bernd. "'But to *Do* Right . . .': Why the Language of 'Rights' Does Not Do Justice to Justice." *Studies in Christian Ethics* 23 (2010) 138–46.

———. "Conversing with the Saints as They Converse with Scripture: In Conversation with Brian Brock's *Singing the Ethos of God*." *European Journal of Theology* 18 (2009) 125-36.

———."Die ethische Dimension der Liturgie." In *Gottesdienst der Kirche; Handbuch der Liturgiewissenschaft; Teil II, Band 2: Theologie des Gottesdienstes*, edited by M. Klöckener et al., 359-402. Regensburg: Friedrich Pustet, 2008.

———. *Die Freiheit der Ehe: Das Zusammenleben von Frau und Mann in der Wahrnehmung evangelischer Ethik*. Neukirchen-Vluyn: Neukirchener, 1993.

———. "Ecclesiology and Ethics." In *The Oxford Handbook of Theological Ethics*, edited by Gilbert Meilaender and William Werpehowski, 57-73. Oxford: Oxford University Press, 2005.

———. "'Members of One Another': *Charis*, Ministry and Representation; A Politico-Ecclesial Reading of Romans 12." In *A Royal Priesthood? The Use of the Bible Ethically and Politically: A Dialogue with Oliver O'Donovan*, edited by Craig Bartholomew et al., 196-220. Carlisle: Paternoster, 2002.

———. "Owning Our Bodies? The Politics of Self-Possession and the Body of Christ (Hobbes, Locke, Paul)." *Studies in Christian Ethics* 26 (2013) 50-65.

———. "Political Love: Why John's Gospel Is Not as Barren for Contemporary Ethics as It Might Appear." In *"You Have the Words of Eternal Life": Transformative Readings of the Gospel of John from a Lutheran Perspective*, edited by Kenneth Mtata, 93-105. Lutheran World Federation Documentation 57. Minneapolis: Lutheran University Press, 2012.

———. *Political Worship*. Translated by Margaret Kohl. Oxford: Oxford University Press, 2004.

———. "Sin as Forgetting: Negotiating Divine Presence." *Studies in Christian Ethics* 28 (2015) 3-20.

Watson, Francis. *Paul and the Hermeneutics of Faith*. London: T. & T. Clark, 2004.

Wiemer, Axel. *"Mein Trost, Kampf und Sieg ist Christus": Luther's eschatologische Theologie nach seinen Reihenpredigten zu 1. Korinther 15 (1532/33)*. Berlin: de Gruyter, 2003.

Witherington, Ben. *Conflict and Community in Corinth: A Socio-Rhetorical Commentary on 1 and 2 Corinthians*. Grand Rapids: Eerdmans, 1995.

Name Index

Adam, 16
Agamben, Giorgio, 160, 161n28
Ambrosiaster, 4n6, 6n8, 10n17, 22n34
Apollos 18, 20, 65, 74–75, 78
Aquinas, Thomas, 81nn7, 9, 107n24, 123n15, 131n27, 165n30, 166, 206, 206nn16, 18
Arendt, Hannah, 6n10, 217n40
Aristotle, 52, 209n23
Atkinson, Tyler, 71n11
Augustine xvii, xvii*nn*2–3, 95–96, 95n6, 96nn7–10, 117, 137n2, 171, 171n3, 175, 176n7, 198n7, 206, 214n38, 222n45

Baal, 42n4
Bach, Johann Sebastian, 208
Badiou, Alain, 33n46
Banner, Michael, 74n14
Barnabas, 195
Barrett, C. K., 82nn12–13, 83, 83n14, 116, 116n6, 130, 130nn24–25, 131–32, 131n28, 143n13, 172n2, 177, 181
Barth, Karl, 30n44, 81n7, 213n35
Barton, Stephen, 7, 7n12, 25n40
Bayer, Oswald, 30n43, 153n20, 221n44
Beethoven, Ludwig van, 208
Bennett, Jana, 134n30
Bonhoeffer, Dietrich, 11n19, 12n19, 22, 22n36, 40n1, 54n16, 68n6, 69–70, 70n8, 72n12, 83n15, 84n16, 91n2, 135n31
Bray, Gerald, 35n50
Brock, Brian, ix, x, 54n15, 64n3, 80n6, 96n10, 115n5
Bultmann, Rudolf, 12n20, 38

Calvin, John, 45n9, 81n7, 98n11, 117, 117n8, 120–21, 120nn11–13, 126n17, 128n20, 129n21, 130, 131n26, 155n20, 175, 202n13, 206, 206n19, 222n45
Cephas, 18, 74–75, 196
Cervantes, 127, 127n18
Chappell, Timothy, 212n29
Chrysostom, 20, 20nn29–30, 21, 21n31, 22n35, 24n38, 68n5, 81n7, 100n16, 103n19, 104n20, 193, 193n4, 202n13
Clement of Alexandria, 64
Cloe, 18
Collins, Raymond F., 47n11, 155n21, 213n37, 223n47, 224n51
Conzelmann, Hans, 10n16, 47n12, 77n4, 81, 81nn8, 10
Crispus, 22
Cyril, 34n49, 45n8

Dahl, Nils A., 53n14
Deluz, Gaston, 211n28
Deming, Will, 140n9, 143n12, 155n23
Descartes, René, 40
Dix, Gregory, 104nn22–23
Dolbeau, François, 202n13
Donatus, 4n6
Dorner, Isaak, 190, 191n1
Du Boulay, Juliet, 104n22
Dysinger, Luke, 64n2

Elijah, 42n4
Elisha, 91n1
Elliot, Carl, 139n8
Elliot, Jim, 214
Engberg-Pederson, Troels, 38n54
Eve, 16

235

Name Index

Fee, Gordon D., 200n10, 213n37
Fitzmeyer, Joseph A., 94n4
Foucault, Michel, 212, 212n33
Fowl, Stephen E., 58n20
Furnish, Victor P., 93n3

Garland, David, 13n22, 111n1, 126n1, 137n3
Garver, Eugene, 23n37
Girard, René, 183
Givens, Tommy, 33n47
Gooch, Paul W., 218n42
Goodrich, John, 197n6, 210n25
Goossen, Rachel Waltner, 132n29

Hadot, Pierre, 58n21
Hamann, Johann G., 30, 30n34
Handelman, Susan A., 56n19
Hauck, 209n24
Hauerwas, Stanley, v, xi, 37n53, 102n17, 198n8
Hays, Richard, 1n2, 9n13, 12, 12n21, 18, 18n28, 45n7, 91n1, 95n5, 104n21, 119, 119n9, 168n31, 192n3, 197n6, 201n12, 204n14
Heidegger, Martin, 7, 7n11, 212, 212n31
Heil, John Paul, 13n23
Heller, Kevin Jon, 213n36
Hodge, Charles, 27n42
Horrell, David, 103n18, 129, 129n22,
Husserl, Edmund, 210

Ignatius of Antioch, 64
Illich, Ivan, xix

James, William, 34, 34n48
Jennings, Willie J., 217n41, 224n50
Jerome, 15n26, 137n2
Johnson, Kelly, 200n11
Jones, Gregory L., 58n20
Julian, 113n3, 114–15
Jungmann, Josef, 104n22

Kant, Immanuel, 140n10
Kierkegaard, Søren A., 14n24
Kim, Yung Suk, 36n51
Kingsolver, Barbara, 194–95, 194n5

Lebron, Tim, 71n10
Lietzmann, Hans, 130
Lindbeck, George, 188n14
Lindemann, Andreas, 211n27
Locke, John, 139n6
Longenecker, Richard, 1n1
Luther, Martin, xvi, xvin1, 15n25, 16n27, 40n2, 61, 64n1, 76–77, 76n1, 77n2,5, 108, 115, 115n4, 127n19, 153–54, 153n20, 161, 175, 175n6, 176n8, 182, 206n17, 207n21, 222

MacIntryre, Alasdair, xviiin4
Malesic, Jonathan, 46n10
Marion, Jean-Luc, 175n5
Martinez, Florentino G., 47n12
Martyn, J. Louis, 55n17
Maximus Confessor, 37, 37n53
McCain, John, 188–89
McCarthy, David Matzko, 144n14
McClendon, James Wm., Jr., 184, 184n12
Melanchthon, Philipp, 81n7
Merleau-Ponty, Maurice, 156nn25–26, 158n27
Miller, Colin D., xviiin4, 38n55, 68n7
Moses, 195
Murphy-O'Connor, Jerome, 1n3, 153–54, 153nn17–19, 156, 180n9, 192n2, 200n9

Nietzsche, Friedrich, 2, 36, 37n52, 212, 212n30.31
Novatian, 4n6

Oecumenicus, 45n8
O'Donovan, Oliver, 206n20
Origen, 10, 10nn15, 17, 37n53, 44n6, 45n8, 64, 77n3, 205n15, 213, 213n37, 216n39, 221, 221n43, 224n49

Pfitzner, Victor, 224nn51–52
Plato, 24

Qoheleth, 72

Rhees, Rush, 30, 30n45, 140n11
Richards, Ernest R., 1n1
Rienecker, Fritz, 124n16, 174n4
Rosenzweig, Franz, 55, 55n18

Schleiermacher, Friedrich D. E., 10n14, 179
Serres, Michael, 130, 130n23
Severiano of Gabala, 222n46
Smith, James, 184, 184n12
Sosthenes, 1–3, 22
Spaemann, Robert, 139n5
Stephanas, 22
Stout, Jeffrey, 198n8
Stuhlmacher, Peter, 44n6, 60, 60n22
Swartley, Willard, 151n16

Taylor, N. H., 2n4
Tertullian, 137n2
Theodoret, 1n3, 68n4, 121, 122n14
Thistleton, Anthony, 109n25, 112n2, 113n3, 138n4, 142–43, 160, 168, 168n32, 172, 174, 177, 182n10, 194, 202n13, 208, 208n22, 210n26, 222n44, 223, 223n48
Timothy, 84

Ulrich, Hans G., xv, xvi, 145, 213n34

Verhoef, Eduard, 1n3

Wannenwetsch, Bernd, ix, x, 3n5, 4n7, 21n32, 26n41, 71n10, 74n13, 82n11, 116n7, 119n10, 139n7, 156n24, 163n29
Warren, Rick, 188
Watson, Francis, 109n26
Weber, Max, 2, 224
Wiemer, Axel, 40n2
Witherington, Ben, 213n37

Yoder, John Howard, 132n29

Subject Index

abortion, 188
abstinence, 137, 137n3, 138, 142–44
accountability, accountable, 75, 77–80
adultery, 127, 165, 205
adventure, xxii
aesthetics, aesthetical, 12, 176, 208–9
agency, xiin4, 3, 38, 66–67, 68n7, 116, 170, 177–79, 182, 186, 208, 213
alliance, xxi, 73, 84, 215
anthropology, anthropological, 48, 127, 138, 171n1
apocalyptic, xviiin4, 47n12, 55n17
apology, *apologia*, apologetic, 109, 192, 198, 203, 215, 223
apostolate, 1, 2, 5–7, 44, 57, 78, 82, 84, 97, 190, 192, 196, 203, 210n25, 215, 221, 223
apostolicity, apostolic, xx–xi, 2, 5–8, 22–24, 43, 53, 56–59, 63, 66, 82, 86, 113, 137–38, 141, 145, 166–67, 192–93, 196–99, 210, 222
arbitration, 111–18, 120
asceticism, ascetic, 50, 137–38, 190, 195, 211, 214
authority, ix, x, xviii, xix–xx, 2, 3, 5–9, 6n9, 21, 34n49, 53, 58–59, 86–87, 97, 109, 115n4, 122, 135–36, 139–40, 145, 148–49, 159, 166–67, 181–82, 185, 188, 193, 195–98
authorship, 2, 6n9

baptism, baptismal, 4n6, 22–23, 91, 102–4, 110, 121–22, 155–56, 155n23, 177
belief, believe, xvi, 5, 14, 33, 47, 47n12, 66, 68, 88, 127, 139, 167, 182, 184–85, 188, 220

belong, 18–19, 21, 25, 63, 65, 73–75, 122, 128, 135, 148, 151, 154, 168, 175n6
Bible, xvi, xviin3, 22n36, 68n6, 83n15, 135n31, 194n5, 195, 218
biblical, xiii–xiv, xviin2, 44, 48, 54–55, 60–62, 71, 74, 80, 88–89, 194n21, 108–10, 136n1, 158, 177, 198, 202
boasting, xviii, 1, 14, 37, 45n7, 72–73, 80, 83, 93–94, 102, 133, 203–5, 210n25, 215
body, bodiliness, xviin2, 29, 40n2, 64, 69, 97, 107, 125–31, 135–36, 138–40, 142, 151–52, 156, 159, 213–14, 221–22
Body of Christ, ix–x, xiii–xiv, xviin2, xviii, xviiin4, xix, xx, 6, 9, 11, 20–23, 25, 31–32, 50, 57, 59, 64, 68n7, 74–75, 93–97, 100–104, 104n23, 108, 116, 118–19, 122–25, 134, 146, 166, 176, 182, 187, 189, 199, 213, 216
bread, 102–5, 108, 213
building up, xix, 67, 109, 166, 171, 186–87. See also *oikodome*
buyer, buy, 16, 158, 162–64, 194

canon, canonical, xv, 23, 47, 62, 74, 117, 120
casuistry, casuistic, 38, 99
Cartesian, xvi, 40, 139, 157n25
celibacy, celibate, 136–37, 137n3, 140n9, 141–43, 143n12, 149, 152, 155n23, 165, 197
chastity, chaste, 89, 136–37, 136n2, 141–42, 144, 146–56, 164, 166–68, 206

Subject Index

child, xvii*n*2, 6n8, 8, 67, 77n3, 82, 85–86, 107, 133, 147, 152–53, 155, 155n23, 161, 218
chronos, chronological, 160–62, 167–68
Christology, christological, 40, 40n1–2, 49, 54n16, 95, 213
circumcision, circumcise, 147, 149, 151, 161
coauthor, xxi
commandment, 16, 114, 122, 148–49, 165
commentary, ix–x, xiii–xv, xxi–xxii, 53–54, 61, 157, 201
commodity, commodification, 20–21, 34n49
communication, communicant, 27, 29, 39, 44–45, 53, 89, 104n23, 107, 122, 129–30, 132n29, 134–35, 157, 180, 186, 209, 218
community, xviii–xix, 4–5, 7–19, 9n13, 21–22, 24–26, 30–31, 36–37, 41–42, 45n9, 49–51, 53, 57, 63–64, 67, 72n12, 75–76, 78, 84, 84n16, 86–87, 91–96, 98–106, 108–110, 112, 118–19, 125, 133–34, 146, 156, 167, 169, 181, 187, 196–97, 197n6, 210, 213n37, 222–25
competition, competitiveness, competitive, 15, 20, 71, 141, 190, 214, 224–25, 224n49
concession, 7, 15, 113, 116, 136–38, 141–43, 145–46, 165–66
condescension, condescending, xxii, 113, 119
confession, confessional, xvii–xviii, 17–18, 154, 156, 176–78, 183, 188–89
conflict, conflicted, conflictual, ix–x, xii, xix, 2, 2n4, 4, 6–7, 12–13, 16, 18–19, 25, 28, 30–31, 34, 37, 39, 42, 57, 112–13, 115, 151, 176n8, 213n37
conformation, conformity, conform, xiv, 32–33, 72, 78, 93, 163, 175–76, 178–79, 184, 201, 212–14, 216, 223

congregation, congregationalism, xix, xxi, 6, 8, 14, 57, 75, 85–86, 99–101, 109n25, 124–25, 144
conscience, 70, 78, 116, 119–21, 169–70, 171n1, 173, 176, 176n8, 179–84, 186, 188–89, 206
convention, xiii, xvii*n*3, 8, 53, 145, 197
conversion, xxii, 2–3, 7
conviction, x, xv, xvii, 58–59, 157, 166, 183–84
counsel, 15, 89, 114, 145, 161, 164–65, 205
court, 7, 76, 79, 108, 111–17, 119–23, 125, 127, 218
covenant, covenantal, 9n13, 33, 100n16, 123, 140, 155, 172
co-worker, 1, 66
creation, creator, create, creaturely, ix, xv, xviii, xx, 7–8, 11, 13, 17, 21, 24, 26, 29–31, 38, 43, 50, 52, 72, 84n16, 87, 92, 105, 109, 138, 139n6, 141, 152–53, 157–58, 160–63, 168, 172–73, 175, 178–80, 185, 194, 202, 207, 216, 217n40
criticism, critic, criticize, critical, xiii–xiv, xvi–xviii, xx, xxiii, 1n3, 10n17, 11, 15, 21, 21n33, 26, 40, 45, 54, 57, 60–62, 77, 80, 88–89, 98, 101, 106, 115, 120–21, 140, 143, 146, 153, 155n23, 156, 160, 162, 164–65, 168, 179, 189, 212, 224
cross, 13–14, 23–24, 26–31, 34–36, 41, 46, 95, 195
crucifixion, crucify, crucified, xiv, 21–22, 25–26, 27n42, 29, 31–32, 35–37, 39–41, 42, 44, 45n8, 46–47, 53–54, 60, 80–81, 135, 151, 157, 214
cruciformity, cruciform, 25, 27, 37, 41–42, 46–47, 53
culture, cultural, xiv, 20, 47, 55–56, 58–59, 127, 130, 132–34, 137n3, 139, 189, 191, 194–95, 197, 204, 207, 211, 213–21, 224

Decalogue, 16
deism, deist, 46

Subject Index

democracy, democratic, 21n33, 75, 198n8

die, dying, 25, 180–81, 203–4

diet, dietary, xix–xx, 124

discernment, discern, xv–xvii, 24, 27, 39, 50, 51–53, 55–57, 60, 63–64, 67, 69, 74, 83, 96–97, 99, 108, 119, 158–59, 162, 166–68, 193, 199–200, 217

discipline, xvi–xvii, 23, 50, 61, 98n11, 99, 104, 104n21, 110, 138, 141, 143–44, 152, 190–93, 211–14, 216

discovery, discover, ix–x, xiii, xv–xvii, xx–xxii, 1, 4, 7–8, 11, 14, 17, 30, 34, 51, 56, 58n21, 59, 61–62, 72, 88–89, 98, 104n22, 110, 118, 146, 151–52, 155, 157, 187, 198, 201, 211, 213, 219

dispute, xviii, 6–7, 11–13, 19, 28, 50, 67, 74, 91, 111–14, 116–20, 126, 170

divorce, 34, 146–48

death, 29, 40n2, 69, 73–74, 81, 83, 100n15, 160, 176n8

doctrine, doctrinal, xv, xviii, 96, 161, 176–78, 183–86, 188n14, 205, 207, 224n49,

Donatist, 4, 103

doubt, xvi, 40, 158n27

dough, 93, 101–4, 103n18, 106, 108

doxology, doxological, 9–14, 16–17, 19, 26, 38, 64, 79–80

duty, 70, 120, 140, 146, 206n19

eat, xviii, 58, 64, 107–8, 124, 127, 170, 173, 176, 178, 180–83, 185, 204

ecclesia, ecclesial, ecclesiastical, xviii, xxi, 7–8, 15–16, 24–15, 37n53, 38, 60, 66, 69, 73, 76, 95–96, 99, 101, 105, 109, 111–17, 119, 125, 134, 216, 225

ecclesiology, ecclesiological, xx, 4n7, 35–36, 49

economy, economic, 15, 34, 54, 56, 73, 79, 124, 161–63, 179, 185, 207, 209, 210n25, 224

empiricism, empirical, 12, 14, 32, 97–98, 157n25

epistemological, 27, 36, 54n16, 157

epistle, epistolary, xiv–xvii, xx, xxii, 1–2, 5, 8, 11, 16, 23, 35, 57, 62

eschatology, eschatological, xix, 23, 29, 82–83, 126, 161, 210–13, 210n25, 219, 222

exegesis, exegete, exegetical, xiii–xvii, xx–xxi, 3n5, 44, 54, 58, 60–61, 73, 88–90, 99, 107n24, 111, 128, 130, 136, 145, 150, 158, 163n29

exousia, 124, 140, 181, 193, 196, 199, 222

experience, xiii, xv, xvii, 7, 13, 26, 30, 34n48, 52, 61–62, 78, 91n1, 135, 139, 158, 160–61, 164, 169, 172–73, 176n8, 189–90, 208, 217

explanation, explain, explanatory, xvi–xvii, xviin3, xxi, 1n1, 7–8, 28, 43, 45, 46n10, 56, 74, 82, 88, 90, 93, 99n13, 107, 109, 130, 136, 137n3, 149, 154–55, 157, 160–61, 163–64, 166, 172, 174, 176, 184, 193, 196, 213, 215, 222

ethics, ethical, xviiin4, xx, 4n7, 14, 38, 40n1, 50, 92, 94, 98–99, 106, 129, 135, 146, 166, 169, 189–91, 191n1, 209n23, 212, 212nn32–33, 213, 224

ethos, xiv, xviii, 6, 54n15, 64n3, 80n6, 92–94, 100–101, 103–4, 110, 114–15, 118, 120, 122, 127, 135

Eucharist, eucharistic, 64, 95, 100, 102, 104–5, 108, 110, 127, 134–35, 221

evangelism, 218–19

excommunication, 77n3, 99–101, 102n17, 104

existence, 3, 8–9, 29–30, 36, 40n2, 63, 71, 79, 94, 111–13, 117, 125, 128, 131, 135, 139, 150, 153, 155, 157, 162–63, 168, 173–75, 178–79, 181, 189, 196, 220–21, 223

faction, factionalism, xiv, xviii–xix, 1, 4, 6–7, 9, 12–14, 19–21, 23–25, 31–32, 34, 36, 46, 63, 65–66, 69–74, 76, 80, 188

Subject Index

faith, xiv, xvi, xviii, xx, 9–10, 15–16, 19–20, 36, 39, 42n4, 43, 46, 46n10, 49, 50, 59–60, 67, 73–74, 84, 88, 99, 100, 102n17, 109n26, 119, 153–54, 157, 167, 175n6, 176, 176n8, 178–79, 184–85, 189–91, 198n8, 207, 214n38
faithful, faithfulness, 4, 9, 12, 14, 59, 74, 77–79, 81–82, 85, 93, 112, 163, 190, 196, 210n25, 212–14
family, familial, ix–xi, 86, 118–19, 169, 172, 180–81, 187–88, 194–95
father, fatherhood, fatherly, xxi, 3, 5–6, 8, 14, 17, 21, 26, 28–29, 34n49, 43, 47, 75, 82, 85–88, 91–92, 94, 95, 173, 178–79, 194–96, 218
Fathers (Church), 21n32, 35, 45, 46n10, 61, 64, 74, 76, 136n2, 197
flight, flee, 90, 129, 131–35, 132n29, 150–51, 168
freedom, 32, 78, 88, 94, 117, 134, 148, 151, 153n20, 167, 181, 183, 187–88, 190–95, 200–201, 203–7, 206n17, 209–11, 215–17, 219, 222
friend, x–xi
food, 16–17, 58, 63–64, 104–5, 124–26, 131, 169–70, 173, 176, 179–83, 185, 187–88, 191, 195–97
folly, fool, foolishness, 13–14, 23, 24, 26–29, 31, 32–33, 35–36, 51, 54, 71–72, 77n3, 81, 84–85
formation, x, 40n1, 153, 184, 189, 211
fornication, 125–26, 128–31
foundation, foundational, 65–68, 70, 78, 85, 87, 97, 129, 174, 188, 196
foundationalist, 33

gift, xix, 8–10, 12–16, 19–20, 28, 31, 38, 40, 48–49, 51–52, 75, 80–81, 84, 101, 134–35, 142–43, 156, 158, 164, 180n9, 208, 211, 214, 218, 224
gnosis, Gnosticism, gnostic, 13, 15, 24–25, 27–29, 46–47, 47n11–12, 50–52, 57, 59–61, 73, 135, 143n12, 176, 186–87, 189
Golden Calf, 71, 73
gospel, ix, xvii–xviii, 10–11, 23, 26, 27n42, 28, 34n49, 36–37, 64, 69, 77n3, 85–86, 92, 101, 119n10, 147, 149, 185, 191–96, 198–211, 213, 215–24
grace, 3, 8–9, 11–12, 16–17, 25–26, 41, 53, 64–66, 105, 150, 153, 206, 220
greed, greedy, 105–8, 121
Greeks, 31–33, 35, 54, 107, 160
growth, 34, 65–66, 68, 152, 176, 183, 190

habit, habituation, habitual, x, xv, xvii, xx, 9, 15, 54, 55, 57, 76, 107n24, 110, 124, 132, 135, 147, 150, 153–54, 176, 179, 181, 184, 189–90, 201, 211–12, 214, 218
heart, xviin3, xix, 38, 48, 76, 77n3, 79, 109, 175, 175n6, 184, 195, 217
Hellenistic, 13, 146
hermeneutic(s), hermeneutic, hermeneutical, xiii–xvi, 44, 58–59, 60n22, 87, 89, 109, 109n26, 145, 184, 201–2, 211
heroic, 190, 193–95
historicist, 53
history, historical, x, xvii, xx, 2, 11, 45–46, 47n12, 48, 53–57, 59–61, 67, 69, 94, 96, 112, 137n3, 143n12, 155n23, 168, 197n6, 201
homiletic, xxi
homosexual, 112
hope, hopeful, xvi–xvii, 1, 11–12, 14, 26, 29, 34, 72–73, 79, 82, 84n16, 99–101, 118, 127–28, 131, 137, 144, 152, 154, 157, 163–64, 169, 175, 187, 191, 196–98, 202, 210–12, 222–23
horizon, xiii, xx–xxi, 29, 46, 59, 74, 89, 95, 103, 106, 128, 144, 185, 210–11, 222n45
household, 21–22, 76
husband, 128, 136, 139–41, 147, 152, 159, 165–66, 218, 221
idealism, idealist, 114, 157, 190
identity, 3, 18–19, 56, 59, 93, 114, 219
idol, 58, 71, 124, 169–70, 173–83, 185, 187, 189, 192, 204
idolatry, idolater, idolatrous, xviii, 19–20, 64, 69–73, 99n13, 105, 107, 121, 152, 189

Subject Index 243

imitation, imitator, 56, 85–86
immorality, immoral, 4, 91–92, 101, 105–7, 122, 128–30, 135–36, 141–42, 218
indicative-imperative-scheme, 12, 38, 103
individual, xix, 10–11, 19–20, 25, 28–29, 33, 51–52, 74, 98–99, 108, 115–16, 118–19, 122–26, 128, 135, 144, 156, 167, 171, 186, 214, 216, 220, 222, 224
individualist, individualistic, 9, 20, 22, 123, 135, 180, 210
infant, 63, 155
intercourse, 137, 139, 141–42
interpretation, interpretative, xiii, xv–xvi, xx–xxii, 10–12, 30, 47n12, 49, 61–62, 67, 77, 80–81, 87–91, 105–6, 108, 110–11, 113–17, 129–30, 132, 141, 145, 162, 165, 174, 190, 196, 198, 200–203, 208, 210, 221–22
intimacy, intimate, 87, 97, 129–30, 138, 140, 146, 193
irony, ironic, ironical, xxii, 2–3, 10, 16, 32–33, 36, 44–47, 45n7, 52, 81, 81n7, 82–85, 87–88, 97, 124, 134, 143

Jew, Jewry, Jewish, 31–33, 33n46, 34n49, 35, 45n8, 47n12, 54–56, 56n19, 101n16, 108, 112, 146, 214, 216, 219–20
judge, xiii, 44, 58, 60, 67–69, 76–78, 77n3, 80, 89, 97, 105–6, 111–13, 116, 121, 150, 170, 187
judgment, 8, 11, 15, 17, 24, 33, 36, 61, 64–73, 75–80, 77n3, 97–102, 105–6, 108, 112, 116–17, 121, 132n29, 133, 144–45, 152, 159, 165, 167–70, 222
justice, injustice, 37, 88, 112–18, 120–26, 135, 145, 198, 200
justification, xviiin4, 36, 38, 80, 94, 120, 122, 148, 153–56

kairos, kairotic, 160–64, 166, 168, 189

kenosis, kenotic, 23–24, 27, 41, 44, 84, 157, 192, 196, 215, 218–19, 221–23
kingdom, 8, 82–83, 85, 121–23, 160, 161n28, 162
knowledge, xiv, xvi, xviin3, xxii, 2, 7, 9–10, 13, 19, 24–25, 28, 30n43, 39–41, 43–44, 46–52, 46n12, 47n12, 57, 59–63, 67, 72, 97–98, 169–73, 171n2, 176–89, 218n42

labor, xv, 1n1, 62, 65, 67–68, 104, 187, 195, 199–200, 202, 204, 208, 224
lament, 95–96, 96n10, 201
law, lawful, xviii, 11, 36, 99n13, 100n16, 101–2, 109–12, 120n12, 123–24, 138, 142, 149, 151, 195, 198, 200n9, 202, 214–15, 218–20
lawsuit, 111–19, 122–24, 123n15
leader, leadership, xix, 19–20, 26, 68, 70–76, 78, 187, 197, 201
legal, xviii, 98, 111, 113–15, 117, 119–21, 125–26, 140, 188
liar, 129
liberalism, liberal, 87, 93, 107, 133, 215
liberation, 72, 78–79, 127, 132, 144, 147, 176, 178
libertarian, 50, 168
liberty, 124, 179–83, 191
life, ix, xiii, xix–xx, 2, 4, 6n9, 7n11, 12, 12n19, 18, 36–38, 37n53, 40n2, 46, 50, 52, 54–55, 55n18, 57, 58n21, 63–64, 68–74, 72n12, 77, 79, 83, 84n16, 86, 90, 93–95, 97, 102n17, 104n22, 105, 112, 112n2, 117, 126, 128, 138–142, 144–47, 149–56, 157n25, 158–59, 161–62, 164–68, 176, 178, 181, 183–84, 188–91, 193, 196–97, 200, 205, 208–12, 214, 219–22
linguistic, xxii, 29, 42, 50, 86, 99–100, 163, 169, 217, 219–20
literal, xviin3, 6n9, 17, 23, 27, 41, 72, 79, 85, 89, 90, 105, 116, 152, 160, 164, 167, 186, 202, 209, 217, 220
literary, xvi, 8, 53
literature, xviin3, 37n52, 101n16

liturgy, liturgical, ix, 70, 104nn22–23, 156n24, 177–78
love, (be)loved, xix, 5–7, 14, 14n24, 16, 19, 28, 31, 35, 38, 48–49, 67, 72n12, 82, 85, 87–88, 96, 119n10, 144n14, 146, 150, 152, 154–56, 165–67, 169, 172, 175, 179, 182, 187–88, 206, 208, 213
Lutheran, xxi

malady, xiii, xvii, xix
management, managerialism, managerialist, 34, 39
marriage, marry, 133, 136–38, 136n1, 140–46, 143n12, 148–50, 152–54, 155n23, 159, 161, 164–66
maturity, mature, immaturity, immature, 8, 16, 24, 44, 45n8, 46, 50–51, 63, 67, 176, 181, 183, 185, 189
medicine, medical, xix, xx, 1n3, 64, 137n3
medieval, xiv, 50, 115, 193, 206
member, membership, ix, 3, 3n5, 22, 26, 26n41, 31, 44, 50, 59, 80, 82n11, 88, 93, 95–97, 100, 104n23, 105, 116, 119, 122–28, 134–35, 138, 142, 169, 177, 180–82, 186–88, 195, 197n6, 199, 220, 225
merit, meritorious, 193, 205
method, methodological, x, xiii–xvi, 17, 35, 40–42, 53, 55, 57, 61, 73, 87, 89–90, 99, 108–9
minister, ministerial, 34, 69, 75, 197, 200–202
ministry, ix, 5, 34, 75–76, 192, 196, 197n6, 200–202, 213
misogynist, xxi, 147
mission, missional, xix, 18, 43, 66, 82, 191, 194, 196, 199, 204, 207, 211–13, 215–17, 219, 221, 223–24
missionary, 42, 56, 194–95, 200, 216–20
mourn, mournful, 25–26, 94–97, 95n5, 105, 158, 162–64
modernity, modern, modernist, xiii–xvi, xvii*n*3, xx, 1–2, 9–11, 32–36, 44–45, 47, 50, 53–55, 59–61, 75, 82, 87, 95, 103n18, 104n22, 111, 114, 116, 123, 125, 131, 132n29, 136, 136n1, 139–40, 143, 143n12, 157, 169–70, 171n1, 179, 187, 193–94, 198, 198n8, 200n9, 213n37, 222n45
moralist, moral, xviii–xx, xviii*n*4, 4–5, 16, 38, 50, 55–56, 58–59, 65, 69–70, 74, 87–89, 91–95, 97–100, 102–110, 114–15, 118–19, 122, 125, 128, 130–33, 140, 140n10, 143n12, 144, 154, 156, 164–65, 169–71, 182, 188–89, 195, 203, 206–8, 212
moralize, 95, 108, 122, 128, 133, 200
mystery, xxii, 39, 47, 76
mystic, mysticism, mystical, 40, 47n12, 91, 91n1, 152

name, 1, 3–4, 4n6, 6, 9, 16–17, 21, 21n33, 29, 35, 37n53, 46, 59, 73, 94, 97, 101, 105, 121–22, 124, 173
naming, 1–2, 4, 14, 94, 101, 107, 121, 143, 146, 160, 163, 212
narrative, narrate, xx–xxii, 14, 32, 34n49, 54, 56, 97, 191, 193–94, 209
New Testament, 12n20, 101n16, 110, 154, 160, 172, 184, 193, 198, 209n24
nothing, nothingness, xiv, xvi, 15, 37, 39–43, 50, 53, 57, 67, 77–81, 89, 98, 107, 111, 130, 147, 157, 175n6, 180, 195, 201, 204–5
nervous system, xix

obligation, 12, 65, 203–5, 207
offertory rite, 104n22
oikodome, oikodomic, xix, 2, 18, 20, 24, 26, 49–50, 64, 95–96, 127, 146, 166, 182, 186. *See also* building up
oikos, 165
Old Testament, 48, 72, 80, 98–100, 98n12, 100n16, 109, 172, 175, 202
ontology, ontologize, ontological, 11n17, 12, 104, 140, 151, 153, 155n23, 165, 167, 177

organ, organic, xix, 29, 126, 131, 141, 154, 156
organism, xx, 29
owner, ownership, 125, 139–41, 144, 151–52

pagan, 20, 91–92, 106, 111, 116, 120, 153, 175, 179
paraenesis, 3
paraklesis, 82, 85
parent, parenting, parental, 3, 8, 16, 61, 70, 85–87, 132–33, 155, 177
parochialism, parochial, 18, 59, 72–73
parousia, 159, 168
passion, passionate, 14–15, 32, 95–96, 120, 142–45, 152, 159, 192
pastor, pastoral, xiii, 2–3, 37, 42, 92, 96, 161, 164, 166–67, 183, 188, 197, 206n19
patience, xvii, 79, 184
patriarchism, patriarchal, 58, 146–47
patristic, xiv, 10, 22n34, 45n8, 46n10, 61, 104, 193, 213
patron, patronage, patronize, 63, 197, 200–201, 204, 215
peace, xviii, xix, 3, 8–9, 9n13, 27n42, 31, 119, 146–47, 152, 185
pedagogue, pedagogy, pedagogical, xxi, 11, 16, 41, 82, 86–88, 95, 145, 183–84, 187, 224
perish, (im)perishable, 27–29, 27n42, 33–34, 44, 90, 184, 186, 210, 221–23
person, personal, ix, xviin2, 5–6, 9, 20, 27, 32, 35, 37, 40, 51, 53, 56, 65, 70–71, 72n12, 73, 75, 77n3, 79, 87, 89–90, 98n12, 99–100, 102, 103n19, 105–6, 116–19, 125–29, 133, 135, 139n5, 144, 146, 148, 151–54, 171–72, 178–79, 182, 186–87, 192, 194, 205, 208–9, 211, 215–16, 223–24
phenomenology, phenomenological, 7n11, 144, 154, 156–58, 158n27, 163, 212
philosopher, philosophy, philosophical, 20, 24, 30n43, 30n45, 32–33, 56, 56n19, 58n21, 85, 130, 139n7, 140, 143n12, 157, 160, 165, 179, 205, 208, 211–12, 224n49
pneumatology, pneumatological, 23, 49, 216, 220
political, xviii, 1, 6n10, 19, 21n33, 23, 45n8, 69–70, 85, 91–94, 99–100, 102–3, 106, 118–19, 119n10, 121, 127–28, 145–46, 152, 162–63, 197n6, 225
politics, xviii, xix, 18, 70–71, 219, 225
porneia, 131–36, 141–42, 144–45, 148, 151, 163, 168
pornography, 132
possession, possessiveness, possess, 2, 13n22, 20, 23, 27–28, 32, 37, 43, 46–47, 47n12, 49–51, 74–75, 84, 123–25, 133, 135, 139–41, 146, 158, 163–64, 168–69, 171, 173, 177, 180, 182, 185–86, 188, 211
postmodern, postmodernity, postmodernist, xiii, xvi, 33, 35
power, powerful, xv, xviii, xxi, 2, 4–6, 6n10, 8, 15, 17, 19–21, 23–24, 27–28, 31–32, 35–36, 39–40, 42–43, 46, 51, 57, 71–73, 83, 85, 90, 97–99, 98n11, 105, 123–24, 125–27, 129, 131n27, 132–35, 138, 143, 145–46, 152, 172, 175–76, 179, 181, 185, 189, 193, 197, 199, 208, 210, 212n31, 213n36, 214n38, 218–20, 222–23
powers (and principalities), xviiin4, 99, 125, 133, 214
pragmatism, pragmatist, 32, 34, 34n49, 36
praise, praiseworthy, 10, 10n17, 11–14, 16, 20, 30–31, 38, 55, 64, 76, 79–80, 84, 128, 205, 219n25
prayer, xv, 12, 37n52, 62, 64n2, 136–37, 142, 156
preach, preacher, xviin2, xix, 2, 23–24, 27–28, 45n9, 95–96, 152, 192–93, 201–2, 208–9, 211, 217–18, 222, 224
presence, xv, xx, 5–6, 8, 17, 29, 37, 41–42, 82, 91n1, 97–98, 135, 160, 164, 200n10, 219

Subject Index

pride, prideful, 4, 32, 91, 93–94, 100–101, 104–5, 184, 186–87, 197, 206n19, 218, 224
private, 70, 92, 98, 108, 118, 122–23, 125, 129, 204, 210n25
prize, 13n22, 190, 195, 210n25, 213–14, 213n37, 218, 221, 222n45, 223
prophet, prophetic, 40, 42n4, 48, 71, 100, 164
proprietor, propriety, (non)proprietary, 139–41, 144–46, 151, 163, 168, 205
prostitution, prostitute, 121, 125–28, 130–31, 134, 140, 146, 148
psychology, psychological, 38, 41, 72–73, 82, 90, 120, 138, 144–45, 172, 184, 195
public, 2, 43, 46n10, 56, 80, 91–92, 95, 99, 107, 112, 119, 125, 135, 182

rationalism, rationalist, 31, 33–34, 140
reader, xiii, xv–xvi, xvii$n$3, xx–xxii, 13–14, 26, 44–45, 47, 50, 58–62, 64, 68, 80, 83–84, 87–88, 90–93, 106, 118, 122, 126, 145, 148, 152, 158, 160, 167, 170, 182, 186–87, 190, 203, 210, 215, 222
reconciliation, 18, 31, 35, 100–101, 110–11, 113, 116–22, 124, 146, 179, 185
redeem, redeemer, redemption, xxii, 16, 27n42, 37, 43, 55n18, 56n19, 179
Reformation, Reformer, xiv–xv, 40n2, 43, 43n5, 45, 114–15, 153, 176n8, 184, 205–6
reign, 8, 56, 84, 145, 163
remember, 172
reputation, 23–24, 91
responsibility, responsible, xvii, 34, 62, 69, 77, 98–99, 115, 118, 132, 140, 150, 152, 165, 167, 169–71, 179, 189
resurrection, 25–26, 40n2, 81n7, 126–28, 223
retaliation, 122, 220
revelation, revelatory, xv, xxii, 42–44, 46–47, 49, 51

reward, xxii, 37n53, 65, 68–69, 190–91, 194–95, 198–200, 202–3, 205, 207–11, 215, 217, 222–24
rhetoric, rhetorician, rhetorical, 2, 8, 20, 23–24, 36, 41–42, 42n3, 58, 67, 71, 78, 83, 92, 106, 109, 112, 149, 181, 198, 203
right, xx, 2, 5, 7, 23, 75, 111–16, 120, 120n12, 122–23, 127, 129, 135–36, 139n6, 140, 146, 187, 190, 193–98, 198n8, 200, 203, 206n19, 207, 210–11, 210n25, 215, 217

sacrifice, sacrificial, 4, 28, 36, 57–58, 72n12, 102–3, 105, 123–24, 169, 173, 180, 182, 190, 193–96, 198, 203–5, 210–11, 215, 217
saint, 3–4, 9–10, 21n32, 33n46, 74, 74n13, 82, 90, 111
salvation, 26, 27n42, 29, 59, 64, 72, 80, 99–100, 153–55, 224
sanctification, sanctify, 3–4, 9, 28, 37–38, 121–23, 153–56
scholasticism, 38
scripture, scriptural, x, xiv–xvii, xxii, 16, 30, 38, 44–45, 54, 56, 58, 60–62, 77n3, 78, 80, 87–90, 94, 96, 114, 132, 145, 153, 158, 198
secret, 44, 45n7, 46, 46n12, 71, 77n3, 91, 107, 157
secretary, secretarial, 1n1
self, 3, 18–19, 24, 28–29, 32, 37n52, 40, 41–42, 44, 45–46, 51, 53, 54, 60, 62, 68, 71–72, 73, 75, 78, 80, 82, 89, 96, 100, 101, 103–4, 108, 115, 124–25, 130, 133, 135, 139, 143, 145, 151–52, 160, 166–67, 169–73, 179, 181–87, 189, 191, 196, 200, 208, 211–14, 224
self-control, 136, 138, 138n4, 142–44, 211, 213n37
servant, servanthood, 1, 5, 65–66, 76–78, 195
sexuality, sexual, xviii–xx, 50, 70, 91–92, 94, 98–99, 105–7, 121, 124–50, 131n27, 137n3, 140n11, 143n12, 144n14, 161, 164–66, 168

Subject Index

shame, shaming, ashamed, shameful, 31–32, 81n7, 82, 85, 92, 94, 111–12, 119, 131, 183
sin, sinner, sinful, 4, 10n17, 11, 14, 16, 69, 71n10, 79, 88–89, 91, 96, 102n17, 106–7, 107n24, 109, 116, 118–19, 122, 129–31, 134, 144, 158–59, 166–67, 169, 180–81, 187–88, 194, 212, 214, 216
skandalon, scandal, scandalous, 31, 91, 96, 119
slave, slavery, enslavement, enslaved, 86, 125, 132–33, 142–44, 148–49, 151, 151n16, 210n25, 214–16, 221–22
slogan, 45, 126, 136n1, 146, 174, 179–81, 185
sociology, sociological, 19, 25, 90, 103, 201
Son, xix, 9, 14, 17, 49, 94, 179
soul, ensouled, 64, 127–28, 152, 165, 199, 213, 224
Spirit, ix–x, xv–xvii, xviin2, xix, 15, 20, 23, 38–40, 42–49, 42n4, 51–52, 56–58, 64, 70, 72, 74, 85, 88, 90, 91n1, 96–97, 99–100, 102, 107, 112, 121–22, 125–27, 129, 134–35, 141, 156, 159, 167, 178–79, 184–85, 216, 224
spirituality, spiritual, xv, xix, 9–10, 14–16, 20, 38, 40–41, 44, 45n8, 48–52, 57–58, 61, 63, 71–72, 85–86, 89, 93–94, 97–98, 127–28, 138–39, 149, 156, 177, 180n9, 185, 190–91, 195–97, 199, 202–4, 211, 214, 221–23
steward, stewardship, 76–77, 209
stoic, stoicism, stoicized, 120, 124, 143–45, 143n12, 147, 161, 168
strategy, x, xx–xxi, 39, 42, 73, 82, 87, 100, 148, 158, 161, 197n6
strong, 5, 26, 31–32, 57, 73, 81, 84, 91n1, 96, 143, 159, 177, 181–89
stumbling block, xvii, 31, 54, 179–81, 185
suffer, xx, 26, 65, 69, 84, 95–96, 115, 124, 130, 139, 224

supererogation, supererogatory, 114–15, 115n5, 193, 195, 204–7, 206nn19–20
surprise, xviii, xxi–xxii, 57, 95, 146, 154, 161, 194, 200n9
suspicion, xvi, 106, 119, 193, 197, 201

teacher, xv, 19–20, 28, 52, 75, 86–87, 147, 197
teleology, teleological, 126, 170, 212
temple, xix, 65, 69–71, 71n9, 107, 129, 135, 180, 182, 196
temptation, 6, 18, 35–36, 60, 70, 88–89, 106, 112, 131, 133, 135n31, 138, 166, 183, 187, 194, 219
testimony, 9, 13, 60
therapy, xiii–xiv, xviii–xix, 106
theologian, xviii, 53, 60, 117, 157
theology, theological, ix–x, xiii–xxii, xviin3, 2, 3n5, 4–6, 8, 11, 12n20, 14, 17, 21n33, 23–24, 27–28, 33, 36, 38, 42–47, 50–51, 53–55, 57–61, 77–79, 82–83, 86, 93n3, 99–100, 103–5, 104n22, 108–110, 113, 115–17, 120–21, 123, 128–31, 132n29, 133–35, 135n31, 137n3, 139, 139n7, 141, 144–45, 148–49, 153–57, 155n23, 161, 163–65, 167–68, 172, 174, 179, 183, 185, 188, 191–93, 198, 205–8, 209n24, 212, 217, 223–24
tolerance, tolerant, xviii–xix, 94–95, 100, 102, 104–5, 133
tradition, traditioning, traditional, xv–xvi, xxi, 8, 23, 33, 38, 40, 42n4, 44, 58, 60–61, 80–81, 104, 104n22, 114, 117–18, 121, 123, 131, 132n29, 136, 141, 143, 145, 149, 151, 161, 165, 170, 177–78, 185, 190, 198, 198n8, 200, 202, 212, 215, 224
transformation, 12, 25, 38, 156, 161, 186n13, 191, 212
travel, traveler, x, xiv, xxi, 114, 190, 194–98, 200, 203, 218
Trinity, Trinitarian, 38, 42–43, 49, 51, 122, 178

trust, trustworthy, entrusted, xvi, xvii*n*2, 14–15, 26, 51, 57, 76–77, 80, 82, 88, 131, 158, 167, 175, 175n6, 178, 184–85, 203, 205, 207, 218–19

truth, truthful, xix, 3, 5–6, 16, 19, 23–24, 28, 30, 32–33, 35–36, 49, 73–74, 79, 88, 98, 102–3, 105, 109, 133, 157, 164, 183–84, 206, 212, 212n32

unity, xvi, xviii–xix, xxii, 1–4, 11, 16–19, 24–26, 28, 34–36, 66, 71, 96, 105, 115, 141, 149, 184, 189

union, 9, 26, 127–28, 134, 152, 223

virgin, virginity, 136n2, 142, 158–60, 167, 198, 205

virtue, xviii*n*4, 37–38, 37n53, 38n54, 70, 106, 127, 141, 153, 189, 206

vice, 38n54, 106–8, 107n24, 121–22

victory, 214

vocation, xv, 2–3, 62, 141, 150, 152, 160, 165–67, 191, 193, 201, 206–7

wait, await, x, xvii*n*2, 7, 9, 14–15, 24, 32, 44, 47, 79, 83, 125, 152, 164, 223

war, warring, xviii, 6, 56n19, 83n15, 121, 139, 145–46, 151n16, 171

weak, weakness, 5, 7, 12n19, 14, 19, 26, 31–32, 39–42, 57, 73, 81, 84, 96, 119, 167, 169–70, 173, 177, 179–89, 191, 192n3, 195, 197n6, 204, 215, 219–20

wife, 91–92, 94, 126–28, 136, 136n2, 139–41, 147, 152, 158–59, 164, 166, 195–98

wisdom, 20, 23–32, 25n40, 34–37, 39, 42–44, 45n7, 46, 47n12, 48–49, 51–52, 54, 57, 60, 71, 73, 79–80, 85, 133

wise, 20, 27, 31–32, 35, 37, 47, 71–72, 79, 81, 84–85, 111, 113

witness, x, xvi, 4, 7, 28, 30, 48n13, 73–74, 84, 100, 118, 146, 156, 161, 164–65, 192, 199, 208, 223

Word (God's), x, xv–xvii, 14, 23, 37, 51, 61–62, 145, 150, 172, 179, 191, 196, 200, 205

work, ix–x, xv–xvii, xvii*n*2, xviii*n*4, xix, 4, 6–7, 13, 14n24, 17–18, 22–26, 28, 30, 33–35, 38, 40, 42, 44–45, 49, 52–56, 58, 62, 64–70, 74, 78–79, 81, 84, 86, 90, 92, 98, 104n22, 110, 114–16, 122, 137n2, 144, 156, 176n8, 178, 185, 187–88, 192, 195–200, 198n7, 202, 205, 206n17, 206n19–20, 207–9, 214n38, 216–17, 217n40

worship, xix, 17, 34, 70–71, 74, 102n17, 110, 119n10, 135, 174–76, 179, 187, 189

Scripture Index

Old Testament

Genesis
8:1	172

Leviticus
18:18	94

Deuteronomy
17:7;12	99n13
19:19	99n13
21:21	99n13, 100n15
22:21;24	99n13
24:7	99n13
25:4	202
29:29	77n3

1 Kings
18	42n4

2 Kings
5:23–26	91n1

Ezra
10:6	95

Job
5:13	72

Psalms
1:3	64n1
19:1–3	30
69:20	96
94:11	72
102:3	96
105:8	172
115:5	175
119:105	158
135:15–18	175

Proverbs
7:10	165

Ecclesiastes
1:2	72

Isaiah
64:4	48

Daniel
4:18	82
5:13	72

Joel
2:16	164

Amos
5:18;20	100n14
8:9–14	100n14

New Testament

Matthew

5:18	90
5:48	47
6:16	190
6:33	123
7:29	181
10:9–10	195, 200
16:4	8
18	112
18:15	118
18:17	118
19	207
26:22;33	60

Mark

1:15	160

Luke

1:72	172
10:35	206
19:8–9	206
23:29	164

John

14:25	42n4
16:13	45

Acts

15	221
17	33
17:21	33
17:32	33
19:18–19	35
20:34	206

Romans

1:20	30
1:28	31
7:16	23
7:20–23	138
8:25–15	23
12	96
12:1–2	186n13
12:1	82
12:2	74, 163
12:5	26, 88
13	121
14:13	156
15:1	96
15:2	166

1 Corinthians

1	84
1:1	1–3
1:2–3	196
1:2–4	3–8
1:4–10	11
1:4–9	9–16, 26, 64, 79
1:5–7	19
1:5–6	13
1:7	14
1:8	29
1:9	17, 19,
1:10	3, 17, 25
1:11–12	18–21, 211
1:11	76
1:13–16	21–26
1:16–17	209
1:18–20	27–29
1:21	29–31
1:22–27	31–37
1:22–23	54
1:23–2:16	185
1:23	35
1:26	83
1:27	32, 38, 183
1:28–31	37–38
1:31	79
2:1–5	39–43, 196
2:1	40, 46
2:2	xiv, 29, 38, 40, 43, 50, 77, 80, 214

2:3	41	4:15	75, 85–86
2:4	42, 46	4:17	86
2:5	43	4:18–21	87
2:6–8	44–48, 51, 57	4:20–21	8
2:8	44	4:20	83
2:9	46	4:21	2
2:9–12	46, 48–50	5	108, 112, 133
2:10–13	49	5:1	91–94, 101, 106
2:10–11	43	5:2	93–94
2:12	49	5:3–5	97–102
2:13–16	51–62	5:3	97
2:13–15	xiv	5:5	77n3, 99
2:13	52	5:6–8	102–5
3	59	5:6	102, 122
3:1–4	63–64	5:7	38, 93, 103
3:1	77	5:8	105, 108
3:2	16	5:9–13	105–110, 204
3:5–15	65–70	5:11	93, 101, 106, 121–22
3:5–9	1		
3:5	81	5:12	106
3:8	67, 210n25	5:13	98n12, 105, 109
3:6–12	66	6	50, 148
3:10–15	182	6:1–6	111–13
3:10–11	188	6:4	112, 117
3:13	78, 144	6:7–8	113–21, 193
3:14	210n25	6:7	113, 117
3:16–17	70–71	6:9–11	121–23
3:17	65	6:11	119, 122
3:18–19	65	6:12	123–25
3:18–20	71–72, 79	6:12–20	163
3:21–23	72–75	6:13–17	125–29, 181, 185
3:21	83		
3:23	38	6:15	127–28
4:1–5	76–80	6:17	127
4:2	88, 210n25	6:18–20	129–35
4:3	193n3	6:18	107
4:5–9	3	6:19	38
4:5	79, 210n25	7	50, 191
4:6–7	80–81	7:1–9	148
4:6	46, 89	7:1–6	136–42, 198
4:8–13	81–85	7:1	136
4:9–16	7	7:2	141, 145, 152
4:10–13	84	7:4	139, 146
4:8	82–84, 87	7:5	137
4:13	82	7:6	137
4:14	82	7:7–9	142–47
4:10–12	5	7:6	143
4:14–21	xiv, 85–90	7:7	142

1 Corinthians (continued)

7:9	143
7:10–24	147–58
7:10–16	148
7:11	146
7:14	152
7:15	146
7:16	152–53
7:17–24	149–40
7:21–23	153
7:25–40	158–68
7:25–29	159
7:25	167
7:28	164
7:29	160, 168
7:29–31	161–64
7:32–35	164
7:34	165–66
7:36–37	143
7:36	167
7:39	167
7:40	167
8	191
8:1–3	169–73
8:1	67, 187
8:2	171, 177–78, 187
8:4–7	173–79
8:4	173–74, 177
8:5	174, 178
8:6	177, 178, 180
8:7	169, 177, 179, 186
8:8–13	179, 218
8:8	180
8:9	169, 181
8:10	182
8:11	181, 183, 186
8:12	169, 181, 187–88
8:13	187, 204
9	191
9:1–15	210
9:1–3	192–95
9:4–14	195–203
9:7	198, 202
9:10	202
9:11	199
9:12	203, 209, 213
9:14	200
9:15–17	203
9:15	203
9:16–17	205
9:16	194, 204
9:17–18	211–14
9:17	205, 210
9:18	199, 206n19, 207, 223
9:19–23	214–21
9:20	216–17
9:21	218
9:22	211
9:23	209
9:24–27	221–25
9:24–25	210n25
9:24	213–14
9:25	211
9:26	214
9:27	213, 222
10	
10:1–12	55
10:17	213
10:23	124
11	64, 108, 201
11:10–22	201
11:19	7, 25
11:28	191
11:29	64, 108
12	38
12:2	xviin2
12:4–13	97
12:12–13	211
12:12	213
12:14–19	224
12:21–26	96, 220
12:27	213
13	90
13:1–13	64
13:1	175
13:12	172
14	221
14:12	15
14:29	44
15	128, 223
15:22–24	223
16:21–24	xiv

2 Corinthians

1:3–7	26
2:9–10	44
2:15	28
5:20	82
10:10	5
11:29	96
13:5–7	223

Galatians

2	221
3:27	156, 160
3:28	213
5	49
5:18	23
5:22	141
6:2	218

Ephesians

2	147
2:11–22	120
4:17	202
5:30	128

Philippians

1:9	172
2:6–11	52
4:10–18	200

1 Thessalonians

2:3–13	7
2:3–5	42n3
2:5	23
2:8–9	206

Philemon

8	82

Hebrews

11:4	57
12:1	73

Revelation

18:21–23	164

www.ingramcontent.com/pod-product-compliance
Lightning Source LLC
Chambersburg PA
CBHW022003220426
43663CB00007B/938